INTERSECTIONALITY AND HIGHER EDUCATION

INTERSECTIONALITY AND HIGHER EDUCATION

Identity and Inequality on College Campuses

EDITED BY

W. CARSON BYRD,
RACHELLE J. BRUNN-BEVEL,
AND SARAH M. OVINK

RUTGERS UNIVERSITY PRESS
New Brunswick, Camden, and Newark, New Jersey, and London

Library of Congress Cataloging-in-Publication Data

Names: Byrd, W. Carson, editor. | Brunn-Bevel, Rachelle J., editor. | Ovink,
   Sarah M., editor.
Title: Intersectionality and higher education : identity and inequality on college
   campuses / edited by W. Carson Byrd, Rachelle J. Brunn-Bevel, and Sarah M.
   Ovink.
Description: New Brunswick : Rutgers University Press, [2019] | Includes
   bibliographical references and index.
Identifiers: LCCN 2018038053 | ISBN 9780813597676 (cloth) |
   ISBN 9780813597669 (pbk.)
Subjects: LCSH: Discrimination in higher education—United States. | Racism
   in higher education—United States. | Educational equalization—United States. |
   Minorities—Education (Higher)—United States. | Intersectionality (Sociology) |
   Identity (Psychology)
Classification: LCC LC212.42 .I57 2019 | DDC 378.1/982—dc23
LC record available at https://lccn.loc.gov/2018038053

A British Cataloging-in-Publication record for this book is available from the British
Library.

♾ The paper used in this publication meets the requirements of the American National
Standard for Information Sciences—Permanence of Paper for Printed Library
Materials, ANSI Z39.48-1992.

www.rutgersuniversitypress.org

Manufactured in the United States of America

CONTENTS

INTERSECTIONALITY AND HIGHER EDUCATION

PART I   INTERSECTED CAMPUSES

An Introduction

1 · ALWAYS CROSSING BOUNDARIES, ALWAYS EXISTING IN MULTIPLE BUBBLES

Intersected Experiences and Positions on College Campuses

RACHELLE J. BRUNN-BEVEL,
SARAH M. OVINK, W. CARSON BYRD,
AND ANTRON D. MAHONEY

In today's increasingly diverse society, a college degree represents a means of attaining middle-class stability amid changing economic, family, and social structures. The sense that a postsecondary degree is now "required" has grown yet more acute after the Great Recession of 2008. As noted by Ovink (2017), high school juniors surveyed for the High School Longitudinal Survey in 2011 overwhelmingly expected to attain some level of postsecondary training, with just 10 percent reporting that they planned to stop their educational training with high school. Most of the reasons offered to support a college-for-all orientation rest on the assumed economic benefits of completing college. Even so, two recent studies of low-income women attending community colleges argue that college plans also represent a claim to *moral* worth, which explains why low-income women's college aspirations hold steady over time even when progress toward completion is slow and the economic benefits remain unrealized (Deterding 2015; Nielsen 2015). College costs continue to rise, far outpacing inflation, and yet college enrollments maintain their upward trend. What few have examined, however, is what happens—on college campuses, in student-faculty-staff relationships, to academic programming—when increasing numbers of historically underrepresented groups arrive on university campuses to work and study alongside their wealthy majority-group counterparts.

Recent protests on college campuses highlighted persistent concerns among historically underrepresented populations, including African Americans, Latinos/as, women, undocumented immigrants, those from low-income or working-class backgrounds, and other marginalized identities. Responses to these calls to improve diversity and inclusivity have not followed a single pattern. For example, protests at the University of Missouri resulted in the resignation of the president of the Missouri University System, Tim Wolfe, in November 2015. However, these and other movements to push university administrators to pay increased attention to the campus climate prompted the University of Chicago to send a letter to all incoming first-year students in September 2016 that strenuously objected to "trigger warnings" and "safe spaces," among other activities that Dean of Students John Ellison considers antithetical to academic freedom. In this war of words over the meaning of higher education and whether college campuses should have a role in ensuring a civil and inclusive campus climate, students, staff, and faculty with marginalized identities often feel caught in the crossfire.

This book examines the interconnected lives of college students, faculty, and staff on campus to clarify how the cultures and structures of colleges and universities assist or hinder campus group members' academic and social efforts, and simultaneously, institutional efforts to support people from different backgrounds and experiences to reduce inequalities. At the heart of this volume lie two connected questions. First, how do students, faculty, and staff navigate campus communities that often simultaneously pose as open and inclusive but can function as restricted and obstacles to academic, career, and social progress? Second, what institutional changes could assist postsecondary institutions to cease operating as engines of social inequality and instead embody the popular ideal of colleges as bastions of inquisitive minds, scholarly discussion, and enriching academic, career, and social experiences? In addressing these questions, our volume responds directly to the call by Mitchell Stevens, Elizabeth Armstrong, and Richard Arum that beyond identifying higher education as "sieves for regulating the mobility processes underlying the allocation of privileged positions in the society, incubators for the development of competent social actors, and temples for the legitimation of official knowledge" (2008, 128), scholars must fully appreciate the plurality of these institutions and the domains they influence in society.

To accomplish this feat, we must explore how people of different backgrounds, particularly marginalized groups, experience these institutions in relation to identity and social position on campus and in society. The chapters in this volume observe how institutions operate as engines of mobility *and* inequality, inclusion *and* exclusion, progressive *and* conservative thought in order to suggest changes to lead the way forward. In doing so, the authors featured here provide empirically and theoretically grounded approaches to these questions of how the varying student, faculty, and staff groups that live, study, and work on college campuses navigate their social worlds in their pursuits for academic, career, and social success, reaching beyond the most frequently studied areas of college experiences. This volume melds important theoretical perspectives from fields such as sociology, psychology, higher education and student affairs, and organizational studies, among others. Merging these many perspectives together, we provide constituents who operate from different positions on campus with the tools to better support each other to increase their institutions' effectiveness regarding academics, employment, and social life.

INTERSECTIONALITY FRAMING FOR COLLEGE EXPERIENCES

Intersectionality provides a useful framework to discuss how mobility and marginalization exist on our college campuses. Intersectionality has a long history of calling attention to marginality and oppression in different situations, and is not solely housed in the halls of academia (Collins and Bilge 2016). Building on a long history of social justice movements around the globe, the legal scholar and black feminist Kimberle Crenshaw (1989, 1991) introduced the concept of "intersectionality" to contend that race, class, and gender cannot be separated. For example, women of color can face oppression simultaneously based on their race, gender, and socioeconomic status in addition to their sexual orientation, immigrant status, and disability. Crenshaw's work is emblematic of and situated in a tradition of black feminist writing, scholarship, and activism that extends from scholar-activists such as Davis (1981), Lorde (1984), the Combahee River Collective (1982), and Sojourner Truth to the influential Patricia Hill Collins and her book *Black Feminist Thought* (2000).

Collins (2000) weaves together the central tenets of black feminism and broadens the scope of what is classified as knowledge by disrupting the dichotomy between theory and activism. She argues that black feminist thought is critical social theory and advocates for a wider vision of who should be counted as scholars, experts, or intellectuals. Importantly, Collins (2000) links social justice efforts by and for black women with movements for justice by and for other marginalized groups around the world. In more recent work, Collins and Bilge (2016) elaborate the importance of recognizing how women of color around the globe have been engaging in intersectional analyses of their communities and pushing for social justice efforts to rectify the marginalization and oppression that exist around them and their experience daily.

Crenshaw (1991) explicates structural, political, and representational intersectionality as important dimensions of intersectionality. Although all three are relevant for investigating campus dynamics, structural and political intersectionality are especially important for this volume. Crenshaw writes, "An analysis sensitive to structural intersectionality explores the lives of those at the bottom of multiple hierarchies to determine how the dynamics of each hierarchy exacerbates and compounds the consequences of another" (114). For example, how are black lesbian college students excluded from or made to feel unwelcome at mainstream campus activities? Are their experiences underrepresented in curricular experiences? "Political intersectionality provides an applied dimension to the insights of structural intersectionality by offering a framework for contesting power and thereby linking theory to existent and emergent social and political struggles" (Cho, Crenshaw, and McCall 2013, 800).

Andersen and Collins (2013) utilize a matrix of domination approach that conceptualizes "race, class, and gender as systems of power" (2). Andersen and Collins contend that "systems of race, class, and gender have been so consistently and deeply codified in U.S. laws that they have had intergenerational effects on economic, political, and social institutions" (5). The authors problematize diversity and multiculturalism frameworks as they argue for a matrix of domination perspective. They write, "The very term *diversity* implies that understanding race, class, and gender is simply a matter of recognizing the plurality of views and experiences in society—as if race, class, and gender were benign categories that foster diverse experiences instead of systems of power that produce social inequalities" (8). This critique is particularly relevant for postsecondary institutions' missions, strategic plans, and recruitment strategies.

For instance, in Sara Ahmed's (2012) study of university diversity practitioners' experiences and challenges of performing diversity work, Ahmed describes and extends Collins's understanding of intersectionality and an employment of a matrix of domination within a postsecondary institutional critique. For Ahmed, within feminism of color, a focus on intersectionality is a concern with the point(s) in which power relations converge and how these points often recede from view. Therefore, the concept of diversity within higher education is an ideological point and obscures the factors that produce social inequalities. A matrix of domination approach, then, reveals the institutional "walls" that restrict and regulate race, gender, class, and sexuality. Ahmed's critique of how diversity is incorporated within academic institutions builds on other feminist of color critiques made by M. Jacqui Alexander (2005) and Chandra Mohanty (2003) in which Mohanty contends diversity as a discourse "bypasses power" as well as history to suggest a harmonious empty pluralism" (193).

Intersectionality and the matrix of domination, which identifies four domains of power, are related yet distinct theoretical constructs. "Intersectionality refers to particular forms of intersecting oppressions. . . . In contrast, the matrix of domination refers to how these intersecting oppressions are actually organized. Regardless of the particular intersections involved, structural, disciplinary, hegemonic, and interpersonal domains of power reappear across quite different forms of oppression" (Collins 2000, 18). Collins (2000) contends that these domains of power are locations of both domination and empowerment. Women of color both encounter and challenge oppressive structures in ways that vary across time and place. Collins develops the "domains-of-power argument" from the experiences of black women in the United States but argues that it is useful for understanding movements for social justice more broadly (276).

The structural domain of power illustrates how societal institutions intersect to constrain opportunities for black women. Collins (2000) writes, "Historically, in the United States, the policies and procedures of the U.S. legal system, labor markets, schools, the housing industry, banking, insurance, the news media, and other social institutions as interdependent entities have worked to disadvantage African-American women" (277). Radical transformation of these institutions is necessary to bring about widespread systemic change. Collins asserts, "As a way of ruling that relies on bureaucratic hierarchies and techniques of surveillance, the disciplinary domain manages power relations" (280). She discusses how surveillance is a method of social control in a wide array of bureaucratic institutions such as prisons, businesses, and postsecondary institutions. She contends that resistance most often comes from within these organizations as black women negotiate their "outsider-within" social location.

The interpersonal domain focuses on daily interactions between groups of people. Collins argues that individuals can easily identify the source(s) of their own oppression (race, class, gender, sexual orientation, disability, etc.) but rarely see how they subordinate others. "In essence, each group identifies the oppression with which it feels most comfortable as being fundamental and classifies all others as being of lesser importance. Oppression is filled with such contradictions because these approaches fail to recognize that a matrix of domination contains few pure victims or oppressors" (Collins 2000, 287). Resistance and empowerment strategies in the interpersonal domain are numerous. Finally, the hegemonic domain functions as a bridge for the other three domains of power. "By manipulating ideology and culture, the hegemonic domain acts as a link between social institutions (structural domain), their organizational practices (disciplinary domain), and the level of everyday social interaction (interpersonal domain)" (284). Advantaged groups effectively use coercive, but often invisible, means of disseminating ideologies that benefit and legitimate their being in positions of power. This is the essence of hegemony. School curriculum and the all-encompassing reach of mass media are important sites for the production and dissemination of ideologies used to subjugate black women and other marginalized groups (Collins 2000). Importantly, stereotyped groups can resist these negative portrayals. Collins asserts that empowerment in the hegemonic domain of power consists of critiquing dominant ideologies and creating new knowledge.

Hallmarks of intersectional scholarship include an emphasis on simultaneity and the interaction of multiple oppressions; focusing on the importance of context and resisting the urge to rank oppressions; taking into account the salience of both micro-level factors such as social identities and macro-level considerations such as power, privilege, and institutional structures; and linking theory to praxis in the pursuit of social justice (Andersen and Collins 2013; Choo and Ferree 2010; Carbado et al. 2013; Hancock 2007; Landry 2007). Intersectional theoretical frameworks have recently been incorporated into the field of higher education (Berila 2015; Winkle-Wagner and Locks 2013; Lundy-Wagner and Winkle-Wagner 2013; Mitchell, Simmons, and Greyerbiehl 2014; Davis, Brunn-Bevel, and Olive 2015; Jones and Abes 2013; Strayhorn 2013; Griffin and Reddick 2011; Marine 2011; Ovink 2017). Importantly, intersectionality scholars go beyond recognizing intersecting identity categories to discuss structural factors such as power, oppression, and privilege. This lens is especially useful to analyze predominantly white higher education institutions given the aforementioned legacy of exclusion that these institutions must confront. Dill (2009, 248) argues that scholars who conduct research and teach about intersectionality "often embody the differences they write and teach about and are therefore engaged in creating places for themselves and for this scholarship in institutions of higher education." Dill also describes the institutional context as "a predominantly White, male, heteronormative, U.S. academy" (229).

As intersectionality becomes popular in a number of disciplines (sociology, psychology, political science, etc.) and fields (including education), there is a fear that it has become a "buzzword" (Collins and Bilge 2016; Davis 2008). Many intersectional theorists would argue that without focusing on power, oppression, and social justice activism, the work is not intersectional (Collins 1990, 1998; Carbado et al. 2013; Cho, Crenshaw, and McCall 2013; Dill and Zambrana 2009; Jones and Abes 2013). We agree that intersectionality scholars cannot neglect systems of power and oppression in their analyses. Cho, Crenshaw, and McCall (2013) contend that an important goal of intersectionality studies is praxis—going beyond theorizing to make real change in the world by working with and on behalf of marginalized groups. Part of this praxis is interrogating one's own communities, and for scholars, that means examining our college campuses. Although theorizing about intersectionality grew out of the experiences of women of color, scholars such as Browne and Misra (2003) argue that it is a useful lens to interrogate other social locations. The contributors in this volume take up that charge. Although race and gender have been central to intersectional thought, socioeconomic status, sexual orientation, ethnicity, immigrant status, age, and ability (among others) are important identity categories that impact life trajectories (Crenshaw 1991; Collins 2000). Carbado et al. (2013) advocate for a "work-in-progress understanding of intersectionality" (305). This supports Crenshaw's (1989, 1991) conception of intersectionality as "provisional" and "transitional." So while Crenshaw (1989, 1991) theorized about intersectionality being applicable in understanding antidiscrimination law and the experiences of women of color who were domestic violence survivors, it is also useful in understanding structural inequality at postsecondary institutions. As we elaborate below, even a brief examination of higher education utilizing an intersectional lens elucidates many aspects of how institutions can support the social mobility of some at the expense and detriment, even the outright dehumanization, of other campus constituents.

PRIVILEGED AND SUBJUGATED IDENTITIES IN HIGHER EDUCATION

A deployment of intersectionality in its various articulations is contingent on deconstructing a matrix of domination situated in historical privilege, power, and difference. Therefore, to understand the significance of intersectionality in contemporary scholarship on higher education, it is important to account for the historical emergence of minoritized and privileged identities within U.S. higher education. In many instances, higher education has acted as an apparatus of and/ or colluded with the state in the construction of a universal citizen predicated on white capitalist cis-heteropatriarchy. Thus, the intersecting materiality of race, gender, sexuality, and class, among other marginalized identities, demarcates the essentialized ideal student, staff, and faculty. Consequently, colleges and universities have also been a vehicle through which marginalized subjects have reconstituted their humanity, gained agency, and reconceptualized the ideal university subject. Nevertheless, this was not done without a constant reshaping and reworking of the higher education landscape as minoritarian groups challenged dominant ideology and leveraged representational and epistemological stakes in the body of postsecondary institutions.

Higher Education: From a Weapon for Colonization to a Means of Freedom

Early colleges and universities in the United States were instrumental to European American colonization through their consolidation and propagation of racialized ideologies. Originally based on the notion of "divine province" and with the mission to "civilize" and govern the newly discovered world through enslaving Africans and targeting indigenous populations in North America and elsewhere (Graves 2001; Smedley and Smedley 2011; Zuberi 2001), the manifestation of this religious, racialized ideology was prevalent among the founding higher education institutions in the American colonies during the seventeenth century. Many of the early colonial schools were built by enslaved Africans, through both physical labor and economic investments, with the intent to evangelize the "savage" native populations to progress Eurocentric ideology and colonial domain (Wilder 2013).

By the mid-eighteenth century, religious, racialized ideologies were being challenged by notions of democracy and independence in the British American colonies, and higher education institutions provided new justifications for racial hierarchy. As noted by Wilder (2013), with the advent of scientific racism, slave owners and traders engaged in academic inquiry to prove their assertions about race, particularly as it relates to physiological features like skin color. Among those invested in applying pseudoscientific perspectives to justify racial hierarchy and oppression was Thomas Jefferson, who was joined by other prominent members of the political and business elite (Graves 2001; Wilder 2013). For example, Jefferson began collecting, dissecting, and trading African and indigenous peoples' cadavers and laid a foundation for the fields of anatomy and medicine, including establishing a professorship at William and Mary. Furthermore, Jefferson embraced the standpoint of polygenists, who believed there was a genetic basis for multiple stratified races, and posited that it was nature that made Africans inferior. Masked in medical and biological jargon, Jefferson's analysis of Africans went beyond skin color to describe almost every physical feature of Africans as substandard and constituting a different species—making Africans inferior to Europeans and even Indians by Jefferson's framework (Wilder 2013). Jefferson even delved into the anatomy and reproduction similar to that of the later sexualized racialization found in the spectacle of the South African Khoikhoi woman Sarah Bartmann, also known as Hottentot Venus, whose body was put on display throughout Europe during the nineteenth century to signify a savage black female sexuality that would juxtapose an ideal European womanhood. The association of racialized gendered sexualities as perversions would become a hallmark of the type of scientific racism perpetuated by U.S. colleges and universities well into the twentieth century. For instance, Ferguson (2004) outlines how canonical sociology has historically constructed African Americans' fitness for citizenship based on white liberal ideologies of sex, family, and gendered relations.

Despite the use of higher education as a tool of not simply marginalization but also oppression, by the mid-eighteenth century a slow shift took hold in society of utilizing higher education as a means of freedom and social justice. Even before the abolition of slavery, enslaved Africans in the South sought education in secrecy, learning to read and write despite legal and social oppression. In the North, between 1835 and 1865, approximately 140 black women attended Oberlin College (Hull and Smith 1982), and black scholars attended educational institutions established by religious and abolitionist missionaries, such as Cheyney (1837), Lincoln (1854), and Wilberforce (1856) (Anderson 1988). Thus, education has been a means of freedom and empowerment for subjugated people in the United States.

At the end of the Civil War in 1865, the Freedman's Bureau began establishing black colleges in the South to educate the newly emancipated African American population. By 1880, blacks in the South had successfully waged a movement for universal, or public, education. Instead of dismantling the public education campaign, southern whites began devising a strategy to divert black schools from offering a traditional liberal education and instead offer one that would uphold Southern stratified social structures (Anderson 1988). Developed by Samuel Armstrong and championed by Booker T. Washington and white northern industrial philanthropists, "the 'Hampton-Tuskegee Idea' represented the ideological antithesis of the educational and social movement begun by ex-slaves" (Anderson 1988, 33). Thus, Tuskegee and Hampton epitomized the industrial model of black education, aimed at preparing African Americans for lower-class labor positions, while schools such as Fisk, Dillard, and Howard, favored by W.E.B. DuBois, ascribed to a more classic liberal arts curriculum.

Northern industrial philanthropists sought to exploit the financial vulnerability of black colleges. They hoped to develop a conservative black leader constituency that would erode African American political acumen. Even so, when they received support from northern white industrialists, such as the General Education Board (established by John D. Rockefeller), black colleges received only a small percentage of what historically white colleges and universities (HWCUs) received (Anderson 1988). Furthermore, with the passing of the Morrill Act I (1862) and II (1890), states established historically black colleges and universities (HBCUs) under the logic of separate but equal public higher education for blacks and whites, but HBCUs were funded disproportionately less than their white counterparts.

Women and Native Americans faced similar challenges—their educational opportunities were aligned with their expected social role. During colonial times, women were legally excluded from college, and by 1860 only about forty-five institutions offered degrees to women (Thelin 2004). Women's curricular and co-curricular engagement was usually differentiated from men's, and ranged from vocational training to genteel finishing-school programs (Thelin 2004). The Indian Removal Act (1830) formalized the removal of Native tribes to federal territory or reservations west of the Mississippi River as a way to seize land for white settlers (Gasman, Nguyen, and Conrad 2015). Around this time, the Bureau of Indian Affairs was created and tasked with Indian education, continuing the assimilationist educational practices begun by early colonial colleges and missionaries (Gasman, Nguyen, and Conrad 2015). The Bureau of Indian Affairs established boarding schools with the purpose of inculcating Euro-American values and eradicating native languages, names, and faiths. Indian schools outside reservations, such as Carlisle and Haskell, adopted the industrial model of education. Needless to say, the early foundations of higher education were built mostly for exclusion, not inclusion, but these spaces were also crafted by a small group of marginalized and oppressed people for agency and freedom.

Twentieth-Century Challenges and Changes

At the turn of the twentieth century, the majority of college students were elite white men. Likewise, Thelin (2004) writes, the ideal college student was embodied by public figures such as Theodore Roosevelt and Woodrow Wilson. Though Native Americans, African Americans, and women were attending postsecondary institutions, their subjugated role in society often dictated their access to and quality of education. Thus, for many within these social categories, higher education was limited to industrial training, genteel finishing-school programs, and/or assimilationist efforts at institutions under-resourced and segregated from their white male counterparts, who were largely exposed to a broader liberal arts education.

The beginning of the twentieth century also marked the changing demographics of the U.S. population. The nineteenth-century Gold Rush brought Chinese immigrants to the West Coast, where they worked low-wage service jobs once gold became scarce. From 1910 to 1930, nearly one million Mexicans immigrated to the United States as the demand for low-wage labor increased. With an influx of Asian and Latino immigrants, these emerging populations generated white anxieties as U.S. demographics shifted. As a result, racialized sexual discourses, such as eugenics, emerged from academic and scientific communities. Derived from social Darwinism, which suggested that competition among groups was the basis of human progress, eugenics constituted the nexus of evolutionary theory and population administration. Eugenicists such as Francis Galton were fundamentally concerned with increasing the numbers and "quality" of the upper-class white population, which included discouraging miscegenation and procreation among "less fit" populations. Phrases like (white) "race suicide"—which Theodore Roosevelt invoked and made popular—characterized eugenic ideology (Somerville 2000). Subsequently, new immigrant populations were subjected to a variety of state-administered regulations, including assimilation programs, vice surveillance, residential segregation, and immigration exclusion laws (Ferguson 2004).

Education, however, has been a means of liberation and political recognition for subjugated groups in the United States. Even before abolition, enslaved Africans in the South strived for education in secrecy, learning to read and write when it was unlawful, and African American leaders such as W.E.B. Du Bois promoted liberal arts education to fortify African Americans' civic capacity and commitment to social uplift. Accordingly, African Americans pushed back against the regulation of educational structures, working to gain control over their education and challenge industrial models. In the 1920s, black students derailed the plans of northern industrial philanthropists to implement a Hampton-Tuskegee conservative philosophy at the liberal arts–focused Fisk University (Anderson 1988). In 1944 a group of HBCU presidents led by Frederick D. Patterson of Tuskegee created the United Negro College Fund to collaborate on fund-raising efforts and replace the waning support of the U.S. Department of Education—a strategy that would later be replicated by other minority-serving institutions (MSIs) (Gasman 2007). Independent financing further provided HBCUs with autonomy over their curriculum.

College education for women was also changing and gaining acceptance. Between 1880 and 1920 several women's colleges emerged as pillars in the field of women's education, including the elite private northeastern colleges known as the "Seven Sisters." States, particularly in the South, charted women's colleges throughout the first half of the twentieth century. Furthermore, coeducation was the fastest-growing model of women's education at the time (Thelin 2004). Yet, access to college education for women was still almost exclusively white and wealthy. The few black women who did attend elite private women's colleges faced serious limitations in campus life, such as segregated housing. Women of color who attended state-funded coeducational institutions were restricted in myriad ways, such as being forced into "appropriate" majors and barred from campus leadership positions (Thelin 2004).

Radical Shifts

Political and social unrest in the 1960s and 1970s called prevailing ideas of higher education into question. The 1954 *Brown v. Board of Education* Supreme Court decision marked the beginning of desegregation efforts. Though desegregation would be resisted, particularly in the South, the *Brown* decision had a significant impact on historically black colleges and universities (HBCUs) and white institutions. As historically white colleges and universities (HWCUs) started to attract high-achieving black students, students of color began to challenge the dominant structures and barriers on HWCU campuses. HBCUs' relevance began to be questioned, a trend that would continue into the twenty-first century (Gasman 2007). Even so, students at HBCUs continued to play an integral part in galvanizing the civil rights movement. Students at schools such as Howard and North Carolina A&T organized activist groups on campus and participated in local and national racial justice demonstrations (Rojas 2007).

Influenced by radical black nationalism, black students at HWCUs changed the academic curriculum and altered university life (Rojas 2007). Black student activists formed black student unions and demanded that black studies courses be taught. In 1969, San Francisco State University established the first College of Ethnic Studies as a response to a five-month student-led protests in 1968. The founding of ethnic studies at San Francisco State and subsequent universities provided an outlet for alternative epistemological points of view and shifted the intellectual landscape of the academy. Furthermore, the fight for black curricular and co-curricular spaces served as a framework for subsequent campus formations in the decade to come, including unions, centers, and academic departments centering scholarship about women, people with disabilities, Asian Americans, Chicanas/os, Native Americans, and members of the LGBTQ (lesbian, gay, bisexual, transgender, queer) community. For instance, one of the first women's studies programs was established at San Diego State University in 1970 after activist organizing by conscious-raising women's groups.

With historic civil rights legislation in place, majority-white colleges and universities were under increased legal pressure to integrate their campuses, particularly in the South. By 1968, only a minimal gain had been made in integrating many of the southern state flagship institutions (Thelin 2004). Therefore, as students of color began to gain admission, typically after legal challenges, to the former all-white-male state institutions, they faced unprecedented discrimination, and even violence, entering these campuses. For instance, Native American students who attended HWCUs typically returned home without a degree after facing inordinate discrimination and isolation (Gasman, Nguyen, and Conrad 2015).

The Immigration and Nationality Act (1965) changed decades-old immigration policy that privileged immigrants from Europe, and thus more immigrants from Asia, Africa, and Latin American countries were admitted to the United States. The discrimination experienced by new immigrants resulted in Latinas/os pushing for social change, including higher education access and equity (Gasman, Nguyen, and Conrad 2015). The Higher Education Act of 1965 increased federal funding to HBCUs because of historical abuse and neglect, and in 1992 a contemporary iteration of the act established support for Hispanic-serving institutions as a response to the growing population.

For Native Americans, the Indian Civil Rights Act of 1968 provided the agency necessary for tribal communities to establish tribally controlled colleges, leading to a surge in their development between 1971 and 1975. While tribal colleges proliferated, single-gender colleges dwindled as many opted to become coeducational. As Thelin (2004) writes, the transition to coeducation typically rendered greater gains for the former all-male institutions, as former women's colleges lost their appeal for high-achieving female students. By 1970, women made up 41 percent of all undergraduates in the United States, becoming the majority of undergraduate students enrolled in postsecondary institutions in 1979—a trend that endures today. Furthermore, the 1972 Title IX legislation, which prohibits sex discrimination in educational programming, resulted in more equitable inclusion of women in college life. Title IX was eventually extended to include sexual harassment and sexual assault committed on campuses in its definition of sex discrimination. This legislation has been increasingly used to seek redress for such crimes following the 1992 *Franklin v. Gwinnett County Public Schools* Supreme Court case, which ruled that individual victims of sexual harassment could receive monetary damages under Title IX (AAUP 2016).

Furthermore, to challenge the myth of the model minority, Asian American and Pacific Islander (AAPI) communities organized to change the national dialogue and perception of students of Asian descent. Thus, legislative efforts have been geared toward rejecting frameworks that associate AAPI students with whites and recognizing the diversity of ethnicity and class experiences within the subpopulation (Gasman, Nguyen, and Conrad 2015). In 2007, as part of the College Cost Reduction and Access Act, Asian American and Native American Pacific Islander Serving Institutions (AANAPISIs) became federally designated MSIs predicated on institutions having at least 10 percent AAPI enrollment and at least 50 percent of their entire student body demonstrating financial need.

Historical Impact

Though changes initiated in the 1960s and 1970s increased access for minoritized students in higher education, legacies of subjugation and oppression remain relevant even as colleges and universities diversify. Brunsma, Brown, and Placier (2013) argue that HWCUs continue to be "white spaces" in which "walls of whiteness" are constructed through spatial, curricular, and ideological barriers. The authors argue that racialized socialization and white homogenous social networks embed these barriers within the white imagination, leading white students to resist engaging in diverse learning experiences. As a result, these "walls of whiteness" prevent white students from seeing and engaging racial realities on campus while isolating and subjugating marginalized students, faculty, and staff. Moreover, since the 1970s, there have been concerted efforts to dismantle civil rights–era policies, such as affirmative action, slowing or reversing campus integration progress.

Furthermore, as minority differences were absorbed by colleges and universities, the institutionalization of those differences primarily resulted in the isolation and regulation of minority differences. Thus, the more radical reconstructive elements of the social movements of the 1960s and 1970s were neutralized. For instance, Roderick Ferguson (2012) contends sexuality was constituted within sociology and the academy as a single-issue form of difference without regard to gender and race—obscuring "questions of intersectionality and histories" of gay liberation's overlap with critiques of race, U.S. imperialism, and patriarchy" (217). As discussed earlier with concern to the concept of diversity within higher education, Ferguson illustrates how institutional interpretations of difference can resurrect barriers to challenging systems of power. Today, the effects of these historical configurations can be observed at MSIs and HWCUs, influencing all facets of institutional life, including the respective and interrelated experiences of students, faculty, and staff.

ORGANIZATION OF THE BOOK

The aim of this book is to offer a more comprehensive exploration of the intersected experiences of campus community members. Three sections of the volume are divided into student-, faculty-, and staff-focused chapters, while a fourth section discusses institutional efforts for equity and inclusion. However, the reader will find that these are not neat or tidy divisions; multiple chapters consider how staff, faculty, and student experiences cross and connect. As the first chapter on student experiences, chapter 2 explores how students from different racial groups (Asian, black, Latina/o, and white) perceive the campus climate in a seemingly diverse and inclusive college. Marcela Cuellar and R. Nicole Johnson-Ahorlu use a public comprehensive university as a case study, conducting a mixed-methods study utilizing student responses to the Diverse Learning Environments survey and focus group data. Cuellar and Johnson-Ahorlu's study discusses students' perceptions of the campus climate in relation to discrimination and bias, institutional commitment to diversity, and satisfaction with diversity. Altogether, this study further affirms that race matters and can influence student experiences at more diverse campuses.

Terry-Ann Jones provides a unique discussion of undocumented students' experiences in chapter 3. With an estimated 10–12 million undocumented persons living in the United States, it should not come as a surprise that their presence is pervasive in a range of spaces and contexts. Jones discusses a study involving surveys of faculty, staff, and administrators at twenty-eight Jesuit institutions, along with in-depth, qualitative interviews with students, staff, and administrators at six institutions. She elaborates on the experiences of undocumented students, arguing that their concerns extend well beyond the legal and financial realms. Although they contend with financial limitations and fears that their status will be revealed, the students also struggle with the dual identities of being students at elite, private universities and being undocumented immigrants with limited resources, few prospects for employment, and a burdensome secret that places limitations on multiple areas of their lives. This chapter also explores the increasing campus awareness of undocumented students and their role in fostering intersected campus experiences.

Chapter 4 details how social class intersects with race and ethnicity to affect student experiences at liberal arts colleges. Deborah Warnock draws on in-depth, semi-structured interviews with students who had expressed interest or were active in a student-led group for low-income, first-generation, and/or working-class identified students at a selective liberal arts college. Warnock elaborates on how embracing particular class-oriented identities varied by race among students. Students who were part of this program identified a community of support and shared experience largely based on race and ethnicity rather than class, although socioeconomic background was one of the official criteria for membership and race and ethnicity were not. Warnock also expounds on why some students voiced concern about the possibility of organizing effectively and cohesively around social class identity when the needs of low-income and/or first-generation students of color and those of low-income and/or first-generation white students on campus might vary.

In chapter 5, Kristen Clayton explores the experiences of multiracial students on college campuses. Although a growing number of students identify as multiracial or multiethnic, most of the existing scholarship on multiracial college students' experiences focuses on students attending HWCUs, with little research examining such experiences at HBCUs. Drawing on interviews, Clayton explores how biracial students navigate race and negotiate their racial identities within different institutional contexts (HWCU compared with HBCU), and how students discuss this racial identity work in relation to class and gender in reflection of the racial structures of each college that can shape the social interactions and identity work of students. Clayton describes how multiracial students navigate the white privilege and racial discrimination endemic on their HWCU campus, while HBCU students navigated racial privilege in contrasting ways and dealt with isolation from the black community and institutional resources. Further, Clayton discusses how campus programming and student organizations may assist or exacerbate multiracial students' experiences at each type of institution.

In chapter 6, Victor Ray revisits a classic text examining the passage through graduate school for black students by focusing on these experiences in the post–civil rights era. In the immediate and hostile desegregation efforts in higher education, Douglas Davidson, a black graduate student in sociology at Berkeley, wrote an incisive article on racism during his graduate career. Davidson's "The Furious Passage of the Black Graduate Student" combined a searing blend of the personal and the political arguing that integration and equality were far from synonymous as integration was a largely cosmetic response to institutional white supremacy since racism shaped nearly every interracial encounter. Further, Davidson anticipated arguments that have become pivotal to current scholarship on race. Almost fifty years after publication, this theoretically informed rumination on the centrality of racism in higher education is still passed between students of color. Building on Davidson's informative writings, Ray focuses on three main areas of graduate student life for students of color in the post–civil rights era: (1) organizational barriers to admission and matriculation, (2) microaggressions at HWCUs, and (3) how cultural forces impact campus life. Ray highlights the importance of faculty of color and white allies in shaping the campus experience for students of color.

Turning to the identities and experiences of faculty on campus in chapter 7, Elizabeth Lee and Tonya Maynard focus on how faculty members from low-socioeconomic backgrounds similar to those of some of their students can play important roles in integrating students into the college community. While many professors find this kind of connection to students fulfilling, there is also evidence that some faculty members are asked more than others to take on such tasks, specifically those who are female and/or of color. Drawing on interviews with demographically diverse faculty members from low-socioeconomic backgrounds at different campuses, Lee and Maynard examine (1) whether faculty from low-socioeconomic-status (SES) backgrounds seek to support low-SES students themselves, and how they choose to do so; (2) the reasoning for support offered; (3) how faculty members determine which students may need their support; and (4) faculty concerns about sharing personal backgrounds. Through their study, Lee and Maynard elaborate how higher education, and faculty bodies in particular, can be more inclusive of faculty members from low-socioeconomic backgrounds and the importance of cultivating this inclusion for higher education as a whole.

In chapter 8, Denise Goerisch looks at the emotional labor performed by faculty members through an examination of a public comprehensive that has branded itself as an affordable alternative to the private liberal arts college. Their commitment to providing students with a transformative liberal arts education carries forward through institutional initiatives and also encourages the development of meaningful and profound relationships between peers, faculty, staff, and the community. In an effort to aid in the formation of these relationships, faculty performed the gendered practice of emotional labor as they nurtured students' academic, professional, and personal development through advising and mentoring. Goerisch examines faculty members' care work and how it changed after a major budget cut at the institution to better understand how these changes impacted some of the more marginalized populations on campus, and perhaps more significantly, how these changes reproduce difference on this particular college campus. Drawing on ethnographic data, analyses of university policies and discourse, and faculty and the public's responses to changes in state policy and rhetoric, Goerisch argues that despite the systematic devaluing of faculty care work, faculty still believe that emotional labor is essential for student success in college, and the loss of emotional labor increases the likelihood of precarity among students.

In chapter 9, Bedelia Richards describes the perils and pitfalls of merit evaluations of faculty members of color. Through a grounded approach to understand personal experiences, Richards shows how systems of evaluation can function to systematically marginalize, exclude, and disempower faculty of color, and in so doing, function effectively as tools of racial subordination. Richards draws on the academic literature to show how her experiences reflect a broader pattern among other faculty of color recruited to "diversify" predominantly white institutions. These institutions draw on the common discourse of "diversity" as an ideal that is valued and critical to preparing its (white) students to function effectively in an increasingly diverse and globalized world. Yet, diversity for many institutions involves the placement of more black and brown faces in predominantly and historically white institutions, without much thought of how to make historically underrepresented group members feel equally valued as part of campus communities. Thus, Richards notes research-driven, actionable steps that institutions can take to foster a more inclusive environment for marginalized faculty.

In chapter 10, Melanie Gast, Maliq Matthew, and Derrick Brooms grapple with emerging discussions of how faculty can work toward racial inclusion through teaching in light of recent public debates. In the wake of racial strife and numerous student protests on college campuses in conjunction with the aftermath of the 2016 presidential election, college students continue to engage in walkouts, protests, and vocal responses to racial oppression and hate crimes at their institutions. Faculty members work on the ground and regularly interact with students, but faculty members are also constrained by their lack of authority and status in college administration and policy. The authors draw on their experiences and strategies as faculty who regularly teach about race, inequality, and diversity to offer approaches for discussing and educating about these issues, while promoting safe environments and advancing the cause of true inclusion through our work in the classroom. The authors further consider how their approach to class discussions of these aspects of everyday life shifted in light of the 2016 presidential election. Through a consideration of their varied backgrounds and those of their students, the authors explore strategies for engaging these important issues and navigating race relations and dialogue in the modern-day era.

In chapter 11, Orkideh Mohajeri, Fernando Rodriguez, and finn schneider provide insights into their experience teaching required undergraduate leadership courses at a HWCU. The curriculum focused on identity exploration through self-reflection, critical analysis of social dynamics, and leadership development and community building. Having taught sections of the course together and individually over several semesters, the authors explore how they alternatively took up or masked various identities as a pedagogical tool for connection to learners and curriculum. Mohajeri, Rodriguez, and schneider broaden the scope of intersectionality to include the multiple identities faculty navigate in their classroom instruction, specifically their own experiences. The authors present vignettes to exemplify the ways in which they individually used intersectionality and self-reflection to prepare for instruction. Intersectionality and performativity, then, become instructional tools that continually inform how and when the authors choose to embody particular aspects of identity. Mohajeri, Rodriguez, and schneider elaborate how co-instruction can be a policy solution, and recommend the institutionalization of team teaching as a policy solution with particular training and emphasis on intersectionality and performativity. Through these approaches, the authors advocate for an applied usage that can help move both instruction and learning forward in concrete ways.

An understudied and somewhat invisible group of the campus community is staff members. Ophelie Rowe-Allen and Meredith Smith address the role of student affairs professionals in managing student development and other institutional priorities in chapter 12. Student affairs professionals play a critical role in creating and implementing high-impact practices resulting in positive student engagement. In addition, student affairs professionals are continually reshaping the campus environment. To accomplish these tasks, student affairs professionals must be skilled in managing institutional commitments in concert with the ever-changing needs of student populations. Despite the quantity of research on student engagement, there is little understanding of the intersection of the student affairs competencies with the identities of student affairs professionals. The authors describe not only their journeys into the student affairs profession but also their successes and challenges when navigating their work experiences through the lens of their diverse backgrounds. Utilizing research and personal experiences, Rowe-Allen and

Smith conclude with promising practices for student affairs professionals that build on the consideration of identities and positions as staff members within campus communities.

Tonisha Lane provides a window into the lives of staff members working in science, technology, engineering, and mathematics (STEM) programs in colleges in chapter 13. Significant attention has been devoted to the recruitment and retention of underrepresented groups in the STEM fields. What is less known is the role administrators can play in helping students understand and navigate these racialized environments. Lane's qualitative case study utilizing interviews with administrators and an instructor who were part of a STEM enrichment program describes how administrators help students of color make meaning of college STEM environments. The study's findings reveal that while the institutional agents provided some useful strategies for navigating racial climates, additional efforts should be geared toward unpacking institutional and systemic racism. Lane concludes her chapter by elaborating on the implications for institutional policies and practices that can increase the inclusiveness of campus communities, particularly in STEM programs.

In chapter 14, Annemarie Vaccaro and Ezekiel Kimball examine the experiences of staff members working with students who have various forms of disabilities. The percentage of students with disabilities pursuing a postsecondary degree has grown rapidly, and they often face a chilly campus climate while contending with prevailing societal disability stigmas. Little research has documented how support for students with disabilities is infused into student affairs practice or how staff members navigate multiple (and sometimes competing) needs of students with and without disabilities to create inclusive and affirming campus environments for all students. This chapter rectifies this problem by sharing the findings from a constructivist grounded theory study about the ways postsecondary staff members from twenty-one institutions conceptualized and responded to disability on campus. During focus groups, professionals described a range of observed behaviors directed toward students with disabilities by campus peers without disabilities. To combat the largely uncivil and exclusionary peer behavior, staff members navigated their liminal role to foster inclusion by teaching, modeling, and creating conditions for civil behavior and perspective taking. Thus, Vaccaro and Kimball offer insight into the intersected nature of campus inclusion and exclusion through the lens of both social identities (i.e., disability) and positions (i.e., staff, students).

In chapter 15, Megan Nanney explores the emergence of trans* policies on college campuses, particularly as they relate to college admissions. Outcry and protest arose in 2013 when Smith College, a women's college in Massachusetts, denied admission to Calliope Wong, a trans* woman, because her financial aid form indicated her sex as male. Since then, at least ten women's colleges have adopted explicit admissions policies outlining varying biological, social, and legal criteria for who may apply to the institution. Previous literature on this topic focuses primarily on legal issues, administrative perceptions, and student and alumni activism around trans* students on campus. Nanney complicates our understanding of gendered policies as a relationship among identity, biology, and legal status leading to trans* precarity. Rather than sex/gender serving as the sole institutional barrier for trans* individuals at these institutions, the utilization of an intersectional analysis can highlight how even seemingly inclusive institutional policies may still exclude the most marginalized students. Nanney calls for a rethinking of best practices beyond the mere addition of identities to pre-existing nondiscrimination practices that invite students into broken systems. They also emphasize trickle-up justice and policy building led by the students to assist with addressing the multiple, interlocking systems of inequalities preventing full inclusion and participation within postsecondary systems of education.

Chapter 16, written by Susan Iverson, discusses why expanding intersectional analyses in higher education is important for the study of organizations and how to combat the reproduction of inequalities. Iverson shares findings from an intersectional analysis of diversity action plans at U.S. flagship universities using an Intersectionality-Based Policy Analysis. This analytic framework centers eight guiding principles in the analysis and represents a ten-year follow-up to a similar study examining diversity action plans at land-grant universities (Iverson 2007, 2008, 2012). Iverson provides campus constituents with vital information on how diversity action plans can assist or hinder equity efforts, and poignantly notes how these policies (diversity action plans) must not only assess and critique what exists but also create new ways of thinking and doing in order to reduce inequities.

In the concluding chapter, the editors coalesce the many findings, implications, and policy suggestions provided across the volume into a discussion of how researchers, administrators, and policy makers can move forward with utilizing intersectionality to improve the inclusivity of college campuses, and combat social inequalities embedded within and perpetuated by the institution. Throughout the discussion, the editors identify potential areas of research that could extend the current volume's findings and provide more insight into the multiple identities and positions of campus community members in higher education. They also elaborate on possible policies that could be utilized on different campuses with slight adjustments to fit the specific campus contexts. Last, the editors provide final commentary to situate this volume's findings and implications for conversations of intersectionality and social inequalities in broader society.

On the whole, this volume provides a challenge to the segmented approach frequently used to investigate topics of diversity and inclusion among campus communities. Students do not pursue their degrees without interacting with faculty and staff. Faculty cannot complete their research and teach their classes effectively without the support of staff members and students. Staff members balance the needs of faculty and students with the larger mission and organization of the institution. By examining how people on campus with different identities and positions approach their everyday life in the classrooms, offices, laboratories, dining halls, and other spaces on campus, our volume provides a more holistic view of campus life. We hope that readers will build on this comprehensive foundation to one day eliminate the marginality pervading our campuses.

REFERENCES

Alexander, M. Jacqui. 2005. *Pedagogies of Crossing: Mediations on Feminism, Sexual Politics, Memory, and the Sacred*. Durham, NC: Duke University Press.

American Association of University Professors (AAUP). 2016. "The History, Uses, and Abuses of Title IX." *Bulletin of the AAUP* 102: 69–99.

Andersen, Margaret, and Patricia Hill Collins. 2013. "Why Race, Class, and Gender Still Matter." In *Race, Class, and Gender: An Anthology*, 8th ed., edited by M. Andersen and P. Hill Collins, 1–14. Boston: Cengage Learning.

Anderson, James D. 1988. *The Education of Blacks in the South, 1860–1935*. Chapel Hill: University of North Carolina Press.

Berila, Beth. 2015. *Integrating Mindfulness into Anti-oppression Pedagogy: Social Justice in Higher Education*. New York: Routledge.

Browne, Irene, and Joya Misra. 2003. "The Intersection of Gender and Race in the Labor Market." *Annual Review of Sociology* 29 (1): 487–513.

Brunsma, David L., Eric S. Brown, and Peggy Placier. 2013. "Teaching Race at Historically White Colleges and Universities: Identifying and Dismantling the Walls of Whiteness." *Critical Sociology* 39 (5):717–738.

Carbado, Devon W., Kimberle Williams Crenshaw, Vickie M. Mays, and Barbara Tomlinson. 2013. "Intersectionality: Mapping the Movements of a Theory." *Du Bois Review* 10 (2): 303–312.

Cho, Sumi, Kimberlé Williams Crenshaw, and Leslie McCall. 2013. "Toward a Field of Intersectionality Studies: Theory, Applications, and Praxis." *Signs: Journal of Women in Culture and Society* 38 (4): 785–810.

Choo, Hae Yeon, and Myra Marx Ferree. 2010. "Practicing Intersectionality in Sociological Research: A Critical Analysis of Inclusions, Interactions, and Institutions in the Study of Inequalities." *Sociological Theory* 28 (2): 129–149.

Collins, Patricia Hill. 1990. *Black Feminist Thought: Knowledge, Consciousness, and the Politics of Empowerment*. Boston: Unwin Hyman.

———. 1998. "It's All in the Family: Intersections of Gender, Race, and Nation." *Hypatia* 13 (3): 62–82.

———. 2000. *Black Feminist Thought: Knowledge, Consciousness, and the Politics of Empowerment*. 2nd ed. New York: Routledge.

Collins, Patricia Hill, and Sirma Bilge. 2016. *Intersectionality*. Cambridge, UK: Polity Press.

Combahee River Collective. 1982. "A Black Feminist Statement." In *All the Women Are White, All the Blacks Are Men, but Some of Us Are Brave: Black Women's Studies*, edited by G. Hull, P. Bell-Scott, and B. Smith, 13–22. New York: Feminist Press at the City University of New York.

Crenshaw, Kimberle. 1989. "Demarginalizing the Intersection of Race and Sex: A Black Feminist Critique of Antidiscrimination Doctrine, Feminist Theory and Antiracist Politics." *University of Chicago Legal Forum* 1989:139–168.

———. 1991. "Mapping the Margins: Intersectionality, Identity Politics, and Violence against Women of Color." *Stanford Law Review* 43 (6): 1241–1299.

Davis, Angela Y. 1981. *Women, Race, & Class*. New York: Random House.

Davis, Dannielle Joy, Rachelle J. Brunn-Bevel, and James L. Olive, eds. 2015. *Intersectionality in Educational Research*. Sterling, VA: Stylus.

Davis, Kathy. 2008. "Intersectionality as Buzzword: A Sociology of Science Perspective on What Makes a Feminist Theory Successful." *Feminist Theory* 9 (1): 67–85.

Deterding, Nicole M. 2015. "Instrumental and Expressive Education: College Planning in the Face of Poverty." *Sociology of Education* 88 (4): 284–301.

Dill, Bonnie Thornton. 2009. "Intersections, Identities, and Inequalities in Higher Education." In *Emerging Intersections: Race, Class, and Gender in Theory, Policy, and Practice*, edited by B. T. Dill and R. E. Zambrana, 229–252. Piscataway, NJ: Rutgers University Press.

Dill, Bonnie Thornton, and Ruth Enid Zambrana, eds. 2009. *Emerging Intersections: Race, Class, and Gender in Theory, Policy, and Practice*. Piscataway, NJ: Rutgers University Press.

Ferguson, Roderick A. 2004. *Aberrations in Black: Toward a Queer of Color Critique*. Minneapolis: University of Minnesota Press.

———. 2012. *The Reorder of Things: The University and Its Pedagogies of Minority Difference*. Minneapolis: University of Minnesota Press.

Gasman, Marybeth. 2007. *Envisioning Black Colleges: A History of the United Negro College Fund*. Baltimore: Johns Hopkins University Press.

Gasman, Marybeth, Thai-Huy Nguyen, and Clifton F. Conrad. 2015. "Lives Intertwined: A Primer on the History and Emergence of Minority Serving Institutions." *Journal of Diversity in Higher Education* 8 (2): 120–138.

Graves, Joseph L. 2001. *The Emperor's New Clothes: Biological Theories of Race at the Millennium*. New Brunswick, NJ: Rutgers University Press.

Griffin, Kimberly A., and Richard J. Reddick. 2011. "Surveillance and Sacrifice: Gender Differences in the Mentoring Patterns of Black Professors at Predominantly White Research Universities." *American Educational Research Journal* 48 (5): 1032–1057.

Hancock, Ange-Marie. 2007. "Intersectionality as a Normative and Empirical Paradigm." *Politics & Gender* 3 (2): 248–254.

Hull, Gloria T., and Barbara Smith. 1982. "Introduction: The Politics of Black Women's Studies." In *All the Women Are White, All the Blacks Are Men, but Some of Us Are Brave: Black Women's Studies*, edited by G. Hull, P. Bell-Scott, and B. Smith, xvii–xxxii. New York: Feminist Press at the City University of New York.

Iverson, Susan V. 2007. "Camouflaging Power and Privilege: A Critical Race Analysis of University Diversity Policies." *Educational Administration Quarterly* 43 (5): 586–611.

———. 2008. "Capitalizing on Change: The Discursive Framing of Diversity in US Land-Grant Universities." *Equity & Excellence in Education* 41 (2): 182–199.

———. 2012. "Constructing Outsiders: The Discursive Framing of Access in University Diversity Policies." *Review of Higher Education* 35 (2): 149–177.

Jones, Susan R., and Elisa S. Abes. 2013. *Identity Development of College Students: Advancing Frameworks for Multiple Dimensions of Identity*. San Francisco: Jossey-Bass.

Landry, Bart. 2007. "The Theory of Intersectional Analysis." In *Race, Gender, and Class: Theory and Methods of Analysis*, edited by B. Landry, 1–15. Upper Saddle Creek, NJ: Prentice Hall.

Lorde, Audre. 1984. *Sister Outsider*. Berkley, CA: Crossing Press.

Lundy-Wagner, Valerie, and Rachelle Winkle-Wagner. 2013. "A Harassing Climate? Sexual Harassment and Campus Racial Climate Research." *Journal of Diversity in Higher Education* 6 (1): 51–68.

Marine, Susan. 2011. "Reflections from 'Professional Feminists' in Higher Education: Women's and Gender Centers at the Start of the Twenty-First Century." In *Empowering Women in Higher Education and Student Affairs: Theory, Research, Narratives, and Practice from*

Feminist Perspectives, edited by P. A. Pasque and S. Errington Nicholson, 15–31. Sterling, VA: Stylus.

Mitchell, Donald Jr., Charlana Y. Simmons, and Lindsay A. Greyerbiehl, eds. 2014. *Intersectionality and Higher Education: Theory, Research and Praxis*. New York: Peter Lang.

Mohanty, Chandra T. 2003. *Feminisms without Borders: Decolonizing Theory, Practicing Solidarity*. Durham, NC: Duke University Press.

Nielsen, Kelly. 2015. "'Fake It 'til You Make It': Why Community College Students' Aspirations 'Hold Steady.'" *Sociology of Education* 88 (4): 265–283.

Ovink, Sarah M. 2017. *Race, Class, and Choice in Latino/a Higher Education: Pathways in the College-for-All Era*. New York: Springer.

Rojas, Fabio. 2007. *From Black Power to Black Studies: How a Radical Social Movement Became an Academic Discipline*. Baltimore: Johns Hopkins University Press.

Smedley, Audrey, and Brian Smedley. 2011. *Race in North America: Origin and Evolution of a Worldwide View*. Boulder, CO: Westview Press.

Somerville, Siobhan B. 2000. *Queering the Color Line: Race and the Invention of Homosexuality in American Culture*. Durham, NC: Duke University Press.

Stevens, Mitchell L., Elizabeth A. Armstrong, and Richard Arum. 2008. "Sieve, Incubator, Temple, Hub: Empirical and Theoretical Advances in the Sociology of Higher Education." *Annual Review of Sociology* 34: 127–151.

Strayhorn, Terrell, ed. 2013. *Living at the Intersections: Social Identities and Black Collegians*. Charlotte, NC: IAP.

Thelin, John R. 2004. *A History of American Higher Education*. Baltimore: Johns Hopkins University Press.

Wilder, Craig Steven. 2013. *Ebony & Ivy: Race, Slavery, and the Troubled History of America's Universities*. New York: Bloomsbury Press.

Winkle-Wagner, Rachelle, and Angela M. Locks. 2013. *Diversity and Inclusion on Campus: Supporting Racially and Ethnically Underrepresented Students*. New York: Routledge.

Zuberi, Tukufu. 2001. *Thicker Than Blood: How Racial Statistics Lie*. Minneapolis: University of Minnesota Press.

PART II BEYOND EXAMS AND PARTIES

Student Identities and Experiences

2 · THE CONTINGENT CLIMATE

Exploring Student Perspectives at a Racially Diverse Institution

MARCELA G. CUELLAR AND
R. NICOLE JOHNSON-AHORLU

Institutions of higher education, particularly public four-year universities, enroll student populations that are increasingly diverse (Deil-Amen 2015). In these contexts, diversity in terms of race, gender, class, enrollment patterns, and so on is the norm; yet, discussions of diversity in higher education largely exclude the experiences of students in these institutions, despite their critical role in educating a majority of undergraduates (Deil-Amen 2015). Understanding how students perceive and experience diverse campuses is essential to enhancing student success. Perceptions of hostile campus climates can adversely affect students' sense of belonging (Hurtado, Carter, and Spuler 1996), help-seeking behaviors (Johnson-Ahorlu 2012), and retention (Johnson et al. 2014; Museus, Nichols, and Lambert 2008). Although diversity within the student body is a catalyst for a welcoming environment (Hurtado et al. 2008), how students from different racial groups view the campus climate within racially diverse contexts and how intersecting identities shape these perceptions require more research.

This chapter explores how African American, Asian, Latina/o, and white students perceive the campus climate in a seemingly inclusive college. As students experience diversity along multiple dimensions, we consider how the intersections of gender, students' pathways into college as a first-time freshman or transfer student, and race inform these perceptions. Our case study is set at Basin University,[1] a public comprehensive university with a majority nonwhite student population. The campus is also unique in its architectural reflections of African American history and culture, appearing on the surface as inviting to students of color. However, our mixed-methods exploration reveals differing views of the campus climate that are contingent on students' racial backgrounds, which further intersect with students' pathways into the university. The fact that our methodological approach uncovered these multiple perspectives indicates the importance of layered examinations of the campus climate to yield more accurate conclusions.

THEORETICAL PERSPECTIVES

The Multi-Contextual Model for Diverse Learning Environments (MMDLE) highlights the importance of the campus climate in universities (Hurtado et al. 2012). The MMDLE details the internal and external factors, such as sociohistorical, political, and institutional contexts, shaping the academic experiences of undergraduates and ultimately affecting student success. Within the institutional context, the campus climate is central and comprises several interrelated dimensions. The *historical dimension* captures the historical context detailing when diverse groups were included or excluded on campus, the *organizational dimension* reflects structures and practices that support group-based privilege or oppression, the *compositional dimension* refers to the number of diverse students on campus, the *psychological dimension* is the perception of intergroup relations and discrimination, and the *behavioral dimension* constitutes the interactions among or between different groups on campus (Hurtado et al. 2012). Each dimension of the climate shapes and influences student experiences within an institution. On racially diverse campuses, we might assume that students of color are more likely to view climates positively and perceive fewer instances of discrimination. However, compositional diversity alone is insufficient in the cultivation of a welcoming climate. Institutions must consider how multiple dimensions of campus environments affect students' perceptions.

At the center of the MMDLE are student identities, which influence perceptions and experiences. As students possess multiple social identities, considering the intersectionality of these identities in how students perceive and navigate campus climates is essential. Intersectionality theory argues that multiple systems of oppression overlap to differentially shape the experiences of individuals (Crenshaw 1991). When intersections of identities and experiences are not considered, critical intragroup differences may be masked and further perpetuate inequities. These perspectives underscore the importance of accounting for socially constructed identities, such as race and gender, in students' perceptions and experiences on campus. Additionally, colleges ascribe other statuses that further distinguish students, such as first-time freshmen and transfers, which may also shape perceptions of campus climates. Thus, we examine how students from different racial backgrounds perceive the climate at a racially diverse campus, considering variations in perception along intersections of race, gender, and pathway into college as a first-time freshman or transfer student.

PERCEPTIONS OF CAMPUS CLIMATE THROUGH DIVERSE METHODOLOGIES

Several studies examine student perceptions of campus climate, largely situated at predominantly white institutions. A majority of studies employ quantitative approaches (Harper and Hurtado 2007; Hart and Fellabaum 2008), using measures assessing campus climate perceptions (Hurtado et al. 2008). In this section, we highlight scholarship that examines student perceptions of the campus climate through a variety of methodological approaches across different racial groups and a range of institutional contexts. We reference a few studies that include intersectional analyses. We begin with a review of scholarship employing quantitative research, followed by qualitative approaches, and more recent scholarship that combines both methods.

Based on quantitative studies, students of color and white students perceive the campus in distinct ways (Hurtado et al. 2008), with students of color reporting more racial conflict. These differing perceptions are often shaped by the quality of interactions students have with students from different racial groups (Locks et al. 2008). Although students of color share similar perceptions of climate in some contexts (Reid and Radhakrishnan 2003), African American students consistently report more hostile environments than other racial groups (Hurtado et al. 2008). Most large-scale quantitative studies, however, do not fully explore the unique experiences of all historically marginalized groups (Hurtado et al. 2008). Nonetheless, emerging research suggests that Asian college students may experience more bias than their peers (Hurtado, Ruiz Alvarado, and Guillermo-Wann 2015). While few climate studies consider intersecting identities, one study finds that among Mexican American students, females and transfer students perceive less discrimination (Ruiz Alvarado and Hurtado 2015). Further, most quantitative climate research reflects student experiences at predominantly white campuses with relatively little exploration of more racially diverse campuses.

Qualitative approaches are less frequently used as the sole method examining campus climate (Harper and Hurtado 2007; Hart and Fellabaum 2008). Scholarship employing qualitative methods provides more nuanced views of students' perceptions. Students of color at less racially diverse institutions generally report unwelcoming climates and may question an institution's commitment to diversity when their curricular and co-curricular experiences do not positively align (Harper and Hurtado 2007; Jones, Castellanos, and Cole 2002). However, qualitative studies also expose critical differences across racial groups. For instance, white and Asian students at predominantly white campuses are generally most satisfied with the climate, while Latina/o, Native American, and African American students express less satisfaction (Harper and Hurtado 2007). However, students of color may also share positive and negative views, suggesting that perceptions of climate are multifaceted in more diverse institutional contexts (Santos et al. 2007). On campuses with larger representations of a racial minority group, prejudicial views of the minority group may be perpetuated by the dominant group. For example, white students maintain stereotypes about Asian peers at institutions with a substantial proportion of Asian students (Cabrera 2014). Consequently, Asian students still encounter discrimination at institutions where they constitute a majority (Poon 2011). Despite the tremendous contributions of qualitative research, much of this work does not focus on racially diverse campuses or consider variations across multiple racial groups and identities.

Though using mixed methods is common to unpublished institutional research, it remains rare in peer-reviewed research on campus climate (Hart and Fellabaum 2008). Mixed-methods studies highlight the complex nature of the campus climate since findings using more than one approach can deepen understanding or offer alternative perspectives (Allan and Madden 2006). For example, within a racially diverse community college in the West, Asian and Latina/o students perceive discrimination, but these views emerge through different methodological approaches (Cuellar and Johnson-Ahorlu 2016). Mixed-methods approaches can be particularly useful in intersectional analyses (Griffin and Museus 2011). One study, for example, exposes different views of campus climate and sense of belonging according to gender and class year among Filipino students (Maramba and Museus 2011). Although these few mixed-methods studies provide valuable additional perspectives on campus climate, they do not address intersecting identities across different racial groups.

METHODS

Our case study employs a parallel mixed-methods research design (Creswell and Plano Clark 2011) to examine student perceptions of the campus climate at a racially diverse university. In a parallel design, the quantitative and qualitative data are collected simultaneously and analyzed independently. Respective findings are compared for validity as well as theory building around similar or contrasting findings (Creswell and Plano Clark 2011). Given a lack of research on racially diverse campuses and the utility of mixed-methods in intersectional analyses, the goal of the study was to examine how different racial groups perceive the climate as well as how gender and student pathways into college additionally influence their perceptions.

Data Source

The data for the current study originated from a larger project, Diverse Learning Environments (DLE), conducted by the Higher Education Research Institute (HERI) at the University of California, Los Angeles. A pilot of the DLE survey was administered online in the spring of 2010 at several institutions across the United States. The DLE survey was designed to capture dimensions of the climate outlined in the MMDLE. The survey targeted currently enrolled undergraduates from all class standings who had attended the institution for at least a full semester to ensure familiarity with the campus climate. Focus groups were also conducted at five campuses administering the survey. Only data from Basin University are highlighted in this chapter.

Setting

Basin University is a large public comprehensive university in an urban area. In the fall of 2009 the university accepted more than 50 percent of applicants and enrolled approximately 18,000 undergraduates. Asian students made up the majority, with approximately 34 percent of the undergraduate population. The remaining population was composed of 27 percent white students, 28 percent Latina/o students, and 5 percent African American students. African Americans made up a substantially smaller proportion of the student body but reflected a higher representation than the surrounding region. The campus also showcased architectural features honoring civil rights figures, such as Martin Luther King Jr. and César Chavez. In addition, monuments and memorabilia prominently honored alumni of color. To a campus visitor, these physical representations may signal an institutional commitment to diversity. With more than 75 percent of the campus identifying as students of color and public displays that espouse diversity-related values, Basin University is a unique setting for examining how students from different racial groups—and across intersecting identities—perceive the climate.

Quantitative Design: Survey

A total of 782 students completed the DLE survey, reflecting a 29 percent response rate among students who opened the email invitation. The racial composition of the sample was as follows: 3 percent African American, 35 percent Asian, 24 percent Latina/o, and 38 percent white. Asian and white students were overrepresented, while African American and Latina/os were underrepresented relative to their campus population. The majority of students were enrolled full time (92%). More than half of the respondents were female (62%) and transfer students (53%). All class standings were represented, with 26 percent of respondents indicating they were freshmen, 21 percent sophomores, 31 percent juniors, and 22 percent seniors.

Variables. The dependent variables were three factors capturing student perceptions of the campus climate: Satisfaction with Diversity, Institutional Commitment to Diversity, and Discrimination and Bias. The Satisfaction with Diversity factor ($\alpha = .92$) was composed of six items measuring the extent to which students were satisfied with the racial/ethnic composition of the faculty and student body. The Institutional Commitment to Diversity factor ($\alpha = .86$) contained seven items representing how much students agreed that their institution valued diversity through the appreciation of differences among social identities, such as cultural, sexual orientation, and gender. Finally, the Discrimination and Bias factor ($\alpha = .88$) was composed of nine items assessing the frequency with which students observed discriminatory actions and heard insensitive remarks from students, staff, and faculty. Each measure was standardized and rescaled to a score ranging from 0 to 100 with a mean of 50 and a standard deviation of 10. The independent variables were students' racial/ethnic group (African American, Asian, Latina/o, and white), gender (male or female), and pathway into college (first-time freshman or transfer).

Analysis. A two-way analysis of variance (ANOVA) was conducted to determine whether there were interaction effects among racial groups, gender, and pathway into college on the three factors capturing perceptions of the climate. In addition, post hoc tests were included to identify significant subgroup differences.

Qualitative Design: Focus Groups

Focus group participants were sampled from the population invited to complete the DLE survey. Participants were recruited by campus administrators through email, flyers, and word of mouth. Four focus groups were organized by racial identity (African American, Asian, Latina/o, and white).

Twenty-six students participated in the focus groups. The number per focus group was as follows: African American, six females and two males; Asian, three females and two males; Latina/o, five females and three males; and white, four females and one male. African Americans and Latina/os were overrepresented in the focus groups, while Asian and white students were underrepresented as compared with campus populations. Unfortunately, we were not able to document focus group participants' pathways into college. Focus groups lasted approximately ninety minutes. Each used the same protocol: two open-ended questions that prompted students to share their perceptions about issues related to diversity and discrimination on campus:

- What are your experiences on campus related to issues of diversity, such as race, class, gender, sexual orientation, and other group identities?
- Are there any other experiences that you have had regarding diversity that you would like to share with us?

Through these questions, students were invited to discuss their satisfaction with diversity on campus, whether they felt the institution was committed to diversity, and whether they perceived discrimination and bias. Our approach aimed to capture students' perceptions of the climate broadly, but our design grouped students by race, thereby likely making this the most salient identity in students' responses.

Focus groups were audio recorded and transcribed. Two researchers independently and deductively coded each transcript according to the various dimensions of campus climate, and compared coding analyses to ensure agreement on appropriate coding. When discrepancies arose, the researchers discussed them in depth. This method resolved discrepancies in coding decisions, producing 97 percent intercoder agreement.

Cross-case Analysis. We conducted a cross-case analysis to look for patterns of similarity or difference across racial groups and multiple identities. First, quotes related to satisfaction with diversity, institutional commitment to diversity, and discrimination and bias were examined to align with the survey factors. These quotes were then organized by each racially homogenous focus group into a table (Miles and Huberman 1994). Quotes were then categorized further into themes and organized into a new table displaying corresponding themes by focus groups. Thus, the table displayed overlapping themes and stark contrasts across focus groups, including possible intersectional differences.

FINDINGS

We present our quantitative and qualitative findings according to the three campus climate factors. The two-way ANOVAs showed no significant differences on students' Satisfaction with Diversity and Institutional Commitment to Diversity. Most students' views on these two aspects of campus climate within the focus groups mirrored these quantitative findings. In contrast, a minor difference in perceptions of Discrimination and Bias was observed. Based on similarities, we discuss findings for Satisfaction with Diversity and Institutional Commitment to Diversity together before proceeding to the Discrimination and Bias findings.

Satisfaction with Diversity and Institutional Commitment to Diversity

Our quantitative analysis on satisfaction with diversity and institutional commitment to diversity revealed generally positive views across racial groups. Tables 2.1 and 2.2 display the means and standard deviations by race and gender as well as race and pathway into college, respectively, for Satisfaction with Diversity and Institutional Commitment to Diversity. African American students, regardless of gender and pathway into college, indicated lower levels of satisfaction and institutional commitment to diversity as compared with the other racial groups, but not to a level of statistical significance. The intersectional trends indicated that these negative views were pronounced for African American students who entered as first-time freshmen, also just missing the significance cutoff perhaps owing to the smaller sample size. Thus, students were essentially satisfied with

TABLE 2.1   Descriptive Results by Race and Gender

| | Satisfaction with diversity | | | | | |
| | Male | | Female | | Total | |
	M	SD	M	SD	M	SD
African American	47.64	7.48	46.12	11.08	46.74	9.59
Asian	49.88	9.81	50.12	9.00	50.01	9.35
Latina/o	52.19	9.02	49.24	9.33	50.19	9.31
White	50.61	9.65	50.37	9.72	50.46	9.68
Total	50.55	9.54	49.87	9.43	50.13	9.47

| | Institutional commitment to diversity | | | | | |
| | Male | | Female | | Total | |
	M	SD	M	SD	M	SD
African American	46.37	10.37	46.73	10.11	46.58	9.97
Asian	49.18	8.80	51.93	8.30	50.73	8.62
Latina/o	51.24	8.61	50.35	8.64	50.64	8.62
White	50.14	8.87	51.23	8.36	50.82	8.55
Total	49.87	8.84	51.10	8.49	50.63	8.64

TABLE 2.2   Descriptive Results by Race and Pathway into College

| | Satisfaction with diversity | | | | | |
| | Freshmen | | Transfer | | Total | |
	M	SD	M	SD	M	SD
African American	41.93	10.95	49.61	7.06	46.93	9.14
Asian	51.77	9.23	48.35	9.27	50.31	9.39
Latina/o	50.90	8.84	49.62	9.58	50.20	9.25
White	51.19	9.89	50.03	9.67	50.45	9.75
Total	51.18	9.43	49.46	9.46	50.24	9.49

| | Institutional commitment to diversity | | | | | |
| | Freshmen | | Transfer | | Total | |
	M	SD	M	SD	M	SD
African American	41.09	10.99	51.09	6.39	47.59	9.38
Asian	51.32	8.91	49.93	8.36	50.73	8.69
Latina/o	50.69	7.91	50.48	9.18	50.57	8.61
White	51.25	8.71	50.54	8.43	50.80	8.53
Total	50.94	8.74	50.38	8.53	50.63	8.62

the racial and ethnic composition of the student body, staff, and faculty as well as the university's commitment to diversity regardless of racial background, gender, and pathway into college. These positive views also aligned with Asian, Latina/o, and white student focus group responses.

In contrast, the majority of African American focus group participants, regardless of gender, expressed dissatisfaction with the level of diversity among African American staff, students and faculty. One student expressed, "I don't see African Americans [on campus]. When I go to Student Services I don't see African Americans. Even [among the maintenance workers] cleaning up outside, I don't . . . that's the truth." Another student said, "That's the first thing you [do] when you walk into a room [on campus]. . . . You look for other black students and usually I don't see none." Another student added, "In my department, Psychology . . . there are no Black faculty. . . . There's one psychologist who is African American, but he actually works in the counseling department, so if you never go to [the counseling center], you never see him, but we have no black faculty. And so being here, I think it's been difficult for me to connect with faculty. Although I get As in all my classes and I sit in the front and stuff like that, I still feel it's a little difficult to make those connections or feel that they want to make those connections with me." The other focus group participants nodded in agreement to the concerning lack of African American presence on campus.

Subsequently, students alleged that African Americans were purposefully marginalized. One student stated, "This campus is not friendly to Blacks," and when referring to the lack of presence of Black faculty and staff on campus, he went on to say "[Blacks are] weeded out . . . and what they do on this campus now is that when a Black is here and he leaves or she leaves, they don't replace them. They replace them with somebody white." Another student seconded this opinion by adding "I personally feel that Blacks are being weeded out or pushed to the side in favor of other cultures." This perceived intentional exclusion made students feel that the institution was not truly committed to diversity.

When students were encouraged by the interviewer to speak more about the institution's lack of commitment to diversity and how it related to the African American community, several gave examples about the university's reluctance to celebrate Black History Month or Martin Luther King Jr. Day, or to support African American cultural awareness activities altogether. The interviewer was surprised given the distinct architectural features celebrating African American history. Probed further about how these monuments represented an institutional commitment to diversity, students responded that the monuments appeared to be the extent of that commitment. One student stated, "I think the school [leans on] the fact that we have [statues] and the Martin Luther King [Center]. . . . I know during orientation they'll be like, 'You know, we have this statue and stuff.' 'Oh, you do? Oh, OK,' but after that it's kind of done because I don't think I've heard one thing about Black History Month on campus." Thus,

African Americans perceived a superficial commitment to diversity through its architecture.

The lack of African American presence on campus also affected students' sense of belonging. There were no African American Greek organizations on campus, which was disappointing to many in the focus group. Some students blamed the commuter campus culture. Others felt the university could do more to help African Americans build campus community. All in all, students expressed feeling out of place with such a low representation on campus. The interviewer asked the students to specifically share how they felt about being a minority. Some responses included:

STUDENT 1: You're the elephant in the room.
STUDENT 2: You feel like you don't belong.
STUDENT 3: Like you have to represent . . .

Similar sentiments were shared by all focus group members (with the exception of one) that the low numbers of African Americans on campus led to their dissatisfaction with diversity and fueled their sense that the institution lacked a commitment to diversity. Despite these challenges, African American students strived to succeed academically and represent their community well.

Discrimination and Bias

The quantitative findings showed minor differences on perceived discrimination and bias according to race. Though perceptions of discrimination and bias were low overall, Asian and African American students perceived slightly more discrimination and bias. However, post hoc tests revealed significant differences only between Asian and white students. While no intersectional differences emerged along gender lines, Asian transfer students reported more discrimination and bias as compared with white transfer students. Figure 2.1 illustrates the general patterns for discrimination and bias by race and pathway into college. Similar to our findings regarding satisfaction and institutional commitment to diversity, Latina/o and white focus group participants did not perceive any discrimination on campus, aligning with their survey responses.

Interestingly, Asian students did not report personally experiencing any form of discrimination on campus, in contrast with survey responses among this racial group. Although Asian participants spoke about gender, none shared experiencing or witnessing gender discrimination. One student stated, "I haven't seen anything like [discrimination] against females or males." However, two students were acutely aware of prejudice based on secondhand accounts. One shared, "I haven't noticed any kind of discrimination. I've been here for four years, but I have read on RateMyProfessor[2] that some of the professors I've had are real discriminatory." The interviewer followed up by asking, "Discriminatory by gender, by

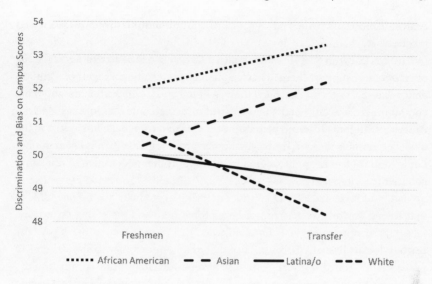

NOTE. – Significant difference between Asian and white transfer students $(p < .05)$

FIGURE 2.1. Mean differences for discrimination and bias by race and pathway into college

race . . . ?" and the student answered "by race." Another student felt there was discrimination based on sexual orientation. He relayed a story about two of his friends holding hands on campus and being harassed. He said: "I remember my two friends, they're gay, and they were holding hands and some guy from Campus Dorms threw a rock at us and he said, 'Fuck you.' . . . Not many people on campus are out. . . . It's just you can't be gay and yourself on campus. Race is acceptable, but sexuality is not." Thus, perceptions of racism and homophobia emerged in these examples, but students did not identify intersectional differences in these forms of oppression.

Unlike their counterparts, African American students perceived several instances of racial discrimination, which manifested according to racial stereotypes for males and females. From their perspective, many faculty felt that African Americans were intellectually inferior based on racial stereotypes encountered in the classroom. One student shared hearing stereotypes in classes all the time. Another student stated, "Going into some classes where maybe you're looked down upon or there's an assumption that you're not going to achieve at a high level." A third student indicated, "Like in class if you ask questions or if you're taking notes, I feel like everyone's just looking at me to see if I'm doing the work, you know." African American students were thus keenly aware of others' views in class.

Students further elaborated on how racial bias inhibited connections to faculty and guidance. Responding to what the biggest barrier to academic achievement was, a male student said, "[the racial] attitudes [of professors] and those you can't control. . . . It's hard to deal with, but what can I say, you're going to have to deal with it." Others shared that faculty did little to explain academic coursework or support them in navigating higher education altogether. One student relayed, "With the teachers, they [will tell you] 'Oh, well, I can only help you so much. . . . You need to go to [the tutoring center].'" Instead, African American students received help from students to navigate the university, as the following example shows: "The biggest barrier is having guidance. . . . [For example,] I didn't know I had to apply for graduation. . . . Another peer told me, 'You know, you have to write a letter. . . .' I was like, 'What?' She's like, 'You better hurry up and do that,' and I was just like, 'OK, wait, I'm trying to graduate and no one told me that I need to do this?' . . . I'm not going to sit here and blame my skin or my race. . . . I'm not going to sit here and say, 'Well, I'm black, so that's why my teacher doesn't like me,' because I use that as an opportunity to show them [to prove them wrong]." African American students' feelings of discrimination did not appear to stem from overt gestures but through implicit racial biases shaping ambivalent interactions on the part of faculty (Dovidio and Gaertner 2004). This lack of faculty support felt by African American students diverged greatly from Asian, Latina/o, and white students, who generally felt that faculty were supportive and provided them with academic opportunities. Despite these challenges, African American students were committed to resisting these stereotypes and succeeding.

DISCUSSION AND IMPLICATIONS

Though many universities enroll diverse student populations, few studies examining campus climates focus on more racially heterogeneous campuses or account for intersectional identities among students. Our mixed-methods study attempts to fill these gaps by capturing student perspectives at one racially diverse institution according to racial background, gender, and pathways into college. We find similarities in how students from certain groups view the climate positively at Basin University as well as others who perceive a less than welcoming environment. Specifically, our case study shows how perceptions of campus climate are largely contingent on racial identities, which intersect with students' pathways into college. Further, these divergent perspectives emerge through a mixed-methods examination, perhaps indicating that views may also be contingent on the approaches used to examine campus climate.

Student perceptions of campus climate largely differ along racial lines even within racially diverse campuses. Latina/o and white students consistently indicate a generally positive view of the climate, which may not be surprising given that campuses with a larger Latina/o representation are perceived as less hostile, particularly among white students (Hurtado 1992). Yet, African American and Asian students at Basin University perceive more marginalization, reflecting larger systemic inequities and the presence of racism within college environments despite a diverse backdrop. These findings further shed light on the marginalization of racial groups beyond a black/white binary. Interestingly, no intersectional differences by race and gender emerged, underscoring the apparent salience of race as a primary organizing identity on this campus. Although Asian students at Basin University acknowledge instances of racism in the classroom and homophobic verbal attacks in dorms, these forms of oppression do not appear to intersect or students may not fully note the interplay between different social identities. Consequently, diverse campuses may appear welcoming, but some students of color continue to feel the enduring remnants of racism, regardless of level of representation on campus.

Yet, intersectional differences emerged along other axes—in this case, student pathways into college. Asian transfer students, in particular, expressed more negative views of the climate as compared with white transfer students. Another concerning intersectional trend surfaced among African American students and pathways into college, but it was not statistically significant. African American first-year students consistently expressed lower levels of satisfaction with diversity and institutional commitment to diversity than all other students. These findings show how students' pathways into the university may intersect with racial identity to additionally shape perceptions of campus climate.

African American student narratives at Basin University clearly portray dissatisfaction with campus diversity, institutional commitment to diversity, and perceptions of racial bias. Though African Americans make up a significantly smaller proportion of the student body, visible emblems celebrating African American history are prominent on campus. While such architectural gestures of inclusivity are notable, according to students, the presence of more black faculty and staff on campus would more aptly demonstrate a commitment to diversity. African American students resiliently navigate college while combatting racial stereotypes. Support from faculty would give these underrepresented students a greater sense of belonging. Access to faculty who share cultural backgrounds and who could serve as mentors to undergraduates would further bolster these students' success. Beyond the classroom, African American students also indicate a need for more institutional support of student organizations. Thus, institutions must demonstrate an explicit commitment to better serve a racially diverse student body in both academic and social spaces, especially for students who identify as members of marginalized groups.

Our different modes of data collection expose racial differences in perceptions, indicating that uncovering such perspectives may be contingent on the researcher's methodological approach. Negative views among Asian students surfaced in the survey and emerged prominently through focus groups for African American students. Combining quantitative and qualitative data provides a more comprehensive account of how racialized groups, particularly those that remain numerical minorities or targets of societal discrimination, experience campus environments. The most marginalized groups on a campus are often hesitant to share negative views on a survey (Hurtado et al. 2008; Shammas 2009). Some groups, such as African American students, may be more open to sharing harsh experiences of racism in focus groups, where trust is built with a researcher, and may purposely avoid sharing negative perceptions through surveys for fear of affirming external judgments about their academic skills (Johnson 2008). Thus, employing multiple approaches to examine the campus climate allows for more layered and accurate examinations across multiple dimensions of student diversity.

Several implications for research and practice emerge from our case study. Because critical self-assessment is essential for transforming campuses to better engage students of color (Jayakumar and Museus 2012; Rankin and Reason 2008), future campus climate research should consider the intersectionality of various social identities in student perceptions. Too often, campus climate studies and reports present findings according to a particular identity, which can overlook critical differences in views or experiences at the intersection of multiple identities. Also, future explorations of campus climate should consider the use of a mixed-methods approach to maximize the likelihood that students will share informative insights, especially negative sentiments, in a format that feels safe. In using mixed-methods approaches, researchers should also be mindful to include questions that probe into the intersectionality of identities, which may require the development of new measures. Through integrated intersectional climate assessments, institutions can gather more nuanced views of how students perceive and navigate campuses.

As a result of more comprehensive campus climate assessments, institutions can identify intersectional differences and develop targeted approaches to effectively support students within the classroom and beyond. For example, given the intersection of race and pathway into college at Basin University, institutions can address possible challenges students of color perceive based on their pathway into the institution by developing interventions targeting different populations. As several universities offer first-year seminars to help students transition to college, one approach could be to create sections that address intersecting identities. In the case of Basin University, a first-year seminar aimed at African American freshmen and Asian transfer students could help these students navigate possible hostile encounters and increase their sense of belonging. In addition, universities must consider how to address the microaggressions students of color continue to face across campus. Providing professional development on systemic inequities and inclusive pedagogies can help faculty and staff critically reflect on their own assumptions or possible deficit views and identify ways to modify instruction and interactions to enhance student success. Additionally, universities can invest in support structures, such as student resource centers and student organizations, that foster students' sense of belonging on campus.

Though colleges are more diverse than in previous generations, race continues to matter in how students view these environments. Moreover, racial identity intersects with other identities and positions that students hold. In turn, negative and positive perceptions influence student experiences and outcomes. Cultivating postsecondary environments where all students, regardless of racial background, pathway into college, and other social identities, feel supported requires intentional action. Mixed-methods and intersectional approaches to assessing the campus climate provide a richer picture of student experiences to inform how institutions can enact interventions that intentionally foster inclusive and empowering environments.

NOTES

1. A pseudonym.
2. RateMyProfessor.com is a website that allows students in the United States (and select other countries) to review and rate the teaching performance of faculty.

REFERENCES

Allan, Elizabeth J., and Mary Madden. 2006. "Chilly Classrooms for Female Undergraduate Students: A Question of Method?" *Journal of Higher Education* 77 (4): 684–711.

Cabrera, Nolan L. 2014. "Beyond Black and White: How White, Male, College Students See Their Asian American Peers." *Equity and Excellence in Education* 47 (2): 133–151.

Crenshaw, Kimberle. 1991. "Mapping the Margins: Intersectionality, Identity Politics, and Violence against Women of Color." *Stanford Law Review* 43 (6): 1241–1299.

Creswell, John W., and Vicki L. Plano Clark. 2011. *Designing and Conducting Mixed-Methods Research.* 3rd ed. Thousand Oaks, CA: Sage Publications.

Cuellar, Marcela, and Robin N. Johnson-Ahorlu. 2016. "Examining the Complexity of the Campus Racial Climate at a Hispanic Serving Community College." *Community College Review* 44 (2): 135–152.

Deil-Amen, Regina. 2015. "The 'Traditional' College Student: A Smaller and Smaller Minority in Its Implications for Diversity and Access Institutions." In *Remaking College: The Changing Ecology of Higher Education,* edited by M. W. Kirst and M. L. Stevens, 134–165. Stanford, CA: Stanford University Press.

Dovidio, John F., and Samuel L. Gaertner. 2004. "Aversive Racism." *Advances in Experimental Social Psychology* 36: 1–52.

Griffin, Kimberly A., and Samuel D. Museus. 2011. "Application of Mixed-Methods Approaches to Higher Education and Intersectional Analyses." *New Directions for Institutional Research* 151: 15–26.

Harper, Shaun R., and Sylvia Hurtado. 2007. "Nine Themes in Campus Racial Climates and Implications for Institutional Transformation." *New Directions for Student Services* 120: 7–24.

Hart, Jeni, and Jennifer Fellabaum. 2008. "Analyzing Campus Climate Studies: Seeking to Define and Understand." *Journal of Diversity in Higher Education* 1 (4): 222–234.

Hurtado, Sylvia. 1992. "The Campus Racial Climate: Contexts of Conflict." *Journal of Higher Education* 63 (5): 539–569.

Hurtado, Sylvia, Adriana Ruiz Alvarado, and Chelsea Guillermo-Wann. 2015. "Thinking about Race: The Salience of Racial Identity at Two- and Four-Year Colleges and the Climate for Diversity." *Journal of Higher Education* 86 (1): 127–155.

Hurtado, Sylvia, Cynthia L. Alvarez, Chelsea Guillermo-Wann, Marcela Cuellar, and Lucy Arellano. 2012. "A Model for Diverse Learning Environments: The Scholarship on Creating and Assessing Conditions for Student Success." In *Higher Education: Handbook of Theory and Research*, edited by J. C. Smart and M. B. Paulsen, 41–122. New York: Springer.

Hurtado, Sylvia, Deborah F. Carter, and Albert Spuler. 1996. "Latino Student Transition to College: Assessing Difficulties and Factors in Successful College Adjustment." *Research in Higher Education* 37 (2): 135–157.

Hurtado, Sylvia, Kimberly A. Griffin, Lucy Arellano, and Marcela Cuellar. 2008. "Assessing the Value of Climate Assessments: Progress and Future Directions." *Journal of Diversity in Higher Education* 1 (4): 204–221.

Jayakumar, Uma M., and Samuel D. Museus. 2012. "Mapping the Intersectionality of Campus Cultures and Equitable Outcomes among Racially Diverse Populations." In *Creating Campus Cultures: Fostering Success among Racially Diverse Student Populations*, edited by U. M. Jayakumar and S. D. Museus, 1–22. New York: Routledge.

Johnson, Dawn R., Timothy H. Wasserman, Nilay Yildirim, and Barbara A. Yonai. 2014. "Examining the Effects of Stress and Campus Climate on the Persistence of Students of Color and White Students: An Application of Bean and Eaton's Psychological Model of Retention." *Research in Higher Education* 55 (1): 75–100.

Johnson, Robin N. 2008. "The Psychology of Racism: How Internalized Racism, Academic Self-Concept, and Campus Racial Climate Impact the Academic Experience and Achievement of African American Undergraduates." PhD diss., University of California, Los Angeles.

Johnson-Ahorlu, Robin N. 2012. "The Academic Opportunity Gap: How Racism and Stereotypes Disrupt the Education of African American Undergraduates." *Race, Ethnicity and Education* 15 (5): 633–652.

Jones, Lee, Jeanett Castellanos, and Darnell Cole. 2002. "Examining the Ethnic Minority Student Experience at Predominantly White Institutions: A Case Study." *Journal of Hispanic Higher Education* 1 (1): 19–39.

Locks, Angela M., Sylvia Hurtado, Nicholas A. Bowman, and Leticia Oseguera. 2008. "Extending Notions of Campus Climate and Diversity to Students' Transition to College." *Review of Higher Education* 31 (3): 257–285.

Maramba, Dina C., and Samuel D. Museus. 2011. "The Utility of Using Mixed-Methods and Intersectionality Approaches in Conducting Research on Filipino American Students' Experiences with the Campus Climate and on Sense of Belonging." *New Directions for Institutional Research* 151: 93–101.

Miles, Matthew B., and A. Michael Huberman. 1994. *Qualitative Data Analysis: An Expanded Sourcebook*. Thousand Oaks, CA: Sage Publications.

Museus, Samuel D., Andrew H. Nichols, and Amber D. Lambert. 2008. "Racial Differences in the Effects of Campus Racial Climate on Degree Completion: A Structural Equation Model." *Review of Higher Education* 32 (1): 107–134.

Poon, OiYan A. 2011. "A Critical Race Theory Case Study of Asian Americans, 'Critical Mass,' and Campus Racial Climate." In *Asian American Education: Identities, Racial Issues, and Languages*, 6th ed., edited by R. Endo and X. L. Rong, 101–130. Charlotte, NC: Information Age Publishing.

Rankin, Susan R., and Robert D. Reason. 2008. "Transformational Tapestry Model: A Comprehensive Approach to Transforming Campus Climate." *Journal of Diversity in Higher Education* 1 (4): 262–274.

Reid, Landon D., and Phanikiran Radhakrishnan. 2003. "Race Matters: The Relation between Race and General Campus Climate." *Cultural Diversity and Ethnic Minority Psychology* 9 (3): 263–275.

Ruiz Alvarado, Adriana, and Sylvia Hurtado. 2015. "Campus Climate, Intersecting Identities, and Institutional Support among Mexican American College Students." In *The Magic Key: The Educational Journey of Mexican Americans from K–12 to College and Beyond*, edited by R. Zambrana and S. Hurtado, 168–189. Austin: University of Texas Press.

Santos, Silvia J., Anna M. Ortiz, Alejandro Morales, and Monica Rosales. 2007. "The Relationship between Campus Diversity, Students' Ethnic Identity and College Adjustment: A Qualitative Study." *Cultural Diversity and Ethnic Minority Psychology* 13 (2): 104–114.

Shammas, Dianne S. 2009. "Post-9/11 Arab and Muslim American Community College Students: Ethno-religious Enclaves and Perceived Discrimination." *Community College Journal of Research and Practice* 33: 283–308.

3 · MORE THAN IMMIGRATION STATUS

Undocumented Students in U.S. Jesuit Higher Education

TERRY-ANN JONES

With an estimated 11 million undocumented persons living in the United States, it should not come as a surprise that their presence is pervasive in a range of contexts: in the food industry, including agriculture, meat processing, and restaurants; construction and landscaping; housekeeping and child care; and maintenance and services, among others. Undocumented children and youth are also present in the U.S. school system. As a result of the Supreme Court ruling on *Plyler v. Doe* (457 U.S. 202 [1982]), undocumented children have a legal right to free public education, and states and school districts have an obligation to provide it at the K–12 level. At the tertiary level, however, there are no expectations or obligations that determine the enrollment of undocumented students. Although it is legal to admit undocumented students into universities in most states, states have the right to restrict access to financial aid and to determine their tuition rate (in-state or out of state). Some states, including South Carolina and Alabama, passed legislation restricting undocumented students from accessing public universities (Ovink, Ebert, and Okamoto 2016), compounding their lack of legal access to federal financial aid. However, private universities are legally able to admit and award scholarships to undocumented students, and the presence of undocumented students in Jesuit institutions in particular embodies the commitment to social justice and inclusiveness to which so many of them profess to aspire.

Attempts over the years to regularize the status of undocumented people in the United States include most notably the proposed Development, Relief, and Education for Alien Minors (DREAM) Act, variations of which have been considered and rejected since 2001. The most recent failure of the bill's passage signified a tremendous disappointment to students and young adults hoping to emerge from the underground life that characterizes the existence of undocumented immigrants. Some of this hope was restored when, on June 15, 2012, the Obama administration announced the Deferred Action for Childhood Arrivals (DACA). While DACA represented the most tangible possibility for undocumented youth to obtain legal status, it is also criticized for its limitations: it does not grant legal immigration status, it does not offer a path to citizenship or legal permanent resident status, and it excludes undocumented youth who started living in the United States on June 16, 2007, or later. Furthermore, it does not allow access to health insurance, nor do students qualify for federal financial aid. However, two of the main and most positive aspects of DACA are temporarily preventing the removal of undocumented immigrants and creating the possibility of employment authorization. However, the Trump administration's September 2017 announcement that DACA would be rescinded within six months barring a legislative solution was a stark reminder of the harsh climate facing undocumented students.

This chapter is based on data collected through a study of the twenty-eight private Jesuit colleges and universities in the United States, which are enabled to admit and grant private scholarships to undocumented students. Furthermore, access to higher education is a value that is deeply embedded in the Jesuit tradition. The study involved surveys of faculty, staff, and administrators at the twenty-eight institutions, along with in-depth, qualitative interviews with students, staff, and administrators at six of the schools, representing three different regions in the United States.

This chapter argues that the concerns of undocumented students at Jesuit tertiary institutions, while nuanced, extend well beyond the legal and financial realms and reflect the intersection of identities that they and their families embody. Although they contend with financial limitations and fears that their status will be revealed, these students also struggle with the dual identities of being students at elite, private universities and being undocumented immigrants with limited resources, few employment prospects, and a burdensome secret that places limitations on multiple areas of their lives. Further, in addition to navigating their status as undocumented and consequently marginalized students at private institutions of higher education, they also deal with the complexities of other forms of identity such as race, ethnicity, gender, sexuality, religion, language, and socioeconomic class, among others. Intersectionality has been critiqued for its emphasis on individual experiences with marginalization rather than on the power dynamics that create this marginalization and perpetuate inequality (Núñez 2014). Thus, this study recognizes the role of institutions of higher education in shaping students' identities and their responsibility for cultivating a more inclusive environment. This chapter explores increasing campus awareness of undocumented students and their role in fostering intersected campus experiences. While the institutions surveyed generally value the diversity that undocumented students add through their experiences, they have not as readily recognized the multiple layers of diversity these students represent. Consequently, they are unable to fully support the students in the ways that they need to be supported.

THE LITERATURE ON UNDOCUMENTED STUDENTS

Literature on the undocumented student population is limited, often emphasizing legal contexts, especially as some states demonstrate their recognition of the value of undocumented populations through various policies (Flores 2010; Gonzales, Heredia, and Negrón-Gonzales 2015). Quantitative studies provide a broad perspective of undocumented students' experiences (Suárez-Orozco et al. 2015), while a small body of qualitative literature explores the experiences, challenges, and realities of undocumented students, underscoring the resilience of undocumented students in spite of many obstacles.

Much of the literature on undocumented college students emphasizes the barriers they encounter as they attempt to pursue tertiary-level education. Foremost among these barriers are the financial constraints undocumented students often confront, given their restricted access to employment and ineligibility for federal financial aid (Kantamneni et al. 2016; Perez and Cortes 2011; Perez 2009; Frum 2007; Jones and Nichols 2017). Financial barriers are compounded by structural barriers related to the students' status. For example, in most states undocumented students (who tend to live off campus with their families) are not legally permitted to drive, further limiting their ability to seek employment and restricting their opportunities to participate in extracurricular activities on campus (Kantamneni et al. 2016; Jones and Nichols 2017).

While much of the literature consistently underscores the barriers resulting from financial constraints, our study reaches beyond the material challenges that undocumented students face to explore the social-psychological burdens that they also bear. Though our research did not explicitly seek to engage these questions, it was a finding that emerged consistently in the qualitative data. The students expressed considerable fear that they or their family members would be deported, and some students exhibited discomfort with their socioeconomic status in relation to that of other students at the private institutions they attended. Arbona et al. (2010) use the term *acculturative stress* to define "the level of psychosocial strain experienced by immigrants and their descendants in response to the immigration-related challenges (stressors) that they encounter as they adapt to life in a new country" (364). Further, Dillon, de la Rosa, and Ibanez (2013) assert that "these stressors result from circumstances such as immigration status, language barriers, economic deficiencies, and discrimination" (484). The student participants in this study represent a positively self-selected group that used their intellectual abilities and networks to circumvent obstacles to their education. Nevertheless, the responses from these students are consistent with Arbona et al.'s (2010) findings that an undocumented status exacerbates the experience of acculturative stress because of the added fear and worry, even among those who have attained the academic standing and social capital needed to attend private universities.

METHODS

The current chapter's research took place over a two-year period, from 2010 to 2012, as collaboration among Fairfield University, Santa Clara University, and Loyola University Chicago. Each of the three institutions partnered with another university in the same region, so the research occurred at six Jesuit institutions in three regions across the United States (East, Midwest, and West). A basic premise of this study is Jesuit institutions have a particular role—perhaps even a responsibility—to welcome undocumented students, given their historical commitment to fostering the education of immigrants. Historically, Jesuit institutions served as a place of refuge for Catholic immigrants, most of whom immigrated from Ireland and Italy. Although the dominant countries of origin have shifted from Europe to Latin America, today's marginalized immigrants are still from predominantly Catholic countries and drawn to the values that Jesuit institutions uphold.

Our approach utilized a combination of qualitative and quantitative data. The former featured the six institutions, where members of the research team conducted in-person interviews with forty-seven key staff members and twenty-five undocumented students. The data analysis involved the recording and transcription of all the interviews, and then used NVivo® software to assist with the organizing and coding of interview transcripts. Staff interviews explored experiences with and attitudes toward undocumented students, while student interviews examined migration experiences, students' on-campus experiences, family situations, and students' general concerns. An online survey of staff members at all twenty-eight Jesuit colleges and universities comprised the quantitative portion of the study. The survey, which included both open- and closed-ended questions, was distributed to 200 people, of whom 110 responded. The survey gauged staff members' attitudes toward undocumented students and also produced information regarding the admissions process.

FINDINGS

The interviews revealed the main challenges that students encountered. While we expected that financial need would be central to the difficulties undocumented students faced, we did not anticipate the pervasiveness of the social-psychological burdens they carry regarding their own precarious situations and those of their families. On the part of the staff, there was consensus that undocumented students are welcome at their institutions, but also an acknowledgment that the admissions process was informal and sometimes clandestine, and possibly excluded some qualified students who did not have the social capital to navigate the process. Social capital, defined as "the ability to gain access to resources by virtue of membership in social networks and larger social structures" (Portes and Rumbaut 2001, 353n47), is a key determinant of undocumented students' access to universities, in addition to their own efforts and determination (Jones 2017). Below, I discuss some of the main themes that arose from the interviews.

Childhood Arrival

All twenty-five undocumented students who participated in this study arrived in the United States as children; with the exception of two who arrived as teenagers, most students were under the age of nine, with the youngest arriving as an infant. Some of the students grew up with awareness of their status as undocumented immigrants. However, others had not been told. In each case, the full realization of the limitations of their status became apparent in their adolescent years when they began to seek employment, driver's licenses, or college admissions and financial aid. Our interviewees expressed their determination to realize their dreams of attending college. However, one student shared that there were others in her social circle who reacted less optimistically upon discovering their undocumented status. The news led to depression and reluctance to complete secondary school (Nichols and Guzman 2017). Another shared her disappointment with each failure of the DREAM Act: "And this thing just happened . . . when the Dream Act wasn't passed. The first time, I had my hopes up so high, I was so happy, and when it didn't I don't know what happened to me. I just became this different person. Because I kept saying to myself why did you just do that to yourself? You been waiting 10 years, and nothing has happened. Why did you . . . Even for the second, I did the same thing. I was so happy. I had my plans, I had dreams, again, and that was crushed, and I think every time it gets crushed, I get crushed with it, I just don't know what to do anymore." Students who participated in the study had attended secondary school in the United States and entered college or a university around the age of eighteen or nineteen. They very much identified as American, and although they had family members in their countries of origin whom they expressed a desire to see again, they conveyed no real sense of connection to their home countries, nor had any compelling memories related to them. As one student stated, "I feel more American than anything, and to be constantly reminded that I'm not, and I can't do everything that an American can, it's like a slap in the face."

Fear

We expected students would show some concerns about their status being revealed. However, the level of fear seemed to be an impediment to their integration into the campus community. Furthermore, they not only feared their own predicaments as undocumented students but also expressed a great deal of concern for family members. Most students lived in households that included family members with different immigration statuses. In some cases, there were family members fighting deportation orders, while in others there were younger siblings who were born in the United States. Interviewees were concerned about the well-being of the family as a whole, rather than just themselves or individual family members. For example, despite the assumption that they may not need to worry about younger, U.S.-born family members, students expressed great trepidation regarding the possibility that the family may be separated. One student interviewee, for example, stated: "I am okay now within my status, but my parents and my sister, they are not. So, I'm basically the base. I am the one that they are holding onto. And basically, I am a second mom, in a way. And I am a student but I am a second mom. It's like I have my own family already even though it's not like I have kids or anything." Keeping the family intact was a priority, and concerns that younger siblings who are U.S. citizens could require foster care or be compelled to live in an unfamiliar country if parents and older siblings were deported was a source of fear. The extent to which students expressed such selflessness, showing equal or greater concern for other family members, was notable.

Ambiguous College Application and Admissions Process

A major complaint heard repeatedly from student interviewees was the lack of a structured application process for the colleges they attended. Misinformation and doubt were pervasive. As one interviewee put it:

> For a while you kind of doubt, well if I can't, because there are lots of rumors as well, people say you can't get into college, or they say that if you get into college you won't get your diploma, or of course most of the time you won't be able to work here, and that's still a reality. So it kind of makes you second-guess yourself and whether or not you should apply, because if you're not going to have the opportunity to work, why go to college, when I can get a job now? For most of the time I always knew that I wanted to go to college and I wanted to get a better education because they know that either the United States or anywhere else in the world you do have better opportunity if you have a college degree. So I said, well, no is the answer that I already have, so I might as well try yes.

In all of the cases studied, there was an informal process relying heavily on students' access to the few individuals who were aware that undocumented students could be admitted and were eligible for private scholarships. These individual advocates varied from teachers, guidance counselors, and clergy to other members of students' places of worship or communities. In each locale, there seemed to be a specific routing process beginning with the student contacting an advocate, and continued with a staff member at the university level who provided further guidance through admissions and scholarship processes. Of course, the students we interviewed had all made it through this process successfully and were grateful to the network of supporters who had advocated for them. However, they were also quick to acknowledge that there was some degree of good fortune involved in their process—they were at the right place and/or had connections, and unveiled their undocumented status to the right people. They spoke of friends and classmates who did not have the same connections. Several expressed concern for undocumented students who were unaware that there were channels to lead them to tertiary education, and for those who may have been aware but lacked the connections that the rather clandestine process requires. For example, one student remarked on her attempt to help another undocumented student: "Because I made it, I made it well known to some people . . . there was this other girl, she doesn't have her papers and she can't even go to college right now. So, like, I was able to guide her, and tell her the procedure and like what I did, and I tried to help her to apply . . . but she thought she wouldn't get in, so she just gave up." As a result of this perspective from the students, our recommendations underscore the need for a more structured and transparent system that would provide access to a wider range of undocumented students.

Limitations on Participation

Students shared their appreciation of the many ways in which they can engage with the academic communities on their campuses, but noted limitations on such activities they can participate in. Most commonly, students expressed disappointment that study abroad was not accessible to them, and even domestic air travel was a challenge because of required government-issued identification. Furthermore, they were reluctant to explain to professors and peers the reasons for their travel aversion. Internships that require background checks also proved unfeasible, limiting the options of majors they were able to pursue. For example, students who major in fields such as nursing, education, engineering, or accounting are required to complete internships, and participation typically requires background checks and/or a social security number. This requirement serves as a deterrent for some undocumented students who are otherwise drawn to these majors. However, there are students who continue to engage in the majors that represent their interests, optimistic that there will be a change in policy that allows them to pursue their careers of choice. Other students were less optimistic, yet remained adamant about choosing their majors on the basis of interest rather than practicality. The rationale students offered to support the latter perspective is that being undocumented limits all of their career options, so they may as well use the college opportunity to study what interests them (Nichols and Guzman 2017). Further, they recognized the value in what they were learning in their college courses. For example, one student stated: "I was just like, ha ha, I'm going to go to college and hopefully they don't kick me out. I said, I am just going to make the best of this. Get involved, and meet great people, and you, know if [it] ends at any time, not because I want it to, but because of my situation, at least I can say I went to college and I took college courses." These participants were rewarded for their optimism when, in 2012, the data collection period for this study coincided with the implementation of DACA.

Lack of Awareness

The student participants lamented the lack of awareness regarding what is legal and what is not. In addition to their own uncertainty, exacerbated by fear, students also expressed frustration regarding misinformation concerning the general assumption that most rights were out of their reach. For example, we learned that many teachers and counselors at the secondary school level are unaware that undocumented students can legally attend college in most states: "I did talk to my guidance counselor, and when I told her that I was undocumented and I wanted to see if there was a way I could go to college at least, she said no. She said that there is no way to go to college. Forget about it. There is no way because of my status. There is no way. . . . So that really brought me down. And from that point I did not go with her at all or with any guidance counselor, I just did everything through the people I knew through my pastor." The uncertainty and ambiguity regarding which activities are available to undocumented students continued through their tertiary education, as most campuses lack readily available information on undocumented students' rights. In their efforts to protect the students, faculty and staff often err on the side of caution, advising students to avoid fields of study that require background checks or social security numbers, and generally supporting their anonymity. Not only does this well-meaning cautiousness limit the students' career prospects, but the fear that it incites also obstructs the students' integration into the university communities, prevents them from embracing other parts of their identities, and reinforces their sense of being outsiders. Although most tertiary institutions have personnel dedicated to working with international students, this category typically offers support with visas and does not apply to undocumented students. Only 10 percent of the twenty-eight institutions surveyed indicated that they provide legal support for undocumented students. Consequently, at most of the institutions there is no explicitly known office or person with whom undocumented students can consult, which underscores the challenges students face, even at elite, private institutions committed to supporting the underserved.

The staff interviews revealed considerable concern for protecting students' privacy, coupled with a lesser degree of fear of repercussions for the university and/or the individuals who offer guidance and support. Consequently, the admissions process for undocumented students is largely a clandestine process; in the majority of cases, no instructions are provided on university websites for undocumented student admission. In reference to citizenship information on the application form, one student explained, "My pastor and the advocate from here, they told me to say the truth and not lie, so I left that blank. I didn't put international or citizen or noncitizen, I left it blank. I did not lie."

Some enter "other" when asked to state their citizenship status, while other students leave the response line blank. Although the Common Application asks for a social security number, it is required only if applying for financial aid. Knowing that they are ineligible for federal aid, undocumented students leave this line blank. These subtle indicators cause university staff who are aware of the admissions process for undocumented students to follow up with these students. As one staff interviewee noted, "What do we look for? Do we look for zeros on their Social Security, do we look for 'other' on visa, do we look for mentions on their personal essays, letters of recommendation? Different factors that we can flag them by." In some cases a counselor or community advocate may have already made college personnel aware of the incoming application.

Several staff members suggested certain measures were taken to protect the institutions from any obligation to reveal undocumented students' status, while another mentioned some reticence exists toward publicizing institutions' policies on undocumented students to avoid alienating other students. Another staff member mentioned they avoid keeping any records alluding to undocumented status. Although fear and secrecy permeate the process, the admission of undocumented students is also characterized by informal and interpersonal connections that are intended to protect the students but carry the consequence of creating a shroud of secrecy limiting information to those fortunate enough to have gained access. While pragmatic, the emphasis on the students' immigration status has the effect of reducing them to their immigration status, causing other aspects of their identity to be overlooked. This prevents them from expressing and seeking support for other components of their identity in ways that other students are able to do. While not explicitly making reference to intersectionality, one student stated: "I wouldn't want to be treated differently. I worked so hard to be treated the same. I work so hard not to have an accent. I worked so hard to learn English. I always try to push myself academically, socially, so I don't really like people having sympathy for me, I guess. I want them [to] treat me as they treat anyone else." Implicit in her comment is her desire to have the range of identities available to students who do not share her undocumented status.

Discrimination

Most undocumented students are, out of necessity, quite discreet about their status and selective about whom they share this information with. On the one hand, their discretion protects them from legal repercussions and avoids labels associated with their status, but on the other hand, undocumented students shared they are sometimes forced to quietly endure bigoted, anti-immigrant comments from their classmates and others on campus.

For example, as noted by Nichols and Guzman (2017, 114–115), who were also researchers in this study, one student stated, "I'm a Political Science major and we talked about immigration policy and there were a lot of students in the class who were like, oh we should just deport them all, there should be someone there just to shoot them." To protect their privacy, most of the students refrain from engaging in what would inevitably be a very personal debate.

Beyond the more explicit forms of discrimination, there also exist more subtle, unintentional ways in which the campus communities exhibit a lack of sensitivity to undocumented students' experiences. Several students described the emotional toll of creating excuses for their lack of participation in activities that were inaccessible to them, such as travel and internships. Others felt pressured to participate. One student described her experience participating in a student club:

> For one of the clubs for example, Model UN, I have hesitated going to most meetings and actually becoming a really active member because I know that they take trips outside of the country and I don't want to be in that position to explain or have an excuse every time, so if I actually take a really active role, and I know that they participate in competitions, so if I become a good candidate for the competitions, I am going to have to explain, come up with some kind of an excuse as to why I couldn't go. So it's kind of a sticky situation for that, and I hesitate participating in some of those. . . . And the service trips is something that I really, really want to do, and I was even considering going to either New York, New York wouldn't be too bad, but I wanted to be able to go to New Orleans, and it's always a risk to leave the place, to leave Connecticut and get on a plane, it's always a risk. So I kind of hesitated doing it.

These types of experiences intensify fears among undocumented students and foster the secrecy that encumbers their integration into the university community.

Financial Need

A common concern among students was financial difficulty. The overwhelming majority of students interviewed reported facing financial challenges, with only one exception. However, what is remarkable is that neither the financial challenges nor the rewards (e.g., jobs, scholarships) were perceived as individual gains or responsibilities. Implicit in the students' statements was the sentiment that their finances could not be considered separate from the household economy. Several students worked in order to contribute to their family's income. Others (though fewer) received financial help from family members. Most students received scholarships from their universities, and six mentioned resourceful ways they were able to legally supplement their incomes, such as participating in surveys in exchange for gift cards or doing on-campus activities for which they could be compensated with stipends that were not considered taxable income (Nichols and Guzman

2017). For example: "Well, I can't do work-study obviously, and it's just my parents are usually the ones who pay for my books and everything, but sometimes . . . I found ways around that, because I have a tax ID so I'm not completely undocumented, but anyone can get a tax ID because the government wants you to pay taxes. Pay taxes without being able to work, right? But I used that and I was able to get paid for my summer job two years ago, and this last year actually someone at this university got a grant and paid for myself and the other people that worked."

Some institutions were also strategic about establishing private scholarships that could be awarded to undocumented students, although they tended to be discreet about details. Loyola University Chicago (n.d.), for example, states, "International and undocumented students are not eligible to receive federal or state financial aid. However, students may qualify for other types of financial aid and/ or scholarships." Similarly, Fairfield University's (n.d.) FAQs page for the Immigrant Student Project states, "Private universities may offer both merit-based and other scholarships to undocumented students." In both cases, a list of scholarships for which undocumented students are eligible follows, but without explicitly drawing attention to the funding sources. A segment on the Fairfield University FAQs page alludes to the reason for the discretion:

Q: Isn't it unfair to use private scholarship money to help undocumented students when there are U.S. citizen students in equal need of scholarships?

A: Nothing in the Christian tradition tells us that poor citizens should be given a preference over poor non-citizens. On the contrary, both the Old Testament and Jesus Christ urge us to broaden our concept of neighbor to include aliens. This concept of solidarity, that we are all part of the same human family, has deep roots in our Jesuit identity and in our way of educating students. We have a local and a global responsibility to help the poor. Schools can differ on the criteria by which they hand out scholarships to the poor but Catholic schools in particular must stand in solidarity with the most marginalized applicants. Sometimes the most marginalized, as well as most qualified, are not U.S. citizens.

These statements suggest that universities strive to strike a balance between supporting undocumented students and avoiding offending students, parents, and alumni who may not share their perspective.

THE CURRENT LANDSCAPE
FOR UNDOCUMENTED STUDENTS

The challenges undocumented students confront constrain and are burdensome, yet there exist positive trends indicating an increase in the number of undocumented students who have found access to higher education (Abrego and Gonzales 2010). The anti-immigrant rhetoric of the Trump administration understandably serves as a source of anxiety for many immigrants, with undocumented immigrants being the most vulnerable among them. While the majority of the undocumented population in the United States is from Latin America, the executive orders issued in early 2017 restricting the immigration of people from seven predominantly Muslim countries is a reminder of both the precariousness of the lives of immigrants and their vulnerability to the whims of political leaders. Further, the Trump administration's September 2017 announcement of a six-month plan to rescind DACA confirmed the administration's stance on undocumented youth. Given the recent and ongoing changes, the data are anecdotal at this point, but strongly indicate that fears of deportation among undocumented students have intensified as the administration makes its hostility to immigrants apparent. Yet in spite of their fears, undocumented students continue to pursue their education and win support among allies as they show that their presence enriches their classrooms and the nation in general.

CONCLUSIONS

Among the estimated 11 million undocumented immigrants in the United States, those who arrived as children accompanying their parents face the unique challenge of not having a voice in their migration process. Many undocumented youth do not learn of their status until adolescence. In many cases, the discovery of their status is a traumatic experience that signifies their inability to participate in typical activities with their peers. Overall, the findings of the study that forms the basis of this chapter suggest that the students' challenges not only are material but also are steeped in fear for their own lives and futures as well as those of their family members, including those whose presence in the United States is authorized. The students are consequently burdened with financial obstacles that limit their access to full integration in these private institutions, and also saddled with the emotional encumbrance of protecting a potentially life-altering secret. They face limitations on the majors they choose and the activities they can engage in. Furthermore, despite their need for financial support, they are not legally permitted to accept positions for which they will be paid, unless they have been granted permission through DACA, which was rescinded in September 2017.

Jesuit universities straddle a set of identities that make them a natural fit for undocumented students while simultaneously being unable to fully integrate them into the college experience. While these institutions are limited in their power to improve the experiences of undocumented students, part of the challenge lies in the shift from their original mission of helping the marginalized to a mission that sometimes inadequately recognizes the immediate need for social justice on campus. Although Jesuit universities have historically emphasized the importance of educating underserved populations, including immigrants, as the early European immigrant population has attained upward socioeconomic mobility, their descendants are now able to enjoy the privilege of attending these schools without the similar need for refuge. As private institutions, Jesuit institutions enjoy an identity that is not necessarily focused on educating the marginalized but rather on educating a privileged population that is interested in helping the marginalized. Social justice is an integral part of the mission and identity of these schools, but the diverse populations that they strive to support are largely absent from the classrooms.

Institutions are increasingly acknowledging the concept of intersectionality, but its definition and application remain limited to race, class, gender, and sexual identity and orientation. Undocumented students, like other diverse populations, enrich the classrooms and campuses with the prolific set of identities they embody and perspectives they bring to these spaces, yet they remain excluded from conversations about intersectionality. Many private liberal arts institutions pride themselves on their ability to send students abroad for semester-long programs or short-term immersion and service trips to broaden their perspectives on other cultures and other realities. These institutions value the presence of diverse populations such as racial or ethnic minorities and LGBTQ (lesbian, gay, bisexual, transgender, queer) students and increasingly seek to increase the socioeconomic diversity, recognizing that exposing students to various forms of diversity within the context of higher education better prepares them as professionals and as global citizens than education in the context of a homogeneous academic community. Undocumented students need to be part of that narrative. Given the awareness, or even hyperawareness, of their presence in the United States, their presence in and desire for education should not come as a surprise. Undocumented students should be welcome in institutions of higher education that purport to embrace diversity and social justice, not only to satisfy the sense of moral obligation they may have, but also to recognize the richness of experience that they bring to these campuses. Yet in welcoming and supporting undocumented students, institutions also need to acknowledge the full range of intersecting identities that these students embody and add to the college experience.

REFERENCES

Abrego, Leisy J., and Roberto G. Gonzales. 2010. "Blocked Paths, Uncertain Futures: The Post-secondary Education and Labor Market Prospects of Undocumented Latino Youth." *Journal of Education for Students Placed at Risk (JESPAR)* 15 (1–2): 144–157.

Arbona, Consuelo, Norma Olvera, Nestor Rodriguez, Jacqueline Hagan, Adriana Linares, and Margit Wiesner. 2010. "Acculturative Stress among Documented and Undocumented Latino Immigrants in the United States." *Hispanic Journal of Behavioral Sciences* 32 (3): 362–384.

Dillon, Frank R., Mario de la Rosa, and Gladys E. Ibanez. 2013. "Acculturative Stress and Diminishing Family Cohesion among Recent Latino Immigrants." *Journal of Immigrant and Minority Health* 15 (3): 484–491.

Fairfield University. n.d. "Immigrant Student Project." Accessed August 8, 2017. https://www
.fairfield.edu/undergraduate/academics/centers/center-for-faith-and-public-life
/research-based-solutions/immigrant-student-project/.

Flores, Stella M. 2010. "State Dream Acts: The Effect of In-State Resident Tuition Policies and
Undocumented Latino Students." *Review of Higher Education* 33 (2): 239–283.

Frum, Jennifer L. 2007. "Postsecondary Educational Access for Undocumented Students:
Opportunities and Constraints." *American Academic* 3: 81–108.

Gonzales, Roberto G., Luisa L. Heredia, and Genevieve Negrón-Gonzales. 2015. "Untangling
Plyler's Legacy: Undocumented Students, Schools, and Citizenship." *Harvard Educational
Review* 85 (3): 318–341.

Jones, Terry-Ann. 2017. "Theoretical and Conceptual Considerations for the Study of Undoc-
umented College Students." In *Undocumented and in College: Students and Institutions in a
Climate of National Hostility*, edited by Terry-Ann Jones and Laura Nichols, 13–29. New
York: Fordham University Press.

Jones, Terry-Ann, and Laura Nichols, eds. 2017. *Undocumented and in College: Students and Institutions in a Climate of National Hostility*. New York: Fordham University Press.

Kantamneni, Neeta, Kavitha Dharmalingam, Jessica M. Tate, Beth L. Perlman, Chaitasi R.
Majmudar, and Nichole Shada. 2016. "DREAMing Big: Understanding the Current Con-
text of Academic and Career Decision-Making for Undocumented Students." *Journal of
Career Development* 43 (6): 483–497.

Loyola University Chicago. n.d. "Student Diversity and Multicultural Affairs." Accessed
August 8, 2017. http://www.luc.edu/diversity/resources/undocumentedstudentresources
/tuitionandscholarships/.

Nichols, Laura, and Maria Guzman. 2017. "Getting, Staying, and Being in College: The Experiences of Students." In *Undocumented and in College: Students and Institutions in a Climate
of National Hostility*, edited by Terry-Ann Jones and Laura Nichols, 104–133. New York:
Fordham University Press.

Núñez, Ann-Marie. 2014. "Employing Multilevel Intersectionality in Educational Research:
Latino Identities, Contexts, and College Access." *Educational Researcher* 43 (2): 85–92.

Ovink, Sarah M., Kim Ebert, and Dina Okamoto. 2016. "Symbolic Politics of the State: The
Case of In-State Tuition Bills for Undocumented Students." *Socius: Sociological Research for
a Dynamic World* 2: 1–15.

Perez, William. 2009. *We Are Americans: Undocumented Students Pursuing the American Dream.*
Sterling, VA: Stylus.

Perez, William, and Richard Douglas Cortes. 2011. *Undocumented Latino College Students: Their
Socioemotional and Academic Experiences.* New York: LFB Publishing.

Portes, Alejandro, and Rubén G. Rumbaut. 2001. "Conclusion: The Forging of a New America: Lessons for Theory and Policy." In *Ethnicities: Children of Immigrants in America*, edited
by Rubén G. Rumbaut and Alejandro Portes, 301–318. New York; Berkeley: University of
California Press.

Suárez-Orozco, Carola, Dalal Katsiaficas, Olivia Birchall, Cynthia M. Alcantar, Edwin Hernan-
dez, Yuliana Garcia, Minas Michikyan, Janet Cerda, and Robert T. Teranishi. 2015.
"Undocumented Undergraduates on College Campuses: Understanding Their Challenges
and Assets and What It Takes to Make an Undocufriendly Campus." *Harvard Educational
Review* 85 (3): 427–463.

4 · RACE-BASED ASSUMPTIONS OF SOCIAL CLASS IDENTITY AND THEIR CONSEQUENCES AT A PREDOMINANTLY WHITE (AND WEALTHY) INSTITUTION

DEBORAH M. WARNOCK

There is this kind of unspoken, and sometimes spoken, assumption that students of color at the school are either in SOP [a scholarship program] or are here on financial aid and the White students are here because their parents are paying for it.   —Bianca

In this chapter I detail the extent to which social class intersects with race and ethnicity to affect college student experiences. I draw on in-depth, semi-structured interview data collected from sixteen students who were involved in a student-led group for low-income, first-generation, and/or working-class (LIF-GWC) students at a small private college. I found that students' assumed class identities on campus are tied to their racial identities. Specifically, students of color are overwhelmingly assumed to come from low-income backgrounds, and white students are assumed to possess class privilege. Because of this, students of color report feeling further marginalized, and white students feel as though their identities and needs as LIFGWC students are ignored. I examine how this conflation of race and class is encouraged by institutional practices as well as question the extent to which students are able to successfully organize around social class. Finally, I conclude by offering a summary of policy suggestions for institutional change provided by student participants.

REVIEW OF THE LITERATURE

Social class is a contested concept in social science. While some see it purely as a macroeconomic category, others view it as one of many identities individuals can claim, and still others have declared it "dead" entirely (Lareau and Conley 2008). Sociologists argue about the conceptualization of class, identifying various organizing concepts such as job autonomy, income, assets, or education as primary (Wright 2005). My work is guided by Bourdieu (1990), who allows for human agency while acknowledging the unconscious predispositions that one's class of origin shapes, which he terms *habitus.*

Just as other identities, such as race or gender, may become more salient to an individual when he or she is surrounded by difference, new college students from LIFGWC backgrounds may find their class identities resonate more strongly than they previously had. Elite institutions in the United States enroll overwhelmingly white and wealthy student populations, and the setting for this study is no exception (Chetty et al. 2017). Previous studies found that LIFGWC students feel out of place at elite colleges (Aries and Seider 2005; Lee 2016; Stuber 2011). Jensen (2012) argues that the values of the working class, such as loyalty and community, clash with traditionally middle-class values of ambition and individualism, which are more likely to be espoused on college campuses. Some research suggests that the dislocation students from disparate backgrounds experience in these settings manifests as a cleft habitus, or "the experience of transitioning and holding two habitus at one time" (Lee and Kramer 2013, 19). In a study of working-class students at a public university, Hurst (2010) found that students develop adaptive strategies for navigating this habitus dislocation.

Seeking out similar peers in student-established affinity groups has been one strategy of coping that LIFGWC students employ (Warnock and Hurst 2016). Part of the function of these groups is to provide a place for storytelling and awareness raising about the experience of socioeconomic minorities on campus. However, as some studies note, many campuses organize diversity affinity groups within a celebration framework, wherein identities are applauded for their difference (Lee 2016; Warnock and Hurst 2016). Some LIFGWC students struggle to find their place in this narrative (Hurst and Warnock 2015).

Another way LIFGWC students struggle with their identities relates to the invisibility of class (Warnock and Hurst 2016). While race can be highly visible, class is often invisible. However, the extent to which class is visible may depend on a person's race. Black and Latino students, in particular, are often assumed to be poor, while whites are associated with more economically advantaged backgrounds (Lee 2016; Lewis and Diamond 2015). While data confirm racial and ethnic income and wealth disparities, a sizable percentage of blacks and Latinos identify as middle class or higher (Lui et al. 2006). While race and class are certainly linked owing to current and past policies of racial discrimination, racial identity does not determine class identity.

Intersectionality theory posits that students experience race and class not as separate identities but as intersecting identities that simultaneously shape their social standpoints and frame the inequalities they may face on campus (Collins 2000). Therefore, the experiences of students of color may vary depending on their background, just as the experiences of LIFGWC students may vary depending on their race and ethnicity. Jack (2016) demonstrates the importance of background in his study of LIFGWC students of color at an elite university. Students matriculating from private schools moved with relatively more ease into college, whereas those from public schools found the transition to be more tenuous.

LIFGWC white students also struggle to adapt to predominantly wealthy campuses. Stuber (2011) showed that these students were less likely to integrate socially by participating in extracurricular activities. Armstrong and Hamilton (2013) demonstrated that institutional practices served to disadvantage white women from low-income backgrounds who lacked the cultural and social capital to be successful in an environment that assumed its students possessed a healthy supply of each.

In her study of upwardly mobile Mexican American and white high school students, Bettie (2003) found that white students articulated their feelings of discomfort and distance from their communities as individualized. However, the association of whiteness with class privilege also smoothed the transition of whites across class boundaries by making it easier for them to "pass" (Bettie 2003, 161–162). Meanwhile, the Mexican American girls in Bettie's study were "more consciously aware of themselves as a community of people" with a shared history of oppression (161). Mexican American girls were marked as different in college prep classes populated by economically privileged and white students.

If students' experiences of upward mobility, and of campus, vary across intersecting racialized and class identities, how should campuses address these students' needs? Some students start campus affinity groups to address issues related to socioeconomic diversity. Part of establishing an activist group is developing a sense of collective identity among members (Leondar-Wright 2014). If students' experiences and standpoints vary on the basis of race and class intersections and the separate needs experienced by each, is it possible for a single campus group to successfully address the needs of LIFGWC students?

In this chapter I argue that the conflation of race and class leads to the further marginalization of race and class minorities on campus. Students of these backgrounds face difficulties organizing around social class on a campus where institutional practices contribute to this conflation.

THE SETTING

The site of the study is Primrose College,[1] a private, coeducational institution located in a small, affluent city in the Northeast. Primrose is a small, selective liberal arts college with a student body that is predominantly white and wealthy. At the time of the study, 12 percent of the student body was eligible for a Pell grant, and 22 percent identified as students of color.

The "special opportunity program," or SOP, described throughout this chapter was started in the 1970s with the goal of recruiting students who face academic and financial challenges. To qualify for SOP, students must apply for admission, their families must meet financial eligibility requirements, and they must score below Primrose's average admissions standards in grades and/or test scores. Admissions officers refer eligible applicants to SOP staff, who then create a ranked list of students, with a cohort target of forty students each year. SOP students constitute about 6 percent of the student body, and the program produces better retention and graduation rates than in the general Primrose population.

The data presented here were collected as part of a larger case study examining the role of a student group for LIFGWC students on campus. At the time of the study I was on faculty at Primrose and was instrumental in working with a student to found the group Class at Primrose (CAP).[2] CAP began meeting in the fall of 2011, and I attended the first few meetings. However, it became apparent that students looked to me for approval when they spoke, and so to avoid affecting the group's dynamics, I stopped attending meetings but continued to act as an informal advisor.[3]

RESEARCH DESIGN AND METHOD

In the fall of 2012 I received approval from Primrose College to conduct interviews with students who were members of or had expressed interest in CAP. I interviewed the three most active members of CAP at the end of the 2012 fall semester. In the spring of 2013 I used CAP's email list to recruit additional participants. Thirteen students completed interviews in the spring, for a total of sixteen participants. Each student received ten dollars for participating. Of the sixteen participants, twelve identified as working class, lower class, or low income, and four identified as middle or lower middle class. Seven participants identified as white, and the other nine as students of color. Eleven participants identified as women, four as men, and one as agender. Three of the sixteen participants were enrolled in SOP.

Interviews took place in a private study room in the campus library and ranged in length from thirty minutes to two hours. I asked students to self-identify as they chose by inviting them to describe their social class background, as well as their race and ethnicity. I also asked them to reflect on how social class affected their experiences on campus, and how their race and ethnicity intersected with their class locations. In addition, students discussed the extent to which they participated in CAP and how Primrose could better serve students like them. I recorded each interview and transcribed them for analysis.

Using an inductive approach to coding the data (Bogdan and Biklen 2003), I open-coded each transcript line by line. I then identified a set of emergent codes related to social class and racial and/or ethnic identities and intersectionalities, as well as campus and group experiences. I recoded the transcripts using these codes and produced memos related to each theme that informed the current study's findings.

In analyzing these data, I sought to remain aware of my own positionality as a white woman from a low-income background who attended a similar undergraduate institution. As I discuss elsewhere (Warnock 2014, 2016a, 2016b), I identify as a "working-class academic," a term coined by Ryan and Sackrey (1984) and shared by a community of like-minded scholars. During many of the interviews my own experiences were echoed back to me and I found myself nodding in shared understanding (Hurst 2008). I also sought to remain aware of my difference from students, particularly my privileged positionality as a white faculty member. Students either knew I had helped start CAP or had worked with me directly to do so, and I sought to create a nonjudgmental atmosphere in which they felt free to share critiques of CAP and campus. Later analysis of the transcripts reveals many points in which students were indeed critical of both, although I cannot be completely sure whether their comments would have taken a different tone with another interviewer. Still, I consider my "insider status" to be more a source of greater understanding of than a hindrance to my analysis.

FINDINGS

I uncovered three major themes regarding the extent to which the intersection of race and class affected both students' experiences of college and their willingness to become involved in CAP. First, I found that race was often conflated with class. Students with multiple marginalized identities tended to more openly identify with an identity that was not class-based, and this was particularly true for students of color. White students, however, identified more strongly with their social class identities and felt stigmatized on a campus that lacked a venue for open dialogue around class inequality. For white students, openly embracing a marginalized class identity appeared to be a choice. Students of color expressed that they were often assumed to lack class privilege by virtue of their race and/or ethnicity.

Second, I found that conceptualizations of class on campus depended on whether students were enrolled in SOP. Students in SOP identified a community of support largely based on race/ethnicity rather than class, although socioeconomic background was one of the official criteria for membership and race/ethnicity was not. Students who were not in SOP were envious of the resources SOP students had access to, with some expressing that they felt unsupported at Primrose.

Finally, some students voiced concerns about the possibility of organizing effectively around social class identity, especially when the needs of LIFGWC students of color and those of LIFGWC white students on campus might vary.

Conflating Race with Class

Many students in the study expressed discomfort with the perceived campus-wide assumption that whiteness meant economic privilege. As Tanya,[4] a low-income white student, put it: "There's definitely the perception that all the White kids at Primrose are the same and I wouldn't say I identify with that. . . . Being rich or wealthy or having an affluent family, that's totally the opposite of how I am. And it's solely because I'm White."

Students of color, meanwhile, were more likely to identify the perceived campus-wide assumption that they lacked economic privilege. Many students of color, regardless of SOP membership, shared that they were automatically assumed to be in the program and, therefore, socioeconomically disadvantaged. Katrina, who identified as "lower class,"[5] shared: "I feel like a lot of students expect a Black student or a Latino student to be poor. They automatically think that student is from [SOP]. I've been suspected to be a part of [SOP] just because I'm Asian." Faculty were also guilty of stating this assumption. When asked about the challenges he has faced on campus based on his class background, Evan, a multiracial student from the middle class, stated, "I don't have much trouble with any faculty. Every now and then, being assumed [SOP], which I don't take as a bad thing. It's just having to correct and say I'm not [SOP]. They say, 'Oh, that's interesting.'"

What is important to note is that this assumption not only conflates race with class but also presumes that students of color were admitted to Primrose solely as part of a special program for the "disadvantaged." By assuming all students of color are affiliated with the SOP, students and faculty are also implying that those students did not gain admission through the mainstream admissions process, an additional way in which students of color may be marginalized. Class, then, while often described as an invisible identity, is made visible through assumptions based on a student's race. However, while white students are assumed to make up the majority of the predominantly wealthy on campus, students of color are *othered* on the basis of race and assumed class, including implicit assumptions about how these students gained admission.

Students in the study more strongly identified with the most salient marginalized identity in the context of the predominantly white institution (PWI). Students of color were more likely to identify with their race or ethnicity, which was especially true for SOP members. Although SOP admissions criteria did not include race or ethnicity, the majority of students in SOP were students of color.

Many SOP students, who participate in a summer bridge program before their first year, develop close-knit relationships and identify similarities that appear to be more at opposition with a predominantly white campus than a predominantly wealthy one. Perhaps this was because these students enjoyed generous scholarships and extra funds for books. The additional resources made social class differences, which were more salient to non-SOP LIFGWC students, regardless of race or ethnicity, less troublesome to SOP students. SOP students, then, appeared to identify their main difference from the majority of students on campus as being due to race and not class. In fact, Salma, a low-income Dominican and African American woman enrolled in SOP, shared that her best friend from high school, who was not in SOP, had found college to be socially difficult until she pulled him into the SOP "clique," where other members "automatically assume he's in SOP." When I asked if all people who hang out with SOP students are assumed to be SOP, she replied, "Not all people. Only if you're a person of color."

As Freddy, a low-income Mexican American student shared, "I feel more comfortable with the people of color . . . especially with the ones that got the SOP grant as well." While he goes on to state that "the reason we all got it was because we came from low socioeconomic statuses," he later mentions that he "feels more comfortable with them than . . . with other people, for example, White people." He continues, "I don't want to generalize that all White people are rich. . . . Obviously, they are from the middle class or middle-upper class." This type of statement, which appears to conflate the race and class of students at Primrose, was more commonly voiced by SOP students, who framed their differences on campus in terms of race and not class. This belief perpetuates the invisibility of LIFGWC white students on campus and may reduce the likelihood of interracial, intraclass interactions.

Jessica, a white student from the "lower class," found it difficult to integrate socially at Primrose. She shared, "I don't want to hang around a group of people who I know are really privileged because it just feels weird." However, when she tried to seek out others with the same socioeconomic background, she encountered difficulties: "A lot of the low-income students here are not White. A lot of them are—everyone knows—in the SOP. I feel funny sometimes because I'm not in SOP, but I don't fit in in the non-SOP population. So, it feels like I don't really have a place sometimes. . . . I know that specifically in the group, I find that most of us are in that position." She also shared that she has had some frustrating experiences interacting with SOP students: "I've noticed that they can kind of judge people by the color of their skin. I've spoken with students and they didn't know that I was poor, because I don't tell people that. I could feel by the way they talk to me, they just assumed that I'm rich. Not just in SOP, anyone as a whole, if people see you're White, they just assume and it's frustrating when that happens because it's kind of ignorant." The conflation of race and class on campus allowed Jessica's class identity to remain invisible, which made it difficult for her to connect with students from similar backgrounds.

White students in the study, with the exception of one who was very involved in racial justice dialogues on campus, tended to identify most strongly with their class and to view themselves as disadvantaged because of this identity. They took issue with others' assumptions of their economic privilege, but were unlikely to challenge assumptions or to openly identify with their class background. Their whiteness served as a cloak of invisibility, aided by the campus-wide conflation of race and class. This allowed white students the option of choosing to confront classism on campus, which only one white student reported doing repeatedly, or to silently stew. Not saying anything was a form of privilege, but also one that was reinforced by the fear of being stigmatized on the basis of class (Aries and Seider 2005; Lee 2016; Warnock and Hurst 2016). Hiding a stigmatized identity can certainly be painful in and of itself, and this tendency to stay "in the class closet" had consequences in that these white students lacked access to needed resources. However, choosing to stay silent is also a form of privilege that was not often afforded to students of color.

Conceptualizations of Class

The fraught nature of class identity and its conflation with race was on full display at a conflict that ensued at a CAP-organized all-campus discussion panel, which included three students and one faculty member. The students on the panel were all CAP members who identified with some form of economic disadvantage and took turns describing their experiences on campus. Javier, a student of color from the "lower class" who was not in SOP, stated that "being poor teaches you how to be better at being poor." Two students of color in the audience who were members of SOP took issue with his statements, charging that he was arguing that poor people were not good enough. They stated that he had an inferiority complex and should be proud of his identity. The two students also accused him of seeking to pass on campus (Javier is biracial and light-skinned) and charged that he had internalized his oppression. Javier repeated that he believes that poverty is harmful to those who experience it. The students argued that growing up in poverty makes you driven to succeed and questioned why Javier did not see himself as special for being at Primrose.

Javier discussed the panel later with a friend in SOP and this friend confirmed that SOP teaches students they are special rising stars on their way to success— that they have "escaped."[6] Javier, however, struggled with being at Primrose, feeling that he was leaving his family behind. He identified forces beyond his control as the reasons he matriculated at Primrose, such as being offered a generous financial aid package. He was loath to identify himself as special if doing so would imply that those in his neighborhood were not.

This incident illustrates the ways in which the institutional context that sought to celebrate diversity on campus and encourage students to be proud and grateful was contrary to the experience of many members of CAP, who felt unsupported. They did not see their socioeconomic status as something to celebrate. In fact, for two of the three students on the panel, the experience was scary, as it was the first time they had publicly shared their class identity.

The racialized aspect of this conflict is telling. The two young women who took issue with Javier's statement accused him of lacking not only class pride but also racial pride, arguing that he was denying his race by being critical of the social class structure. Ironically, Javier was not trying to insult his community by acknowledging socioeconomic stratification and its consequences. However, this acknowledgment did not conform to a rhetoric of pride espoused by the SOP, a rhetoric that was also distinctly racial. The delicate ways in which class and race intertwine and the institutional context that advocated a celebration framework did not allow for a critical reading of upward mobility.

Though participants' circumstances differed, I found many parallels between Primrose students and Bettie's (2003) study of mobility-seeking high school girls. Bettie's important findings about the intersections of race and class can be seen in the alienation of the LIFGWC white students at the college and in the use of racial terms to describe class differences among students on campus. The lack of a collective language or visible identity for all LIFGWC students made establishing solidarity among this group a formidable task.

Organizing around Class

Warnock and Hurst (2016) found that CAP faced difficulties in recruiting and maintaining membership. For example, many students indicated they wanted to be more involved with CAP, but their work schedules prohibited them from participating in extracurricular activities, a finding also reflected in Stuber (2011). Tanya shared her frustration: "It would be nice if I could work fewer hours. . . . I have this huge time commitment that you won't know unless you ask me." Students' workloads interfere not only with participation in activities but also in their ability to meet assignment deadlines that, too often, assume an open schedule. Tanya continued: "Yes, our job is school, but maybe our job is also supporting ourselves." Javier quit his work-study job because he found the time commitment too stressful, yet he worried about paying for books and supplies. He described an art class in which he was encouraged to "be free with the materials." He was, however, consumed with worry about the costs of doing so. SOP students whose books and materials were paid for through the program did not cite such worries.

Bianca, CAP founder and a working-class white first-generation immigrant from eastern Europe, expressed concern that CAP membership was "predominantly white." She was frustrated "because we had a lot of students of color coming to our first meetings." She wondered if "our goals are disproportionately addressing the needs of *White* low-income and working-class students or maybe just the fact that the leadership is White." Given the concerns discussed by the white students in this study, one explanation for the racial disparity in membership could be because LIFGWC white students had no other space on campus where they felt they could find the support of similar others. As discussed above, white students tended to stay silent while simultaneously experiencing the campus as a deeply classed place. In fact, when pushed to embrace a more openly activist identity, one white student, who had relied on CAP as her sole social tie to campus, left the group. Among CAP students of color, some were in SOP and some were not. Those not in SOP, similar to the white students, appeared to rely on CAP as a source of interaction with similar peers more so than the already-bonded SOP students.

However, Bianca was also correct in assuming that the overwhelmingly white makeup of CAP could be alienating for students of color who might otherwise become involved. When asked about her perceptions of CAP, with which she had been peripherally involved, Minnie, a working-class Caribbean American student, shared that she "didn't know if CAP appealed to people of color." She cited discussions of class on campus that elided the important effects of race and her discomfort with the term "working class." Even though Minnie identifies as working-class, this label read as "white, rural, and male" to her. Minnie's concerns—that in a group devoted to exploring and discussing social class, race would be marginalized—demonstrate the importance of acknowledging the intersectionality of students' identities. These intersections shape students' campus experiences, as well as their involvement with an organization that hoped to organize around class-based marginality across racial and ethnic identities.

CONCLUSION AND POLICY IMPLICATIONS

The student participants suggested several institutional policies, including increasing socioeconomic diversity, expanding access to institutional resources and mentoring, orientation programming for LIFGWC students and their families, and dialoguing events to increase awareness of socioeconomic diversity on campus. Finally, this chapter provides evidence that students' needs are affected by the intersections of race and class identities, which campuses can do a better job of supporting.

Many students called for increased socioeconomic diversity on campus. Tanya shared, "I think what would make Primrose a lot better was if there were more middle income students here, so it's not such a huge gap." Bianca advocated for Primrose to adopt a need-blind admissions policy to get "more students from lower classes to come here."

Non-SOP students suggested Primrose expand the SOP. Jessica, a white student, "had a really hard time freshman year and it would have helped a lot" and suggested Primrose should make "more resources available for first-generation or low-income students, even just to have specific advisors [like SOP students]." Also enviable to her were the "summer component before college" that SOP offered and the fact that "they get their books and health insurance paid for." Further, Jessica shared, "I feel like they [SOP students] have so much support and I really love the program. . . . I just wish Primrose could afford to open it up more." Minnie echoed Jessica, noting that "there needs to be some guidance for a student of color and working-class students that aren't part of SOP." Continuing, Minnie "felt like [she] wasn't as prepared" when she got to campus and did not learn about many important resources until much later. Similar to Jack's (2016) work on low-income students of color, this chapter demonstrates that LIFGWC students' experiences vary by race and the accessibility to institutional support.

Contrast Jessica's and Minnie's comments with those of SOP student Nadine, who, when asked what improvements Primrose could make, said she "didn't know." She continued, "I feel like I am very supported here . . . so maybe I'm blind to seeing some things that could be changed." However, Nadine, who identified as working class, acknowledged that "that's not true for every low-income student on campus." Salma described this difference in more detail: "My best friend—we went to the same high school and had the same background. Although I got into SOP, he did not. For him, it's harder, because he has to buy his own books. He has to work more hours and he doesn't have as much financial support so it's more difficult for him to assimilate into the crowd as well because when we come in from SOP we already have a good group of friends, so his experience has been way more difficult than mine financially and socially." This two-tiered system of support for LIFGWC students made some feel unsupported, while others entered their first year of college with reduced financial and social worries. Those who do not benefit from SOP, which utilizes an "individual" rather than an "institutional" approach (Fox, Sonnert, and Nikiforova 2009), have entirely different, and much more difficult, experiences at Primrose. Applying a more institutional approach to the problems facing LIFGWC students could make the campus more inclusive for all LIFGWC students, regardless of race and ethnicity, and reduce the conflation of race and class on campus.

It came as no surprise that, when asked what changes could be made on campus, many students cited expanded access to institutional resources. Chad suggested a food stipend for students suffering from food insecurity, stating that "it gets scary when you don't have access to food." Emma noted the need for an airport shuttle, which was an "$80 cab drive" from campus. Katrina argued that many resources exist on campus but are not well publicized. A few students reported the Office of Financial Aid as being particularly unhelpful. Jessica shared that she has "formally requested to have certain [fees] waived [because she] really [doesn't] have the money . . . and usually they don't allow [her] to." Although she is not in

SOP, they may believe that "maybe I do not need this waived," a frustration shared among other non-SOP students not identified and supported as suffering from economic insecurities.

This lack of accommodation from campus offices is compounded by the need for self-advocacy by many LIFGWC students. Jessica must advocate for herself, and believes this is fairly ineffective. "I work in residential life and I witness it myself. When a student calls, the tone of the administrator's voice is way different from when there's a parent on the phone. I don't have a parent to advocate for me when I need something. I have to do it myself. I feel like I'm just not treated the same as if my dad had come in." Crystal's parents were uncomfortable attending orientation events, and suggested "an open forum . . . for parents of first-generation students" to counter an assumption that parents were familiar with navigating college offices and events.

The lack of dialogue about class issues on campus was a concern many participants shared. CAP members suggested that "more dialogues, more public, open events" would help inform the campus community about the characteristics and needs of all students. Bianca thought it was particularly important to invite staff to every awareness event. Echoing Minnie's concerns about discussing social class without taking into consideration important intersections with race and ethnicity, Katrina argued that first-year peer mentors should be trained "to talk about social class issues as well as other social identities."

Bianca questioned how the campus defines diversity, how those definitions are reflected in its perceived admissions priorities, and the consequences of this for the student body. "Primrose defines diversity as just racial diversity and diversity comes in so many different forms and there are the invisible diversities and class differences that should be represented. . . . It's not just like 'Let's bring these students of color who are low-income so we're killing two birds with one stone,' because low-income students of color and low-income White students also have very different experiences and I think bring very different perspectives. . . . That doesn't only benefit the students who are getting here, but all of the students who don't even share those identities, by having variety." Bianca's quote encapsulates the main arguments of this chapter. Colleges often identify and treat students as a monolithic group. Even when different needs and experiences are acknowledged, they tend to be painted in broad strokes without attention to the intersections of identities that define individual student experiences.

In this chapter I sought to tease race from class, interrogating assumptions made on the basis of each. To be sure, race and class intersect to shape students' experiences, but the ways in which they do so are not always, or correctly, acknowledged in campus policies. The conflation of race and class, both through interpersonal assumptions and the implementation of campus initiatives, erases important differences within and between students. Attending to students' intersecting identities on an unequal campus assists with creating institutions that can better serve a diversity of student needs. Importantly, class similarities are often erased, impairing students' attempts to build class solidarity.

In this chapter I build on Bourdieu's habitus and Collins's intersectionality theory to suggest that the two are more effective when combined. Just as Bettie (2003) demonstrates, both race and class matter to students' mobility projects. For upwardly mobile LIFGWC students struggling with Bourdieu's "cleft habitus," race and ethnicity play a large role in determining the ways in which this is experienced. The (in)visibility of class makes navigating a predominantly white and wealthy campus difficult for LIFGWC students, but students' challenges also vary by racial/ethnic identity. Therefore, upward mobility that results in a "cleft habitus" cannot be considered a homogenous experience. Researchers and practitioners must also take into account, and heed Collins's call by doing so, the intersection of identities that contribute to varying lived realities of class. These intersecting identities affect not only the students' own experiences of class mobility, including the ease or difficulty with which they are able to transition to a PWI, but also the extent to which they are identified by others as belonging on campus. Although an LIFGWC white student may feel like an outsider and face obstacles in finding a home on campus, this process is more easily hidden than is the mobility experience for an LIFGWC student of color. The split identity articulated by Bourdieu's "cleft habitus" may be experienced on the basis of not only class but race as well, as Bettie (2003, 156) discusses in the extent to which Mexican American girls "articulated their difference clearly in terms of race." Because of the marked difference of race and ethnicity, these girls carefully navigated class transitions using a strategy of "accommodation without assimilation" (158).

As demonstrated in this chapter, race and class intersect to shape not only students' own experiences of campus but also how they are identified and viewed by others on campus. To know one does not belong is different from being identified as not belonging. Arguably, LIFGWC students on predominantly wealthy campuses, regardless of race or ethnicity, experience a kind of "double consciousness," viewing themselves through the eyes of an institution that does not explicitly make space for them, and may instead regard them with contempt and pity in both interpersonal and institutional practices (DuBois 1903). However, students of color often experience this feeling of "otherness" or "two-ness" imposed on the basis of both race and ethnicity and assumed class difference, regardless of the accuracy of this assumption, as well. Whereas LIFGWC white students are likely aware of this difference, there are fewer salient visible markers by which to name it. Indeed, white students are often assumed to be race and class congruent with the majority of the campus by virtue of their race alone. White LIFGWC students, although they might inwardly question their legitimacy and belonging on campus, experiencing the split identity described by Bourdieu's "cleft habitus," are not as often explicitly marked as other by the campus. Therefore, the "cleft habitus" is moderated by the intersections of race and class within a context that legitimates the white and (assumedly) wealthy student.

Through the conflation of race and class at predominantly white and wealthy institutions, these campuses deny belonging on the basis of both race and class. By not providing support to LIFGWC white students who suffer from a "cleft habitus," they are invalidating the needs of students based on class, while not openly questioning the legitimacy of the white student presence. Simultaneously, by assuming students of color come from LIFGWC backgrounds, they are invalidating the legitimacy of these students by twice "othering," once on the basis of race and ethnicity and again on the basis of assumed class. While lived experiences of class vary on the basis of race, to tie one without question to the other is also to deny the interracial solidarity around class location that might otherwise be possible. Similarly, to deny differences in lived experiences of class on the basis of race is also to miss the importance of intersectional identities in shaping one's habitus. Future research should continue to explore how campus practices differentially affect students across intersecting identities and how Bourdieu's concept of habitus might be expanded to allow for raced differences in experiences of class and upward mobility.

NOTES

1. This is a pseudonym chosen by the author.
2. This is a pseudonym chosen by the author.
3. For more detail about CAP, see Warnock and Hurst (2016).
4. All names are pseudonyms either chosen by or assigned to participants.
5. While some find the term "lower class" to be pejorative, I include it here because the student chose to self-identify in this way.
6. See Hurst and Warnock (2015) for further discussion of the narratives of upward mobility used by SOP at Primrose.

REFERENCES

Aries, Elizabeth, and Maynard Seider. 2005. "The Interactive Relationship between Class Identity and the College Experience: The Case of Lower Income Students." *Qualitative Sociology* 28, no. 4 (Winter): 419–443.

Armstrong, Elizabeth A., and Laura T. Hamilton. 2013. *Paying for the Party: How College Maintains Inequality*. Cambridge, MA: Harvard University Press.

Bettie, Julie. 2003. *Women without Class*. Berkeley: University of California Press.

Bogdan, Robert, and Sari K. Biklen. 2003. *Qualitative Research for Education*. Boston: Allyn and Bacon Press.

Bourdieu, Pierre. 1990. *The Logic of Practice*. Palo Alto, CA: Stanford University Press.

Chetty, Raj, John Friedman, Emmanuel Saez, Nicholas Turner, and Danny Yagan. 2017. "Mobility Report Cards." The Equality of Opportunity Project. http://www.equality-of-opportunity .org/papers/coll_mrc_paper.pdf.

Collins, Patricia Hill. 2000. *Black Feminist Thought*. New York: Routledge.

Du Bois, W.E.B. 1903. *The Souls of Black Folk*. Chicago: A. C. McClurg.

Fox, Mary Frank, Gerhard Sonnert, and Irina Nikiforava. 2009. "Successful Programs for Undergraduate Women in Science and Engineering: Adapting versus Adopting the Institutional Environment." *Research in Higher Education* 50 (4): 333–353.

Hurst, Allison L. 2008. "A Healing Echo: Methodological Reflections of a Working-Class Researcher on Class." *Qualitative Report* 13 (3): 334–352.

———. 2010. *The Burden of Academic Success*. Lanham, MD: Lexington Books.

Hurst, Allison L., and Deborah M. Warnock. 2015. "*Les Miraculés*: 'The Magical Image of the Permanent Miracle'—Constructed Narratives of Self and Mobility from Working-Class Students at an Elite College." In *Sharing Space, Negotiating Difference: Contemporary Ethnographies of Power and Marginality on Campus*, edited by Elizabeth Lee and Chaise LaDousa, 102–117. New York: Routledge.

Jack, Anthony Abraham. 2016. "No Harm in Asking." *Sociology of Education* 89 (1): 1–19.

Jensen, Barbara. 2012. *Reading Classes: On Culture and Classism in America*. Ithaca, NY: Cornell University Press.

Lareau, Annette, and Dalton Conley, eds. 2008. *Social Class*. New York: Russell Sage Foundation.

Lee, Elizabeth M. 2016. *Class and Campus Life*. Ithaca, NY: Cornell University Press.

Lee, Elizabeth M., and Rory Kramer. 2013. "Out with the Old, in with the New? Habitus and Social Mobility at Selective Colleges." *Sociology of Education* 86 (1): 18–35.

Leondar-Wright, Betsy. 2014. *Missing Class: Strengthening Social Movement Groups by Seeing Class Cultures*. Ithaca, NY: Cornell University Press.

Lewis, Amanda E., and John B. Diamond. 2015. *Despite the Best Intentions*. New York: Oxford University Press.

Lui, Meizhu, Barbara Robles, Betsy Leondar-Wright, Rose Brewer, and Rebecca Adamson. 2006. *The Color of Wealth*. New York: New Press.

Ryan, Jake, and Charles Sackrey. 1984. *Strangers in Paradise: Academics from the Working Class*. Boston: South End Press.

Stuber, Jenny M. 2011. *Inside the College Gates: How Class and Culture Matter in Higher Education*. Lanham, MD: Lexington Books.

Warnock, Deborah M. 2014. "On the Other Side of What Tracks? The Missing Discussion of Social Class in the Academy." *Rhizomes: Cultural Studies in Emerging Knowledge*, no. 12 (December). http://www.rhizomes.net/issue27/warnock.html.

———. 2016a. "Capitalizing Class: An Examination of Socioeconomic Diversity on the Contemporary Campus." In *Working in Class: Recognizing How Social Class Shapes Our Academic Work*, edited by Allison L. Hurst and Sandi K. Nenga, 173–183. Lanham, MD: Rowman & Littlefield.

———. 2016b. "Paradise Lost? Patterns and Precarity in Working-Class Academic Narratives." *Journal of Working-Class Studies* 1, no. 1 (December). https://workingclassstudiesjournal.files.wordpress.com/2016/06/jwcs-vol-1-issue-1-december-2016-warnock.pdf.

Warnock, Deborah M., and Allison L. Hurst. 2016. "'The Poor Kids' Table': Organizing around an Invisible and Stigmatized Identity in Flux." *Journal of Diversity in Higher Education* 9 (3): 261–276.

Wright, Erik Olin. 2005. *Approaches to Class Analysis*. Cambridge: Cambridge University Press.

5 · BIRACIAL COLLEGE STUDENTS' RACIAL IDENTITY WORK

How Black-White Biracial Students Navigate Racism and Privilege at Historically Black and Historically White Institutions

KRISTEN A. CLAYTON

The face of higher education is changing as more multiracial students enter college. On the 2000 U.S. Census, individuals could indicate membership in more than one racial category for the first time; 2.4 percent of individuals indicated they were multiracial. Between 2000 and 2010, the number of people identifying with two or more races increased from about 6.8 to 9.0 million people, and those identifying as both white and black increased by 134 percent (Jones and Bullock 2012). Relatedly, the multiracial college student population has grown each year since 2010 and is projected to increase through at least 2025 (National Center for Education Statistics 2015).

Despite increasing scholarly attention to multiracial students (e.g., Renn 2004; Renn and Shang 2008; Museus, Yee, and Lambe 2011; Kellogg and Liddell 2012; Museus, Sarinana, and Ryan 2015; Jones 2015), little research focuses on multiracial students at historically black colleges and universities (HBCUs). This lack of attention to HBCU students' experiences not only ignores a subset of the biracial student population; it also prevents a full understanding of how institutions of higher education as racialized organizations shape how students manage and negotiate their racial identities. HBCUs and historically white colleges and universities (HWCUs)[1] have different racial structures, or "set[s] of social relations and practices based on racial distinctions" (Bonilla-Silva 1997, 474).

Thus, comparing the experiences of students within these institutions will contribute to a more complete understanding of the interaction between racial identity and educational contexts. This study specifically addresses the following questions: (1) How do black-white biracial students navigate race and negotiate their identities within HBCUs and HWCUs? and (2) How do they describe their racial identity work in relation to class and gender?

To address these questions, I draw on data from interviews with fifty-five black-white biracial students attending an HBCU or HWCU. I present an intersectional account of the ways that skin color and biracial background shape experiences across institutional contexts. I show how the HWCU's privileging of whiteness disadvantaged biracial students (particularly women) because of their relative blackness. In contrast, biracial HBCU students (particularly women) occupied a high position within their campus racial structure because of their lightness and/or biraciality. Much of biracial students' identity work at HWCUs focused on navigating racism, while in the HBCU context, it involved navigating privilege. Moreover, I show how race intersects with gender and class to affect biracial students' experiences and identity work.

STRUCTURAL RACISM'S EFFECTS ON INTERACTIONS WITHIN HISTORICALLY WHITE AND HISTORICALLY BLACK INSTITUTIONS

This study draws on Bonilla-Silva's (1997) conceptualization of structural racism, which posits that racism has both ideological and structural components. In a racialized social system, actors are placed into hierarchically ranked racial categories based on socially defined indicators, such as skin color (Bonilla-Silva 1997). Actors placed in the category deemed superior receive economic, social, political, and psychological benefits (Bonilla-Silva 1997). A racial ideology underpins this structure, guiding actors' behavior (Bonilla-Silva 1997).

I apply Bonilla-Silva's concept of racial structure to universities. The racial structure of HWCUs privileges whiteness. HWCUs are institutions "whose histories, traditions, symbols, stories, icons, curriculum, and processes were all designed by whites, for whites, to reproduce whiteness via a white experience at the exclusion of others who, since the 1950s and 1960s, have been allowed in such spaces" (Brunsma, Brown, and Placier 2013, 3). Many students of color view HWCUs as unaccepting, culturally insensitive, and/or hostile environments (Karkouti 2016). For much of U.S. history, multiracial blacks have been classified as black in accordance with the rule of hypodescent (Davis 1991). Because others often classify them as nonwhite, biracial HWCU students may experience racial discrimination (Kellogg and Liddell 2012).

Structural racism also affects interactions in HBCUs. Racial hegemony and the U.S. valorization of whiteness have led to colorism: "the allocation of privilege and disadvantage according to the lightness or darkness of one's skin" (Burke and Embrick 2008, 17). Colorism in black communities is a result of institutional racism and will likely exist so long as the U.S. racial structure continues to privilege whiteness (Hunter 2007).

Historically, light skin was associated with attendance at elite HBCUs, perpetuating the association between lightness and status within black communities (Gasman and Abiola 2016). For instance, Gasman and Abiola (2016, 42) state that lighter-skinned blacks attended the highest-ranked HBCUs "above the others, thus creating clusters of light-skinned Blacks and making their presence the norm on campus early on." Additionally, membership in high-status organizations (e.g., sororities or fraternities) was often contingent on having skin lighter than a brown paper bag (Gasman and Abiola 2016). While the civil rights and black power movements were accompanied by increased pride in blackness and appreciation of all skin tones, research suggests that colorism still exists within HBCUs (Gasman and Abiola 2016). Because individuals with one black and one white parent are often perceived as light-skinned within black communities, they likely receive social advantages within HBCUs.

Importantly, research suggests that colorism is gendered such that lightness is associated with more benefits for women than men. The association between lightness and perceived attractiveness is stronger for black women than black men (Hill 2002). Relatedly, black men are more likely than black women to desire a light-skinned spouse (Ross 1997). Some theorize that the increased importance of lightness for women is related to the feminization of whiteness within black communities (Hill 2002). This analysis considers whether and how colorism might differentially shape the advantages of biracial men and women within HBCUs.

BIRACIAL IDENTITY WORK

Biracial individuals may engage in identity work to negotiate their position within racialized social systems. Racial identity work refers to strategies individuals use to present racial identities during interaction (Khanna and Johnson 2010). Strategies include "verbal identification/disidentification, selective disclosure, manipulation of phenotype, highlighting/downplaying cultural symbols, and selective association" (381). The idea that individuals work to affect how they are racially categorized highlights the socially constructed nature of race. Far from being static and natural, racial meanings are constructed and revised through interaction. Biracial individuals may engage in identity work to have their internal identity validated, achieve status, avoid discrimination, and/or evade stigmatized racial identities (Khanna 2011).

Historically, attention to biracial identity work focused on individuals who "passed" as white. Passing refers to "a deception that enables a person to adopt specific roles or identities from which he or she would otherwise be barred by prevailing social standards" (Kennedy 2003, 283). A biracial individual, defined as nonwhite by norms of hypodescent, who portrays herself as white could be described as passing. While many biracial Americans shun the idea of attempting to live as white, some describe passing situationally to avoid discrimination (Khanna 2011). Others do not conceal their blackness but work to distance themselves from stigma surrounding this identity (Khanna 2011). Whiteness can also be stigmatized when it is associated with oppression, presumed superiority, or other negative characteristics (Storrs 1999). In such settings, biracial individuals may "pass" as black to avoid the stigma of whiteness (Khanna and Johnson 2010).

The stigma of blackness is often connected to the stigma of poverty; race and class are frequently conflated in American culture such that blackness is associated with lower-class status and whiteness with middle- or upper-class status (Bettie 2000). Blackness may also be stigmatized because of its association with deviant gender identities. Dominant ideologies depict black women as more masculine than white women and black men as *too* masculine compared with white men (Ridgeway and Kricheli-Katz 2013). Black women are disadvantaged by this association with masculinity, particularly within the dating scene (Ridgeway and Kricheli-Katz 2013). Black men are also disadvantaged by their association with hypermasculinity and associated images of violence and criminality (Ridgeway and Kricheli-Katz 2013). Whiteness can also become stigmatized through association with deviant gender identities. For instance, the feminization of whiteness in some black communities can lead to the stigmatization of white and/or light-skinned men, who are perceived as insufficiently masculine (Hill 2002).

This analysis explores how race, class, and gender ideologies intersect to create stigmatized and/or privileged identities within different educational contexts and how these ideas of stigma and status affect biracial students' identity work. Knowledge of these processes is limited owing to scholars' lack of attention to HBCUs. Comparing the experiences of biracial HBCU and HWCU students advances understanding of how racial and gendered meanings, and the resulting location of black-white biracial students within campus racial structures, change depending on the racialized nature of institutional contexts.

METHODS

I conducted semi-structured interviews with students who reported having one black (non-Hispanic) and one white (non-Hispanic) biological parent. I recruited participants from one HWCU and three HBCUs. The HWCU is a public university in the Southeast. It enrolls over 26,000 undergraduates, approximately

73 percent of whom are white. The HBCUs are private schools in the Southeast, enrolling between 2,000 and 4,000 students, over 80 percent of whom are black. I recruited most participants through advertisements posted on campuses and emailed to student mailing lists. Eleven students were referred by others. The sample includes fifty-five respondents: twenty-two HBCU students (seven men and fifteen women) and thirty-three HWCU students (nine men and twenty-four women). Most respondents were underclassmen (89 percent), and most were middle class (69 percent).

Interviews ranged from 37 to 160 minutes. After asking broad questions about students' racial experiences in college, I asked targeted questions designed to explore identity work. I used MAXQDA qualitative analysis software to assist with coding. I began with a list of codes generated from the interview guide; however, I also used the inductive approach emphasized by grounded theorists (Corbin and Strauss 2008). I engaged in open coding, "breaking data apart and delineating concepts to stand for blocks of raw data" (195). I also utilized in vivo coding, using participants' exact words as codes. These techniques allowed data to drive analysis.

During analysis, I utilized a constant comparative method; this method increases the credibility of qualitative studies by requiring researchers to identify common themes that reoccur across the data as opposed to drawing conclusions from singular cases (Corbin and Strauss 2008). By comparing interviews within and across institutions I show how context shapes identity work; specifically, I show how much of biracial students' identity work at HWCUs focused on navigating racism, while in the HBCU context, it involved navigating privilege. By comparing interviews within and across gender categories, I show how race and gender intersect to shape students' location in campus racial structures and their resulting identity work. Additionally, when appropriate, I cross-checked students' accounts of institutional policies/practices and their descriptions of racial inequality against other sources; this use of triangulation further increases credibility[2] (Creswell and Miller 2000).

Throughout analysis, I remained reflexive about how my positionality may influence the study. As a black-white biracial woman, I am a member of the racial group I studied. I worked to ensure that I did not project my experiences onto participants. I also encouraged participants to expand on questions even when I and/or the participant assumed I knew the answer based on my lived experiences. For the most part, however, I believe my insider status to be an advantage in that many respondents reported feeling comfortable with me because of perceived racial similarity. While many perceived me as a racial "insider," my gender (woman) and class (middle class) differentially situated me as an insider or outsider depending on the respondent.

In the remainder of this chapter, I describe the results that emerged from analysis. Thick description enhances credibility in qualitative research (Corbin and

Strauss 2008; Creswell and Miller 2000); thus, I provide detailed descriptions of biracial students' experiences within different institutional contexts, using direct quotations when possible to highlight respondents' voices and perspectives.

BIRACIAL HWCU STUDENTS

The HWCU Racial Structure

The HWCU racial structure privileged whiteness. Consistent with Bonilla-Silva's (1997) description, whites' superior position in the societal and campus racial structures allowed them to draw boundaries between themselves and those defined as nonwhite. This was most evident within Greek life and the surrounding bar scene.

Alicia described the racialized rules that excluded black people from bars white students attended, saying: "Like you can't have braids. . . . Of course, white people aren't gonna have braids. . . . So, it just seems like it's like directly centered to keep like black people out of the bars." Alicia's account highlights how whites' power gives them license to exclude black people from certain spaces surrounding the campus, virtually marking those spaces as "white." Students described similar processes of exclusion within predominantly white Greek organizations. For instance, Thomas said: "I mean there were [fraternities] where you knew you weren't going to get in if you weren't white." Similarly, Emma said: "It's not like a boy's club, but it kinda is where you have to be this sort of person, this sort of color, this sort of, you know, background to get into the Greek associations."

The discriminatory practices of bars and Greek organizations aided in the formation of separate white and black social worlds, which students perceived as unequal with regard to resources. Emma described status differences between white and black Greek organizations, saying: "A lot of people just see the black Greek organizations as less than the white Greek organizations. . . . A lot of people are like oh well they don't even have houses . . . and then the white . . . sororities and fraternities they've got the massive houses." Visible racial disparities in resources (e.g., possession and size of fraternity houses) contributed to racial differences in organizations' status and power on campus.

Relatedly, respondents believed that among the predominantly white Greek organizations, those with the most status were the least accepting of nonwhite members. For instance, Candace described a conversation with a white member of a high-status sorority: "I was asking her if I should rush. . . . I was like, 'Do you think I would get in?' She goes 'Yeah, somewhere.' And she rushed for [Eta].[3] . . . They . . . have a reputation of being the ones with the more money . . . and they're really pretty girls and like one of the highest if you can rank sororities. . . . I said, 'But, do you think I could get into the one that you want to get into?'—which she is in now. . . . She kind of beat around the bush. . . . But, I think she kind of got the sense that . . . they would choose a white girl over me." This conversation reflects the relationship between race and status in Greek associations; Candace and others believed they may get accepted into a predominantly white Greek organization, but their race would likely bar them from those with the highest status.

Navigating Racism

Students used various strategies to navigate race and negotiate their identities within a campus that privileged whiteness. Importantly, most did not align themselves with the black community. At the time of the interview, only two of thirty-three respondents belonged to a black organization, and 61 percent *opposed* joining such organizations. Thirty percent avoided black organizations because of feelings of cultural and/or racial difference. For instance, Michelle said: "I don't really fit in I guess with just black people because I'm not black." Some of these students feared they would face rejection from black students or were uncertain whether they would even be allowed to join due to their biracial background. Twenty-four percent opposed *all* race-based organizations, finding them unnecessary and/or divisive. For instance, Janelle said: "I find race to be irrelevant. . . . I don't understand the concept [of race-based organizations] because it's 2013 and we're past that."

Later in the interview, however, Janelle mentioned that her peers make racist comments, saying: "People say things that bring out racism, and it's just shocking." Janelle's comments reflect a tension that was common among participants; students described racism ("people say things that bring out racism") while simultaneously downplaying its significance ("it's 2013, and we're past that"). Students like Michelle and Janelle navigated a campus where whiteness was privileged while distancing themselves from organizations and resources designed to support students from marginalized racial backgrounds.

Despite the privileging of whiteness on campus and some students' disidentification with blackness, no respondents reported attempting to "pass" as white. For some, concealing their blackness was impossible because of phenotype. Moreover, nearly three-quarters of respondents believed that presenting themselves as solely white would be morally wrong. Nevertheless, many attempted to highlight their whiteness and/or downplay their blackness. For instance, Ellie identified as biracial and believed that claiming to be solely white was "wrong." Yet, she wore her hair in a way that allowed her to blend in with white students, thus covering her blackness and highlighting her whiteness. She said: "I'll straighten my hair when I remember to because I don't like how big my hair is. . . . I don't want people to look at me for being different." While Ellie did not deny her blackness when asked about her race, straightening her hair had the effect of accentuating her whiteness and covering a physical marker associated with racial difference.

Approximately 21 percent of students reported purposefully altering their hair to highlight their whiteness and/or downplay their blackness within their HWCU. An additional 26 percent reported styling their hair in a way that effectively highlighted their whiteness or covered their blackness but claimed these racial effects were unintentional. For instance, Jada said: "I don't like my hair curly, period. . . . So, I do try to straighten it a lot. But, I never thought about it from a point of view as I'm gonna do this to . . . seem more white." While Jada said she did not straighten her hair to appear white, she later acknowledged that straightening her hair covered her primary physical marker of racial difference. Straightening her hair thus had the effect of covering her blackness, regardless of her intentions.

While men and women used their bodies as sites of racial identity work, women were more likely to situate this discussion in relation to dating. For instance, Isabelle said: "I do feel like it would be harder for me to date a white guy than a black guy unless I kept my hair straight all the time." No men described altering their appearance in relation to dating; instead, men most often described altering their appearance in relation to work and ideas of professionalism. For instance, Thomas said: "It's not professional and frowned upon . . . to have like an afro." In a context where interracial dating more frequently involves black men and white women than black women and white men (Crowder and Tolnay 2000), biracial women may feel heightened pressure to conform to white beauty standards if they desire a white man.

Women's discussion of their appearance also highlights the intersection of race and gender with class. Alicia said: "When I did have my braids . . . I really did kinda feel like I was being judged by people, like they might have thought I was ghetto." Alicia's comments suggest that hairstyles associated with black women (e.g., braids) not only distanced women from white feminine beauty standards but could also signal a lower-class identity owing to the cultural conflation of race and class. Within such a context, women often straightened their hair, distancing themselves from stigmatized race, gender, and class identities.

In addition to manipulating their physical appearance, students responded to the stigmatization of blackness through verbally highlighting their whiteness. While both men and women used this identity work strategy, women were more likely to do so for purposes of securing a white dating partner, again suggesting that blackness was particularly devalued for women (compared with men) within the campus dating scene. For instance, Kia said: "When skin tone comes up, I'll say something about like a white parent. . . . I want them to know that I'm mixed and not fully black, just because of like the guys that were at my high school did not date black girls and I've always been attracted mostly to white guys." While Kia identified as biracial, her desire to highlight her whiteness was not just an attempt to have this identity validated but also a response to her perception of racial discrimination in the dating scene. She believed white men did not date black women and that her relative whiteness may make her more acceptable within a dating scene that privileged whiteness.

BIRACIAL HBCU STUDENTS

The HBCU Racial Structure

The U.S. racial structure's privileging of whiteness also influenced biracial HBCU students' experiences. I describe the HBCU racial structure in terms of its social relations and practices based on race *and color* distinctions. I use the term "racial structure" to include distinctions based on color because these distinctions are intricately tied to structural racism and the U.S. privileging of whiteness.

Students' descriptions suggest that the HBCU racial structure was characterized by social relations that sometimes privileged lightness while at other times condemning biracial and light-skinned individuals for their perceived sense of superiority. Students said their peers frequently discussed colorism and the benefits of lightness. For many respondents, the idea that they occupied a privileged position was surprising. For instance, Omar said: "It was really shocking to me that African-Americans and I think [my college] is sort of emblematic of the sort of general thoughts about race in the African-American community, with this idea that certain African-Americans are looked down upon by other African-Americans because they might be able to pass or might have different opportunities solely because of their skin color." Having grown up in a predominantly white neighborhood, Omar was unaware that black communities viewed lighter-skinned black individuals as privileged. Importantly, Omar's comments illuminate the relationship between colorism and structural racism; he describes how light skin is viewed as a privilege because lighter individuals may be able to pass as white and reap the rewards of whiteness in a racist society.

While distinctions based on skin color and associated privilege may characterize the structure of many predominantly black environments, these ideas were likely particularly salient within HBCUs because of the academic focus on race and the legacy of colorism within Greek life. Every student reported taking classes that discussed race. Sometimes this discussion addressed the privileges or disadvantages associated with skin tone. Students were also aware of skin color stereotypes attached to Greek organizations. Specifically, high-status organizations associated with ideas of attractiveness were also associated with lightness. For instance, Wendy said: "Growing up I heard that light skin girls are part of the [Betas], the pretty girls are part of the [Betas], you know, everything like you want to be is to be a [Beta].... [Alphas] were the ones like average kind of like women.... And so, it was kind of always put into my head that it's better to be a [Beta] than it is to be an [Alpha]." Wendy's comments highlight the association among lightness, attractiveness, and status. She was taught that the high-status, most desirable sorority was composed primarily of light-skinned, attractive women. Regardless of the extent to which stereotypes about skin color played out in contemporary Greek organizations, students' shared knowledge of these stereotypes likely heightened the salience of color distinctions on campus.

Respondents' accounts of their experiences suggest that their lightness and/or biraciality did result in some privilege, especially in relation to dating. Importantly, while there was variation in respondents' skin color, all respondents said they were at least sometimes described as light-skinned by peers. Consistent with theories of gendered colorism (Hill 2002), the advantages of lightness were particularly evident for women. Respondents described an ideology favoring light over dark women. Nicholas said: "A lot of women who are lighter-skinned, they are put on a pedestal, and [people] say that they're more attractive than dark-skinned women." Moreover, some women reported instances when men cited the women's skin color or biracial background as a reason for romantic interest in them. For instance, Tiana said: "[My boyfriend] has mentioned before that he always wanted to be with a mixed girl."

Biracial men were not as advantaged in the dating scene owing to the feminization of lightness (Hill 2002). When describing stereotypes of light-skinned men, Joshua said: "They try to be just as pretty as the girls." Quinton said: "They're soft, pretty boys." Tiana said: "They're sensitive. They're crybabies." These comments suggest that biracial and light-skinned men were feminized. While they were sometimes advantaged within the dating scene owing to their association with attractiveness, this advantage was attenuated by their association with devalued, feminine attributes (e.g., "softness," sensitivity). Some respondents even perceived that dark-skinned men had an advantage within the dating scene. For instance, Cameron said: "They say that [at this college] every girl wants a dark-skinned man and every man wants a light-skinned girl." Thus, students' comments suggest that within HBCUs, whiteness and lightness were not as beneficial for men's status as they were for women's status.

Navigating Privilege

Compared with biracial men, biracial women occupied a more privileged position in the campus racial structure. Relatedly, navigating privilege was a more salient concern for women than for men. Some women navigated privilege by joining or avoiding high-status sororities associated with lightness. Most women who mentioned a desire to become a Beta cited the sorority's status and association with beauty and femininity as motives for joining. For instance, when asked which sorority she was interested in, Aurora replied: "At first I was like [Beta] because they're pretty." As described above, this association between Betas and beauty was intertwined with ideas privileging lightness. Students like Aurora were aware that Betas were depicted as light-skinned, beautiful women; they were also aware that they fit this image. Joining this sorority could increase their status by further aligning them with ideas of beauty and femininity.

The Betas, however, were also stereotyped as stuck-up and elitist. In joining this sorority, women would likely increase their association with these negative stereotypes, which were already sometimes applied to them because of their phenotype or biracial background. Aware of this possibility, some avoided this sorority.

Women also used verbal identification/disidentification to maximize privilege or distance themselves from ideas of elitism. Realizing the privilege attached to biraciality, Leah verbally identified as "mixed" within the dating scene. She said: "Black boys have this thing about mixed girls. So, I feel like I really tried to emphasize the fact that I was mixed." Alternatively, some concealed their biracial background to avoid preferential treatment and problematize the valorization of whiteness and lightness. Nyesha said: "When dudes ask me like 'Are you mixed?' I'll say no, I'm black. And they'll be like nah you gotta be mixed. . . . I'm like 'I have to be mixed to be cute? . . . Like I can't just be a . . . black pretty girl?'" Nyesha's comments indicate that she is aware of the status attached to being biracial within the campus dating scene. She takes issue with this and engages in identity work to assert a black identity and problematize the association between biraciality and attractiveness.

Relatedly, some women feared that others would perceive a statement of biracial identity as an attempt to claim racial superiority over black people. As a result, some engaged in selective disclosure, telling only close friends about their biracial background or revealing it when specifically asked. Two women went as far as saying they were *not* biracial. For instance, when asked if anyone identifies her as biracial, Tiana replied: "They do, but then I correct them. . . . Then they'll be like okay wait you're black. . . . Because I'd rather be seen as black than to be mixed because I don't want them to think that oh I think I'm superior because I'm mixed or oh I'm better than anybody else because I'm mixed."

Women's discussions of navigating privilege also reflect the conflation of race and class in American society (Bettie 2000). In listing stereotypes about biracial people, Camryn said: "I've heard that we must have money or . . . more money than the average black person." Within a context that conflated racial with socioeconomic privilege, students sometimes presented working-class identities to distance themselves from accusations of racial elitism. For instance, when arguing against the accusation that she was a white supremacist, Rebecca mentioned her mother's socioeconomic status. Rebecca said: "She started calling me a white supremacist. . . . I was like what are you talking about? And, we just got into an argument. And, like both of her parents are like doctors. . . . And, I was telling her how my mother grew up very poor and like worked in the fields." Rebecca discussed how her mother grew up poor, using this presentation of class to counter accusations of racial supremacy. Such identity work highlights the cultural association between "authentic" blackness and working-class struggles (Lacy 2007) and shows how students drew on these intersecting ideologies of race and class to negotiate their position within campus racial structures.

Fifty percent of HBCU women reported engaging in identity work to distance themselves from ideas of privilege and/or internalized racial superiority. No HBCU men described this type of identity work. This difference reflects how race and gender intersect to influence students' position in campus racial structures and their resulting identity work. Compared with biracial women, biracial men were less likely to believe they occupied a privileged position in the campus racial structure or that their peers believed them to be stuck-up or pretentious. As a result, their discussion of identity work did not focus on distancing themselves from ideas of privilege.

CONCLUSION

My findings illuminate how biracial students' identity work related to their school's racial structure. Situated in a context that privileged whiteness, biracial HWCU students navigated racism. In contrast, much of biracial HBCU students' identity work involved navigating the privilege attached to lightness and/or biraciality.

These results highlight the contextual nature of racial meanings. While all respondents had similar racial backgrounds, this background carried different meanings depending on the social environment. Additionally, I highlight how gender and racial identities intersect to affect individuals' placement within racialized social systems. Specifically, the data suggest that biracial women were more advantaged than biracial men within HBCUs, especially with regard to dating. Alternatively, the data suggest that biracial women were more disadvantaged than biracial men within HWCU dating scenes. Biracial men thus experienced college contexts differently than did biracial women, despite having similar racial backgrounds.

Bonilla-Silva (1997) states that despite gender variation within racial groups, the group as a whole occupies a particular position within a racialized social system's hierarchy. My analysis, however, elucidates the importance of taking an intersectional approach to understanding racial structures. I show how individuals' location in racialized structures is dependent not solely on socially defined indicators of race (e.g., skin color) but also on how those indicators of race intersect with gender ideologies in different social contexts. To discuss biracial students' position within campus racial structures without mentioning gender would mask important gender differences in students' experiences and obscure understanding of how racial and gender ideologies intersect to shape students' relative privilege and disadvantage.

This study also adds to the literature on intersectionality by showing how gender and class identities are invoked in the negotiation of racial identities.

Studying biracial individuals is particularly informative for illuminating these processes of racial identity negotiation because biracial individuals occupy a unique social location, where racial identity may be less certain and stable and more strongly tied to ideas of class and gender (Davenport 2016). Thus, studying multiracial students provides unique insight into the ways that racial identities are created and negotiated in relation to gender and class identities in different contexts.

My findings also suggest that institutional policy changes could improve biracial students' experiences. Segregation and discrimination at HWCUs would be reduced if Greek life were dismantled. Greek life is divided along color lines, and organizations do not have equal access to resources. HWCU students reported that the wealthiest organizations were white, while more diverse and predominantly black organizations had fewer resources. Greek organizations' financial resources affect their social power and campus visibility. Thus, Greek life can create an institutionally supported race/class hierarchy on campus, where wealthy whites maintain the most social power (Armstrong and Hamilton 2013).

While HWCU students discussed how the campus racial structure privileged whiteness, many simultaneously downplayed the impact of racism. Additionally, many reported feeling uncomfortable around black students and/or isolated from the black campus community. Without an awareness of the longevity and impact of institutional racism and without the support of the black campus community, biracial students may be particularly vulnerable to the effects of racism should they experience it. Educating biracial students on the reality of structural racism and facilitating their access to resources and organizations designed to assist students of color could help them cope with any marginalization and/or discrimination they experience.

Some respondents did not know whether they could participate in programs for black students; administrators should clearly indicate that these programs are open to multiracial students. Additionally, some did not participate because they did not identify as black; establishing multicultural organizations could provide these students with a group to help them cope with the challenges of being a racial minority at an HWCU. Additionally, biracial students may benefit from increased dialogue about racism and intersectionality within racially diverse spaces (e.g., academic courses).

While biracial HBCU students generally did not experience racism on campus, they sometimes struggled to comprehend the history of colorism and its lasting impact within black communities. This left many unprepared for accusations of privilege and elitism. A more sustained, institutionally supported dialogue on colorism could be beneficial; this conversation should emphasize how colorism is the result of systemic racism and encourage students to fight against all forms of race- and color-based injustice. Students may also benefit from having diversity counselors available to help them navigate any race- and/or color-based challenges they experience.

Researchers should continue to explore how biracial students draw on race, class, and gender identities to negotiate their placement within institutional racial structures. Future studies could explore how underclassmen and upperclassmen differ in their identity work strategies and/or implement longitudinal designs to capture how students' identity work may change over time.

NOTES

1. I use the term HWCU instead of PWI (predominantly white institution) to shift emphasis from schools' racial composition to their racial history and accompanying racialized structure.
2. For example, I compared HWCU students' accounts of racial discrimination in the businesses surrounding campus with newspaper articles that similarly described widespread racial profiling in the college town. Additionally, I cross-checked HWCU students' descriptions of racial disparities in Greek organizations' resources against campus newspaper articles on this topic.
3. Names of Greek organizations are pseudonyms.

REFERENCES

Armstrong, Elizabeth A., and Laura T. Hamilton. 2013. *Paying for the Party: How College Maintains Inequality*. Cambridge, MA: Harvard University Press.

Bettie, Julie. 2000. "Women without Class: Chicas, Cholas, Trash, and the Presence/Absence of Class Identity." *Signs* 26 (1): 1–35.

Bonilla-Silva, Eduardo. 1997. "Rethinking Racism: Toward a Structural Interpretation." *American Sociological Review* 62 (3): 465–480.

Brunsma, David L., Eric S. Brown, and Peggy Placier. 2013. "Teaching Race at Historically White Colleges and Universities: Identifying and Dismantling Walls of Whiteness." *Critical Sociology* 39 (5): 717–738.

Burke, Meghan A., and David G. Embrick. 2008. "Colorism." In *International Encyclopedia of the Social Sciences*. Vol. 2, edited by William Darity, 17–18. Detroit: Macmillan Reference USA.

Corbin, Juliet, and Anselm Strauss. 2008. *Basics of Qualitative Research: Techniques and Procedures for Developing Grounded Theory*. 3rd ed. Thousand Oaks, CA: Sage.

Creswell, John W., and Dana L. Miller. 2000. "Determining Validity in Qualitative Inquiry." *Theory into Practice* 39 (3): 124–130.

Crowder, Kyle D., and Stewart E. Tolnay. 2000. "A New Marriage Squeeze for Black Women: The Role of Racial Intermarriage by Black Men." *Journal of Marriage and Family* 62 (3): 729–807.

Davenport, Lauren D. 2016. "The Role of Gender, Class, and Religion in Biracial Americans' Racial Labeling Decisions." *American Sociological Review* 81 (1): 57–84.

Davis, James F. 1991. *Who Is Black? One Nation's Definition*. University Park: Pennsylvania State University Press.

Gasman, Marybeth, and Ufuoma Abiola. 2016. "Colorism within the Historically Black Colleges and Universities (HBCUs)." *Theory into Practice* 55 (1): 39–45.

Hill, Mark E. 2002. "Skin Color and the Perception of Attractiveness among African Americans: Does Gender Make a Difference?" *Social Psychology Quarterly* 65 (1): 77–91.

Hunter, Margaret. 2007. "The Persistent Problem of Colorism: Skin Tone, Status, and Inequality." *Sociology Compass* 1 (1): 237–254.

Jones, Nicholas A., and Jungmiwha Bullock. 2012. "The Two or More Races Population: 2010." Washington, DC: U.S. Census Bureau.

Jones, Veronica. 2015. "The Black-White Dichotomy of Race: Influence of a Predominantly White Environment on Multiracial Identity." *Higher Education in Review* 12: 1–22.

Karkouti, Ibrahim M. 2016. "Black Students' Educational Experiences in Predominantly White Universities: A Review of the Related Literature." *College Student Journal* 50 (1): 59–70.

Kellogg, Angela H., and Debora L. Liddell. 2012. "'Not Half but Double': Exploring Critical Incidents in the Racial Identity of Multiracial College Students." *Journal of College Student Development* 53 (4): 524–541.

Kennedy, Randall. 2003. *Interracial Intimacies*. New York: Vintage Books.

Khanna, Nikki. 2011. *Biracial in America: Forming and Performing Racial Identity*. Lanham, MD: Lexington Books.

Khanna, Nikki, and Cathryn Johnson. 2010. "Passing as Black: Racial Identity Work among Biracial Americans." *Social Psychology Quarterly* 73 (4): 380–397.

Lacy, Karyn. 2007. *Blue-Chip Black: Race, Class, and Status in the New Black Middle Class*. Berkeley: University of California Press.

Museus, Samuel D., Susan A. Lambe Sarinana, and Tasha K. Ryan. 2015. "A Qualitative Examination of Multiracial Students' Coping Responses to Experiences with Prejudice and Discrimination in College." *Journal of College Student Development* 56 (4): 331–348.

Museus, Samuel D., April L. Yee, and Susan A. Lambe. 2011. "Multiracial in a Monoracial World: Student Stories of Racial Dissolution on the Colorblind Campus." *About Campus* 16 (4): 20–25.

National Center for Education Statistics. 2015. "Digest of Education Statistics: 2015." Accessed August 1, 2017. https://nces.ed.gov/programs/digest/d15/tables/dt15_306.30.asp.

Renn, Kristen A. 2004. *Mixed Race Students in College: The Ecology of Race, Identity, and Community on Campus*. Albany: State University of New York Press.

Renn, Kristen A., and Paul Shang, eds. 2008. *Biracial and Multiracial Students: New Directions for Student Services*, Number 123. San Francisco: Jossey-Bass.

Ridgeway, Cecelia L., and Tamar Kricheli-Katz. 2013. "Intersecting Cultural Beliefs in Social Relations: Gender, Race, and Class Binds and Freedoms." *Gender & Society* 27 (3): 294–318.

Ross, Louie E. 1997. "Mate Selection Preferences among African American College Students." *Journal of Black Studies* 27 (4): 554–569.

Storrs, Debbie. 1999. "Whiteness as Stigma: Essentialist Identity Work by Mixed-Race Women." *Symbolic Interaction* 22 (3): 187–212.

6 · THE STILL FURIOUS PASSAGE OF THE BLACK GRADUATE STUDENT

VICTOR E. RAY

The difficulty of "proving" that an individual is racist reflects the insidious nature of "civility" and "tact" in the American way. It is his awareness of and sensitivity to the operation of covert, institutionalized racism that accounts for the "furious passage" of the Black student through graduate school. (Davidson 1970, 194)

STILL FURIOUS IN THE WHITE SPACE OF GRADUATE SCHOOL

American universities were founded as white spaces (Wooten 2015; Wilder 2013; Moore 2008). Campuses were a central front in battles over racial equality because higher education provided basic access to skills, networks, and credentials necessary for mainstream jobs and opportunities. During the civil rights movement, years of coordinated protests, including litigation, civil disobedience, and occasional campus takeovers, successfully compelled integration into what Eduardo Bonilla-Silva (2012) calls "historically white colleges and universities." Campuses were designed such that the presence of people of color in service positions advanced white education and ensured occupational apartheid. In response to protest, campuses adopted policies to recruit students of color as they were forced to adjust to new racial realities.

This story of college desegregation is often retold as a simplistic morality tale. The forces of good—valiant black student activists and their allies—defeated backward racists who feared change. Once universities recognized their errors[1] they designed policies hoping to diversify (Berrey 2011). Through outreach to communities of color, affirmative action, and diversity programs, organizations attempted to repent their racial mistakes and move, however slowly, toward integration.

Like all morality tales, the story of desegregation hides a more complex—and fraught—historical reality. Desegregation was largely forced on reluctant colleges and universities that needed to maintain legitimacy. Desegregation undoubtedly created opportunities for people of color, providing a degree of access to white educational spaces and their resources. Yet, many educational organizations did the minimum necessary to include students of color, refusing to fundamentally transform university racial relations more broadly. The whiteness of university symbols, rituals, and curriculum remained largely unchanged (Moore 2008; Hordge-Freeman, Mayorga, and Bonilla-Silva 2011). Even structural interventions such as African American and ethnic studies programs often remain tenuously institutionalized and threatened by conservative legislatures questioning their legitimacy (Kendi 2012, 2016; Rojas 2007). Moreover, the backlash to even small gestures of inclusion was severe. Affirmative action policies were demonized to the point where researchers used attitudes toward affirmative action as a proxy for racial animus more generally. Ultimately, white resistance to the civil rights movement never ended (Anderson 2016; Steinberg 2001).

Douglas Davidson (1970), a black graduate student in sociology at the University of California, Berkeley, wrote during this transition from the overt exclusion of the Jim Crow era to the tenuous inclusion of the post–civil rights era. His "Furious Passage of the Black Graduate Student" was a searing blend of the personal and the political. Davidson argued that students of color integrating campuses in the wake of the civil rights movement bore the brunt of racialized organizational contradictions. Davidson claimed integration and equality were not synonymous, and black students were in, but not of, the university. Racism shaped nearly every interracial encounter, and integration was a largely cosmetic response to institutional white supremacy. Further, Davidson anticipated arguments that have become pivotal to current scholarship on race—that covert discrimination is no less effective in producing and perpetuating racial inequality (Bonilla-Silva 2010). For example, gatekeeping exams and the structure of historically white colleges and universities still put students of color at a disadvantage (Miller and Stassun 2014). Thus, "The Furious Passage" is a classic primer on how race shapes opportunities and outcomes for students of color.

This essay revisits some of the key insights of Davidson's work to show their contemporary relevance. To construct my argument, I begin with the claim that the university—its foundations, internal hierarchies, and processes—is structured by racial inequality. Although universities often claim that they are based on neutral, abstract principles of merit and the pursuit of knowledge, they are deeply shaped by racial concerns. To show this, I briefly review the literature on educational inequality to show how the pathways into higher education are racialized. I then highlight the relationship between individual and structural racism on campus, including organizational barriers to admission and matriculation. Although individual acts of discrimination are by no means eradicated, the structural bases of racial inequality have often shifted—altered in form but not function (Ray and Seamster 2016)—but still serving to exclude promising students of color. Next, I show how environmental microaggressions (including the symbolic resources of campus life) remain a constant reminder of second-class citizenship for people of color on these campuses. Narratives of being followed by campus police, assumptions of intellectual inferiority, and the overwhelming whiteness of the curriculum and campus traditions help keep students of color "in their place" (Mitchell 2015).

After outlining the social forces compounding racial inequality on campuses, I then move to show how actors are attempting to undermine and reshape race relations. More hopefully, wider cultural forces, including social movements such as Black Lives Matter, can positively influence campus life. I highlight the importance of faculty of color and white allies in shaping the campus experience for students of color. Through mentoring, personal example, and transmitting the cultural history of resistance to racism, faculty of color and white allies (Warren 2012) committed to racial equality continue to attempt to transform the historically white university.

STRUCTURAL RACISM ON CAMPUS OR INSTITUTIONALIZED RACISM IN "LIBERAL" ACADEMIA

Almost fifty years after its publication, Davidson's theoretically informed rumination on the centrality of racism in American higher education is still passed, like contraband, between mentors and students of color. During my second year of graduate school I considered leaving. Goals that had led me to graduate school—the application of sociological knowledge to social problems and the pursuit of social justice—were considered distractions. Both the official and "hidden" curriculum are studies in normative whiteness, although rarely acknowledged as such (Brunsma, Brown, and Placier 2013). The socialization of graduate school asked not simply for an understanding of the methods and theory of my discipline. Success meant adopting a detached, faux objective stance that often pathologized (Wilson 1978) or erased the intellectual contributions of people of color (Mills 1997; Morris 2015). I slowly began to withdraw from public conversations and seriously considered leaving the program or transferring. I was, in a word, furious. In this context, a senior mentor told me to read Davidson's work.

The "Furious Passage" reads, in many ways, as if it were written yesterday. Of course, Davidson's language and theoretical commitments are marked by the intellectual trappings of the era. Terminology drawn from social movements, such as "the man" and "the colonizer," is rare in current sociological scholarship. And Davidson's writing is untouched by feminism and intersectionality, with little time spent discussing how the experience of graduate school for students of color varies by gender. Colleges and universities are also marked by deeply gendered exclusion (Dancy, Edwards, and Davis 2018) that shapes the experiences of black women through increased service expectations, and the presumption of incompetence (Gutierrez y Muhs et al. 2012). Intersectional perspectives have drawn attention to the overlapping and mutually constitutive nature of oppressive systems, a perspective that Davidson largely neglects.

But despite these flaws, Davidson was grappling with ideas that have become central to current thought on higher education and race scholarship generally. Davidson's description of white gatekeepers and covert racism, as I show below, is resonant with current thinking on testing regimes and microaggressions. Davidson's distinction between individual and structural racism continues to animate debates about university diversity and inclusion. Current black graduate experiences are a difference of degree, not kind.

Davidson showed the utility of furious counternarratives in forging a shared sense of community across geographic distance and historical time. Davidson's work was also methodologically and theoretically prescient, anticipating several aspects of critical race theory (CRT), including Derrick Bell's (1991) notion of the permanence of American racism and the technique of using personal narrative to illuminate the peculiarities of racial inequality. This narrative style is a staple of current iterations of CRT (Delgado and Stefancic 2012) by using counternarratives to uncover the often racialized assumptions of stories about people of color. Rather than accepting stories from racially dominant groups, counternarratives "examine, critique, and counter" (Harper 2009, 701) sociological "just-so" stories that explain racial exclusion as a function of the culture or innate characteristics of people of color.

As an homage, I adopt Davidson's polemical style and use of personal narrative because the "fury" Davidson expresses is still central to the experience of graduate school. Even naming this "fury" goes against the rules of graduate training and undermines the dominant understanding of graduate school as a genteel place where scholars dispassionately debate ideas and issues (Steinberg 2007). Although the construction of knowledge is one key function of graduate school, a lesser recognized function of graduate training relates to also reinforcing and reproducing racial hierarchies. The most insidious ideas about people of color, and the most profound rationalizations for racial inequality, were (and are) developed in institutions of higher education (Kendi 2016; Wilder 2013).

REVISITING DAVIDSON'S COLONIAL MODEL APPLIED TO GRADUATE SCHOOL

The history of higher education in the United States rests on a largely unacknowledged debt to slavery (Wilder 2013). Higher education was funded by slavery's proceeds. Black exclusion from higher education was a given as educated people of color were seen as potential threats to the racial order (Williamson 2004). After emancipation, segregation, differential resource allocation, and outright interpersonal racism were institutionalized (Wooten 2015). Racial inequality marked the curriculum, shaping pedagogy and choice of subject matter. Teacher training and educational funding were separate and unequal, further negatively affecting black peoples' educational opportunities.

The landmark *Brown v. Board of Education* (1954) (eventually enforced in the face of massive resistance and white violence) created a brief period when segregation levels declined and the test-score gap between black and white students began to narrow (Hannah-Jones 2014). Although in an absolute sense white achievement remained ahead, the relative change in group position (Blumer 1958) threatened whites. Thus, tracking programs (Tyson 2011), "segregation academies" (Harper and Reskin 2005), anti-busing initiatives (Bobo 1983), and a host of other covert measures led to school re-segregation surpassing pre-*Brown* levels (Ravitch 2013; Hannah-Jones 2014). White Americans and the Supreme Court have always had, at best, an ambivalent commitment to desegregation. Each level of the American education system remains separate and unequal. Despite the success of desegregation in decreasing the test-score gap, many contemporary reformers see racial segregation and inequality as unsolvable problems (Ravitch 2013). This "racial apathy" (Forman and Lewis 2006) allows white reformers to acknowledge the deeply racialized nature of the U.S. education system while simultaneously avoiding advocating for integration. Ultimately, racial inequality is not an unfortunate deviation from neutral norms in the American education system. Racial inequality is a bedrock principle of the American educational system. White educational opportunity has been premised on the exclusion of people of color.

America's history of racial inequality is imprinted on our colleges and universities. Organizational theorists typically argue that organizations are "imprinted" by the environment in which they arose (Stinchcombe 1965). That is, the concerns of an organization's founders and the wider culture in which organizations develop—in this case, racial exclusion or subordination—are constitutive of the subsequent organization. Assumptions about racial superiority are central to this process of imprinting, as notions of racial hierarchy shape the allocation of educational resources. Research on racial inequality in schools often conceptualizes the problem narrowly, for instance, as the result of discriminating teachers or prejudiced parents. Rather than seeing racially unequal educational opportunities and outcomes as the result of individual prejudice aggregated, racial inequality is part of the structural base of education in the United States. In claiming that educational inequalities are structural, I do not mean they are simply empirically patterned. Rather, the educational system, at all levels, is designed around basic principles that (re)produce racial inequality. Designed under the regimes of slavery and Jim Crow, which assumed racial inferiority, inequality in the American educational system is "stamped from the beginning" (Kendi 2016). This racial inequality is institutionalized through custom, policy, and law and expressed through local organizational variations.

Americans, as an article of faith, typically see schooling as a way to minimize racial stratification (Johnson 2006). But, schools are central to reinforcing the racial status quo. Class theorists have adopted this position for nearly forty years (Bourdieu and Passeron 1977). Yet, many still argue that education as the purported "great equalizer" is the primary way out of America's racial quagmire. Schools also reinforce patterns of segregation in communities, enforce the racialized policing of students' bodies (Ferguson 2001; Shedd 2015; Lewis and Diamond 2015), and socialize people into menial roles or the acceptance of privilege (Khan 2012).

Davidson recognized some of these structural issues in 1970, arguing that the relationship between universities and black students was colonial. By invoking colonialism, Davidson showed the social relations of colonial orders (including a strict racial hierarchy) were recapitulated within the university setting. Colonial administrators often relied on local deputies, or "native informants," to help legitimate the colonial system. Incorporation helped colonial administrators gain local legitimacy and provided a relief valve of social mobility for subjugated peoples. Davidson recognized a similar dynamic, as university integration was part of a logic of political pacification aimed at undermining support for the more radical elements of the civil rights and black power movements (Bloom and Martin 2013). The language of colonialism sounds dated to current scholarship, although some are pushing for an updated revitalization of this theorization and language (Glenn 2015). The basic claims Davidson makes resonate with contemporary scholarship, which claims that selective integration helped defuse civil rights tensions (Bloom and Martin 2013). While invoking colonial relations may appear hyperbolic to contemporary mainstream scholars, the relations described in Davidson's essay still deeply resonate for black graduate students. So far, I have argued that the U.S. educational system is a central factor in the reproduction of racial inequality. Below, I show how race shapes the graduate school experience before one even begins the formal application process.

EXPLANATIONS FOR CONTINUED RACIAL INEQUALITY IN ACADEMIA

Explanations for continued underrepresentation usually focus on three main causes. First, so-called pipeline issues claim that underrepresentation or selection into a different career track at earlier stages of their education leads to few qualified students of color or women attending graduate school.[2] Second, cultural explanations tend to claim that minority groups adopt maladaptive behavior—such as claiming that those with high academic achievement are "acting white" (Ogbu

1987). This behavior then leads minorities to spurn scholastic excellence. Conveniently, these explanations leave gatekeepers themselves off the hook, as they are not responsible for the leaky pipeline or bad culture within schools and colleges. Finally, and most convincingly, are explanations that focus on discrimination. Davidson (1970) claimed that although blacks in higher education "seldom encounter the overt racism that his [sic] people experience on the outside" (194), covert mechanisms of racial discrimination still shaped the graduate experience for students of color.

Recent research shows systematic discrimination in professors' responses to inquiries about graduate school even before these students apply (Milkman, Akinola, and Chugh 2014). Using an experimental audit (considered the gold standard for discovering covert discrimination) allowed these researchers to isolate and eliminate causal confounding factors. These scholars randomly assigned fake student names signaling race and gender (for instance, Brad Anderson and Mei Chen) and then sent fictitious emails to professors. The email content was identical—researchers varied only the students' names—thereby isolating racialized names as the cause of any observed differences in responses. Emails were sent to 6,548 professors at 259 top universities. The authors found that across nearly every discipline, professors were significantly more likely to ignore requests from applicants who were not white men.

For academic outsiders, ignoring potential graduate students may not seem consequential. However, this mimics the processes undertaken before applying to graduate school in reality. Prospective students routinely reach out to professors to inquire about potential mentorship, and graduate admissions documents often ask applicants to list any professors with whom they have corresponded. Connecting with professors during the applications process establishes rapport and potentially gives the student an advocate on admissions committees. Being ignored at this stage sends a signal to students of color that they are unwelcome. This feeling of being unwelcome may be compounded if potential students are ignored by multiple potential mentors, particularly within the same department. At a minimum, this type of discrimination indicates that *students of color face entry barriers before they have even applied to graduate school.* Students of color must work harder than similarly situated white students.

Importantly, Milkman, Akinola, and Chugh (2014) examined the current demographic makeup of an institution, hypothesizing that discrimination would decrease in institutions with higher numbers of minority faculty and students. Contrary to this hypothesis, they found that the current proportion of women and minorities had no effect on whether professors ignored potential graduate students. Even in relatively diverse academic spaces, stereotypical biases influence access to resources and opportunities. It is impossible to know whether the racial biases these researchers measured are explicit or implicit (Quillian 2006). But in practice, the distinction between implicit and explicit racial attitudes hardly matters: they both produce unequal access to educational opportunities and contribute to the reproduction of racial inequality. A large body of research on racial bias shows that discrimination continues to deeply shape organizational inclusion despite stated intent (Pager 2007). It might be surprising to some that such systemic discrimination exists in higher education given popular narratives describing colleges as bastions of liberalism with a strong commitment to diversity (Berrey 2015). Yet, because racial inequality is imprinted on higher education organizations, even good-faith efforts at intervening in racial inequality may be undermined in practice. As Davidson (1970) argued, the covert nature of much discrimination in graduate school led to a kind of "inner turmoil" for graduate students trying to decipher whether there was a racial character to their exclusion. This inner turmoil can influence one's ability to complete their research or prepare for class, and can even lead students to discontinue their graduate education.

THE SMOKE SCREENS OF GRADUATE ADMISSIONS

> We know that the immediate reasons we are so few in numbers are the various "smoke screens" set up by the colonizer to prevent us from entering his institutions in the first place ... his college boards, his Graduate Record Exams. (Davidson 1970, 195)

Once students of color move from initial interest in graduate school to the actual process of applying, they are met with another set of systematic barriers. The gatekeeping mechanisms in higher education were *designed to be covert and discriminatory*. Davidson called these gatekeeping mechanisms "smoke screens" that created a plausibly deniable, facially neutral, way to exclude black students. As Khan (2011) notes, we are more likely to accept inequality considered the result of a fair competition as opposed to a rigged game. Thus, universities' organizational legitimacy is tied to the belief that opportunities are equal, and that the meritorious fill coveted admissions spots. Yet Khan notes that ideas about meritorious characteristics are historically variable, shifting to match the backgrounds of those at the top of racial and economic hierarchies. For instance, when Jewish students began to outcompete Anglos on standardized tests and administrators wanted to curtail Jewish matriculation in the Ivy League, Harvard's president altered admissions criteria, intending to disadvantage Jewish students (Khan 2011).

One unfortunate effect of popular notions of meritocracy is that measures *designed to privilege* one racial or economic group are taken as evidence of *inherent inferiority*. Take, for instance, so-called intelligence tests, which were partially developed to prove nonwhite intellectual inferiority (Gould 2006). It is well known that these tests continue to correlate with economic and racial inequality, such that family income is the best predictor of achievement and racial gaps remain stark. Achievement gaps are constructed through the deployment of these exams.

Although these empirical outcomes are often interpreted as individual failings (for example, students did not study hard enough), admissions tests showing racial and economic inequality in outcomes are working as designed. Yet, as Kendi (2016) notes, these tests attribute structural inequalities to personal inadequacies, blaming students of color for the results of a test designed to harm them.

So, we continue to rely on tests that were developed to prove the racial inferiority of nonwhite groups as key organizational gatekeepers for graduate school. These tests influence not just admission but the distribution of important educational resources once a student is admitted. Admissions tests influence who receives prestigious university fellowships and who gets assigned to research experiences (which are valued) or teaching (which is devalued). Thus, tests designed to prove racial inferiority are now considered organizationally neutral measures of a student's preparation and ability to compete in graduate school. Institutionalized racism is presented as a natural fact.

Although these tests may be, as Davidson states, "smoke screens" for the continuation of racial inequality, they exert real psychological and material consequences on students of color. Social psychologists have chronicled the pervasiveness of "stereotype threat" (Steele 1997), under which widely shared cultural ideas about intellectual inferiority cause black students to underperform as they try to combat them. In a series of experiments, Steele (1997) shows that black students who are "domain identified," or committed to doing well academically, fear confirming pernicious stereotypes about black intellectual inferiority when faced with a standardized test. Simply telling black students that the test measures innate aptitude is enough to induce fear that ends up causing them to underperform relative to similarly situated whites. This underperformance has real implications for where one ends up in the academic hierarchy. Similarly, the material consequences can extend beyond graduate school as early inequalities are compounded across a research career.

Ultimately, the "smoke screens" of admissions tests legitimate organizational inequality. Despite widespread awareness of the biases embedded in these measures, we continue to use standardized test justifications for racial exclusion. Describing this as institutionalized racism is simply correct.

MICROAGGRESSIONS AND DIVERSITY

> The black graduate student usually reaches his most intense anger at the departmental level because it is here that he is most intimately exposed to the workings of institutional racism. (Davidson 1970, 197)

Davidson, of course, could not have anticipated that diversity in higher education would become a rhetorical selling point that often falls short in practice. Once black students are admitted to graduate school, they are greeted with a new set of racialized organizational and individual practices. These include microaggressions and a focus on cosmetic, rather than substantive, diversity.

Universities are central to the production of racial ideologies promulgated in the rest of the society and culture. Although education is often put forward as the best way to combat racism, the most sophisticated defenses for racism have been developed by society's most educated. Black graduate students often bear the brunt of rationalizations for the relative absence of people of color in the academy. One common way racialized ideologies are expressed occurs through microaggressions that question the existence of students of color in the university and their academic pursuits.

Davidson (1970) describes social interactions now typically considered to be *microaggressions*, or racial slights that remind people of color of their alleged subordinate status (Sue et al. 2007). Individually, microaggressions are expressed in sentiments such as questioning the intelligence of black students or the widespread belief in black cultural inferiority. Organizationally, the overall whiteness of sociological theory and methods as a type of passive hostility influences their academic pursuits (Zuberi and Bonilla-Silva 2008). The overwhelming whiteness of university symbols (Brunsma, Brown, and Placier 2013), comments subtly undermining the intelligence or expertise of black students (Sue et al. 2007), or party themes that use racist caricatures (Mueller, Dirks, and Picca 2007) contribute to a university environment of racial exclusion. Although critics of this concept—mostly on the right, but some from the left—diminish the effects of racial interactions as coming from a sense of entitlement, a large body of research shows there is nothing small about their effects.

Part of the insidiousness of microaggressive interactions is the simple fact that many whites can remain ignorant of the ways their behaviors reinforce racial stereotypes against people of color. Microaggressions do not require intent; rather, their significance lies in their impact on students who experience these interactions. In the case of a drunk driver accidentally killing a child, the driver's intent plays little role in their guilt. Similarly, microaggressions can unintentionally wound targets. For instance, a classic—and controversial—discussion of microaggressions concerns the overwhelming symbolism of whiteness on campus. This symbolism, including walls with photographs featuring only white faces, styles of music and food that neglect minority cultures, and the denigration of nonwhite styles as "unprofessional" or inappropriate (Carbado and Harris 2008), contributes to a sense of alienation among nonwhite students. They are reminded that this space was not built for them, and in many cases, they control little.

Microaggressions continue to mark the furious passage through graduate school for black students. The literature on students of color in graduate school is rife with reports of their being considered affirmative action admits or being told they are less qualified than their peers (Hordge-Freeman, Mayorga, and Bonilla-Silva 2011; Harper 2009). The curriculum itself can sometimes feel like a microaggression in the humanities and social sciences with the whiteness of the so-called mainstream curriculum remaining unmarked. Syllabuses remain thoroughly racialized, and victim blaming is a staple of sociological theories that blame black culture for racial inequality. The work of foundational black scholars, such as W.E.B. Du Bois and the Atlanta school, remains neglected (Morris 2015). Similarly, sociological theory remains deeply Eurocentric (Go 2014; Connell 1997). Each of these is a (not so subtle) reminder that whiteness remains the assumed default in graduate education, and the standard with which all other knowledge is compared.

Scholars are increasingly questioning the divergence between universities' stated commitment to diversity and their actual response to documented discrimination. Universities often use the presence of students of color as a "moral credential" (Bendick and Nunes 2012) to insulate the organization against claims of discrimination. Scholars argue that moral credentialing is a process whereby the inclusion of members of a stigmatized group provides a preemptive defense against later claims of discrimination. Diversity programming is central to this strategy. Diversity has become dogma in university publications, statements, and talking points (Berrey 2015). Yet, when it comes to actually diversifying faculty or the student body, the rhetorical commitment to diversity remains, in many cases, just words.

During graduate school I repeatedly witnessed a pattern in university responses to racial incidents. Responses typically included a rhetorical recommitment to principles of diversity that was decoupled from concrete actions. The pattern is predictable. First, a racist event occurs and students of color respond with demands for organizational change. Next, the administration counters by stating its commitment to diversity and forming a committee to study the problem. Some of the more radical or outspoken students of color are asked to sit on the committee, effectively silencing the protest and occupying students' time. Then, the committee ends up reframing or abandoning the initial demands, and protest is channeled into a difficult-to-navigate bureaucracy where students have little power. The committee briefly functions but soon devolves into simple organizational inertia. Finally, students are reassured that the university is "doing all it can" to address their concerns.

Sometimes the committee issues a set of recommendations that fall short of the initial demands for more faculty and students of color or improving the overall racial climate. When another racist incident erupts, the administration can point to the committee for evidence of its commitment to diversity, regardless of the outcome. In essence, having a diversity program *is* the entire program, as it serves university public relations. University responses to racist incidents on campus are essentially repressive—they manage the people of color already on campus. Because diversity programs typically treat difference as unrelated to societal hierarchies, the "white center in most discourse on diversity" (Bell and Hartmann 2007, 908) remains unbothered. This process allows white students to come away with the impression that people of color are on campus for their edification.

CONCLUSION: TOWARD A LESS FURIOUS GRADUATE SCHOOL

Thus far, I have described a rather pessimistic view of race relations on graduate school campuses. Using Davidson's "Furious Passage" as inspiration, I have argued that many of the racialized patterns of exclusion he outlined have changed little in the almost fifty years since the article's publication.

But I would be remiss if I neglected to mention the scholars of color (and their allies) who have been working against the mainstream of historically white colleges and universities for generations. Despite my pessimism, strong mentoring practices and drawing connections between local campus struggles and larger movements can help make the passage of graduate school, if not pleasant, at least less furious. Recent work by David Brunsma, David Embrick, and Jean Shin (2017) shows that although sociology departments tend to recruit more students of color than other graduate programs, these students are not necessarily happy in their departments or in how they are treated by colleagues. These authors argue for an overhaul that would create a more inclusive curriculum, a focus on a real dedication to increasing the numbers of underrepresented scholars, and a departmental and university climate that is responsive to the needs of students of color (Brunsma, Embrick, and Shin 2017). Beyond these measures, broader movements for racial justice can have an impact on the academy.

Ultimately, Davidson recognized that the presence of black students at schools like Berkeley was a result of movement pressure. Movements such as Black Lives Matter—which call for structural interventions in the mechanisms reproducing racial inequality—help push universities toward making diversity more than just a buzzword. Universities have never become more inclusive out of benevolence. A more racially just university is possible. Recent examples of successful student protest, such as those at the University of Missouri, where a coalition of student athletes and activists forced a reluctant administration to increase student-body diversity, show that activism works.

NOTES

1. Many whites argue that universities went too far and are now characterized by a "reverse discrimination" that disadvantages whites. The claim that people of color are now advantaged relative to whites in college admissions falls apart under minimal scrutiny. Universities show only a limited commitment to diversifying their students and faculty, and affirmative action

policies have actually been quietly dismantled outside of a few elite schools (Hirschman and Berrey 2017).

2. I see so-called pipeline issues as a type of discrimination that simply happened earlier in one's educational trajectory.

REFERENCES

Anderson, Carol. 2016. *White Rage: The Unspoken Truth of Our Racial Divide.* New York: Bloomsbury.

Bell, Derrick. 1991. "Racial Realism." *Connecticut Law Review* 24 (2): 363–380.

Bell, Joyce M., and Douglas Hartmann. 2007. "Diversity in Everyday Discourse: The Cultural Ambiguities and Consequences of 'Happy Talk.'" *American Sociological Review* 72 (6): 895–914. doi:10.1177/000312240707200603.

Bendick, Marc, and Ana P. Nunes. 2012. "Developing the Research Basis for Controlling Bias in Hiring." *Journal of Social Issues* 68 (2): 238–262. doi:10.1111/j.1540-4560.2012.01747.x.

Berrey, Ellen C. 2011. "Why Diversity Became Orthodox in Higher Education, and How It Changed the Meaning of Race on Campus." *Critical Sociology* 37 (5): 573–596. doi:10.1177/0896920510380069.

———. 2015. *The Enigma of Diversity: The Language of Race and the Limits of Racial Justice.* Chicago: University of Chicago Press.

Bloom, Joshua, and Waldo E. Martin. 2013. *Black against Empire: The History and Politics of the Black Panther Party.* Oakland: University of California Press.

Blumer, Herbert. 1958. "Race Prejudice as a Sense of Group Position*." *Pacific Sociological Review* 1 (1): 3–7.

Bobo, Lawrence. 1983. "Whites' Opposition to Busing: Symbolic Racism or Realistic Group Conflict?" *Journal of Personality and Social Psychology* 45 (6): 1196–1210. doi:10.1037/0022-3514.45.6.1196.

Bonilla-Silva, Eduardo. 2010. *Racism without Racists: Color-Blind Racism and the Persistence of Racial Inequality in the United States.* 3rd. ed. Lanham, MD: Rowman & Littlefield.

———. 2012. "The Invisible Weight of Whiteness: The Racial Grammar of Everyday Life in Contemporary America." *Ethnic and Racial Studies* 35 (2): 173–194. doi:10.1080/01419870.2011.613997.

Bourdieu, Pierre. 1977. "Cultural Reproduction and Social Reproduction." In *Power and Ideology in Education,* edited by Jerome Karabel and A. H. Halsey, 487–511. New York: Oxford University Press.

Bourdieu, Pierre, and Jean C. Passeron. 1977. *Reproduction in Education, Society and Culture.* London: Sage Publications.

Brunsma, David L., Eric S. Brown, and Peggy Placier. 2013. "Teaching Race at Historically White Colleges and Universities: Identifying and Dismantling the Walls of Whiteness." *Critical Sociology* 39 (5): 717–738. doi:10.1177/0896920512446759.

Brunsma, David L., David G. Embrick, and Jean H. Shin. 2017. "Graduate Students of Color: Race, Racism, and Mentoring in the White Waters of Academia," *Sociology of Race and Ethnicity* 3 (1): 1–13. doi:10.1177/2332649216681565.

Carbado, Devon W., and Cheryl I. Harris. 2008. "The New Racial Preferences." *California Law Review* 96 (5): 1130–1214.

Connell, Robert William. 1997. "Why Is Classical Theory Classical." *American Journal of Sociology* 102 (6): 1511–1557. doi:http://dx.doi.org/10.1086/231125.

Dancy, T. Elon, Kirsten T. Edwards, and James Earl Davis. 2018. "Historically White Universities and Plantation Politics: Anti-blackness and Higher Education in the Black Lives Matter Era." *Urban Education* 53 (2): 176–195.

Davidson, Douglas. 1970. "The Furious Passage of the Black Graduate Student." *Berkeley Journal of Sociology* 15: 192–211. doi:10.2307/41035174.

Delgado, Richard, and Jean Stefancic. 2012. *Critical Race Theory: An Introduction*. New York: New York University Press.

Ferguson, Ann. 2001. *Bad Boys: Public Schools in the Making of Black Masculinity*. Ann Arbor: University of Michigan Press.

Forman, Tyrone A., and Amanda E. Lewis. 2006. "Racial Apathy and Hurricane Katrina: The Social Anatomy of Prejudice in the Post-Civil Rights Era." *Du Bois Review: Social Science Research on Race* 3 (1): 175–202. doi:10.1017/S1742058X06060127.

Glenn, Evelyn Nakano. 2015. "Settler Colonialism as Structure." *Sociology of Race and Ethnicity* 1 (1): 52–72. doi:10.1177/2332649214560440.

Go, Julian. 2014. "Sociology's Imperial Unconscious." In *Sociology and Empire: The Imperial Entanglements of a Discipline*, edited by George Steinmetz, 1–41. Durham, NC: Duke University Press.

Gould, Stephen Jay. 2006. *The Mismeasure of Man*. Revised and expanded. New York: Norton.

Gutierrez y Muhs, Gabriella, Yolanda Flores Niemann, Carmen G. Gonzalez, and Angela P. Harris, eds. 2012. *Presumed Incompetent: The Intersections of Race and Class for Women in Academia*. Logan: Utah State University Press.

Hannah-Jones, Nicole. 2014. "Segregation Now." *The Atlantic*. May 2014.

Harper, Shannon, and Barbara Reskin. 2005. "Affirmative Action at School and on the Job." *Annual Review of Sociology* 31 (1): 357–379. doi:10.1146/annurev.soc.31.041304.122155.

Harper, Shaun R. 2009. "Niggers No More: A Critical Race Counternarrative on Black Male Student Achievement at Predominantly White Colleges and Universities." *International Journal of Qualitative Studies in Education* 22 (6): 697–712. doi:10.1080/09518390903333889.

Hirschman, Daniel, and Ellen Berrey. 2017. "The Partial Deinstitutionalization of Affirmative Action in U.S. Higher Education, 1988 to 2014." *Sociological Science* 4: 449–468. doi:10.15195/v4.a18.

Hordge-Freeman, E., S. Mayorga, and Eduardo Bonilla-Silva. 2011. "Exposing Whiteness Because We Are Free: Emancipation Methodological Practice in Identifying and Challenging Racial Practices in Sociology Departments." In *Rethinking Race and Ethnicity in Research Methods*. Edited by John H. Stanfield, II, 95–122. Walnut Creek, CA: Left Coast Press, Inc.

Johnson, Heather Beth. 2006. *The American Dream and the Power of Wealth: Choosing Schools and Inheriting Inequality in the Land of Opportunity*. New York: Routledge.

Kendi, Ibram X. 2012. *The Black Campus Movement: Black Studies and the Racial Reconstruction of Higher Education*. New York: Palgrave Macmillan.

———. 2016. *Stamped from the Beginning: The Definitive History of Racist Ideas in America*. New York: Nation Books.

Khan, Shamus. 2011. *Privilege: The Making of an Adolescent Elite at St. Paul's School*. Princeton, NJ: Princeton University Press.

Lewis, Amanda E., and John B. Diamond. 2015. *Despite the Best Intentions: How Racial Inequality Thrives in Good Schools*. New York: Oxford University Press.

Milkman, Katherine L., Modupe Akinola, and Dolly Chugh. 2014. "What Happens Before? A Field Experiment Exploring How Pay and Representation Differentially Shape Bias on the Pathway into Organizations." *Journal of Applied Psychology*, Forthcoming 1–74. doi:10.2139/ssrn.2063742.

Miller, Casey, and Keivan Stassun. 2014. "A Test That Fails." *Nature* 510 (7504): 303–304. doi:10.1038/nj7504-303a.

Mills, Charles W. 1997. *The Racial Contract*. Ithaca, NY: Cornell University Press.

Mitchell, Koritha. 2015. "Keep Claiming Space!" *College Language Association Journal* 58 (4): 229–244.

Moore, Wendy Leo. 2008. *Reproducing Racism: White Space, Elite Law Schools, and Racial Inequality*. Lanham, MD: Rowman & Littlefield.

Morris, Aldon. 2015. *The Scholar Denied: W.E.B. Du Bois and the Birth of Modern Sociology*. Oakland: University of California Press.

Mueller, Jennifer C., Danielle Dirks, and Leslie Houts Picca. 2007. "Unmasking Racism: Halloween Costuming and Engagement of the Racial Other." *Qualitative Sociology* 30 (3): 315–335. doi:10.1007/s11133-007-9061-1.

Ogbu, John U. 1987. "Variability in Minority School Performance: A Problem in Search of an Explanation." *Anthropology & Education Quarterly* 18 (4): 312–334. doi:10.1525/aeq.1987.18.4.04x0022v.

Pager, Devah. 2007. "The Use of Field Experiments for Studies of Employment Discrimination: Contributions, Critiques, and Directions for the Future." *ANNALS of the American Academy of Political and Social Science* 609 (1): 104–133. doi:10.1177/0002716206294796.

Quillian, Lincoln. 2006. "New Approaches to Understanding Racial Prejudice and Discrimination." *Annual Review of Sociology* 32 (1): 299–328. doi:10.1146/annurev.soc.32.061604.123132.

Ravitch, Diane. 2013. *Reign of Error: The Hoax of the Privatization Movement and the Danger to America's Public Schools*. New York: Vintage Books.

Ray, Victor, and Louise Seamster. 2016. "Rethinking Racial Progress: A Response to Wimmer." *Ethnic and Racial Studies* 39 (8): 1361–1369. doi:10.1080/01419870.2016.1151540.

Rojas, Fabio. 2007. *From Black Power to Black Studies: How a Radical Social Movement Became an Academic Discipline*. Baltimore: Johns Hopkins University Press.

Shedd, Carla. 2015. *Unequal City: Race, Schools, and Perceptions of Injustice*. New York: Russell Sage Foundation.

Steele, Claude M. 1997. "A Threat in the Air: How Stereotypes Shape Intellectual Identity and Performance." *American Psychologist* 52 (6): 613–629.

Steinberg, Steven. 2001. *Turning Back: The Retreat from Racial Justice in American Thought and Policy*. Boston: Beacon Press.

———. 2007. *Race Relations: A Critique*. Stanford, CA: Stanford University Press.

Stinchcombe, Arthur L. 1965. "Social Structures and Organizations." In *Handbook of Organizations*, edited by James G. March, 149–193. Chicago: Rand McNally & Company.

Sue, Derald Wing, Christina M. Capodilupo, Gina C. Torino, Jennifer M. Bucceri, Aisha M. B. Holder, Kevin L. Nadal, and Marta Esquilin. 2007. "Racial Microaggressions in Everyday Life: Implications for Clinical Practice." *American Psychologist* 62 (4): 271–286. doi:10.1037/0003-066X.62.4.271.

Tyson, Karolyn. 2011. *Integration Interrupted: Tracking, Black Students, and Acting White after Brown*. New York: Oxford University Press.

Warren, Mark R. 2012. *Fire in the Heart: How White Activists Embrace Racial Justice*. New York: Oxford University Press. doi:10.1093/acprof:oso/9780199751242.001.0001.

Wilder, Craig Steven. 2013. *Ebony and Ivy*. New York: Bloomsbury Publishing USA.

Williamson, Joy Ann. 2004. "'This Has Been Quite a Year for Heads Falling': Institutional Autonomy in the Civil Rights Era." *History of Education Quarterly* 44 (4): 554–576. doi:10.1111/j.1748-5959.2004.tb00020.x.

Wilson, William Julius. 1978. *The Declining Significance of Race*. Chicago: University of Chicago Press.

Wooten, Melissa E. 2015. *In the Face of Inequality: How Black Colleges Adapt*. Albany: State University of New York Press.

Zuberi, Tukufu, and Eduardo Bonilla-Silva. 2008. *White Logic, White Methods*. Lanham, MD: Rowman & Littlefield.

6

PART III

BETWEEN RESEARCH, TEACHING, AND SERVICE

Faculty Identities and Experiences

7 · FACULTY MEMBERS FROM LOW-SOCIOECONOMIC-STATUS BACKGROUNDS

Student Mentorship, Motivations, and Intersections

ELIZABETH M. LEE AND TONYA MAYNARD

Research suggests faculty members are important sources of connection for students, crucial to academic and social integration on campus (Astin 1993; Schreiner et al. 2011). This role has been highlighted for faculty members holding particular demographic traits that are minoritized within specific educational contexts, such as faculty members of color at predominantly white institutions (PWIs) and female faculty members within majority-male departments or study areas (Tierney and Bensimon 1996). Indeed, faculty members of color and female faculty members are often expected to play both formal and informal roles supporting students who share their demographic characteristics, above and beyond those of their white and/or male colleagues (Griffin and Reddick 2011; Hirschfield and Joseph 2012; Moore 2017; Padilla 1994). Faculty members of color and/or female faculty members may both be pressured by colleagues or department chairs to perform this work (even when it is personally gratifying to them) and yet also reap negative consequences such as loss of time for research and emotional exhaustion, adding to other microaggressions and challenges faced as a minoritized department member (see Cole and Griffin 2013 and Moody 2004 for reviews).

Considering these findings, we might expect a similar role for faculty members from low-income, working-class, and/or first-generation college backgrounds in supporting low-socioeconomic-status (SES) students. Recent research shows that faculty members with low-SES backgrounds, regardless of race or gender status, may face similar stigma-based challenges in the middle- or upper-middle SES and white-collar environs of faculty life on many campuses (Haney 2015, 2016; Lee 2017; see also Grimes and Morris 1997). This mirrors findings about classism in academia more broadly (e.g., Langhout, Drake, and Rosselli 2009; Langhout, Roselli, and Feinstein 2007; Spencer and Castano 2007), as well as echoing alienation and isolation experienced by low-SES undergraduate and graduate students (e.g., Aries and Seider 2005; Armstrong and Hamilton 2013; Smith, Mao, and Deshpande 2016). However, this comparison is complicated by differences between perceptions of race and gender, on the one hand, and class, on the other. Despite sociological understandings of race and gender as being socially constructed, interactional, and often contingent (West and Fenstermaker 1995), Americans typically approach gender and racialized positions as being visible and embodied in day-to-day settings. That is, we approach gender and race as qualities we can *see*. By contrast, class is often presumed to be a constant among faculty members by students and colleagues alike, who tend to believe that faculty members come from middle- or upper-SES backgrounds (Haney 2015), making other statuses largely invisible.

Based on these possible conflicts between expected supportive roles rooted in publicly available identities and a potential desire to keep class identity private, we ask whether faculty from low-SES backgrounds seek to support low-SES students and how they choose to do so, and we examine the way these choices may also be influenced by racialized and gendered positions. Through interviews with forty-six demographically diverse faculty members from low-SES backgrounds at varying campuses, we found that low-SES faculty members often seek to support students who share their low-SES backgrounds and that, indeed, respondents' processes of sharing and concerns about doing so are shaped by their gender and race positions. It is especially important to understand this intersectionality because significant scholarship already shows that female faculty members and faculty members of color experience particular burdens, what Padilla (1994) calls "cultural taxation" (e.g., Padilla 1994; Moody 2004; Zambrana et al. 2010; Gutierrez y Muhs et al. 2012; Hirschfield and Joseph 2012). Though little work examines faculty members' socioeconomic backgrounds specifically, we know that race, class, and gender are deeply interrelated and cannot be understood separately (Crenshaw 1991). We therefore consider the experiences of white faculty members who might more easily "pass" as a majority in their predominantly white middle-class employment settings, and of faculty members of color, who are already minoritized.

THE IMPORTANCE OF FACULTY MEMBERS

Faculty members affect student life in ways that stretch beyond academic instruction. As education scholars have long shown, faculty members' interactions with students contribute to student retention and campus involvement broadly (Astin

1993; Schreiner et al. 2011). This may be especially important for students who are statistically at greater risk of dropping out, including underrepresented students of color and low-SES students (Strayhorn 2008; Schreiner et al. 2011). A number of studies have examined this effect in the cases of students of color noting that minoritized faculty may be key sources of support for demographically similar students (Gershenson et al. 2017; Milner 2006; Umbach 2006).[1] Just (1999) argues that faculty members from racialized minority groups can help students by constituting a racially diverse campus, which will then be more welcoming and a better "fit" for students. Similarly, Zambrana et al. (2010) found that faculty members of color recalled the importance of their own academic mentors vividly. Others find that minoritized faculty may place special emphasis on the importance of teaching and student mentorship as a crucial aspect of academic life and mission, benefiting their students (Antonio 2002; Milner 2006; see also Moore 2017). We therefore see a powerful role for faculty mentors and, specifically, professors who personally understand the experiences that racially marginalized students face in predominantly white academic spaces.

However, this area of scholarship also shows that faculty members of color and female faculty members who are called on or elect to do this work may accrue negative outcomes resulting from this student-centered focus. These negative outcomes include less research time and lower productivity, emotional exhaustion, and lower evaluation from colleagues and institutions that do not value this level of service (Hirschfield and Joseph 2012; Joseph and Hirschfield 2011; Moore 2017; Williams and Williams 2006) and are compounded by other systemic problems, including lower levels of mentorship and greater levels of scrutiny for faculty members of color and/or female faculty members (Chang et al. 2013; Cole and Griffin 2013; Griffin and Reddick 2011; Moody 2004). Moreover, these effects are intersectional: women, and specifically women of color, are likely expected to play more caring or nurturing roles, take on heavier teaching loads, and even among faculty advisors are expected to utilize more personal interaction with students (Gregory 2001; Griffin and Reddick 2011; Menges and Exum 1983; Hirschfield and Joseph 2012). As Chang et al. (2013) discuss, student-centered service may be a double-edged sword in that female faculty of color do more work that "matters" but "doesn't 'count,'" but may nonetheless provide crucial spaces of meaning in that "extra" work of, for example, advising students and student groups who share their ethnic, racialized, gender, or other social positions (see, e.g., Griffin et al. 2011; see also Moore's 2017 discussion of her own experiences).

Class and SES have rarely been empirically examined as an important aspect of faculty background or a factor shaping faculty-student interaction, or as part of what shapes faculty work life (for exceptions, see Gutierrez y Muhs et al. 2012; Haney 2015; Hurst and Nenga 2016; and Lee 2017). However, it is clear that low-SES students often feel alienated on campus (Aries and Seider 2005), lack a sense of belonging (Ostrove 2003), and are often unfamiliar with campus resources (Stuber 2009), suggesting that faculty support might be especially important. This raises crucial questions in that faculty members from low-SES backgrounds may face stigma if they reveal their backgrounds (Lee 2017). As Haney (2015, 2016) notes, faculty members are presumed to be from middle- or upper-SES backgrounds. Moreover, faculty members have undertaken long periods of socialization into white-collar employment (Margolis and Romero 1998), providing them with the cultural capital and interactional skills needed to operate in this particular professional setting. Given these circumstances, faculty members from low-SES backgrounds might choose to keep their backgrounds private, rather than risk discomfort or alienation, which would reduce the possibility of providing status-specific mentorship to low-SES students. We examine the dynamics of this potential relationship here.

METHODS

This research grew out of the first author's larger project comprising interviews and fieldwork with low-SES undergraduate students. During that research, the first author began to see the role of faculty members as important to students and contingent on faculty members' choices to be "out" about their backgrounds and class statuses. Indeed, in conversations with student respondents, they often reported that low-SES faculty members are difficult to locate. While faculty of color (and female faculty members in certain fields) are often shockingly few in number, students at least believe that they are visibly observable and therefore locatable. Moreover, for better and for worse, they are also institutionally recognized as a source of "diversity," which provides an institutionalized pathway to different forms of involvement (O'Hearn 2015).

The first author conducted interviews between 2012 and 2016, building on five that had been collected in the earlier project. Interviews were conducted by phone or Skype, and typically recorded and transcribed. In cases where interviews were not recorded, they were typed in note form in real time. In cases where the interviews were recorded, they were subsequently transcribed by a research assistant or a professional transcriptionist. Institutional Review Board approval was obtained from the first author's home campus; interview respondents were asked to choose pseudonyms and were informed that the interview data would be confidential and anonymous. Respondents' names, fields of research, employers, graduate programs, and other possible identifiers were changed or omitted. If the respondent did not select a pseudonym, the first author assigned one during the course of data analysis.

We sought to include faculty members working across fields and at varied types of campuses. Interview respondents include faculty members working in the following categories: private liberal arts colleges, private research universities,

TABLE 7.1   Faculty Respondent Characteristics

Characteristic	Frequency	Percentage
Employer campus type		
Community college	5	10.87
Public, non-/moderately selective	16	34.78
Public flagship	4	8.70
Private nonprofit	21	45.65
Gender		
Male	16	34.78
Female	30	65.22
Race and ethnicity		
African American	2	4.35
Asian American	4	8.70
Hispanic/Latina/o	5	10.87
Native American/Indigenous	1	2.17
Pacific Islander	1	2.17
White	33	71.74
Field		
Social sciences	23	50.00
Natural sciences	5	10.87
Humanities	17	36.96
Professional	1	2.17
N	46	

public research universities, and two- and four-year public colleges and universities focused on teaching. Respondents' disciplines include natural sciences, social sciences, humanities, and professional fields. Female respondents are somewhat overrepresented, as are faculty members in the social sciences and humanities. Although we purposively sampled faculty members of color both through online recruitment and through snowball sampling, the sample is predominantly white, with twelve respondents of color out of forty-six. Table 7.1 provides an overview of our respondents' characteristics.

The first author contacted potential respondents through a working-class faculty Facebook page, public college first-generation faculty listings, and faculty who had made public presentations about their experiences as low-SES background faculty. After approximately twenty-five interviews she focused on newer faculty members, faculty of color, and faculty in the natural sciences, relying largely on snowball sampling to avoid biases in the overall sample. By nature of these recruitment processes, respondents typically self-identified as low-SES; basic background questions such as parent education level and occupation were asked as part of the interview protocol.

The second author joined the research project during the analysis phase. Both authors developed codes while reviewing the transcripts, working both deductively (looking for specific themes) and inductively (reviewing for themes that arose from the data). We then discussed the coding process and our observations of themes together.

One limitation of the research is that these data likely overrepresent the experiences of faculty members who are willing to speak with students about their backgrounds, given the recruitment process and the nature of the interview subject, and may therefore not sufficiently speak to the experiences of those faculty members for whom class background remains private. A second limitation is that, because we have fewer respondents of color than white respondents and a disproportionately female sample, we cannot undertake in-depth comparisons within racialized demographic groups (e.g., variation among African American respondents) or across groups (i.e., comparing Latina/o and Asian American respondent experiences or male vs. female responses).

FINDINGS

Support for Low-SES Students

Faculty members described offering types of support that we consider to be either *pragmatic* or *performative*. Pragmatic support included student employment or concrete opportunities—for example, a summer job in a lab—while performative support included the explicit or implicit presentation of the faculty member's low-SES background. While about a quarter of the respondents described using pragmatic support approaches, often in addition to performative efforts, the majority of respondents indicated that they made efforts to support their low-SES students specifically through the disclosure of class identity.

Nearly two-thirds of the sample described making themselves visible as (formerly) low-SES persons by talking about personal history and experiences. Many spoke openly about their backgrounds when teaching or advising, drawing on personal background for anecdotes or simply telling students about their background as first-generation and/or low-income people. Mary, for example, responded, "I always come out on day one to my class." Others indicated that they were not explicit about their background in class on a regular basis, but selectively informed students when the lecture called for it. Roy noted that opportunities to talk about his background come up organically because of the subjects he teaches: "So I try to teach on this subject in just about every class that I teach. Like I talk about social networking being [unclear], social and cultural capital being important." Reflecting further, he added, "I haven't made a habit of like describing my whole situation the first day of class, but when we get to the topics, I'll share a lot about [my background]."

We refer to this as performative support—that is, making themselves visible as (formerly) low-SES persons through the disclosure of that specific identity or discussion of their history. The operative theory of representation on campus posits an important role for visibility: having members of the faculty from selected demographics (e.g., racialized minority groups, presenting as female) provides indirect support for students who may feel encouraged or better understood by having an adult who in some particular way "matches" them and potential for direct support should the student or faculty member reach out based on that shared status. As noted above, faculty members are assumed by colleagues and students alike to come from middle- to upper-class backgrounds. For students, this may both make the faculty member seem alien and remove the sense of professional attainment as something that is reachable, something that they might envision for themselves. Making a shared class background clear may require more intentional or deliberative exposure.

A smaller number of faculty respondents offered what we call pragmatic support, providing opportunities for work, making pedagogical choices about texts assigned or how to structure their courses, connecting students to campus resources, or advocating for students. Many of these also spoke about their own backgrounds; the approaches were not mutually exclusive.

Visibility in Classed, Gendered, and Racialized Terms

Whether or not faculty members choose to be open about class identity, that is, of course, not the only salient demographic marker, nor the only one being displayed. As previous studies have established, faculty members from racially minoritized backgrounds and female faculty members are often subject to expectations for greater care and representational work, what Padilla (1994) describes as "cultural taxation." Because our respondents include so few faculty members of color and a disproportionate female-to-male ratio, a rigorous comparison would be impossible to do. Rather, we discuss the ways in which intersectional concerns of race, class, and gender became evident in respondents' narratives.

Class and race are profoundly related in American society, and faculty members of color described intersecting or multiplied concerns in supporting low-SES students. Similar to findings in other literature (see Moody 2004), one such concern was becoming overwhelmed by service requests from colleagues and from students because of their race, ethnic, and in some cases gender statuses, which then might become exacerbated by taking on similar roles supporting low-SES students. Mai, for example, teaches at a campus serving high numbers of students of color and low-income students. Her classes include high proportions of these students, who seek out either the course or her specifically. Knowing that these students are not likely to get support through home communities or elsewhere on campus, Mai works hard to be available to them. However, this takes its toll on her in emotional costs, stress, and time: "And, one of the things

I, like as a faculty member, I felt really bad being in this program because I felt like the students weren't getting the support that they needed, so that's why I ended up like working myself like crazy, to try to support them. . . . I mean, I really enjoyed working with the students, it's just the numbers. I mean, how can you be on 60 doctoral thesis committees?" Mai's position as one of only a small number of professors of color in her program made her visible to students who wanted support. She was caught between wanting to "work with" students to help them through the program successfully and the impossibility of meeting workload demands that that effort presented.

In many cases, as Mai pointed out, class and race statuses are inseparable in students' lives and therefore in faculty members' teaching, advising, and support work. Mai reported that when she asks students how they came to enroll in her class, "They told me that they chose me because I was a faculty member of color. . . . [And] the reasons why they're interested in doctoral education, and the topic, specifically, is 'cause they want to focus on diversity issues because they might be first gen." For Mai's students, her status as a professor of color is important, and in many cases intertwined with their background as first-generation, which drives their broader scholarly goals and interests. For Wallace, his own experiences of race and class were intertwined, which informed his decision to speak with students about their own backgrounds. When asked how he began speaking with students openly, he described an early teaching moment in which "I just kind of said, 'Okay, show of hands, people who are from community college, or first generation, or you know, who come from a family of immigrant parents.' And people were just very open talking about these things. So, it was just a way for me to say, 'Hey, you know, I come from a similar background too.'" For Wallace, each of these is interrelated, and his thinking about the importance of these statuses came directly from his own undergraduate career as a first-generation student raised in an immigrant family: "I think that the kind of point of departure for me was cultural difference and, you know, stereotypes Chinese students may have about American students, and stereotypes American students have about Chinese students. And so I think, I mainly just started talking about, you know, like American identity. But then, you know, American identity is a very diverse thing where there's many things that intersect, so there's this sort of intersectionality when it comes to, you know, what it means to be 'American'—you know, put that in quotes just to be safe." His awareness of the complexities of these identities informed his thinking about how these statuses might matter and be similarly intersectional for his students.

Respondents of color also described issues of specifically racist microaggressions. For example, Maria spoke about being misidentified as another African American professor by members of her own department, who addressed her using the wrong name or spoke to her about issues related only to the other person. However, in many cases, the implications of race and class are hard to separate for respondents of color—what is "about" race and what is "about" class? Indeed, when asked about his experiences as a professor, Raul related a story about being presumed to be custodial staff by a visiting speaker in his department. Was that about race or class, he asked rhetorically during his interview. In a similar example, Roberto spoke about the caution he feels in speaking with colleagues about his background as a working-class Latino, now working at a predominantly white and middle-class campus: "I think being a person of color, you have to guard yourself . . . [from] the stereotypes and the assumptions and misperceptions." Because of this caution, he holds back from speaking with colleagues about his background, and reserves sharing his personal stories for advising. One concern, he reported, was that white and middle-class colleagues will misperceive his intentions—they may think that "Roberto is sharing nice stories about his struggle, and maybe he's trying [to] achieve being seen as something else," or "he's playing the race card, or the poor card, like 'Oh I struggled so much,' like 'the whole pity story thing.'" Roberto's concern here is very squarely situated at the intersection of race and class—people will think he is "playing the race card or the poor card." His guardedness stems from being minoritized both racially and socioeconomically in ways that might be impossible to separate. Similarly, Veronica noted that because they are so few in number, "every professor of color has a following of students who will come to them consistently." She is therefore already sought out by students sensing a connection with her because of a shared racialized status. Making another minoritized status clear, or speaking in personal terms about her life by talking about her socioeconomic background, would open her up only further to students seeking her help, wanting a personal connection, or treating her as a "buddy," thus diminishing the respect typically accorded to a faculty member. Veronica's experience may further be contextualized within a broader expectation that female faculty members perform what Tierney and Bensimon (1996, 85–87) call "mom work"—namely, the performance of caring for students.

For white respondents, by contrast, it was easier to distinguish between racialized privilege (or perceived neutral location) and lack of class privilege. While the entanglement of race and class in students' and their own lives led to these roles conjoining for professors of color (e.g., students sought professors because of their visible race status and also because of their class background), white respondents described being assumed to be middle class by colleagues and by students. Beth, for example, was asked to speak specifically about her socioeconomic status during a meeting with students at her job talk at a minority-serving institution. She was prompted by the faculty member coordinating the search process to "tell 'em about your background." After she had shared a bit of her history, he again prompted, "Okay, why don't you tell 'em the other part about your background." Beth told the group, "Well, I grew up in rural poverty" and noted that "he stopped everyone and said, 'I want to ask how many people here, with a show of hands, assumed that she was an upper-[class woman]?'" As Beth recounted, most students assumed that she was from a class-advantaged background. Likewise, Brittany noted that she speaks openly with her students about her class background because she knows that they will perceive her as middle class because of her raced and gendered self-presentation: "I want to sort of immediately sort of challenge people a little bit and just point out that, you know, I might look like a prissy, upper middle class, white woman but I actually grew up dirt poor, white trash." Michael recounted that even some of his faculty colleagues of color expressed surprise that he, a white male, had grown up poor: "I have found that some people are really surprised for a number of different reasons. I find my colleagues of color are sort of surprised because they think that, well, I had one person say, 'I thought all white people were rich. Like I never thought about having, like how being poor and white would be different from being rich and white.'" In these cases, racialized privilege is read as long-term economic privilege, allowing the holder to potentially "pass" as affluent or compelling them to clarify their background.

The intertwined nature of racialized and classed privilege was also reflected in some white respondents' perception that their racialized status was construed as mutually exclusive to speaking about or being sensitive to race. Some white respondents described either feelings of hesitation to engage in discussions or pushback from others when bringing up the importance of class to discussions of campus diversity and/or privilege. Tori spoke about being part of an intergroup dialogue training session on her campus: "We were talking about race, and gender, and sexual orientation, and class was not part of this. And so I wanted to talk about class and I was told, point blank, 'You're bringing up class because you don't want to deal with your white privilege.' So, I just felt like, I mean, I felt like it was basically like you're being racist because you want to talk about class." In this instance, talking about race seems to be mutually exclusive from talking about class, and for Tori, shut down the possibility of considering how these two statuses intersect.

Several white respondents also acknowledged the privileges that their racialized position provided them—in some cases, the same respondents who voiced concerns about how to talk about class alongside race. Dennis, for example, whose research focuses on aspects of class inequality, reflected that, "I'm a white male. A white, heterosexual male [*laughter*]. . . . You know, it's like what do I have to say about anything? But, the fact is that I grew up in poverty [through] high school, which [led to becoming a] working class laborer for years before [grad school]. . . . But frankly, even growin' up I didn't think that—I saw myself, while I was barely inching out a living trying to get an associate's degree, I saw myself as privileged 'cause I am a white male and I was also a liberal." Dennis is aware of the contradictions between his status as a white, heterosexual male and his status as a working-class person, but he does not know how, precisely, to manage that contradiction. Victoria also had concerns about how her race and SES intersected in others' evaluation of her advocacy for students. She mused, "I don't know how widely, but I am recognized by some people as taking risks, going out on a limb for students." Did this recognition, she wondered, come from her position as a white woman? By contrast, she has friends who are "people of color on faculty who feel like they get some backlash for doing the same thing." She referred to this as "the good daddy benefit," alluding to the phenomenon in which men are lauded as "good daddies" for completing basic childcare tasks that would receive no notice if women were doing them. This, she noted, is "a positive effect I feel weird about." Race, class, and gender are therefore not only intersectional but also juxtaposed sources of privilege or lack thereof.

Gender also appears to play a role both in faculty members' decision making and in responses to their presentations of class. This is most clearly evident in the differences by gender in likelihood of disclosure: while most respondents spoke at least sometimes about their background, female respondents were more likely to do so. This distinction may come in part because of the distribution of fields and gender disparity in the sample, which reflects a broader disparity across fields. In our sample, of five respondents in natural sciences, three are male. These respondents described having less opportunity to incorporate socioeconomic status into their lectures. Moreover, female respondents were more likely to use language that evoked care work in the language of parenting—for example, Lara described herself as being "mama-like."

CONCLUSION

We find that low-SES professors report their work with students as meaningful and fulfilling, sometimes more than their research and broader teaching responsibilities. Here our findings echo what Griffin et al. (2011) call acts of "critical agency": faculty members disengaging from or sidestepping traditionally white, male, upper-class practices of the academy and instead finding connections to serve as "home places" or "safe spaces." While we did not see evidence of a "cultural tax" around socioeconomic status (Padilla 1994), we see three ways in which these dynamics are important.

First, to the extent that shared experience matters to students, as other scholars suggest is the case, having faculty members who are open about their low-SES backgrounds is important for students, graduate and undergraduate alike. Longtime findings show that connections with faculty members are significant for student retention. Low-SES faculty members who are able to make their background available to students provide support that may be lacking elsewhere. Here again, we see the importance of intersectionality: for graduate students already struggling with marginalization around gender and/or race (Margolis and Romero 1998), the lack of faculty mentors who can speak to their experiences, and the overall lack of inclusion of their experiences, is significantly problematic

(Richards 2018). Of course, this matters not only for graduate students but also for undergraduates, junior faculty members, and indeed all those who are members of these scholarly communities (Richards 2018).

Second, these dynamics are important in understanding the experiences of faculty members themselves. For professors who feel they cannot be direct about their backgrounds, this is a substantial burden and source of discomfort, and possibly an inducement to leave the field. For faculty members who are able to be open, there are risks of overcommitment to student support, or of stigma from students and colleagues. Both are problematic. Indeed, these data suggest that low-SES faculty members may experience dueling pressures: on the one hand, to perform middle class-ness for colleagues; but on the other hand, to provide support to low-SES students by making their class background and identity clearly visible. These dueling impulses are perhaps more complicated for faculty members of color and female faculty members, who already experience what Griffin and Reddick (2013) call higher levels of "surveillance" of their work than white male colleagues; the intersection of race and/or gender and class may be an even greater source of struggle in this context. Accordingly, questions about whether and how to talk about one's socioeconomic background as a person of color, in particular, seemed to be shaped by this intersectionality and, at least for some, this higher level of surveillance. While white respondents sometimes described feeling compelled to engage in the performative support of making their class background clear, some respondents of color were hesitant specifically because they were already being judged on one demographic category. Thus the intersectional positions of class, race, and gender are important to understand—the experience of being a low-SES faculty member varies across other statuses. Future research should more closely examine these dynamics, as well as consider statuses such as immigration history.

Finally, these dynamics matter for the state of higher education and its cross-generational contours. Academic departments remain largely class-homogenous: only a third of all doctoral degrees were awarded to first-generation graduates, and of these, roughly half took positions in academe, including postdoctoral fellowships (National Science Foundation 2015). Moreover, only very small percentages of faculty members are racialized as nonwhite (National Center for Education Statistics 2017): particularly among faculty members who are tenured, the majority are white, and among those, most are men. The number of faculty members who share multiple minoritized statuses is small, providing ample evidence of the intersectional costs and challenges accrued in the process of seeking to become a faculty member and thrive in the professoriate. When low-SES voices are "silenced" (Brook and Michell 2012), we see the closure of the academy to low-SES people across racialized and gendered statuses: faculty members and students who perceive the space as elite and elitist fear discomfort or sanction if they are open about their backgrounds, which discourages other students and faculty to be open and to stay in academia, which then leads to a continuation of these dynamics, stymieing efforts to diversify the professoriate.

NOTE

1. However, see Gay's (2000) cautionary note that sharing a demographic status does not automatically equip teachers with better skills or bring success, nor does responsibility for teaching students rest with those who share something in common with students.

REFERENCES

Antonio, Anthony Lising. 2002. "Faculty of Color Reconsidered: Reassessing Contributions to Scholarship." *Journal of Higher Education* 73 (5): 582–602.

Aries, Elizabeth, and Maynard Seider. 2005. "The Interactive Relationship between Class Identity and the College Experience: The Case of Lower-Income Students." *Qualitative Sociology* 28: 419–443.

Armstrong, Elizabeth A., and Laura Hamilton. 2013. *Paying for the Party: How College Maintains Inequality.* Cambridge, MA: Harvard University Press.

Astin, Alexander. 1993. *What Matters in College: Four Critical Years Revisited.* San Francisco: Jossey Bass.

Brook, Heather, and Dee Michell. 2012. "Learners, Learning, Learned: Class, Higher Education, and Autobiographical Essays from Working-Class Academics." *Journal of Higher Education Policy and Management* 34 (6): 587–599.

Chang, Aurora, Anjale D. Welton, Melissa A. Martinez, and Laura Cortez. 2013. "Becoming Academicians: An Ethnographic Analysis of the Figured Worlds of Racially Underrepresented Female Faculty." *Negro Educational Review* 64 (1/4): 97–118.

Cole, Darnell, and Kimberly A. Griffin. 2013. "Advancing the Study of Student-Faculty Interaction: A Focus on Diverse Students and Faculty." In *Higher Education: Handbook of Theory and Research*, 561–611. Editor: Michael B. Paulsen. Dordrecht: Springer Netherlands.

Crenshaw, Kimberle. 1991. "Mapping the Margins: Intersectionality, Identity Politics, and Violence against Women." *Stanford Law Review* 43 (6): 1241–1299.

Gay, Geneva. 2000. *Culturally Responsive Teaching: Theory, Research, & Practice.* New York: Teachers College Press.

Gershenson, Seth, Cassandra M. D. Hart, Constance A. Lindsay, and Nicholas W. Papageorge. 2017. "The Long-Run Impacts of Same-Race Teachers." *IZA Discussion Papers*, No. 10630. Bonn, Germany: Institute of Labor Economics.

Gregory, Sheila T. 2001. "Black Faculty Women in the Academy: History, Status and Future." *Journal of Negro Education* 70 (3): 124–138.

Griffin, Kimberly A., Meghan J. Pifer, Jordan R. Humphrey, and Ashley M. Hazelwood. 2011. "(Re)defining Departure: Exploring Black Professors' Experiences with and Responses to Racism and Racial Climate." *American Journal of Education* 117 (4): 495–526.

Griffin, Kimberly A., and Richard J. Reddick. 2011. "Surveillance and Sacrifice: Gender Differences in the Mentoring Patterns of Black Professors at Predominantly White Research Universities." *American Educational Research Journal* 48 (5): 1032–1057.

Grimes, Michael D., and Joan M. Morris. 1997. *Caught in the Middle: Contradictions in the Lives of Sociologists from Working-Class Backgrounds.* Westport, CT: Praeger.

Gutierrez y Muhs, Gabriella, Yolanda Flores Nieman, Carmen G. Gonzalez, and Angela P. Harris. 2012. *Presumed Incompetent: The Intersections of Race and Class for Women in Academia.* Boulder: University of Colorado Press.

Haney, Timothy J. 2015. "Factory to Faculty: Socioeconomic Difference and the Educational Experiences of University Professors." *Canadian Review of Sociology/Revue Canadienne de Sociologie* 52 (2): 160–186.

———. 2016. "'We're All Middle Class Here': Privilege and the Denial of Class Inequality in the Canadian Professoriate." In *Working in Class: Recognizing How Social Class Shapes Our Academic Work*, edited by Allison L. Hurst and Sandi K. Nenga, 141–156. Lanham, MD: Rowman & Littlefield.

Hirschfield, Laura E., and Tiffany D. Joseph. 2012. "'We Need a Woman, We Need a Black Woman': Gender, Race, and Identity Taxation in the Academy." *Gender and Education* 24 (2): 213–227.

Hurst, Allison L., and Sandi K. Nenga. 2016. "Introduction." In *Working in Class: Recognizing How Social Class Shapes Our Academic Work*, edited by Allison L. Hurst and Sandi K. Nenga, 1–10. Lanham, MD: Rowman & Littlefield.

Joseph, Tiffany D., and Laura E. Hirshfield. 2011. "'Why Don't You Get Somebody New to Do It?' Race and Cultural Taxation in the Academy." *Ethnic and Racial Studies* 34 (1): 121–141.

Just, Helen D. 1999. *Minority Retention in Predominantly White Universities and Colleges: The Importance of Creating a Good "Fit."* U.S. Department of Education report ED439641.

Langhout, Regina Day, Peter Drake, and Francine Rosselli. 2009. "Classism in the University Setting: Examining Student Antecedents and Outcomes." *Journal of Diversity in Higher Education* 2 (3): 166–181.

Langhout, Regina Day, Francine Rosselli, and Jonathan Feinstein. 2007. "Assessing Classism in Academic Settings." *Review of Higher Education* 30 (2): 145–184.

Lee, Elizabeth M. 2017. "'Where People Like Me Don't Belong': Faculty Members from Low-Socioeconomic Status Backgrounds." *Sociology of Education* 90 (3): 197–212.

Margolis, Eric, and Mary Romero. 1998. "'The Department Is Very Male, Very White, Very Old, and Very Conservative': The Functioning of the Hidden Curriculum in Graduate Sociology Departments." *Harvard Educational Review* 68 (1): 1–33.

Menges, Robert J., and William H. Exum. 1983. "Barriers to the Progress of Women and Minority Faculty." *Journal of Higher Education* 54 (2): 123–144.

Milner, H. Richard, IV. 2006. "The Promise of Black Teachers' Success with Black Students." *Journal of Educational Foundations* 20 (3/4): 89–104.

Moody, Joanne. 2004. *Faculty Diversity: Problems and Solutions*. New York: Routledge.

Moore, Mignon. 2017. "Women of Color in the Academy: Navigating Multiple Intersections and Multiple Hierarchies." *Social Problems* 64 (2): 200–205.

National Center for Education Statistics. 2017. "Fast Facts: Race/Ethnicity of College Faculty." *Conditions of Education*. Accessed June 15, 2018. https://nces.ed.gov/fastfacts/display.asp?id=61.

National Science Foundation. 2015. "Doctorate Recipients from U.S. Universities." NSF 16-300. http://www.nsf.gov/statistics/sed/.

O'Hearn, Dennis. 2015. "Campus Diversity Efforts Ignore the Widest Gulf: Social Class." *Chronicle of Higher Education*, June 30. Accessed June 8, 2016. http://chronicle.com/article/Campus-Diversity-Efforts/231233.

Ostrove, Joan M. 2003. "Belonging and Wanting: Meanings of Social Class Background for Women's Constructions of Their College Experiences." *Journal of Social Issues* 59 (4): 771–784.

Padilla, Amado M. 1994. "Ethnic Minority Scholars, Research, and Mentoring: Current and Future Issues." *Educational Researcher* 23 (4): 24–27.

Richards, Bedelia Nicola. 2018. "Is Your University Racist?" *Inside Higher Ed*, May 25. Accessed May 28, 2018. https://www.insidehighered.com/advice/2018/05/25/questions-institutions-should-ask-themselves-determine-if-they-are-operating.

Schreiner, Laurie A., Patrice Noel, Edward Anderson, and Linda Cantwell. 2011. "The Impact of Faculty and Staff on High-Risk College Student Persistence." *Journal of College Student Development* 52 (3): 321–338.

Smith, Laura, Susan Mao, and Anita Deshpande. 2016. "'Talking across Worlds': Classist Microaggressions and Higher Education." *Journal of Poverty* 20 (2): 127–151.

Spencer, Bettina, and Emanuele Castano. 2007. "Social Class Is Dead. Long Live Social Class! Stereotype Threat among Low Socioeconomic Status Individuals." *Social Justice Research* 20 (4): 418–432.

Strayhorn, Terrell L. 2008. "The Role of Supportive Relationships in Facilitating African American Males' Success in College." *NASPA Journal* 45 (1): 26–48.

Stuber, Jenny M. 2009. "Class, Culture, and Participation in the Collegiate Extra-Curriculum." *Sociological Forum* 24 (4): 877–900.

Tierney, William G., and Estela Mara Bensimon. 1996. *Promotion and Tenure: Community and Socialization in Academe.* Albany: State University of New York Press.

Umbach, Paul D. 2006. "The Contribution of Faculty of Color to Undergraduate Education." *Research in Higher Education* 47 (3): 317–345.

West, Candace, and Sarah Fenstermaker. 1995. "Doing Difference." *Gender & Society* 9 (1): 8–37.

Williams, Brian N., and Shaneka M. Williams. 2006. "Perceptions of African American Male Junior Faculty on Promotion and Tenure: Implications for Community Building and Social Capital." *Teachers College Record* 108 (2): 287–315.

Zambrana, Ruth Enid, Rashawn Ray, Michelle M. Espino, Corinne Castro, Beth Douthirt Cohen, and Jennifer Eliason. 2010. "'Don't Leave Us Behind': The Importance of Mentoring for Underrepresented Minority Faculty." *American Educational Research Journal* 52 (1): 40–72.

8 · DOING LESS WITH LESS

Faculty Care Work in Times of Precarity

DENISE GOERISCH

Robin State University[1] (RSU) is a public comprehensive university self-branded as an affordable alternative to private liberal arts colleges. Its commitment to providing students with a transformative liberal arts education is highlighted in its mission statement, which mentions it seeks to engender creativity, critical thinking, empathy, and courage in students to prepare them for their lives after college. To do so, the university encourages students to take on multiple academic and professional pathways, engage civically at the local and global levels, and develop meaningful and profound relationships with peers, faculty, staff, and the community. In an effort to form these relationships with students, faculty and staff perform care work through the practice of emotional labor as they nurture students' academic, professional, and personal development through advising and mentoring. These values and qualities of the university are in a state of precarity due to the recent $250 million cuts to higher education initiated by Governor Scott Walker in the state of Wisconsin. Walker argued the cuts were justified because he believed faculty work less than five hours per week, which he based solely on physical time spent in the classroom (Herzog and Marley 2015). Walker's perception of faculty labor fails to recognize the hours spent on research, preparing course materials, and mentoring and advising students, which in turn further devalues faculty labor. During the 2015 budget cuts crisis, the chancellor of RSU said on multiple occasions that the university would not compromise its mission or its liberal arts education framework in response to the cuts. The chancellor acknowledged that it would be difficult to uphold its mission, but as a university they would have to come together and do "less with less" (observation, winter 2015). While the chancellor felt the university would not waive its standards during this time of crisis, faculty and staff openly responded to the chancellor and one another that the "do less with less" approach would de-invest time spent caring for students' academic, professional, and personal well-being.

The 2015 budget cuts in Wisconsin created a perplexing dilemma for faculty. While the state seemingly devalued their care work with students by claiming its nonexistence, university leadership, on the other hand, claiming to value care work, instructed faculty not to be as invested in care work. This approach created an environment of fear and contradiction in which faculty worried for their positions and for students' well-being if they did not invest more in their teaching, advising, and mentoring. To aid in students' development, faculty perform the practice of emotional labor. Arlie Hochschild (2003) argues that emotional labor is used to suppress or induce certain feelings in order to provide students with support and guidance. Emotional labor is often perceived as gendered because of its emphasis on maternal care (or in many cases, perceived care), which is exhibited more in service-dominated fields. Care work is arguably an extension of emotional labor, as it is the case that faculty can potentially provide a service to students that helps develop their capabilities. Though faculty were deeply affected in profound ways by the cuts and worried how the cuts would impact how they engaged with students, RSU's students, particularly marginalized students (i.e., students of color, women, low income, first generation, LGBTQ [lesbian, gay, bisexual, transgender, queer], disabled, etc.), were concerned with the lack of engagement exhibited by faculty in the months after the budget cuts, as noted in news coverage, campus town halls, and classroom discussions. For students, especially those identified as vulnerable and more likely to transfer or drop out of college, the guidance and support they receive from faculty is instrumental to their success (Gomez et al. 2015). Additionally, forming and maintaining relationships with others, whether it be peers, faculty, or staff, is seen as a positive outcome of a liberal arts education for all students (King et al. 2007). When faculty were told to do "less with less" by university administration, it sent a message not to invest too much care in students' academic, professional, and personal well-being.

Faculty members believe their roles as mentors and advisors have a direct impact on their students. Tinto (2006) argues that institutional contributions such as academic advising and faculty mentoring have a positive impact on student well-being, campus culture, student retention, and graduation rates. Students at RSU stated that positive relationships with faculty were one of their key motivations for remaining in college. Before the cuts, many faculty members stated that even though they observed increases in what they perceive to be anxiety, depression, and stress among students due to socioeconomic forces they faced, such as increasing costs of tuition, racial and sexual violence on campuses, and fear of not being employed after college, faculty felt they had the time, energy, and capacity to be understanding, accommodating, and compassionate with and toward their students. However, because of the cuts and loss of shared governance and tenure, some faculty began to reluctantly detach, act coldly, or in some cases act with hostility and aggression toward students within their advising and mentoring relationships, thus, actually creating more precarity rather than helping facilitate or manage it for their students. During this time, when doing "less with less" was to become the norm, faculty began to question their roles within the university and whether they could or should continue to perform care work, even though they believed it to have a positive impact on students.

Precarity is a multidimensional state that has differential effects on intersectional identities in higher education (Hey 2011) and exacerbates systems and structures of privilege and oppression within higher education (Misiaszek 2015). While there is a considerable breadth of research within higher education on intersectionality, there is a need for more empirically based research, especially as it relates to precarity or crisis (Cabrera 2011). Much of the current research on emotional labor in higher education emphasizes faculty experiences (Bellas 1999; Constanti and Gibbs 2004). However, missing from these conversations regarding care work in higher education is how these practices change during times of precarity and how they differ among faculty populations. I examine both privileged and marginalized faculty's perceptions of care work within the context of advising and mentoring and how it changed in the months after the announcement of the 2015 budget cuts to better understand (1) how faculty come to perceive their precarious positions as care workers in the university, and (2) how faculty manage precarity with their students.

SITUATING THE RESEARCH

This chapter is based on a larger team-based ethnographic research project on college affordability with marginalized students. The majority of the students came from historically underrepresented groups and were marginalized in complex and intersecting ways based on their racial/ethnic identities, gender, ability, first-generation status, and prior academic preparation. While most of the research focused on documenting the lives of fifty low- and middle-income students across four public universities in Wisconsin, additional data were collected to better understand and contextualize the costs of college. These additional data included interviews with faculty, staff, nonfocal students, and alumni as well as observations of academic and social spaces on campuses, and the collection of pertinent documents and digital materials (admissions brochures, student organization agendas, student blogs, etc.).

At RSU, I interviewed nineteen faculty members, whom I met through invited classroom observations of focal students. Nearly 74 percent of the participants identified as male, and all of the participants identified as white, differing from the nearly 50 percent female and 10 percent faculty of color represented at RSU. While many faculty of color welcomed me into their classrooms, several stated they did not want to be interviewed out of fear of being potentially persecuted by the university. As there were few faculty of color on campus, they believed it would be easy to identify them by their race/ethnicity in combination with their gender and/or department affiliation. In addition to the sample being overwhelmingly male and white, I was able to interview only two non-tenure-track faculty members and one part-time instructor, who collectively represent approximately one-third of faculty on campus. Based on their interviews as well as casual conversations with faculty and staff, instructional staff members felt much more vulnerable than tenure-track or tenured faculty as their contracts are renewed every year, and at this time were much more susceptible to layoffs or nonrenewals due to the budget cuts. The sample was also overwhelmingly from the science, technology, engineering, and mathematics (STEM) disciplines. This may be due to the majority of RSU's STEM faculty teaching large lecture general education courses directed toward first- and second-year students, who were the focal population of the larger ethnographic study.

Despite living in a time of cuts and nonrenewals, white male faculty perhaps felt more secure within their positions of privilege to share their opinions without the fear of being singled out, unlike more marginalized faculty. While white male tenured and tenure-track faculty are overwhelmingly vocal about their roles as care workers within the precarious university, female faculty, part-time faculty, and university staff (who also perform faculty duties including teaching and advising) are understandably silent, owing to the precariousness of their positions in the university, which partially accounts for their lack of representation in this chapter.

GENDERING AND RACIALIZING EMOTIONAL LABOR AND CARE WORK IN ACADEMIA

Hochschild (2003) argues that faculty and staff perform substantial amounts of emotional labor through care work such as teaching, service, and to some extent, administration. As higher education becomes further commodified (see Shumar 1997), faculty are increasingly seen as service workers (Wyles 1998). Hochschild (2003) further argues that emotional labor has become a gendered practice, one that is devalued in the workplace as it is often perceived as feminine or "women's work." The gendering of care work is therefore naturalized and essentialized in a postindustrial economy, which contributes to the perpetual devaluing of such work by faculty and staff, particularly among those most marginalized within the university. Faculty members, specifically women, are expected to nurture and mentor students with care, consideration, and empathy despite increasing class sizes and number of advisees. Faculty are expected to perform care work well and do more with fewer allocated resources and with little to no pay increases. Yet, faculty's intersectional performances of emotional labor, especially in these precarious times within higher education, are surprisingly under-theorized.

Emotional labor is not necessarily gender specific, but the overwhelming majority of studies show that women, especially women of color, provide more emotional labor and are subject to expectations that they will perform emotional labor and care work (Bellas 1999; Hochschild 2003; Goerisch and Swanson 2015; Padilla 1994; Hirshfield and Joseph 2012; Griffin and Reddick 2011). Occupations that require workers to perform emotional labor are generally underpaid and also have the potential to be exploitative as well as impose negative consequences on the worker such as exhaustion, anxiety, and depression (Noor and Zainuddin 2011). Emotional labor, therefore, becomes devalued by both employers and society in general. Faculty care work can be considered to be precarious work because it often exists in states of unrest, conflict, or crisis at varying scales (Aronson and Neysmith 1996; Boris and Dodson 2013; Dyer, McDowell, and Batnitzky 2008; Pratt 2004; Uttal and Tuominen 1999; Vora and Boscagli 2013). Boris and Dodson (2013) argue that due to economic downturns, globalization, and changes in state and national policies, care work is much more susceptible to exploitation, manipulation, and devaluation. Therefore, it is imperative to critically analyze the performance of emotional labor in higher education to provide a foundation to understand how dominant power structures and majoritarian cultures, such as those that exist within the university, systematically devalue faculty labor. This examination must specifically include the care work performed by marginalized faculty, such as women and faculty of color, who often carry the burden of care work (Baez 2000; Stanley 2006).

While many care workers' positions are precarious owing to their identity, environmental and contextual realities cannot be dismissed. The few female faculty members I interviewed cited the near-impossible expectations of being a care worker within the university because of the changes in policy and tone at RSU. For example, one white female faculty member argued that policy changes enacted by Governor Scott Walker over the past several years, beyond the most recent round of budget cuts, made it more difficult to teach and advise as her "workload stayed the same or, perhaps even increased" while her "salary actually stayed the same or dropped" (interview, summer 2015). She continued to argue that owing to increased class sizes, she and others will not be able to provide students with the quality education they need. With contract nonrenewals and early retirement contributing to the loss of faculty, certain programs such as the LGBTQ studies minor, which is largely taught by marginalized faculty, were in jeopardy. The loss of such programs would not only delay graduation for students but also take away what many marginalized students perceived to be a safe space. To her and many other marginalized faculty members, the university sent a very clear message that doing "less with less" ultimately means caring less, and less for marginalized students and faculty in general.

Although most tenured faculty positions in higher education are occupied by men (NCES 2016), women faculty members are expected more often than not to perform emotional labor for the benefit of students. These faculty members are often from lower-paying and lower-ranked academic positions and are less likely to receive tenure compared with their white male counterparts (AAUP 2016). Women's work in academia (i.e., teaching and service) is often devalued and not given the same weight as research activities depending on personnel policies, procedures, and practices (Perna 2005). Teaching and service require substantial amounts of emotional labor and care work—labor generally not viewed as involving valuable skills and is consequently poorly rewarded. As a result, teaching and service are either negative factors in compensation or unrelated to compensation; neither do they count as heavily as research or teaching in tenure and promotion considerations (Fairweather 1993; Bellas 1999).

As a direct response to Governor Scott Walker's comments about faculty being grossly overcompensated for their lack of time in the classroom and devaluing the work of namely marginalized faculty (Herzog and Marley 2015), RSU released a series of informative videos detailing a week in the life of a tenure-track faculty member to demonstrate that faculty work up to (and often beyond) fifty to sixty hours a week. The subject of the first set of videos was a white female nursing professor whose responsibilities to the university included teaching in the classroom, online, and in a hospital; advising and mentoring students; learning new pedagogical methods; serving on university committees; and working at a local hospital and clinic. A nursing faculty member seems to be an interesting, and perhaps the ideal and most pragmatic, choice to demonstrate why the general public and state government should (re)value faculty efforts. Nursing is a field and occupation that most Americans are familiar with, and nurses, despite also being underpaid and overworked, are seen as performing a valuable function of care work in society. While challenging Walker's assumptions about faculty labor, the video also further reinforced societal norms of who (i.e., women) should perform emotional labor among faculty (Henderson 2001).

In addition to the university's own expectations of who should perform emotional labor and care work, students, particularly marginalized students, had high expectations of women and faculty of color to carry the burden of emotional labor and care work in comparison with white male faculty. Focal students in the larger ethnographic study rarely cited negative advising experiences with male professors, but few of the focal students actually had male advisors, which speaks to the gendered division of labor in academia (Acker and Feuerverger 1996). While many focal students, namely white and/or male students, had positive experiences with women professors in terms of advising and teaching, several students, mostly women and students of color, had incredibly negative experiences that left them feeling frustrated and abandoned, especially by faculty the students perceived to be their allies.

For example, Sarah, a white low-income, first-generation focal student from the larger ethnographic study, had a poor advising experience with a white female professor that derailed her path from her academic and professional aspirations. Sarah had always wanted to be an actuarial science major as she loved math and business. In her second year, a medical emergency forced her to drop a required class for her major and she did poorly on her midterms just days after surgery. Solely based on Sarah's poor midterm performance and dropping a class, her advisor suggested she switch majors. Sarah's grade point average (GPA) was above the required GPA for the actuarial science program, but her advisor felt that she would not be able to handle the real-world pressures of being an actuary. Her advisor did not offer any suggestions of what she could or should major in to help fulfill her professional goals. Sarah felt her advisor just did not care or want to care about her academic and professional future in light of the medical emergency impacting her academic performance. For Sarah, actuarial science was so deeply embedded as a part of her identity that many of her friends and support networks were from the major and she had made professional connections and commitments in the field. Sarah also grew up in a troubled household with a mother with a substance abuse problem, and hoped to earn a decent living as an actuary after college in order to become a legal guardian over her youngest sister, who was still in the care of their mother. She felt lost without the guidance of her advisor or any faculty member. After a day of coping with the shock of potentially not being an actuary, Sarah went to work to find a major that fit her academic and professional interests. After spending an afternoon looking through the course catalog and her degree audit, she determined she could still graduate within four years with a degree in business economics. While Sarah was able to navigate changing degree programs on her own, many students, particularly marginalized students, are left adrift by their advisors. Students with negative experiences were far less likely to go to their advisors and instead turned to peers for academic advising.

Veronica, a focal Latina student in the larger ethnographic study, was met with apathy and outright discontent when she approached her instructor for clarification on an assignment:

> I went to talk to a teacher today and I was like, "I just needed more instruction in the class." It met once a week and like only for like 50 minutes sometimes, and it's supposed to be 2 hours, you just let us off, you know, a lot and she was like "Well I gave you instructions." And like it would be 2 paragraphs and we would have to write 5 pages, and it gives you a couple of instructions, and so I was like I needed more and I'm sorry I didn't ask for it before, I was just really stressed out, and . . . she was just like "Well you should have come earlier in the semester." . . . She wasn't listening, she was like I had to take full responsibility but . . . she was like, "You can meet with me again." It's like [I] didn't have time. And then she was like, "Well everything else like shouldn't matter as much as academics." And I'm like, "That's so easy for you to say when you don't realize what experience I'm having." (interview, December 2015)

Not only did the faculty member not provide clarification on the assignment, but the instructor was also not meeting with students during the designated class period, as indicated by Veronica when she states that the class is "supposed to be 2 hours" and the professor just "let us off." It is unclear as to why the instructor was regularly dismissing students from class early and why she was so confrontational with Veronica or lacked any sort of empathy. The effects of this interaction added to Veronica's anxieties about academics and interacting with faculty and staff in the future. Veronica, who already felt isolated because of her ethnic identity on the predominantly white campus, believed she could no longer turn to most of the faculty or staff for help with academic, professional, or personal issues. As with Sarah's interaction with her advisor, it is not clear as to why Veronica's instructor engaged in this sort of behavior or if her behavior was any different before the budget cuts. But what is clear is that faculty care work or lack thereof has profound effects on students, especially students from historically underrepresented groups.

Marginalized students in the larger ethnographic study believed that relationships with faculty, particularly with faculty they could identify with (such as women and faculty of color), were not only meaningful but instrumental to their success in college. Several students in the study belonged to different activist groups that attempted to place pressure on the university administration to hire more faculty of color. However, because of the budget cuts, the administrators claimed they were unable to do so and actually eliminated the positions of many marginalized faculty and staff. Shortly after the announcement of the cuts, the Latinx student coordinator and advisor was laid off. Veronica and other Latinx students were then forced to seek advising from the Native American student coordinator and advisor, which was not very effective and placed an additional burden of care on this advisor. Advising has shown to have a positive effect on persistence and graduation for students of color, especially those on predominantly white campuses (Museus and Ravello 2010). If faculty are able to demonstrate an empathic and holistic approach to serve racial and ethnic minority students, then those students are more likely to succeed during their time in college (Guiffrida 2005). However, this seems not to be a priority at RSU during the reactionary changes to budget cuts at the university, despite administrators noting a desire to increase the number of students of color on campus over a five-year period.

Marginalized students already find approaching faculty to be an overwhelming and intimidating experience. When they are met with apathy, lack of care, and sometimes outright contempt, students' academic careers and postcollege futures are at risk. For students like Sarah and Veronica, faculty relationships are crucial for short-term and long-term success in college. However, owing to various forms of precarity, whether it be budget cuts or potential layoffs, faculty may not be able to physically or emotionally support students, especially those who need it most.

That said, the burden of care should not rest solely on marginalized faculty, especially as their positions within the university are often more precarious and vulnerable compared with those of white male tenure-track and tenured faculty. Faculty in positions of power and privilege, such as white male faculty, also need to be concerned with and care for marginalized students. Importantly, more privileged faculty need to demonstrate that care work should not fall to marginalized faculty, especially in times of crisis and precarity.

WHITENESS AND MASCULINITY IN EMOTIONAL LABOR AND CARE WORK

Despite the breadth of scholarship on the gendered and racialized intersections between emotional labor and care work (Boris and Dodson 2013; Dodson and Zincavage 2007; Duffy 2005; Maume, Sebastian, and Bardo 2010), there is a need to explore how workers in positions of privilege and power perceive, understand, and perform emotional labor and care work. Men are particularly less likely to engage in emotional labor based on gendered expectations of service and care work (Barber 2008; Nixon 2009; Smith 2008). When men do perform emotional labor, it is to potentially demonstrate and exert their masculinity, strength, and power by inducing feelings of passion, fear, or contempt (Smith 2008); and when men demonstrate care, concern, or kindness, it is often coded as effeminate by majoritarian cultures.

There are certainly male faculty who perform emotional labor to exert authority and control over their students, but there are also male faculty who would argue that they induce feelings more associated with supposedly feminine traits. One STEM faculty member commented that because he demonstrated so much care and openness with students, particularly marginalized students, many students, faculty, and staff perceived him as "gay" and effeminate. This particular faculty member, while somewhat amused by others' assumptions, took this as a compliment in that marginalized students, particularly women in the sciences, saw him as an ally. Several male faculty from various STEM departments actively tried to provide guidance and support for historically marginalized students in the sciences, specifically women, by serving as advisors for women in STEM student organizations, trying to recruit marginalized students at student orientations, holding office hours on the weekends, and learning more about campus services to better serve marginalized students. Many of these faculty members believed that if they were not supportive of underrepresented students in the sciences, then no one else would be. After the cuts and the tragic death of one of their most prominent female students, STEM faculty began to feel somewhat disillusioned with their roles as advisors and questioned their roles as caregivers. One faculty member who was particular close to the female STEM student who passed away stated that it became increasingly difficult for him to put the time and energy into caring for his students as the number of advisees increased in recent years:

> To me that was somebody who I had spent a lot of emotional energy on for so long and I realized I'm losing the ability to help students in that way. Now obviously it didn't work out with her, but I spent three years helping her through—well, I don't know helping—but trying to navigate systems and trying to navigate life in general and, you know, checking in and, you know, whether we have the ability to have that time and emotional energy to do that starts to ebb away as we have more and more students because, you know, your first thing that you're supposed to do is you are supposed to educate them. (interview, summer 2015)

After the announcement of the budget cuts and another year without a pay increase, STEM faculty believed they could no longer serve marginalized students in the ways they had done previously. For example, they could no longer afford the time and energy to attend additional training or workshops to better educate themselves on how to serve marginalized students. Even so, many white male faculty members continued to provide guidance and support to more privileged students. Male faculty in the STEM disciplines are more likely to collaborate on research with white male students and take the time to groom them professionally (Moss-Racusin et al. 2012). In addition to formal mentoring relationships, STEM faculty members were more likely to engage in informal mentoring relationships with white male students at RSU. For example, I observed several male STEM faculty eating their meals with mostly male students in the "STEM Lounge" and offering professional and academic advice, answering questions about homework, and sometimes discussing pop culture, campus experiences, and everyday life. These formal and informal mentoring relationships between male faculty and students are not surprising given that dominant mentoring models are masculinist in that they are "restricted to instrumentalist, exchange relationships, that work to advance each individual's separate interests and perpetuate gender inequities in organizations" (Buzzanell and D'Enbeau 2014, 698). Therefore, white male faculty members engage in relationships in which they see immediate and long-term benefits such as strengthening their research agendas while still engaging in service.

CONCLUSION

The mission of many public liberal arts universities, such as RSU, is to foster a strong relationship between faculty and students to help ensure student success during and after college. With yet another round of budget cuts and threat of potential layoffs as well as feeling increasingly devalued by the state and society in general, faculty questioned whether they can or even should develop and sustain advising relationships. As the number of advisees increases and pertinent information concerning major requirements or course availability is in a state of flux, faculty are unsure how to (or even if they want to) care. While faculty may want to help manage precarity with their students, it is difficult to do so when they themselves are in a precarious state.

Higher education faculty have become increasingly precarious; yet, some are more at risk than others due to the uneven distribution of privilege within the university. Those in departments, programs, and offices that may no longer be seen as serving the missions and goals of the university are under threat of possibly being let go because of new tenure policies. Additionally, female faculty, faculty of color, and other underrepresented groups within higher education are increasingly marginalized and expected to host additional burdens of care. As we continue to think about how faculty manages or creates precarity, we need to further consider how we frame privilege and power within the context of faculty care work, especially during times of crisis and uncertainty, and how this potentially reframes our understandings of intersectionality within the academy.

To help alleviate some of the uncertainty, universities can do more to better educate and train faculty concerning care work, particularly when serving marginalized students. Universities could reward and/or compensate faculty who participate in training and workshops to further revalue the importance of care work and caring for marginalized students. Universities could also do more (with potentially less) to place value on care work by making service just as important as research and teaching in terms of awarding tenure or granting promotions. Furthermore, faculty in positions of power and privilege could do more to support marginalized faculty by also taking on additional service roles. During times of precarity, the expectation for faculty to do "less with less" is not realistic, nor does it do anything to alleviate uncertainty among marginalized students. Rather than doing "less with less," universities can do more to value and reward care work.

NOTE

1. Robin State University is a pseudonym used to anonymize the institution examined in the current study.

REFERENCES

Acker, Sandra, and Grace Feuerverger. 1996. "Doing Good and Feeling Bad: The Work of Women University Teachers." *Cambridge Journal of Education* 26 (3): 401–422. doi:10.1080/0305764960260309.

Aronson, J., and S. M. Neysmith. 1996. "'You're Not Just in There to Do the Work: Depersonalizing Policies and the Exploitation of Home Care Workers' Labor." *Gender & Society* 10 (1): 59–77. doi:10.1177/089124396010001005.

AAUP. 2016. "List of Tables and Figures for 2013–14 Annual Report on the Economic Status of the Profession | AAUP." Accessed October 12, 2017. https://www.aaup.org/list-tables-and -figures-2013-14-annual-report-economic-status-profession.

Baez, Benjamin. 2000. "Race-Related Service and Faculty of Color: Conceptualizing Critical Agency in Academe." *Higher Education* 39 (3): 363–391. doi:10.1023/A:1003972214943.

Barber, Kristen. 2008. "The Well-Coiffed Man: Class, Race, and Heterosexual Masculinity in the Hair Salon." *Gender and Society* 22 (4): 455–476.

Bellas, Marcia L. 1999. "Emotional Labor in Academia: The Case of Professors." *ANNALS of the American Academy of Political and Social Science* 561 (1): 96–110. doi:10.1177/000271629956100107.

Boris, Eileen, and Leigh Dodson. 2013. "Working at Living: The Social Relations of Precarity." *eScholarship,* July. http://escholarship.org/uc/item/6bk5x0j5.

Buzzanell, Patrice M., and Suzy D'Enbeau. 2014. "Intimate, Ambivalent and Erotic Mentoring: Popular Culture and Mentor–Mentee Relational Processes in Mad Men." *Human Relations* 67 (6): 695–714. doi:10.1177/0018726713503023.

Cabrera, Nolan. 2011. "Using a Sequential Exploratory Mixed Method Design to Examine Racial Hyperprivilege in Higher Education." In *Using Mixed Methods to Study Intersectionality in Higher Education: New Directions in Institutional Research,* edited by Kimberly A. Griffin and Samuel D. Museus, 77–92. Hoboken, NJ: John Wiley & Sons.

Constanti, Panikkos, and Paul Gibbs. 2004. "Higher Education Teachers and Emotional Labour." *International Journal of Educational Management* 18 (4): 243–249. doi:10.1108/09513540410538822.

Dodson, Lisa, and Rebekah M. Zincavage. 2007. "'It's Like a Family': Caring Labor, Exploitation, and Race in Nursing Homes." *Gender & Society* 21 (6): 905–928. doi:10.1177/0891243207309899.

Duffy, Mignon. 2005. "Reproducing Labor Inequalities: Challenges for Feminists Conceptualizing Care at the Intersections of Gender, Race, and Class." *Gender & Society* 19 (1): 66–82. doi:10.1177/0891243204269499.

Dyer, S., L. McDowell, and A. Batnitzky. 2008. "Emotional Labour/Body Work: The Caring Labours of Migrants in the UK's National Health Service." *Geoforum* 39 (6): 2030–2038. doi:10.1016/j.geoforum.2008.08.005.

Fairweather, James S. 1993. "Academic Values and Faculty Rewards." *Review of Higher Education* 17 (1): 43–68.

Goerisch, Denise, and Kate Swanson. 2015. "'It's Called Girl Scouts, Not, Like, Woman Scouts': Emotional Labour and Girls' Bodies." *Children's Geographies* 13 (4): 451–466. doi:10.1080/14733285.2013.849855.

Gomez, Mary Louise, Kelly Ocasio, Amy Johnson Lachuk, and Shameka N. Powell. 2015. "The 'Battlefield': Life Histories of Two Higher Education Staff Members of Color." *Urban Review* 47 (4): 676–695. doi:10.1007/s11256-015-0329-6.

Griffin, Kimberly A., and Richard J. Reddick. 2011. "Surveillance and Sacrifice: Gender Differences in the Mentoring Patterns of Black Professors at Predominantly White Research Universities." *American Educational Research Journal* 48 (5): 1032–1057. doi:10.3102/0002831211405025.

Guiffrida, Douglas. 2005. "Othermothering as a Framework for Understanding African American Students' Definitions of Student-Centered Faculty." *Journal of Higher Education* 76 (6): 701–723. doi:10.1080/00221546.2005.11772305.

Henderson, Angela. 2001. "Emotional Labor and Nursing: An Under-Appreciated Aspect of Caring Work." *Nursing Inquiry* 8 (2): 130–138. doi:10.1046/j.1440-1800.2001.00097.x.

Herzog, Karen, and Patrick Marley. 2015. "Scott Walker Budget Cut Sparks Sharp Debate on UW System." Accessed October 12, 2017. http://www.jsonline.com/news/education/scott

-walker-says-uw-faculty-should-teach-more-classes-do-more-work-b99434737z1
-290087401.html.

Hey, Valerie. 2011. "Affective Asymmetries: Academics, Austerity and the Mis/Recognition of Emotion." *Contemporary Social Science* 6 (2): 207–222. https://doi.org/10.1080/21582041.2011.583486.

Hirshfield, Laura E., and Tiffany D. Joseph. 2012. "'We Need a Woman, We Need a Black Woman': Gender, Race, and Identity Taxation in the Academy." *Gender and Education* 24 (2): 213–227. doi:10.1080/09540253.2011.606208.

Hochschild, Arlie Russell. 2003. *The Commercialization of Intimate Life: Notes from Home and Work*. Berkeley: University of California Press.

King, Patricia M., Marie Kendall Brown, Nathan K. Lindsay, and Jones R. Vanhecke. 2007. "Liberal Arts Student Learning Outcomes: An Integrated Approach." *About Campus* 12 (4): 2–9. doi:10.1002/abc.222.

Maume, David J., Rachel A. Sebastian, and Anthony R. Bardo. 2010. "Gender, Work-Family Responsibilities, and Sleep." *Gender & Society* 24 (6): 746–768. doi:10.1177/0891243210386949.

Misiaszek, Lauren Ila. 2015. "'You're Not Able to Breathe': Conceptualizing the Intersectionality of Early Career, Gender and Crisis." *Teaching in Higher Education* 20 (1): 64–77. https://doi.org/10.1080/13562517.2014.957267.

Moss-Racusin, Corinne A., John F. Dovidio, Victoria L. Brescoll, Mark J. Graham, and Jo Handelsman. 2012. "Science Faculty's Subtle Gender Biases Favor Male Students." *Proceedings of the National Academy of Sciences* 109 (41): 16474–16479. doi:10.1073/pnas.1211286109.

Museus, Samuel D., and Joanna N. Ravello. 2010. "Characteristics of Academic Advising That Contribute to Racial and Ethnic Minority Student Success at Predominantly White Institutions." *NACADA Journal* 30 (1): 47–58. doi:10.12930/0271-9517-30.1.47.

National Center for Education Statistics, IPEDS Data Center. 2016. "Full-Time Instructional Staff, by Faculty and Tenure Status, Academic Rank, Race/Ethnicity, and Gender (Degree-Granting Institutions): Fall 2015," *Fall Staff 2015 Survey*.

Nixon, Darren. 2009. "'I Can't Put a Smiley Face On': Working-Class Masculinity, Emotional Labour and Service Work in the 'New Economy.'" *Gender, Work & Organization* 16 (3): 300–322. doi:10.1111/j.1468-0432.2009.00446.x.

Noor, Noraini M., and Masyitah Zainuddin. 2011. "Emotional Labor and Burnout among Female Teachers: Work–Family Conflict as Mediator." *Asian Journal of Social Psychology* 14 (4): 283–293. doi:10.1111/j.1467-839X.2011.01349.x.

Padilla, Amado M. 1994. "Research News and Comment: Ethnic Minority Scholars; Research, and Mentoring: Current and Future Issues." *Educational Researcher* 23 (4): 24–27.

Perna, Laura W. 2005. "Sex Differences in Faculty Tenure and Promotion: The Contribution of Family Ties." *Research in Higher Education* 46 (3): 277–307. doi:10.1007/s11162-004-1641-2.

Pratt, Geraldine. 2004. *Working Feminism*. Philadelphia: Temple University Press.

Shumar, Wesley. 1997. *College for Sale: A Critique of the Commodification of Higher Education*. New York: Routledge.

Smith, R. Tyson. 2008. "Passion Work: The Joint Production of Emotional Labor in Professional Wrestling." *Social Psychology Quarterly* 71 (2): 157–176.

Stanley, Christine A. 2006. "Coloring the Academic Landscape: Faculty of Color Breaking the Silence in Predominantly White Colleges and Universities." *American Educational Research Journal* 43 (4): 701–736. doi:10.3102/00028312043004701.

Tinto, Vincent. 2006. "Research and Practice of Student Retention: What Next?" *Journal of College Student Retention: Research, Theory & Practice* 8 (1): 1–19.

Uttal, Lynet, and Mary Tuominen. 1999. "Tenuous Relationships: Exploitation, Emotion, and Racial Ethnic Significance in Paid Child Care Work." *Gender & Society* 13 (6): 758–780. doi:10.1177/089124399013006005.

Vora, Kalindi, and Maurizia Boscagli. 2013. "Working under Precarity: Work Affect and Emotional Labor." *eScholarship*, June. http://escholarship.org/uc/item/0m87j6n1.

Wyles, Barbara A. 1998. "Adjunct Faculty in the Community College: Realities and Challenges." *New Directions for Higher Education* 1998 (104): 89–93. doi:10.1002/he.10409.

9 · FACULTY ASSESSMENTS AS TOOLS OF OPPRESSION

A Black Woman's Reflections on
Color-Blind Racism in the Academy

BEDELIA N. RICHARDS

When I started my job as a tenure-track professor of sociology at the University of Richmond (UR), I thought of my colleagues as nice people, and I would have characterized the departmental culture as collegial. My colleagues were gracious about sharing course syllabuses or generously providing feedback on journal articles and grant applications. If I presented my research on campus, they would make an attempt to show up in support. Even so, this interpersonal niceness and collegiality coexisted with and masked increasingly hostile, toxic relationships with my colleagues as a collective. This hostility toward me—primarily reflected in my annual performance reviews—was fueled by my refusal to accept the department's interpretation of the student evaluations it used to assess my teaching effectiveness, and its resistance to acknowledging the distinct challenges I faced as a black woman[1] working at a historically white institution (HWI). Although the impact of gendered anti-black stigmas and ideologies is well documented in academic literatures and testimonials of underrepresented faculty on college campuses (Collins 2002; Desmond and Emirbayer 2010; Gutiérrez y Muhs et al. 2012; Matthew 2016), our experiences with racism are routinely ignored or treated as if they are a tangential aspect of our professional lives (Joseph and Hirshfield 2011). By minimizing the impact of racism on our lives, HWIs engage in a practice that the sociologist Eduardo Bonilla-Silva (2014) describes as color-blind racism.

In contrast to the explicit forms of racism and racial discourse that were dominant before the 1960s civil rights movement, sociologists agree that a more covert form, color-blind racism, has become the dominant racial ideology in the twenty-first century (Bonilla-Silva 2014; Omi and Winant 2014). Dominant racial ideologies exist to both justify and conceal racial dominance and the inequalities it produces. Thus, Bonilla-Silva (2014) argues that white Americans draw on four central frames of color-blind racism—abstract liberalism, naturalization, cultural racism, and minimization of racism—to talk about racial issues with race-neutral language, even while supporting policies or engaging in practices that rationalize and reproduce racist structures.

In this chapter, I draw on my experiences as a black woman teaching at an HWI to illustrate how institutional assessments can function effectively as tools of gendered racial oppression when color-blind frames are used to evaluate the experiences and accomplishments of underrepresented faculty. I do so by highlighting the gendered anti-black stigmas that manifest in students' end-of-semester evaluations of my teaching, and my departmental colleagues' reliance on a color-blind lens to assess these biased comments. In doing so, my colleagues minimized my racialized experiences in the classroom while empowering and legitimizing student biases and converting student evaluations into effective tools of gendered racial oppression. This conversion was particularly effective because excellence in teaching is critical to career advancement at small liberal arts schools like UR, and until recently, student evaluations had been uncritically accepted as a reliable measure of excellence.

There is an abundance of essays and empirical work on the racial and gendered bias embedded in students' evaluations of teaching (Hamermesh and Parker 2005; Smith 2007; Smith and Hawkins 2011; Lazos 2012), as well as the racial microaggressions that faculty of color are subjected to by students or by colleagues on predominantly white campuses (Smith 2004; Sue et al. 2011; Pittman 2012). This chapter expands on this work by showing how (white)[2] students and (white) colleagues function unwittingly as "co-conspirators" in an oppressive system that privileges whiteness. I end this chapter with research-driven, actionable steps that institutions can take to truly foster a more inclusive, anti-racist environment for underrepresented faculty.

GENDERED ANTI-BLACK RACISM, STUDENT EVALUATIONS, AND INCIVILITIES

For pre-tenure faculty, gendered racism manifests most consistently in end-of-semester evaluations of teaching. This bias was strongest in my Introduction to Sociology courses, as this is the first time that students' worldviews are being challenged by readings and discussions revolving around the issues of inequality central to sociological inquiry. Students were particularly resistant to discussions about racial injustice. For example, in 2011, a student complained, "I don't like her teaching style. She constantly brings up race in every subject we talk about." This discomfort emerges from the fact that my students, who are predominantly white[3] and economically privileged, think inequality is a relic of the past. As one student noted in 2014, "She has a close minded view that Blacks and minorities are always discriminated on." Additionally, my white students often felt that they or white people more generally were being targeted unfairly (Bohmer and Briggs 1991; Davis 1992). A quote from a student in 2014 is representative of this perspective: "My fellow students and I come to gain elementary knowledge of sociology, and all we got were sources pointing out racism in this country and why the majority class—being White—should feel like terrible people." These statements persist, despite steady improvement in my evaluations for this course over time, because my social role as a black woman made it difficult for some students to also see me in the role of a credentialed expert imparting sociological knowledge. These students' rhetoric is consistent with prior research that suggests minority and women professors are more likely to be perceived as ideologically driven than their white and male counterparts, and that students penalize professors whom they perceive as promoting a biased (liberal) agenda in the classroom (Kelly-Woessner and Woessner 2006).

Course evaluations were convenient tools for students to express their resentment at having to engage with uncomfortable issues of racial inequity. However, student evaluations are not only tools for expressing their disapproval. They are mechanisms of racialized social control, especially for pre-tenure and short-term faculty, since student evaluations may influence whether we are (re)hired, tenured, or promoted. In particular, (white and male) students use course evaluations to exert power over minority and women professors by penalizing us for not conforming to their racialized and gendered expectations (Harlow 2003; Wingfield 2010; Ford 2011). For example, my no-nonsense demeanor and straightforward communication style were often interpreted as "mean," "rude," and "intimidating" because of the expectation that black women should be nurturing and motherly (Harlow 2003). Additionally, race and gender bias were partially at play in student comments that referred to me as "unfair" or as a "hard grader." Students are more likely to be hostile to a black female professor with rigorous academic expectations because we challenge both racialized and gendered expectations of our incompetence and we disrupt the role expectations of women as nurturers. We are simultaneously violating racial and gendered norms of subservience to our white and male students, respectively. As a whole, these complaints suggest that, while I formally held the title of professor, as a "black woman," I could not be trusted in the role of "credentialed expert" that this position entails.

Students manifest racial and gendered bias in their greater likelihood to challenge the authority of professors who are women and/or faculty of color than that of our white and male counterparts (Johnson-Bailey and Lee 2005; Ford 2011). In my case, these challenges occurred inside and outside the classroom. For example, during classroom discussions students have posed questions for the sole purpose of testing my knowledge rather than engaging in an authentic discourse, or have attempted to talk over me when they disagree with a position I am trying to articulate based on my expertise. White male students are more likely to engage in these overt forms of incivilities, which underscores the significance of both race and gender in shaping these interactions with students (Pittman 2010).

Students are also more likely to challenge the authority of their black female professors by going over our heads, due to the perception that we are not qualified for our positions (Miller and Chamberlin 2000). For example, during my first two years at UR, if students struggled with an assignment, they complained to the department chair instead of speaking with me directly. Instead of requiring students to speak with me, my chair met with students privately, guaranteed them anonymity, and then she conveyed the nature of student concerns to me in a separate meeting. With this approach, my chair encouraged students to further undermine my authority by functioning more as a mediator charged with settling a dispute between peers, which abrogates the professor-student relationship. Additionally, my chair's actions normalized students' biases as legitimate and bolstered their ability to make allegations without ever having to be accountable for them. Her actions reflect an implicit assumption that students would not complain in this manner about "competent" professors. This color-blind reading was possible because she minimized the impact of racial and gendered biases in how students responded to me.

I never accepted my students' or colleagues' presumption of my incompetence as a teacher, but as someone who has always been passionate about teaching, I was open to constructive feedback. So I enthusiastically participated in professional development opportunities offered through the university, educated myself on the impact of racial and gendered bias on student evaluations, and sought mentorship from women colleagues of color on how to minimize these biases. My efforts were rewarded with more positive ratings on items meant to assess student learning. Thus, by the time of my midcourse review in the spring of 2013,[4] the majority of students in my courses either agreed or strongly agreed that my courses stimulated critical thinking and that taking the course increased their knowledge of the subject. Students' racial and gendered biases became even more pronounced as my ratings on these items continued to improve, because they were not consistent with low ratings on items that reflect their feelings for me as a person. For example, the same students who gave high assessments of their learning also said that they would not recommend that others take my course. Students reconciled these inconsistencies in the comment section by distinguishing between how they felt about the course material and how they felt about me with comments such as "The material was interesting and thought-provoking, but the teacher made me hate the course." Admittedly, resentment and distress over the grades students received played a significant role in how students evaluated me (Sinclair and Kunda 2000). Students consistently rated my courses as more challenging than others they have taken at the university, and complaints about workload and grades are the strongest pattern that emerges from reviewing several years' of student evaluation comments.

COLOR-BLIND RACISM AND FACULTY ASSESSMENTS

My colleagues' attempts to craft color-blind interpretations of the inconsistent course evaluations described earlier in this chapter led to a pattern of illogical and contradictory statements in my performance reviews.[5] For example, in the initial draft of my spring 2013 midcourse review,[6] my colleagues point out "there continue to be narrative complaints (by students) that Dr. Richards' knowledge is not always being passed on to them." Yet, elsewhere in the document, the department acknowledges that one of the areas where students evaluate me favorably is "increasing knowledge of course topics." In that same document, my senior colleagues state that students "avoided" my classes because I did not clearly communicate my standards to them. However, this statement contradicted the prior two paragraphs, where these colleagues agreed with my assessment that students complained that I failed to communicate my standards to them due in part to their dissatisfaction with low grades on writing assignments. My chair at the time suggested working more on rubrics in order to better communicate my expectations to students. I pointed out that I had a number of rubrics, and asked whether she could point out what was wrong with them. She could not. In fact, I reminded her that she and another senior colleague had complimented my rubrics the prior semester. Exasperated, my chair finally admitted, "the department thinks that something you are doing is turning students away, but we can't figure out what it is." This statement is a powerful example of how the minimization of racism informed and is informed by the presumption of guilt and incompetence. For in this one sentence my department chair, speaking on behalf of my senior colleagues, conveyed the following three messages:

1. We have no concrete evidence that you have done anything wrong pedagogically, but we believe the students that you are guilty of doing "something" wrong; we just cannot figure out what that is . . . yet (presumption of guilt and incompetence).
2. We do not believe your race or gender has anything to do with how students are evaluating you, and therefore it is logical to believe that "something" you are doing is turning students away (minimization of racism).
3. We do not really know what you have done wrong, but since we are positive that the students are right about your incompetence, we still have to provide a rationale for your low merit review scores because you still need to be punished for whatever it is that you are doing wrong (gendered racism).

In a department of sociologists and anthropologists who prided themselves on our department's coverage of diversity issues in our curriculum, it was striking that bias (racial or gendered) evidently was never considered as one potential explanation. Instead, this interaction exemplifies the strategic maneuvering of departmental colleagues who persisted in putting forth color-blind explanations for student evaluation responses that were themselves contradictory. My colleagues' assessments and suggestions mirrored the inconsistencies in students' evaluations of my teaching because they were just as likely to view me through the anti-black stigma of incompetence as some of my students. And, therefore, they were just as inclined to presume me guilty of whatever students accused me of—even if the evidence did not support the students' perspectives (Johnson-Bailey and Lee 2005; Joseph and Hirshfield 2011). In this regard, my students and my colleagues colluded, albeit unintentionally, in transforming student evaluations of my teaching and my performance reviews into effective tools of gendered racial oppression.

In some cases, the statements my colleagues made in my reviews were blatantly inaccurate. In the first draft of my 2012–2013 annual review and my midcourse review that same year, the department claimed, "Bedelia consistently teaches the least amount of students per capita of anyone else in the department." With help from my mentor, I was able to provide evidence that this statement was inaccurate by reviewing four years of course enrollment data in order to compare mine with those of my sociology colleagues. Although my department amended this statement in the final draft, their new statement expressed their "concern for lower enrollments" in my Introduction to Sociology courses relative to those of other full-time colleagues. Obviously, I could not challenge the fact that they were "concerned." However, insistence on keeping this information in my review showed a lack of support for me as a junior colleague, as this was the very first time that this issue was being raised in an official capacity. Additionally, the department did not acknowledge any external factors that could contribute to lower enrollments, such as teaching in the spring versus fall, being perceived as more difficult than other sociology professors, or racial bias. Thus, my department used this information to undermine rather than support me. As this inaccuracy was part of a pattern, I was constantly using my time to fact-check my reviews in order to defend myself, time that could have been spent more effectively on my research, writing, and teaching.

These narratives demonstrate how the presumption of my incompetence and guilt, rooted in gendered anti-black racial ideologies, became institutionalized into my annual performance reviews. As a result, the performance review process increasingly became a site of conflict with my department because my senior colleagues refused to acknowledge that my being a black woman influenced how students viewed, interacted with, and ultimately evaluated me. I have therefore contested some aspect of my annual performance review almost every year on the tenure track at UR. My colleagues viewed these attempts to secure fair assessments of my accomplishments as insubordination, and resented me for not behaving deferentially, consistent with my role as a junior scholar. My colleagues' response to me was also about race, for they sought to silence and debunk any assertions that students' responses and evaluations of me were filtered through their perceptions of me as a black woman. Their response epitomized the color-blind tendency to minimize the gendered anti-black racism I experienced. Missing from this chapter is the fact that my colleagues' resentment eventually manifested in more overt acts of sabotage and a violent verbal assault by my department chair while I was meeting with one of my students in the fall of 2014. I have also chosen to exclude examples of overt forms of student incivilities, and the long history of racist microaggressions to which I have been subjected by my former chair, in part because these experiences do not fit the color-blind framing I have elected to use here. Finally, because of space limitations, I have not discussed in detail the strong support I received from a black woman colleague in a different department who guided me through appropriately responding to my negative reviews, or the support from my former dean and my official institutional mentor, who, collectively, have contributed to my becoming a tenured professor.

As stated at the beginning of this chapter, racial ideologies, such as the current commitment to color blindness, both justify and conceal racial dominance. In my particular case, color-blind racial discourse rested on the assumption that my experience as a black woman was no different from the experiences of my white and male colleagues. This ideology effectively made it possible for my colleagues to ignore (conceal) the ways in which my professional life was filled with obstacles that did not present themselves to my white and male colleagues. By ignoring the gendered racism that was part of my everyday lived experience as a professor, my department could use student evaluations to justify assigning me lower merit review scores on my annual performance reviews, and reinterpret them as "objective" evidence of my incompetence relative to my white and male colleagues. Since my department functioned in a way that was consistent with the larger institutional culture at UR, there was no resistance from my first dean, who ultimately could have reversed the department's score or, at a minimum, had a conversation with my chairs about my problematic reviews. Thus, the institution as a whole, while avowing to be committed to becoming more diverse and inclusive, contributed to my oppressive circumstances.

The negative experiences I have had at UR have provided me with insight into how institutions can claim to value diversity and inclusivity, on the one hand, while simultaneously contributing to the marginalization of some of its most vulnerable members, on the other hand. I draw on the greater clarity I now have from reflecting on my experiences and the academic literature to provide recommendations in the next section for how institutions like UR can do a better job of acting in ways that are consistent with their own avowed values and priorities.

Today I am a tenured associate professor of sociology at the University of Richmond. I no longer operate in a constant state of crisis and paranoia from feeling perpetually under attack, or exist in an elevated state of insecurity and psychological distress, because the only power I have is the power to resist, not the power to remove the source of my oppression.

The experiences I have described in this chapter reflect a broader pattern among black faculty and other faculty of color who have been recruited to "diversify" predominantly white institutions (Patton 2004). These institutions draw on the common discourse of "diversity" as an ideal that is valued and that is critical to preparing their (white) students to function effectively in an increasingly multicultural and globalized world. Yet, diversity for many institutions involves the placement of more black and brown faces in historically white institutional spaces, without much thought as to how to institute structural changes to counter the systemic bias we inevitably encounter. This happens in part because white Americans tend to view racial discrimination primarily as overt acts of hatred and/or as a relic of past times that has no meaningful impact on the day-to-day lives of black and brown people in the present (Desmond and Emirbayer 2010). White administrators, department chairs, and colleagues are not exempt from internalizing this normative belief that we live in a postracial society, despite the abundance of social science data to debunk this myth.

Inclusivity does not mean treating all demographic groups the same when we clearly face different institutional challenges—in fact, to do so is to engage in the practice of color-blind racism. For, treating everyone "the same" often means treating everyone as if we experience the world in the same way as the average white (male) person. However, since racially and ethnically marginalized scholars do not experience the world in the same way as our white colleagues, treating us the same minimizes the racism that is part of our everyday realities, ensuring that racialized forms of inequality will remain in place. Below I draw on my personal experiences as a black woman, as well as my expertise as a sociologist and race scholar, to offer suggestions for what institutions can do to proactively cultivate a community that is inclusive of racial and ethnically marginalized groups. I suggest that doing so will require institutions to become *proactively anti-racist and anti-sexist*.

RECOMMENDATIONS

An institution that is *proactively anti-racist and anti-sexist* will address racism and sexism as systemic issues, not as a series of individual problems with bigots who are outliers in the campus community. Perhaps more importantly, we should be sensitive to the ways in which these systems of oppression intersect and mutually reinforce each other. All members within our society, which is stratified by race and gender, are subjected to racist and sexist ideologies, symbols, and imagery through socialization in our families, through our school curriculums, and through media (mis)representations. Thus, it is important for university administrators to recognize that higher education institutions reflect these problematic racial and gendered dynamics in the larger society. For example, as a result of anti-black racism in the United States, people of African descent are more segregated from whites than any other racial and ethnic minority group (Massey and Denton 1993). Thus, white Americans who are socialized in predominantly white neighborhoods, schools, and churches have few intimate interactions with black people as equals, and therefore few opportunities for their racial biases to be challenged. This racial isolation means that even white colleagues who may view themselves as racially progressive and committed to racial justice may be complicit in perpetuating a system that is oppressive to people of African descent and other underrepresented groups. Similarly, men and women tend to live segregated lives outside of familial and romantic contexts because of the systemic ways in which gender permeates and stratifies social life and institutions (Risman 2004). Honesty about these basic facts should be the starting point for proactively creating systems of support and mentorship that are explicitly race-conscious, but that also recognize the gendered manifestations of racism. I identify below specific anti-racist and anti-sexist practices for institutions that are serious about creating a campus community that is supportive of racially marginalized faculty.

1. *Fund a position or office to support recruitment and retention of underrepresented faculty.*

The first step toward creating an inclusive environment is appropriately funding a position or office that is responsible for coordinating anti-racist projects across the university that take into consideration how racism intersects with other forms of oppression. Doing so is an explicitly anti-oppression strategy demonstrating institutional commitment to diversity, equity, and inclusion because there is a proactive effort to create an environment that is welcoming and protective of underrepresented faculty (students and staff). An appropriately funded office or position to coordinate anti-racist projects ensures consistency across the university and provides accountability for the university to act in accordance with its avowed values, as is typically reflected in a strategic plan. The alternative is that our issues are addressed as individual anomalies within an otherwise healthy (racism- and sexism-free) system, an approach that is consistent with color-blind ideology.

In my particular case, a more senior black woman colleague was my only source of support for many years. However, since she was not my official university mentor, and because her ability to help me depended on our ability to conceal how closely we worked together, the service she provided has never been recognized. This is particularly exploitative of underrepresented faculty, particularly women, because of the gendered division of service work in our universities (Guarino and Borden 2017). When an institution forces "race work" to be done "underground" in this manner, it is often other marginalized faculty, women of color in particular, who perform this unpaid and invisible labor at the expense of their own scholarly productivity (Joseph and Hirsh-field 2011). Even in cases where this work is visible as service, there is still the potential for exploitation owing to what Padilla (1994) refers to as cultural taxa-tion, a term used to refer to the added service responsibilities that accrue to faculty of color because of our ethnoracial backgrounds and underrepresenta-tion on historically white and male-dominated campuses. Since cultural taxa-tion has negative impacts on the career advancement and job satisfaction of women faculty and faculty of color, having an appropriately funded office or position for this kind of "race work" and "gender work" signifies that the insti-tution values this kind of work and is invested in protecting underrepresented faculty from the negative impacts of cultural taxation. It is equally important for this office or position to be vested with institutional power to make deci-sions that directly impact the well-being of faculty of color and women faculty, such as input into hiring policies and decisions. There is no way to perform effectively as an accountability mechanism without power to transform insti-tutional cultures designed to elevate and protect white male hegemony. This position or office would be responsible for carrying out the proactively anti-racist and anti-sexist agenda items described below.

2. *Institutionalize racism and sexism awareness and cultural competency workshops.*

Underrepresented faculty need access to agents with institutional power to help navigate racist and sexist microaggressions in masculinist, predominantly white, color-blind institutional spaces. Administrators should take seriously that racial and gender microaggressions are a logical outcome of a society that is both stratified and segregated by race and gender (Massey and Denton 1993; Oliver and Shapiro 2006; Risman 2004). Thus, white and male colleagues (and students) often have few opportunities to have their racial and gender stereo-types and assumptions, respectively, challenged. Orientation workshops for new faculty (and incoming students) and mandatory training for tenured faculty can, at a minimum, raise consciousness as to the most common "offenses" and why these are problematic.[7] I view the goal of the racism and sexism aware-ness and cultural competency workshops as minimizing the possibility for underrepresented faculty to be subjected to racial and gender microaggressions in their interactions with colleagues. These workshops will not erase a lifetime of socialization, and so proactively anti-racist and anti-sexist institutions (as opposed to color- and gender-blind ones) should have systems, policies, and mechanisms in place to address situations when they inevitably arise. For example, in the absence of an office or position at my current institution whose work focused on supporting and retaining marginalized faculty, when a colleague told me that my natural (black) hairstyle was unprofessional, there was no one to whom I felt safe reporting this information outside of two black female friends I had on campus who could only listen and empathize. There was no one to whom I felt comfortable reporting what became a pattern of gendered racial microaggressions that contributed to a hostile work environment, and I had no expectation that anything would be done even if I had reported these incidents to my chair or the person who served as dean at that time. If my institution had been proactively anti-racist, my colleague would have had some basic training to increase awareness that her racially insensitive statements were problematic, and why. When this person eventually became my chair, the psychological distress I experienced was magnified by the feeling of powerlessness to confront her abusive behavior because she had the power to harm me professionally. The university could have spared me the countless hours spent processing these offensive statements and strategizing whether or how to address them without causing myself more harm, *time that could have been used more productively on my teaching, research, and writing.*

3. *Institutionalize race talk as an anti-racist practice.*

Being proactively anti-racist means being vigilant about making white racial norms visible so that institutions can actively mitigate their negative impacts on racial and ethnically underrepresented faculty. White Americans' discomfort with, and therefore tendency to avoid, discussions about race and racial injustice is an example of such a white racial norm (Bonilla-Silva 2014). People of African descent talk frequently about racial inequality because it is part of our everyday life experiences. However, this "race talk" is taboo in predominantly white spaces because of the powerful influence of color-blind racial ideology, which equates race consciousness with racial prejudice. To protect our jobs, people of African descent often deliberately minimize our experiences with racism in predominantly white spaces, as drawing attention to our oppression makes our white colleagues uncomfortable and can have serious personal and professional consequences.[8] Yet, our silence causes us psychological distress and makes it possible for color-blind ideology to flourish unchallenged. Thus, creating a racially inclusive environment will require institutions to normalize discussions of racial injustices that manifest in the lives of marginalized faculty, while being attentive to how these experiences are shaped by gender and sexual orientation. This takes the burden off racially marginalized faculty and releases us from the fear that our experiences will be minimized or dismissed, or—worse—will instigate retaliation. Race talk can be institutionalized through the racism and sexism awareness and cultural competency workshops described above, new faculty orientations, and professional development for teaching that focuses explicitly on best practices for teaching about racism, sexism, and other potentially contentious issues.

4. *Provide race- and gender-conscious mentorship and support.*

An institution that aims to create systems of support that are proactively anti-racist and anti-sexist should ensure that the basic professional needs of all faculty are being met in a systematic way. This, at a minimum, entails communicating clear expectations of tenure and promotion standards, creating a strong mentoring program, and offering ample opportunities for professional development. This is important because mentors tend to gravitate to others who are most like them, and because race and gender are generally proxies for "sameness." Therefore, institutions that function on the assumption that mentorship relationships will form organically (i.e., blind to race and gender) are more likely to harm women and faculty of color (Bova 2000; Stanley and Lincoln 2005). Thus, institutionalizing mentoring is an anti-racist and anti-sexist practice because it disrupts the patterned ways in which underrepresented and women faculty tend to be excluded from informal mentoring networks. Even so, an institution that is proactively anti-oppression will design these basic support structures in an explicitly race- and gender-conscious way by addressing issues specific to marginalized faculty and/or by providing interventions for underrepresented faculty on issues that are salient only within this group. In order to do so, proactively anti-racist and anti-sexist institutions should invest in the expert knowledge of anti-racist and feminist scholars and organizations that might help codify a set of anti-racist and anti-sexist best practices. These best practices can guide the professional development of any individual or entity whose job is to mentor and/or evaluate underrepresented faculty, but in a way that is attentive to their intersecting identities.

It is impossible for a doctor to make a patient well if she is continually diagnosing the patient's symptoms incorrectly. Similarly, institutions fail to effectively mentor or support underrepresented faculty when they are unable to identify and diagnose the racist and sexist biases that manifest in the professional lives of underrepresented faculty, and how these biases intersect. While the expert knowledge referenced here can be conveyed in workshops similar to the racism and sexism awareness and cultural competency workshops described above, the goal here is to make visible the ways in which racial and gender biases manifest in the professional lives of marginalized faculty and the implications of this for mentoring and assessments. Thus, a proactively anti-racist and anti-sexist institution will ensure that department chairs, deans, tenure and promotion committees, and entities tasked with professional development of faculty be introduced to scholarship delineating the unique challenges of marginalized scholars in order to design race- and gender-conscious mentoring strategies and systems of evaluation. In particular, since many institutions draw on students' evaluations of teaching to assess faculty for merit pay, tenure, and promotion, it is critical for these entities to be familiar with the academic literature delineating how race and gender bias infuses student evaluations, as well as training on how to identify this bias in student comments.

5. *Institute race- and gender-conscious systems of evaluation.*

Institutions that insist on color- and gender-blind interpretations of marginalized faculty's evaluations are, in fact, practicing color-blind racism and gender-blind sexism. While these systems of evaluation are considered to be objective and neutral, they are more likely to paint us as incompetent, reinforcing dominant narratives of the deficits many assume we already have. This is potentially damaging psychologically to underrepresented faculty who may internalize hostile student comments and, as a result, decide to leave the professoriate. Additionally, poor student evaluations may contribute to racial and gender gaps in salary and promotion outcomes while at the same time concealing the discriminatory racial and gendered mechanisms that contribute to these gaps. Alternatively, institutions that approach student evaluations through a color- and gender-blind lens compel some marginalized faculty to learn literature outside our areas of specialization, just to defend ourselves against biased institutional policies and systems of evaluation. Thus, institutions that claim to value diversity and inclusion need to think about how or to what extent systems of evaluation are designed in ways that privilege whiteness and masculinity, and need to create race- and gender-conscious systems of evaluation. To do so effectively, higher education institutions should codify anti-racist logic and anti-sexist practices into policies and systems of evaluation that impact hiring, tenure, and promotion.

NOTES

I would like to thank my colleagues and writing group members Patricia Herrera and Eric Anthony Grollman for providing valuable feedback on earlier versions of this chapter.

1. I draw on the language of "gendered racism" throughout this chapter to signal that my blackness and my gender identity as a woman are interconnected dimensions of my social identity. For this reason, anti-sexist policies would not have helped address my negative racialized experiences. In fact, most of my departmental colleagues have been white women, and they have participated to varying degrees in the oppressive system that is the subject of this chapter. To make this point even more forcefully, in the fall of 2009 when I began my career at UR, 60 percent of the faculty were men and 40 percent were women. In contrast, 92 percent of the faculty were white and 8 percent were faculty of color. Additionally, I was one of three black assistant professors of the seventy-nine assistant professors at the university in the fall of 2009 (University of Richmond Fact Book 2010). As such, my recommendations at the end of this chapter focus primarily on how to improve the experi-

ences of racially marginalized and underrepresented faculty, even though these experiences are gendered.

2. My point here is to make visible systemic oppression; thus it is possible for faculty and students of color to also be complicit within a system that privileges whiteness, whether they intend to or not.

3. The experiences I describe in this chapter cover the period roughly between the fall of 2009 and the spring of 2014. In the fall of 2009, when I began my career at UR, students of color were 17 percent of the traditional undergraduate population and white students were 78 percent. In the fall of 2014, students of color were 25 percent of the student body (8 percent Latinx, 9 percent Asian, 7 percent black, and 1 percent Native American) and white students were 66 percent (Source: Official enrollment files, Office of Institutional Effectiveness at UR).

4. My midcourse review actually happened in my fourth year, as I had my tenure clock stopped for medical reasons.

5. At UR, all pre-tenure faculty are required to do annual performance reviews of their teaching, research, and service. Department chairs then write their own assessments of faculty and deliver both to the dean of arts and sciences. The dean's office makes the ultimate decision about the final merit score. Since my department is fairly small, it has been the practice for all tenured senior colleagues to weigh in on the narrative and the merit score for junior faculty. In other departments, the chair alone makes this decision. Pre-tenure faculty are told that annual reviews are primarily for the purpose of determining merit raises, since UR does not give standard-of-living raises. Even so, these reviews are included in our tenure package.

6. At UR, the midcourse review is an assessment of pre-tenure faculty's teaching, research, and service. However, the goal of the midcourse review is to provide feedback to pre-tenure faculty on progress toward tenure during the third year on the tenure track.

7. Universities should address microaggressions that target other marginalized groups, such as women and LGBTQ individuals. However, I do think it is more effective to focus on specific target groups in separate sessions.

8. See essays about the experiences of black faculty targeted by hate groups and generally unsupported by their institutions (e.g., Zandria Robinson, Saida Grundy).

REFERENCES

Bohmer, Susan, and Joyce L. Briggs. 1991. "Teaching Privileged Students about Gender, Race, and Class Oppression." *Teaching Sociology* 19 (2): 154–163.

Bonilla-Silva, Eduardo. 2014. *Racism without Racists: Color-Blind Racism and the Persistence of Racial Inequality in America.* Lanham, MD: Rowman & Littlefield.

Bova, Breda. 2000. "Mentoring Revisited: The Black Woman's Experience." *Mentoring and Tutoring* 8 (1): 5–16.

Collins, Patricia Hill. 2002. *Black Feminist Thought: Knowledge, Consciousness, and the Politics of Empowerment.* New York: Routledge.

Davis, Nancy J. 1992. "Teaching about Inequality: Student Resistance, Paralysis, and Rage." *Teaching Sociology* 20 (3): 232–238.

Desmond, Matthew, and Mustafa Emirbayer. 2010. *Racial Domination, Racial Progress: The Sociology of Race in America.* New York: McGraw-Hill.

Ford, Kristie A. 2011. "Race, Gender, and Bodily (Mis) Recognitions: Women of Color Faculty Experiences with White Students in the College Classroom." *Journal of Higher Education* 82 (4): 444–478.

Guarino, C. M., and V. M. Borden. 2017. Faculty Service Loads and Gender: Are Women Taking Care of the Academic Family? *Research in Higher Education* 58 (6): 672–694.

Gutiérrez y Muhs, Gabriella, Yolanda Niemann, Carmen González, and Angela Harris, eds. 2012. *Presumed Incompetent: The Intersections of Race and Class for Women in Academia*. Boulder: University of Colorado Press.

Hamermesh, Daniel, and Amy M. Parker. 2005. "Beauty in the Classroom: Instructors' Pulchritude and Putative Pedagogical Productivity." *Economics of Education Review* 24 (4): 369–376.

Harlow, Roxanna. 2003. "'Race Doesn't Matter, But . . .': The Effect of Race on Professors' Experiences and Emotion Management in the Undergraduate College Classroom." *Social Psychology Quarterly* 66 (4): 348–363.

Johnson-Bailey, Juanita, and Ming-Yeh Lee. 2005. "Women of Color in the Academy: Where's Our Authority in the Classroom?" *Feminist Teacher* 15 (2): 111–122.

Joseph, Tiffany, and Laura E. Hirshfield. 2011. "'Why Don't You Get Somebody New to Do It?' Race and Cultural Taxation in the Academy." *Ethnic and Racial Studies* 34 (1): 121–141.

Kelly-Woessner, April, and Matthew Woessner. 2006. "My Professor Is a Partisan Hack: How Perceptions of a Professor's Political Views Affect Student Course Evaluations." *PS: Political Science & Politics* 39 (3): 495–501.

Lazos, Sylvia. 2012. "Are Student Teaching Evaluations Holding Back Women and Minorities?" In *Presumed Incompetent: The Intersections of Race and Class for Women in Academia*, edited by Gabriella Gutiérrez y Muhs, Yolanda Niemann, Carmen González, and Angela Harris, 164–185. Boulder: University of Colorado Press, 2012.

Massey, Douglas S., and Nancy A. Denton. 1993. *American Apartheid: Segregation and the Making of the Underclass*. Cambridge, MA: Harvard University Press.

Matthew, Patricia A., ed. 2016. *Written/Unwritten: Diversity and the Hidden Truths of Tenure*. Chapel Hill: University of North Carolina Press.

Miller, Joanna, and Marylin Chamberlin. 2000. "Women Are Teachers, Men Are Professors: A Study of Student Perceptions." *Teaching Sociology* 28 (4): 283–298.

Oliver, Melvin L., and Thomas M. Shapiro. 2006. *Black Wealth, White Wealth: A New Perspective on Racial Inequality*. New York: Taylor & Francis.

Omi, Michael, and Howard Winant. 2014. *Racial Formation in the United States: From the 1960s to the 1990s*. New York: Routledge.

Padilla, Amado M. 1994. "Research News and Comment: Ethnic Minority Scholars; Research, and Mentoring: Current and Future Issues." *Educational Researcher* 23 (4): 24–27.

Patton, Tracey O. 2004. "Reflections of a Black Woman Professor: Racism and Sexism in Academia." *Howard Journal of Communications* 15 (3): 185–200.

Pittman, Chavella T. 2010. "Exploring How African American Faculty Cope with Classroom Racial Stressors." *Journal of Negro Education* 79 (1): 66–78.

———. 2012. "Racial Microaggressions: The Narratives of African American Faculty at a Predominantly White University." *Journal of Negro Education* 81 (1): 82–92.

Risman, B. J. 2004. "Gender as a Social Structure: Theory Wrestling with Activism." *Gender & Society* 18 (4): 429–450.

Sinclair, Lisa, and Ziva Kunda. 2000. "Motivated Stereotyping of Women: She's Fine If She Praised Me but Incompetent If She Criticized Me." *Personality and Social Psychology Bulletin* 26 (11): 1329–1342.

Smith, Bettye P. 2007. "Student Ratings of Teaching Effectiveness: An Analysis of End-of-Course Faculty Evaluations." *College Student Journal* 41 (4): 788–801.

Smith, Bettye P., and Billy Hawkins. 2011. "Examining Student Evaluations of Black College Faculty: Does Race Matter?" *Journal of Negro Education* 80 (2): 149–162.

Smith, William A. 2004. "Black Faculty Coping with Racial Battle Fatigue: The Campus Racial Climate in a Post-Civil Rights Era." In *A Long Way to Go: Conversations about Race by Afri-*

can *American Faculty and Graduate Students,* edited by Darrell Cleveland, 171–190. New York: Peter Lang Publishing.

Stanley, Christine A., and Yvonna S. Lincoln. 2005. "Cross-Race Faculty Mentoring." *Change* 37 (2): 44–50.

Sue, Derald, David Rivera, Nicole Watkins, Rachel Kim, Suah Kim, and Chantea Williams. 2011. "Racial Dialogues: Challenges Faculty of Color Face in the Classroom." *Cultural Diversity and Ethnic Minority Psychology* 17 (3): 331–340.

University of Richmond Fact Book 2009-10. 2010. Accessed December 19, 2017. https://ifx .richmond.edu/research/fact-book.html.

Wingfield, Adia H. 2010. "Are Some Emotions Marked 'Whites Only'? Racialized Feeling Rules in Professional Workplaces." *Social Problems* 57 (2): 251–268.

10 · "DIVERSITY" GOALS AND FACULTY OF COLOR

Supporting Racial Inclusion and Awareness in General Education Courses

MELANIE JONES GAST, ERVIN (MALIQ) MATTHEW, AND DERRICK R. BROOMS

"Diversity"—often referring to an increase in minority representation and the integration of students from different racial and ethnic backgrounds—is a well-known term in higher education and public discourse. While diversity is a frequent topic of conversation among Americans, such "diversity talk" often rests on the premise that we have achieved racial equality in American society and no longer need to think about how race intersects with ethnicity, gender, sexuality, class, or other types of social hierarchies (Bell and Hartmann 2007). This rhetoric hinders concrete efforts to implement "diversity" as a goal, especially in higher education (Berrey 2015). Indeed, many Americans believe in the abstract ideals of racial and ethnic integration but eschew connecting race to intersecting hierarchical systems or the need for race-based policies and efforts to address institutional racism, segregation, and oppression (Pew Research Center 2016).

College mission statements and language used by students, administrators, campus offices, and programs circulate ideas about the benefits of diversity and its purpose in higher education (Berrey 2015; Musil et al. 1999; Warikoo 2016). Officials attract students using the goal of diversity in websites, brochures, and other promotional material, and students use the concept as a way to measure campus excellence and worth (Berrey 2015; Warikoo 2016). A large body of research supports diversity as a goal, underscoring the benefits of a diverse undergraduate student body, as well as curriculum and programs focused on the content of race, ethnicity, and intergroup relations (see Gurin et al. 2002; Denson and Chang 2009; Harper and Hurtado 2007).

While administrators espouse diversity goals in mission statements and campus materials, there is often little concerted effort to address college students' awareness (or lack thereof) of race[1] and diversity issues on campus and in society. In this chapter we focus on introductory courses on race, diversity, and inequality, such as those taught in the humanities or social sciences, where college students of different majors and social identities regularly interact with these topics. As part of recent movements to add "diversity" components to undergraduate general education curriculums, these types of courses often fulfill the "multiculturalism" or "diversity" requirement for general-education programs (Nelson Laird 2005). Research suggests these courses provide myriad opportunities for students to develop critical thinking, analytical, and communication skills, and awareness with regard to race and other types of social differences (Musil et al. 1999; Chang 2002; Gurin et al. 2002; Nelson Laird 2005). In these courses, students engage in self-reflection, understand and appreciate social differences, and learn to situate themselves in the broader social world.

In particular, we focus on introductory sociology courses to highlight how faculty members[2] act as conduits through which colleges and universities wish to achieve diversity goals and work toward racial inclusion—the integration, understanding, and valuing of different racial groups as part of efforts to address racism, raise racial awareness, and mitigate oppression and exclusion in the learning environment. We detail our strategies in helping students navigate and understand the social construction of race and its intersection with other social categories, as well as impediments to managing these issues in the classroom, especially in historically white colleges and universities (HWCUs). We begin by discussing dominant frameworks in the United States with regard to race, diversity, and inequality that many students are exposed to before taking a college course on race. We then draw on our experiences as faculty of color who regularly teach these courses, and we detail the pedagogical strategies and issues that we negotiate. Finally, we outline lessons learned and suggestions for addressing these issues and developing institutional support for faculty and pedagogy in these courses.

COLLEGE STUDENTS AND DOMINANT RACIAL IDEOLOGY

Upon entering college, students are exposed to institutional messages about the benefits of diversity via campus websites and mission statements. Berrey (2011, 2015) shows how university administrators often acknowledge the benefits of diversity for a campus community; however, in doing so, they also replace race with other forms of difference—"cultures, religions, nationalities, and beliefs" (2011, 577). This type of rhetoric helps universities make minority representation and diversity goals appealing to campus members, but it also deprioritizes the needs of students, faculty, and staff of color. As Berrey (2015) notes, it "depict[s] racial minorities as culturally distinct from but culturally equivalent to white people" (77). Such rhetoric dismisses the need to tackle racial oppression and to support diverse students' understandings of and experiences with race (see Martínez Alemán and Salkever 2001).

Research on elite college students suggests that students interpret these messages about the value of "cultural" diversity in ways that undermine racial diversity and inclusion goals (Byrd 2017; Warikoo 2016). Warikoo (2016) finds that many elite white students, while drawing on color-blind and integrationist ideals, resent diversity programming unless it directly benefits them, and these students express tensions with and ambivalence toward racial inclusion efforts. This research points to the power of institutional messages and programming, and the interaction of students' race and other social positions, in shaping student interpretations of diversity goals and the contemporary need for race-related programming and curriculum. Colleges need to understand the multiple and intersecting identities of students and their different experiential understandings of diversity goals when implementing diversity programming.

Even while espousing diversity goals, colleges in many ways reproduce racial dominance and other types of oppression, disregard the existence of discrimination and oppression, and limit the achievement of diversity and inclusion goals. For example, research shows that university officials and administrators often downplay or dismiss the pervasiveness of racism and racial structures even while touting the benefits of racial diversity (Berrey 2015; Harper and Hurtado 2007; Brunsma, Embrick, and Thomas 2016). Additionally, a 2016 study of university executives found that higher education officials overwhelmingly provided glowing assessments of race relations on their campuses and believed that they had been addressing student grievances adequately (Jaschik and Lederman 2016). However, recent campus protests and candlelight vigils, such as the ones at the University of Missouri and the University of Virginia, highlight the prevailing nature of institutional racism and hostile racial climates on college campuses, as students demand that university leaders address racism and make colleges more accommodating to racial and ethnic minorities (Wong and Green 2016).

Through policies, practices, and rhetoric (or lack thereof), college leaders and staff, particularly in HWCUs, often inadvertently support white supremacy—the power, domination, and normalization of the white racial group in social institutions and everyday social life as part of our racialized social system (Bonilla-Silva 2001; Desmond and Emirbayer 2009). This occurs through invisible or obscured processes in the organization of higher education (Byrd 2017). As Brunsma, Brown, and Placier (2012) describe, "Most white students enter . . . surrounded by invisible walls that protect them from attacks on white supremacy," and HWCUs "bolster [these invisible walls] through curricular and extracurricular experiences, residential and disciplinary isolation, institutional symbols, cultural reproduction, and everyday practices" (718).

At the campus level, courses, centers, departments, and programs working to break down social barriers and oppression are often separate from core curriculum and main university events, making it difficult for students to routinely encounter and engage in these spaces (see Harper and Hurtado 2007). At the symbolic level, building names, statues, and other markers connected to white male supremacy are normalized into campus culture or are used to uphold the ideals of Jim Crow and white nationalism, as shown during the recent violence in Charlottesville, Virginia (see Bonilla-Silva 2012). Racial domination and other types of subordination also take on subtle forms in campus interactions. Women, racial and ethnic minorities, and LGBTQ (lesbian, gay, bisexual, transgender, and queer) students and faculty experience microaggressions, othering, and discrimination—often in forms that are difficult to name or conceptualize—in residence halls, Greek life, recreation centers, classrooms, offices, and other campus locations (Pittman 2012; Pasque et al. 2016; Harper 2015; Gutiérrez y Muhs et al. 2012). Although diversity goals are widespread across colleges and universities, many racial and ethnic minorities and marginalized populations do not feel safe, comfortable, or included in campus communities, and they face barriers to bringing their experiences to light in the institutional setting.

In contrast, white students often are exempt from racialized experiences in college or lack attention to issues related to race, diversity, and inequality (Harper and Hurtado 2007; Hurtado et al. 1998). Research finds that white youth and young adults tend to be apathetic toward race relations and racial inequality and tend to describe themselves as "raceless" or without a racial position (Forman and Lewis 2015; Warikoo 2016; Bonilla-Silva 2017). Students holding privileged statuses are often unaware of hierarchies related to race, class, gender, and sexuality, having learned before college to normalize privilege and oppression in school interactions and to dismiss power inequality from understandings of "race" in education (Pascoe 2007; Lewis 2003; Byrd 2017; Warikoo 2016).

Especially in HWCUs, college students have few spaces where they can carefully unpack and work through the concepts of race and diversity and the often subtle, persistent realities of racial domination and other types of oppression. Following color-blind logic, college students may believe in the principles of equal opportunity and diversity goals while still assuming that racism and oppression are in the past or operate through prejudiced individuals and overt behaviors (Bonilla-Silva 2017; Byrd 2017). Thus, the rationale is that structural inequality is muted if individuals "don't see color, just people." These students observed the 2008 election of Barack Obama, the first black president of the United States, signaling for many "the arrival of a 'post-racial' period . . . where racial background ceased to be a significant determining factor of one's outcomes . . . and life chances" (Wingfield and Feagin 2012, 143). Few have had opportunities to examine empirical evidence on the structural oppression of racial minorities in U.S. institutions, including housing, politics, and criminal justice (see, for example, Shapiro, Meschede, and Osoro 2013; Brown et al. 2003). Students may go through their college years "completely drained by the mixed-mediated messages about the importance of diversity and the necessity of colorblindness" (Halualani 2011, 47).

These dominant sets of ideas, along with general anxieties about offending others, engaging in confrontations, or relaying personal experiences, can impede engagement, learning, and dialogue in a course on race. Scholars argue that since these topics have long been taboo for whites and distressing for communities of color, "there is very little honest dialogue around race" (Fox 2014, 55). The polarizing nature of discussions about race and other social categories in politics today no doubt incites further emotions, unease, and resistance, especially when students misconstrue information presented in class as moral or political argument (Fobes and Kaufman 2008; Hedley and Markowitz 2001; Warikoo 2016). Students, regardless of racial and ethnic background, have most likely learned to avoid the topic of race or come at it with a heavy guard on.

Additionally, with rising racial segregation across public schools, including what scholars call second-generation segregation—segregation at the academic program or course level—many college students come from schools where they have had little interaction with peers of a different racial or ethnic background (Southworth and Mickelson 2007; Frankenberg and Orfield 2012). Even in diverse and "integrated" public schools that work toward tolerance, curricular tracking fosters racial divisions and limits race-based dialogue (Lewis and Diamond 2015). Students coming from segregated school environments are likely to enter college with a limited understanding of the significance of race in our society and the experiences of other racial and ethnic groups.

Finally, students may enter a college course on race with preconceived opinions about politicized issues, such as the Black Lives Matter movement or immigration policies, and draw on common racial fallacies when confronting course material (Goldsmith 2006; Fox 2014). Others may enter ready to discuss ideas and approaches that overtly challenge the legitimacy of white racial dominance (Wingfield and Feagin 2012). Instructors need to balance the variety of ideologies and assumptions, as well as the tensions and apprehensions, which are sure to play out in a course on race.

CRITICAL RACE PEDAGOGY

The three authors are faculty of color who research topics that include racial and ethnic identity, intersectionality, communities of color, and inequality in education. Together, we represent twenty-five years of independent college teaching experience. We currently teach at large, urban, public four-year universities, and work with students of diverse social backgrounds. Our teaching experiences also include teaching at private Catholic universities and a community college. We have taught courses on race and racial inequality, such as those titled Introduction to Sociology, Social Problems, Diversity and Inequality, Race in the U.S., Race and Ethnicity, The Immigrant Experience, Slavery and Racialization, Black Urban Communities, and Sociology of Education. Our large courses, such as Introduction to Sociology and Race in the U.S., have 55 to 140 students with no pre-requisites (as part of a general-education "diversity" requirement)—we focus on these courses in this chapter.

We engage with Critical Race Pedagogy (CRP) and intersectionality while working through the above-mentioned issues and fostering inter- and intra-racial dialogue and awareness. Lynn (1999) defines CRP as "an analysis of racial, ethnic, and gender subordination in education that relies mostly on the perceptions, experiences, and counterhegemonic practices of educators of color" (615). Playing a fundamental role in our teaching, intersectionality refers to the social, economic, and political structures in which identity-based systems of privilege and oppression connect, overlap, and influence one another. As Crenshaw (1989, 141) articulates, "Any analysis that does not take intersectionality into account cannot sufficiently address the particular manner" in which people's lives are narrowed down. We do not wish to disregard other pedagogical strategies that can be useful in a course on race; rather, we highlight these strategies given dominant ideologies with regard to race, diversity, and color blindness today and the significance of race as it intersects with class, gender, and other forms of domination.

Teaching from an intersectional framework and through a CRP perspective involves conscientious efforts to include work representing diverse scholars and perspectives, to allow opportunities for different student voices and types of engagement, and to connect and integrate different concepts and topics to facilitate and develop students' critical consciousness (see Ladson-Billings 1995). While syllabus length and the semester or quarter system limit us, and we cannot always address all intersecting social identities, we are diligent in the design and application of syllabuses, curriculum, assignments, and activities. In an Introduction to Sociology course or one where race is not the primary topic, we cannot risk treating race as a temporary diversion, and so we integrate the topic of race throughout the entire course. Likewise, analyses that incorporate class, gender, and other identities are infused throughout our courses to help students see how these identities intersect and compound people's experiences. Additionally, we do not simply separate each week based on racial categories (e.g., the "black week" or the "Asian American week"), but, rather, we integrate different racial groups and incorporate gender and class analyses into the study of racialization, racial domination, and other key course concepts.

We also include readings, videos, and discussions that focus on the perspectives of racial and ethnic minorities, while making efforts to include the intersecting nature of class, gender, and other social identities. For instance, we use Patricia Hill Collins (2009) and other women scholars of color to investigate black feminist epistemology, the Black Lives Matter movement, and other ways that gender and sexuality provide us with a lens to interrogate patriarchy and hegemony across social institutions. When we connect racial oppression to other forms of domination, we find that students from marginalized positions based on gender, class, or sexual orientation are able to link their experiences to the course material. These strategies help students look beyond the normalcy of whiteness and understand the significance of race as related to other social arenas and categories.

Teaching from and within a historical perspective is necessary to avoid the ahistorical component of color-blindness. In our current era with visions of a color-blind and "postracial" society, it can be easy to believe that racism, slavery, and colonialism are all part of the distant past and inconsequential for race relations today (Bonilla-Silva 2017). Moreover, while studies have shown the benefits of ethnic studies curriculums and historical perspectives of America's diverse racial and ethnic groups, especially at the high school level, these curriculums remain highly contested and unique to certain cities and school districts (Cabrera et al. 2014; Dee and Penner 2016). Students often enter a course on race with limited historical knowledge and an adherence to common racial fallacies (see Desmond and Emirbayer 2009).

While working through the social and historical constructions of race, we situate institutional structures in discussions of power, privilege, and social justice and help students understand the complexities and significance of racial hierarchy in the United States, as well as intersections with other identity categories and hierarchical systems. We are very methodical in working through racial ideologies that have become commonsense and in providing evidence to counter common racial fallacies, while also allowing students to discuss multiple perspectives and ideas. We use a variety of activities, including journaling, freewriting, multiple writing assignments, problem-oriented questions, and group discussions, that allow for the voicing of real-life experiences and diverse applications of topics and concepts (see, for example, Packard 2013; Goldsmith 2006; Picca, Starks, and Gunderson 2013; Lee et al. 2012).

As noted above, students are often apprehensive about discussing race, revealing personal ignorance or an offensive stance, or being judged based on perceived identities. Some may scorn others' closely held views about the societal relevance of race and racial inequality (or lack thereof) and about policies to address said inequality when it is verified. Therefore, it is important to help students do the following: (1) present ideas that may later be discovered as wrong or simplistic, (2) posit ideas that may offend others, and (3) acknowledge social realities as opposed to moral dichotomies (Hedley and Markowitz 2001; Lee et al. 2012). These strategies are in line with research on the importance of a collaborative pedagogical approach that bridges students' learning about core concepts like whiteness and privilege with intergroup dialogue (Ford 2012). We strive to include different student voices and create a safe space to openly explore ideas without fear of consequences such as threat or stigmatization. We also openly share our own vulnerability and openness to new ideas during these discussions.

Finally, we work toward inclusivity in a variety of other ways. White and middle-class privilege can translate to confidence when interacting with authority figures; meanwhile, racial minority, immigrant, and working-class students face difficulties in communicating with professors (see Jack 2016). We make considerable efforts to keep lines of communication open and engage students through a variety of methods, rather than using the normative form of communication during office hours or class lectures. These strategies can help facilitate engagement and dialogue for diverse students.

CONSTRAINTS AND LIMITATIONS OF FACULTY OF COLOR

Our pedagogical approaches and strategies are not always perfect or free from constraints. It is important to note the limitations that we as faculty, especially as faculty of color, face in acting as the conduits through which colleges and universities hope to achieve diversity goals. There are the external constraints—two of us are untenured faculty and are especially cognizant of things like student evaluations, time spent on teaching, institutional systems of evaluation, and institutional vulnerabilities when adopting a CRP (Fobes and Kaufman 2008). For example, past research shows that in courses on anti-racism and white privilege, "students often reject both message and messenger, projecting their frustrations and emotions about this topic onto instructors" through course evaluations (Boatright-Horowitz and Soeung 2009, 575).

Issues and constraints also exist inside the classroom, especially in a course on race and diversity. Gender, race, ethnicity, age, class, sexuality, political orientation, and other social identities are intersectional and performative. The faculty-student relationship and how students engage with and respond to material are influenced by student perceptions of instructors' social identities (Pittman 2010, 2012). As a small, young-looking Asian American professor, the first author has experienced onslaughts to her authority and status as an expert in the field. In her general-education courses, students have written things in evaluations like "She's a sweet lady," while then discrediting her teaching competence and expertise. In contrast, the second author, an African American male, is able to maintain a casual interactional style without having it influence his course evaluations. However, he has experienced other types of student resistance, such as during discussions about social policies or the Black Lives Matter movement, as students seem to interpret his identity as representing a political standpoint rather than an academic position. While we utilize various strategies to address these issues, we must recognize intersecting faculty identities, as well as students' preconceived ideas about how they understand the credibility of faculty and course material (Hendrix 1997; Gutiérrez y Muhs et al. 2012).

CONCLUSION

Situated between administrators and students, faculty members facilitate inter-actional diversity and, through teaching, help students understand the nature of diversity and racial domination and inequality in society. Faculty members work directly and regularly with students, and their efforts to engage and interact with students can be the primal points of diversity and inclusion that colleges and universities wish to achieve. Thus, faculty members remain on the front lines as critical institutional agents engaging institutional diversity goals.

How faculty incorporate race, racism, and inequality into the curriculum matters. College courses on race provide many students with their first opportunities for meaningful cross-racial interaction and for obtaining in-depth academic knowledge to better understand race, intersectionality, racism, and the current context of diversity in the United States. Studies suggest that diversity courses and initiatives can have positive effects for improving students' interests in racial understanding and appreciation for multiple cultures, as well as for reducing prejudice, especially toward African Americans (Chang 2002; Hurtado 1996; Villalpando 1994). Given the prevailing "walls of whiteness" in higher education, without intentional efforts, students will have difficulty seeing and understanding racial privilege and oppression and making sense of their place and potential in racial justice and diversity efforts (Brunsma et al. 2012).

As researchers contend, institutional efforts must move beyond a focus on compositional and representational diversity and instead create multiple opportunities for interactional diversity and working toward racial dialogue and awareness (Tatum 2015; Harper and Hurtado 2007; Byrd 2017). In these interactions, and in realizing intended benefits of such interactions, attention must be paid to issues of power, privilege, intersectionality, and social justice (Gurin et al. 2002). Critical race pedagogy can help in addressing these issues within and beyond a "diversity" course (Brunsma, Brown, and Placier 2012; Lynn 1999).

Implications for Administrative Efforts, Faculty, and "Diversity" Courses

Given the long-term, multifaceted ways that students have been exposed to dominant ideologies and the limited length of a semester- or quarter-long course, faculty face constraints in breaking down ideological fortifications and working toward racial awareness and inclusion on their own (Brunsma, Brown, and Placier 2012). Based on our experiences as faculty of color teaching issues centered on race and diversity for many years, we make the following suggestions to help faculty teaching within a university's "diversity" agenda and to aid administrators and other university members in supporting faculty pedagogy in "diversity" courses.

First, instead of placing responsibility for executing diversity missions on one office or limiting student exposure to one "diversity" course, creating and sustaining the integration of diverse groups and the inclusion of their histories, voices, and experiences must be part of long-term, multi-pronged institutional efforts across offices, disciplines, and courses. We find that many students have only just begun to understand the salience of race and engage in racial dialogue by the end of our courses. Better integrating offices, courses, and learning goals that focus on race and diversity into the institutional fabric and curricular structures of universities will help students further develop skills to understand and navigate racial realities and issues related to intersectionality. Engagement in racial dialogue and awareness, as well as meaningful social justice work, requires in-depth and prolonged conversations and efforts *across* the curriculum and different university members.

Second, college administrators and curriculum committees should expand required courses and consider their support (and hiring) systems for faculty (tenure-track, term, and adjunct) committed to racial diversity and inclusion goals. College administrators also should establish greater accountability and support for all faculty to engage in these efforts. Faculty must have departmental and institutional support for teaching these types of courses and incorporating effective and inclusive pedagogical strategies. Given the constraints on faculty teaching "diversity" courses, administrators should rethink some of the existing evaluation models to better assess teaching in these courses. Opportunities should be provided for *all* faculty to enhance their teaching praxis and learn from others; tenure-track faculty need additional support during their probationary period. These efforts could include time and resources allocated for co-teaching, exchanging syllabuses, and teaching seminars, workshops, and institutes addressing intersectionality, diversity and inclusion efforts, and teaching praxis.

Third, all faculty members can create spaces for diverse students to come together and engage in difficult conversations about race and other identity categories. Additionally, faculty members should create classroom environments inclusive of authors and perspectives across different identity locations while helping students understand and work through issues related to power inequality, intersectionality, privilege, and oppression. Faculty also should incorporate both historical and contemporary issues to help students make sense of race, other social constructs, and their intersections. We believe that using inquiry-based instruction, discussion-centered teaching practices, and critical and inclusive pedagogy can enhance student learning (Lynn 1999; Ladson-Billings 1995; Fobes and Kaufman 2008).

And, fourth, faculty of color, especially junior or adjunct faculty, who typically are underrepresented, under-resourced, and overstretched on many college campuses, often teach "diversity" courses. Administrators should make structural adjustments to support and enhance the teaching efforts of these faculty members and their engagement in these types of courses. Often, general education and introductory courses that meet a "diversity" requirement are large in size (e.g., 140 students), which can make it difficult to achieve meaningful cross-racial dialogue and interaction. Colleges and universities need to consider how the structure of courses focused on race can be adapted to enhance student engagement in difficult and critical conversations. Faculty pedagogy in these courses requires additional time and effort. Institutional systems of evaluation need to value faculty techniques in these types of courses and consider how faculty of color face barriers to meeting standardized norms for course evaluations. Colleges could provide support and opportunities for these courses to be co-taught, which can enhance students' in-class experiences and the pedagogical techniques used by faculty members. Co-taught classes can allow two faculty members with complementary knowledge bases and skills to create a dynamic and engaging class/classroom environment.

Implications for Institutional Climate

Students take their cues in engaging with and understanding racial diversity and inclusion from the institutional climate. As noted above, recent studies show that university officials often provide glowing assessments of race relations on their campuses or espouse diversity goals without engaging in concrete and concerted efforts to address issues related to intersectionality, inequality, and oppression. While "diversity talk" has become prominent on college campuses, colleges are often exclusionary and hostile to students who hold marginalized statuses. Institutional culture can influence how students engage in discussions on race and racism *even in* classes that focus on these topics. Colleges must move beyond addressing compositional diversity to focus on racial inclusion and awareness and the shared understanding of how race affects the entire campus community. Thus, as a community, institutions need to do more to help students understand how and why racial inclusion and awareness matter, while also offering greater support for faculty working toward those goals.

NOTES

1. We recognize that the concepts of race and ethnicity are interwoven and important in these types of courses. However, given the salience of race and racialization in college and broader society, and the fact that our "diversity" courses center on race, we focus on race in this chapter.
2. While we focus on the conditions and strategies of tenured and tenure-track professors given our own faculty positions, it is important to note that non-tenure-track instructors share similar conditions and strategies.

REFERENCES

Bell, Joyce M., and Douglas Hartmann. 2007. "Diversity in Everyday Discourse: The Cultural Ambiguities and Consequences of 'Happy Talk.'" *American Sociological Review* 72 (6): 895–914.

Berrey, Ellen. 2015. *The Enigma of Diversity: The Language of Race and the Limits of Racial Justice*. Chicago: University of Chicago Press.

Boatright-Horowitz, Su L., and Sojattra Soeung. 2009. "Teaching White Privilege to White Students Can Mean Saying Good-Bye to Positive Student Evaluations." *American Psychologist* 64 (6): 574–575.

Bonilla-Silva, Eduardo. 2001. *White Supremacy and Racism in the Post-Civil Rights Era*. Boulder, CO: Lynne Rienner Publishers.

———. 2012. "The Invisible Weight of Whiteness: The Racial Grammar of Everyday Life in Contemporary America." *Ethnic and Racial Studies* 35 (2): 173–194.

———. 2017. *Racism without Racists: Color-Blind Racism and the Persistence of Racial Inequality in America*. 5th ed. Lanham, MD: Rowman & Littlefield.

Brown, Michael K., Martin Carnoy, Elliott Currie, Troy Duster, and David B. Oppenheimer. 2003. *Whitewashing Race: The Myth of a Color-Blind Society*. Berkeley: University of California Press.

Brunsma, D. L., E. S. Brown, and P. Placier. 2012. "Teaching Race at Historically White Colleges and Universities: Identifying and Dismantling the Walls of Whiteness." *Critical Sociology* 39 (5): 717–738.

Brunsma, David L., David G. Embrick, and James M. Thomas. 2016. "College Leaders Think Race Relations Suck—Except on Their Campuses." *Slate.com*. Accessed November 4, 2016: https://slate.com/human-interest/2016/09/college-leaders-say-race-relations-on-their-campuses-are-just-fine.html.

Byrd, W. Carson. 2017. *Poison in the Ivy: Race Relations and the Reproduction of Inequality on Elite College Campuses*. New Brunswick, NJ: Rutgers University Press.

Cabrera, N. L., J. F. Milem, O. Jaquette, and R. W. Marx. 2014. "Missing the (Student Achievement) Forest for All the (Political) Trees: Empiricism and the Mexican American Studies Controversy in Tucson." *American Educational Research Journal* 51 (6): 1084–1118.

Chang, Mitchell J. 2002. "The Impact of an Undergraduate Diversity Course Requirement on Students' Racial Views and Attitudes." *Journal of General Education* 51 (1): 21–42.

Collins, Patricia Hill. 2009. *Black Feminist Thought: Knowledge, Consciousness, and the Politics of Empowerment*. 2nd ed. New York: Routledge.

Crenshaw, Kimberle. 1989. "Demarginalizing the Intersection of Race and Sex: A Black Feminist Critique of Antidiscrimination Doctrine, Feminist Theory and Antiracist Politics." *University of Chicago Legal Forum* 1 (8): 139–167.

Dee, T. S., and E. K. Penner. 2016. "The Causal Effects of Cultural Relevance: Evidence from an Ethnic Studies Curriculum." *American Educational Research Journal* 54 (1): 127–166.

Denson, Nida, and Mitchell Chang. 2009. "Racial Diversity Matters: The Impact of Diversity-Related Student Engagement and Institutional Context." *American Educational Research Journal* 46 (2): 322–353.

Desmond, Matthew, and Mustafa Emirbayer. 2009. "What Is Racial Domination?" *Du Bois Review: Social Science Research on Race* 6 (2): 335–355.

Fobes, Catherine, and Peter Kaufman. 2008. "Critical Pedagogy in the Sociology Classroom: Challenges and Concerns." *Teaching Sociology* 36 (1): 26–33.

Ford, Kristie A. 2012. "Shifting White Ideological Scripts: The Educational Benefits of Inter- and Intraracial Curricular Dialogues on the Experiences of White College Students." *Journal of Diversity in Higher Education* 5 (3): 138–158.

Forman, T. A., and A. E. Lewis. 2015. "Beyond Prejudice? Young Whites' Racial Attitudes in Post-Civil Rights America, 1976 to 2000." *American Behavioral Scientist* 59 (11): 1394–1428.

Fox, Helen. 2014. *"When Race Breaks Out": Conversations about Race and Racism in College Classrooms*. 2nd rev. ed. New York: Peter Lang.

Frankenberg, Erica, and Gary Orfield. 2012. *The Resegregation of Suburban Schools: A Hidden Crisis in American Education.* Cambridge, MA: Harvard Education Press.

Goldsmith, Pat Antonio. 2006. "Learning to Understand Inequality and Diversity: Getting Students Past Ideologies." *Teaching Sociology* 34 (3): 263–277.

Gurin, Patricia, Eric L. Dey, Sylvia Hurtado, and Gerald Gurin. 2002. "Diversity and Higher Education: Theory and Impact on Educational Outcomes." *Harvard Educational Review* 72 (3): 330–366.

Gutiérrez y Muhs, Gabriella, Yolanda Flores Niemann, Carmen G. González, and Angela P. Harris. 2012. *Presumed Incompetent: The Intersections of Race and Class for Women in Academia.* Logan: Utah State University Press.

Halualani, Rona Tamiko. 2011. "In/visible Dimensions: Framing the Intercultural Communication Course through a Critical Intercultural Communication Framework." *Intercultural Education* 22 (1): 43–54.

Harper, Shaun R. 2015. "Black Male College Achievers and Resistant Responses to Racist Stereotypes at Predominantly White Colleges and Universities." *Harvard Educational Review* 85 (4): 646–674.

Harper, Shaun R., and Sylvia Hurtado. 2007. "Nine Themes in Campus Racial Climates and Implications for Institutional Transformation." *New Directions for Student Services* 2007 (120): 7–24.

Hedley, Mark, and Linda Markowitz. 2001. "Avoiding Moral Dichotomies: Teaching Controversial Topics to Resistant Students." *Teaching Sociology* 29 (2): 195–208. doi: 10.2307/1318717.

Hendrix, Katherine Grace. 1997. "Student Perceptions of Verbal and Nonverbal Cues Leading to Images of Black and White Professor Credibility." *Howard Journal of Communications* 8 (3): 251–273.

Hurtado, Sylvia. 1996. "How Diversity Affects Teaching and Learning." *Educational Record* 66 (4): 27–29.

Hurtado, Sylvia, Jeffrey F. Milem, Alma R. Clayton-Pedersen, and Walter R. Allen. 1998. "Enhancing Campus Climates for Racial/Ethnic Diversity: Educational Policy and Practice." *Review of Higher Education* 21 (3): 279–302.

Jack, Anthony Abraham. 2016. "(No) Harm in Asking: Class, Acquired Cultural Capital, and Academic Engagement at an Elite University." *Sociology of Education* 89 (1): 1–19.

Jaschik, Scott, and Doug Lederman. 2016. *The 2016 Inside Higher Ed Survey of College and University Presidents.* Washington, DC: Inside Higher Ed.

Ladson-Billings, Gloria. 1995. "Toward a Theory of Culturally Relevant Pedagogy." *American Educational Research Journal* 32 (3): 465–491. doi:10.3102/00028312032003465.

Lee, Amy, Robert Poch, Marta Shaw, and Rhiannon D. Williams. 2012. "Special Issue: Engaging Diversity in Undergraduate Classrooms—A Pedagogy for Developing Intercultural Competence." *ASHE Higher Education Report* 38 (2): 1–132.

Lewis, Amanda. 2003. *Race in the Schoolyard: Negotiating the Color Line in Classrooms and Communities.* New Brunswick, NJ: Rutgers University Press.

Lewis, Amanda, and John B. Diamond. 2015. *Despite the Best Intentions: How Racial Inequality Thrives in Good Schools.* New York: Oxford University Press.

Lynn, Marvin. 1999. "Toward a Critical Race Pedagogy: A Research Note." *Urban Education* 33 (5): 606–626.

Martínez Alemán, Ana M., and Katya Salkever. 2001. "Multiculturalism and the Mission of Liberal Education." *Journal of General Education* 50 (2): 102–139.

Musil, C. M., M. Garcia, C. A. Hudguns, M. T. Nettles, W. E. Sedlacek, and D. Smith. 1999. *To Form a More Perfect Union: Campus Diversity Initiatives.* Washington, DC: Association of American Colleges and Universities.

Nelson Laird, Thomas F. 2005. "College Students' Experiences with Diversity and Their Effects on Academic Self-Confidence, Social Agency, and Disposition toward Critical Thinking." *Research in Higher Education* 46 (4): 365–387. doi:10.1007/s11162-005-2966-1.

Packard, Josh. 2013. "The Impact of Racial Diversity in the Classroom: Activating the Sociological Imagination." *Teaching Sociology* 41 (2): 144–158.

Pascoe, C. J. 2007. *Dude, You're a Fag: Masculinity and Sexuality in High School.* Berkeley: University of California Press.

Pasque, Penny A., Noe Ortega, John C. Burkhardt, Marie P. Ting, and Phillip Bowman. 2016. *Transforming Understandings of Diversity in Higher Education: Demography, Democracy, and Discourse.* Sterling, VA: Stylus Publishing. http://public.eblib.com/choice/publicfullrecord .aspx?p=4676917.

Pew Research Center. 2016. "On Views of Race and Inequality, Blacks and Whites are Worlds Apart." Accessed March 1, 2017: http://www.pewsocialtrends.org/2016/06/27/on-views-of -race-and-inequality-blacks-and-whites-are-worlds-apart/.

Picca, L. H., B. Starks, and J. Gunderson. 2013. "'It Opened My Eyes': Using Student Journal Writing to Make Visible Race, Class, and Gender in Everyday Life." *Teaching Sociology* 41 (1): 82–93.

Pittman, Chavella T. 2010. "Race and Gender Oppression in the Classroom: The Experience of Women Faculty of Color with White Male Students." *Teaching Sociology* 38 (3): 183–196.

Pittman, Chavella T. 2012. "Racial Microaggressions: The Narratives of African American Faculty at a Predominantly White University." *Journal of Negro Education* 81 (1): 82–92.

Shapiro, Thomas, Tatjana Meschede, and Sam Osoro. 2013. *The Roots of the Widening Racial Wealth Gap: Explaining the Black-White Economic Divide.* Waltham, MA: Institute on Assets and Social Policy.

Southworth, Stephanie, and Roslyn Arlin Mickelson. 2007. "The Interactive Effects of Race, Gender and School Composition on College Track Placement." *Social Forces* 86 (2): 497–523.

Tatum, Beverly. 2015. "Breaking the Silence." In *White Privilege: Essential Readings on the Other Side of Racism,* edited by Paula S. Rothenberg, 195–201. New York: Worth Publishers.

Villalpando, Octavio. 1994. "Comparing the Effects of Multiculturalism and Diversity on Minority and White Students' Satisfaction with College." Paper presented at the Annual Meeting of the Association for the Study of Higher Education. November, Tuscon, AZ.

Warikoo, Natasha Kumar. 2016. *The Diversity Bargain: And Other Dilemmas of Race, Admissions, and Meritocracy at Elite Universities.* Chicago: University of Chicago Press.

Wingfield, Adia Harvey, and Joe Feagin. 2012. "The Racial Dialectic: President Barack Obama and the White Racial Frame." *Qualitative Sociology* 35 (2): 143–162.

Wong, Alia, and Adrienne Green. 2016. "Campus Politics: A Cheat Sheet." *The Atlantic.* Accessed March 1, 2017: https://www.theatlantic.com/education/archive/2016/04/campus-protest -roundup/417570/.

11 · PURSUING INTERSECTIONALITY AS A PEDAGOGICAL TOOL IN THE HIGHER EDUCATION CLASSROOM

ORKIDEH MOHAJERI, FERNANDO
RODRIGUEZ, AND FINN SCHNEIDER

I sit at my desk before the first class session of the semester, battling internal and external scripts of worthiness, "Who am I to be teaching a course at this institution?" As a first-generation Mexican American gay man from the U.S.-Mexico border, statistically speaking, I should not be in the academy. I scroll through photos of my students to familiarize myself with their names and faces. As I consider my identities and how my students might receive me, it strikes me, I will probably be the only Mexican American instructor these students will see at the university and perhaps their entire journey in higher education.

If I show up "too gay," will I ostracize students? How might my Latinxness/ Mexican heritage come into conflict with students who support building a wall along the U.S.-Mexico border? How will I relate to the many students who come from socioeconomic backgrounds far more privileged than anything I am familiar with? These questions press on me, and no lesson plan, syllabus, or learning objective contains the answers.

The above vignette captures the preparation process for one instructor before teaching his first class session of a course offered at a predominantly white institution (PWI) of higher education in the United States. In this evocative portrait of Fernando's first day of teaching, he pauses to consider the various intersections of his identities in context with the demographic makeup of his class, consciously weighing how these are likely to affect students, his own sense of authenticity, and the curricular materials that this group of learners will cover together over the course of the semester.

What are safe identities? Which intersections of race and class are likely to be welcomed, and which are likely to create distance between instructor and students? How will heteropatriarchy, white supremacy, and other power formations show up in the classroom? How can Fernando use his dress, his performance of masculinity, his positional power as instructor, or his emotional labor of kindness to bridge the gaps of difference? What ideas, images, and enactments of queerness have these students been exposed to in the past, and which do they accept and welcome? What ideas and images of "Mexican" have these students been exposed to? Do they have any idea what it means to live at a physical border between two countries, and these two countries in particular? The classroom becomes a site for the interplay of contentious politics, racial tension, queerness, and class divides. Fernando is simultaneously empowered and disempowered as he takes on roles of authority and expertise in the academic hierarchy.

In this chapter, we use vignettes to provide insight into four years of experience gained while teaching undergraduate leadership courses at a PWI. Having taught sections of the course together and individually, we employ intersectionality as a lens through which we question and explore how we connected to learners and the curriculum. After first describing the course and its participants, we introduce the concepts of intersectionality, power formations, and silence and explore how and when these were taken up in our classrooms. The chapter concludes with possibilities for intentionally taking up intersectionality as a pedagogical tool.

THE COURSE

This course focuses on individual and group leadership capacities (Heifetz and Linsky 2002; Komives and Wagner 2009). One of the threads that run throughout the curriculum is case-in-point teaching, where the classroom is treated as a laboratory for social learning, experimentation, and analysis. This "container" or experimental space is built up over the academic term through a variety of activities, coupled with intentional in-class analysis of social dynamics and default behaviors. Many sections of the course are co-taught, with two instructors teaching, grading, and learning from one another in an integrated manner. Some sections are taught by just one instructor, but only after the instructor has had at least one semester of co-teaching as a foundation to ground and orient them to the course, its culture, and objectives. Even in semesters of individual instruction, there are both formal and informal spaces for instructor training, collaboration, debriefing, and co-learning.

Students from all undergraduate years and diverse majors enroll in this course. They come with a wide range of racial and ethnic backgrounds, including white,

Latinx, Hmong, Somali, African American, Asian American, and multiracial students. A sizable number of the students hail from rural communities in the upper Midwest. Most students tend to be between eighteen and twenty-one years of age. Diversity along spectrums of gender, class, nationality, ethnicity, sexual orientation, religion, ability, and immigration/refugee status shows up in these spaces too. A strong local cultural dynamic values polite, public social interaction above direct communication, especially around potentially contentious topics. We name structural components of the larger social context and our students' lived experiences in an attempt to portray the complex makeup of the class environment. This range of identities and social forces begins to unveil the complex intersections at play in the classroom space.

The three authors have each taught and co-taught sections of this course. Orkideh is a 1.5 generation female immigrant. Her phenotype is not white and generally Middle Eastern, although she is often judged as Latinx, Spanish, or Greek and can be read as Native American. Over the past decade, Orkideh believes she has been increasingly recognized as Middle Eastern. She speaks unaccented English and occupies a position of authority as instructor for the course. She hails from one of the Middle East's numerous religious minority populations, and this complicates how her body is read and understood by others, especially in today's contentious political climate. There is a double consciousness (Du Bois [1903] 2012) that she carries, aware that she is increasingly racialized as Muslim and feeling a desire to counteract new/old Orientalist conceptualizations of Islam and Muslims (Said 1978) while simultaneously representing a marginalized population of the Middle East / North Africa region.

Fernando is a first-generation Mexican American gay man. His phenotype is not white, and he is read as Latinx and male. He speaks unaccented English and occupies a position of authority as course instructor. Fernando can play up or play down his queerness, depending on dress, voice, enactments of masculinity, and other factors. Fernando can play up or play down his "Mexicanness," depending on dress, language, accent, cultural accoutrement, and more. Fernando was born and raised on the U.S.-Mexico border, a space rich with implications of race, class, masculinity, and citizenship. Fernando also feels an obligation and responsibility for how he presents his various identities and for how he is read by others.

finn is a white, queer, transgenderqueer doctoral student from a small town in the Midwest. They were raised in a Catholic, middle-class, blended family by parents with graduate degrees and experience navigating formalized educational contexts. Across time and space, finn's gender and sexuality are perceived in varying ways, ranging from and between butch lesbian, gay cisgender man, heterosexual transman, and queer nonbinary. While their nonbinary gender creates many possibilities for taking up masculinity and/or femininity intentionally to disrupt cisnormative notions of gender, finn is routinely perceived and engaged by strangers as a white (cis)man. The enmeshed power formations of cisgenderism, white supremacy, and heteropatriarchy result in finn experiencing simultaneous privilege and oppression; finn experiences white male privilege based on how students perceive them while at the same time being invisibilized and marginalized in their transness and queerness.

The authors of this piece share some intersections, but not others. Mostly we share the reality that each of us embodies simultaneously subordinated identities and has a history of being othered by enactments of white supremacy and heteropatriarchy. We share the experiences of reflecting on power formations in larger society and our intersectional identities, as we labor in higher education spaces to contribute to the betterment of society.

WHITE SUPREMACY

It is important to position white supremacy at the forefront of our analysis. In brief, white supremacy promulgates "the mythic superiority of Whites and [the] equally false inferiority of people of color" (Leonardo 2013, 95). While U.S. higher education has grown somewhat open to discussions of white privilege, it is still quite resistant to acknowledging the power and operations of white supremacy (Brunsma, Brown, and Placier 2012; Harper 2012). Instead, white supremacy is relegated to the realms of overt hate crimes such as anti-Semitic graffiti sprayed on campus property or KKK and neo-Nazi rallies sensationalized on television. While frameworks focused on white privilege and normative whiteness do shed light on the manifestations of structural racism, we argue they do not go far enough in critiquing the underlying power dynamics of systemic racism and naming whites' role in creating and maintaining structural racism.

Leonardo (2013) uses the framework of "White educational supremacy" to expand possibilities for critiquing institutions that, while not white supremacist in the traditional, active sense, nevertheless prioritize white interests. Education is one such institution. Both historically and contemporarily, education operates with a white supremacy paradigm. In calling for a critical examination of racial inequities in education, Leonardo (2013, 95) asserts that "favoring the explanatory framework of racial supremacy neither exaggerates nor understates this racial predicament but names it in the most realistic way possible that accounts for current racial arrangements."

INTERSECTIONALITY

Intersectionality originates from black feminist scholars and can be conceptualized as "the commitment to centering research and analysis on the lived experiences of women of color for the purpose of making visible and addressing their marginalization" (Alexander-Floyd 2012, 9). Instead of analyzing identities as independent, single-axis (May 2015) categories of difference that can be ranked hierarchically, intersectionality seeks to tell the location of "interlocking structures of oppression" (Collins et al. 1995, 492). Intersectionality emphasizes matrix thinking in a single-axis world and focuses on multiplicity and simultaneity (May 2015). It shows that privilege and oppression can be experienced simultaneously. Intersectionality is a heuristic that can be used to examine how unequal social structures mutually construct each other (Bowleg 2008; Collins and Bilge 2016; May 2015). Intersectionality can be used to examine the operations of power on interpersonal, disciplinary, cultural, and structural levels (Collins and Bilge 2016).

While acknowledging that intersectionality grew out of a call to focus on the multiply oppressed experiences of black women (Crenshaw 1993; May 2015), like other scholars before us, we attempt to bring this concept to bear on our experiences with power and marginalization in the classroom. It is important to note that we do so with hesitation, as we are committed to honoring and learning from the uniquely interlocked positions of black women in the United States. At the same time, there is value in extending this heuristic to new categories of subordination, including "Mexican," "border," "gender," and "Muslim," especially as these interlock with sexuality, class, and race in the context of a settler-colonial, global capitalist U.S. society. Below is a series of vignettes from the classroom. We share this self-reflection and analysis with the hope of complicating the discourse in higher education literature around pedagogy, power formations, intersectionality, and identity.

VIGNETTE: ISLAMOPHOBIA AND SILENCE

We are doing introductions on the first day of class, and I am taken aback by one student's question of another student: "So what holy book do those people follow?" I suck my breath in sharply and hold it. This white, cisgender male student—who had moments earlier identified himself as Christian and devout—was now asking a darker-hued, cisgender female student if she was Muslim! He was forcing her to identify her religion.

What do I do now? Do I interrupt? If I say something, will other students assume that I am Muslim as well, and therefore think I am being defensive? What will this do to my connections with other students for the rest of the term? On the other hand, how can I let this student suffer alone? Before I can decide, the student begins to answer, and oh, she is good! Gracefully, she describes the significant religious diversity of her home country, with percentages, geographic reference, and respect, and then she claims her Muslim identity. She never even answers the question about the Quran directly.

The vignette above captures Orkideh's perception of an instance of othering on the first day of class. Several seemingly white students had just introduced themselves and included Christianity as a primary part of their identities. Moments later, a darker-skinned female student offered up her introduction and mentioned that her parents were immigrants from another country. Mid-introduction, the student was interrupted and pressed to redefine herself. The interruption sought to determine exactly how foreign, how other, and how dangerous the student was. This interaction was clearly a microaggression directed toward the young woman. Sue (2010) describes microaggressions as commonplace, daily slights that are either consciously or unconsciously delivered against people of color. These assaults cause considerable psychological and emotional pain for victims (Byrd 2007; Salvatore and Shelton 2007; Solórzano, Ceja, and Yosso 2000; Utsey and Ponterotto 1996). The questioning, the othering, the requests for justification and explanation build up over time, and remind victims that they are either not comprehensible or not welcome.

For the instructor, there was a significant moment of silence in the episode above. Orkideh wondered if she should shift weight into her Middle Eastern phenotype to defend a student who was being microaggressed, or if she should shift away from her Muslim-looking appearance in order to hold the future possibility of connection with other learners in the classroom community. The silence also held an element of "masking" (Montoya 1994, 2000) as Orkideh chose to mask her own minoritized religious identity. Her dress and demeanor do not belie any specific faith affiliation, and students did not explicitly know her religious affiliation, but possibly assumed that she is Muslim because of her Middle Eastern facial features. Orkideh wonders how much her masking was sourced in fear. Namely, in an increasingly anti-Muslim environment where people are more frequently able to distinguish her from a Latinx or North Indian body, to what extent is masking really an attempt to set herself aside from a group that is increasingly criminalized and scapegoated?

While choosing silence, at least for a time, the instructor was also choosing to let go of other opportunities, such as that of naming Islamophobia, Christian normativity, or the interplay of gender and race in those moments. Orkideh found herself gridlocked by authority, phenotype, gender, and religion. Using the heuristic of intersectionality, we see how subordination and privilege exist simultaneously for the instructor. Her positional authority as course instructor puts her in a position of power, while gender- and race-related power formations work to constrain her agency in this setting. The questions that Orkideh was left to continually consider (often in conversation with her co-instructor) included: How will I use my authority as instructor to connect and make comfortable? Whom do I make comfortable, and whom do I make uncomfortable? What are the edges where discomfort leads to good pedagogy and where it steps beyond that? Who is responsible for comfort and discomfort?

VIGNETTE: HOLDING THE TENSION IN THE CLASSROOM

It is the crunch period after spring break. The decision not to press charges against police officers involved in the shooting death of another young black man was announced yesterday. I forgo today's agenda and open up small and large group discussion instead. Students with dominant identities have notably differing perspectives and experiences with police and the criminal justice system than their counterparts of color. Numerous moments of conflict arise during discussion, and students look to me to break the tension. One particular moment silences the room. A white cisgender female student states that it makes sense for police to stop individuals more frequently in neighborhoods with high crime rates in order to ensure the neighborhood's safety. Further, she clarifies, if they happen to be predominantly black neighborhoods, then it would make sense that police would stop black people more frequently.

Students of color react. Some look to each other, others roll their eyes, and others physically lean in as though making sure they heard correctly. An awkward silence takes hold. Some stare blankly, some at the floor, others to their desks, and some directly at me. Perhaps students expect me to take sides with a particular perspective or to control the conversation in my role as instructor? I hold a neutral position and force the collective to sit in the discomfort.

After a few moments, a cisgender Somali man shares his own perspective. He describes his experiences as a young child, being warned by his parents to always comply fully with police in order to preserve his life. Over the course of his life, he has learned that because of the color of his skin, he will likely be a target for police regardless of dress, education, or which neighborhood he resides in. As a resident of a wealthy, predominantly white suburb, he emphasizes that even on his own block, police officers regularly stop and question him. This includes being pulled over while driving around his neighborhood, and being stopped and questioned as he casually walks through his block.

In the vignette above, Fernando leverages the news to encourage difficult conversations informed by race, class, privilege, and systemic oppression. The instructor's own identity as a Mexican American gay man provides him with personal experiences that would also advance the discussion, but he chooses to withhold these stories. Fernando insightfully asks the class to reflect on the messages and experiences they received about police and the criminal justice system throughout their lives. Here, he calls forth intersections of student identities in order to create connection with curricular concepts of privilege and leadership. In doing so, Fernando positions the conversation within a framework that prioritizes individual lived experience. In this way, the conversation is partially protected from devolving into judgments of right and wrong, true and false.

Fernando shifts weight away from his positional authority and resists the urge to perform the role of instructor in order to create space for students to grapple with their own perspectives. Fernando uses silence to hold tension and to shift back from his own identities and experiences. Fernando's purposeful silencing of his authority allows students to turn to one another in their exploration of the issues at hand. Working our intersectionalities as instructors sometimes means knowing how to use silence to hold productive tension in the classroom.

VIGNETTE: SUBSTITUTE TEACHING AND AUTHORITY

I was sick last Thursday and Orkideh solo instructed in my absence. At the next class, we are having our weekly "presence" check-in with the students to discuss how we are individually and collectively showing up ready to learn with and from one another. It comes to light that class was pretty rowdy last week. Multiple students link this energy, which they describe as "wired," to my absence. More specifically, one student compares the classroom dynamic to days in high school when there was a substitute teacher. Another student notes that there was a missing feeling of "authority." Both of these students are white cisgender women.

Immediately, I have a strong internal emotional reaction to the race and gender power formations at play in this unfolding dialogue. The operation of white supremacy and patriarchy in the students' thinking is clear to me; I, as a white, masculine-presenting instructor, am seen in the students' eyes as having more authority and credibility than Orkideh. For a moment, I am uncomfortable in my uncertainty about the "best" way to proceed. How is Orkideh feeling? Would my pointing to the racism and sexism at play serve to strip her of agency to name her own experience? Does my leading the way in raising questions of power and identity further the students' association of knowledge and authority with my racialized and gendered body?

I decide to speak strictly from my perspective in an effort to simultaneously name what I'm observing without assuming how my co-instructor is feeling. I share my observations about the students' differential perceptions of Orkideh and me as teachers. As I ask the class if they think it is possible that race and gender are at play in the different ways they perceive us as their co-instructors, my question is met with twenty-five blank stares.

After prolonged silence, Violette, an African cisgender woman, turns to Orkideh and asks, "Do you feel hurt?"

Intersections of identity and power formations collide with pedagogical considerations in this classroom exchange. It is clear that at least some of the students granted finn more authority as a co-instructor on a day when finn was not even present in class. Understanding whiteness as both identity and ideology (Leonardo 2013; Mills 1997) and utilizing a white supremacy discourse as a frame of analysis (Lensmire et al. 2013; Leonardo 2013), one could argue that the students were (perhaps subconsciously) calling on the paradigm of normative whiteness that positions whites as most powerful, most knowledgeable, most authoritative, and most deserving of respect. The theme of racial domination is unmistakable here; however, an intersectional analysis adds necessary complexity to considering the exchange. The enmeshed power formations of hegemonic masculinity (Connell and Messerschmidt 2005) and white supremacy shape the ways the students perceive the co-instructors and how the students do or do not grant Orkideh and finn authority.

It is not surprising that the students perceive Orkideh and finn differently through intersectional lenses of gender and race. Students' association of authority and classroom management with finn, a white, masculine-presenting instructor, is a clear and vivid example of internalized racism and sexism. They more or less deem Orkideh, a feminine-presenting cisgender woman of color, a substitute teacher. finn was struck by the blatant manifestation of entangled white supremacist and sexist thinking in the students' perceptions and found it difficult initially to understand how this was not obvious to them. Pedagogically, we had to step back and consider the varying levels of racialized consciousness of the students in the room. Normative whiteness and postracial discourse, mutually constructed and reinforced by hegemonic masculinity, work to invisibilize the ways that racialized and gendered power operate. While some students are acutely conscious of these power formations, others are not.

Adding a layer of considerable complexity to this classroom encounter is finn's identity and experience as a transgenderqueer person. finn's intentional choice to leverage the authority granted them by students (an authority based on the students' not entirely accurate perception of finn as a white man) was conscious and strategic. It was not without costs, however. Stepping into others' projections onto one's body—in this case, projections of normative cis maleness—invisibilizes finn's nonbinary transgenderqueer identity. finn felt uneasy about performing cisnormative masculinity in ways that do not honor their nonbinary gender. There was an acute sense of loss accompanied with intentionally performing as a white cis man. Simultaneous privilege and marginalization characterize this experience for finn, as they concurrently benefit from white masculine privilege and are invisibilized by cisgenderism. Consistent and uncontested, however, is finn's access to whiteness and the power and privilege that racialization entails.

POSSIBILITIES FOR IMPROVED INSTRUCTION

Educators are charged with employing innovative and intentional instructional strategies to support student success and growth in increasingly diverse institutional contexts. The changing demographics of students who attend institutions of higher learning and the emerging national political context require educators to re-envision the academic classroom as an opportunity to grapple with the varying values, beliefs, and perspectives that students bring with them. We build on literature about collaborative teaching and co-teaching (Cook and Friend 1995;

Bacharach, Washut Heck, and Dahlberg 2008) and recommend pursuit and experimentation of co-teaching with an intersectional lens as one of many possibilities for enhancing pedagogy on campus.

Among the elements that should be considered in such work are self-reflection, critical considerations of power formations, adaptability/responsibilities to unfolding dynamics in the classroom, and ongoing dialogue between co-instructors. Below, each of these elements is described and questions are raised about the role of each component in improved pedagogy.

Self-Reflection

Using intersectionality as a heuristic to inform pedagogy relies on continued individual self-reflection on larger societal power formations, issues of equity and inequality, instructor identity intersections, deliberate consideration of how instructors show up and engage with curriculum, the individual and collective identities and experiences of students, and awareness of positional authority as instructors. Self-reflection can be carried out in a variety of ways, from informal musings to more standardized forms of journaling and publications of blog posts. Instructors will be attracted to various forms at various junctures. We have found that self-reflection is most productive when it is combined in a cyclical fashion with the other three elements described below.

Critical Consideration of Power Formations

Consideration of power formations grows over time and is quite dependent on exposure to literature. We recommend texts from Leonardo (2013), Bonilla-Silva (2014), Bush (2004, 2011), Castagno (2014), May (2015), and others. Reading must also be combined with observation of both classroom and nonclassroom spaces and interactions on campus through an intersectional lens. Immersion in this literature is likely to lead to consideration of and experimentation with the ideas and concepts presented therein. This must also be combined with the creation of relationships wherein these ideas can be debated and discussed. These conversations may often feel difficult and challenging.

Adapting to Classroom Dynamics

Meaningful communication within the classroom ought to include considerations of formal texts and class objectives, contextual factors, power formations extant in society, and the individual identities, experiences, and backgrounds of learners and instructors. Both silence and naming can be used at multiple points to bring attention to various dynamics in order to enhance opportunities for learning. In addition to the action inside the classroom, we have found that intentional and meaningful communication with students can be facilitated through other vehicles such as one-to-one conversations outside the classroom, holistic grading, and strategic outreach over the course of the academic semester. Ongoing communication in the form of follow-up and check-in email and/or face-to-face exchanges serve to acknowledge student contributions, identify moments of difficulty, and/or push students to reflect on how they can engage more intentionally. Holistic grading pushes instructors to appreciate the review/feedback process of assignments as a chance to ask questions of reflection, react in conversation with student work, and pose considerations for continued growth. Intentional one-on-one conversations and/or individual student connections are opportunities for student and instructor to begin to understand each other outside the classroom setting in order to gain a broader view of who students and instructor(s) are, and how their identities and experiences impact how they show up in the classroom.

Ongoing Dialogue between Instructors

While co-teaching as a professional development tool for educators has mainly been explored and implemented in teacher education programs focused in the K–12 setting (Bacharach, Washut Heck, and Dahlberg 2007), we draw from the positive implications this model has demonstrated in order to advocate that co-teaching, or paired instruction by two or more instructors in a single academic course, be increased across postsecondary settings. These pairings can provide instructors with supportive and generative relationships where self-reflection, learning about power formations, experimentation with pedagogy, and refinement of pedagogy can be fostered. The co-instructor relationship allows educators to work collaboratively in the classroom and also gives multiple opportunities for each instructor to identify learning moments. Structures can be put in place for debriefing, analysis, and planning by co-instructors. In some cases, co-teaching enables a more seasoned instructor to accompany the learning, experimentation, and development of a new instructor. Co-instruction makes available a broader range of instructor experiences and identities, and thus enhances the co-instructors' ability to leverage perspectives and/or positionalities to best respond to emerging classroom dynamics. In our experience, we have found that co-teaching through the framework of intersectionality allows us to uplevel our pedagogy.

CONCLUSION

The vignettes discussed in this chapter explore intersectionality as a pedagogical tool in the higher education classroom. We considered three moments from the classroom and explored questions and possibilities laid bare through the use of an intersectional lens. With the hopes of framing opportunities for advancing this work, we described elements for collaborative co-teaching in the higher education classroom, including self-reflection, consideration of power formations, responding to classroom dynamics, and collaborative co-instruction. Inclusion of these elements in formal training programs for new and seasoned instructors can lead to improved pedagogy. Further experimentation on intersectionality as a pedagogical tool would also be beneficial. For example, how might these elements be adjusted to work outside of the social sciences, in subject areas a bit further afield, such as the physical sciences? What special considerations need to be planned when co-instruction takes place between more than two instructors? How often do individual instructors need to re-engage in co-instruction across the course of a career cycle? Further exploration and implementation of these issues would add to learning and pedagogical innovation.

REFERENCES

Alexander-Floyd, Nikol G. 2012. "Disappearing Acts: Reclaiming Intersectionality in the Social Sciences in a Post-Black Feminist Era." *Feminist Formations* 24 (1): 1–25.

Bacharach, Nancy, Teresa Washut Heck, and Kathryn Dahlberg. 2008. "Co-Teaching in Higher Education." *Journal of College Teaching & Learning* 5 (3): 9–16.

Bonilla-Silva, Eduardo. 2014. *Racism without Racists: Color-Blind Racism and the Persistence of Racial Inequality in America.* 4th ed. New York: Rowman & Littlefield.

Bowleg, Lisa. 2008. "When Black + Lesbian + Woman ≠ Black Lesbian Woman: The Methodological Challenges of Qualitative and Quantitative Intersectionality Research." *Sex Roles* 59: 312–325.

Brunsma, David L., Eric S. Brown, and Peggy Placier. 2012. "Teaching Race at Historically White Colleges and Universities: Identifying and Dismantling the Walls of Whiteness." *Critical Sociology* 39 (5): 717–738.

Bush, Melanie E. L. 2004. *Breaking the Code of Good Intentions: Everyday Forms of Whiteness.* New York: Rowman & Littlefield.

———. 2011. *Everyday Forms of Whiteness: Understanding Race in a "Post-Racial" World.* New York: Rowman & Littlefield.

Byrd, Marilyn Y. 2007. "The Effects of Racial Conflict on Organizational Performance: A Search for Theory." *New Horizons in Adult Education and Human Resource Development* 21 (1/2): 13–28.

Castagno, Angelina E. 2014. *Educated in Whiteness: Good Intentions and Diversity in Schools.* Minneapolis: University of Minnesota Press.

Collins, Patricia Hill, and Sirma Bilge. 2016. *Intersectionality.* Malden, MA: Polity Press.

Collins, Patricia Hill, Lionel A. Maldonado, Dana Y. Takagi, Barrie Thorne, Lynn Weber, and Howard Winant. 1995. "Symposium: On West and Fenstermaker's 'Doing Difference.'" *Gender and Society* 9 (4): 491–506.

Connell, R. W., and James W. Messerschmidt. 2005. "Hegemonic Masculinity: Rethinking the Concept." *Gender & Society* 19 (6): 829–859.

Cook, Lynne, and Marilyn Friend. 1995. "Co-teaching: Guidelines for Creating Effective Practices." *Focus on Exceptional Children* 28 (3): 1–16.

Crenshaw, Kimberle. 1993. "Mapping the Margins: Intersectionality, Identity Politics, and Violence against Women of Color." *Stanford Law Review* 43 (6): 1241–1299.

Du Bois, W.E.B. (1903) 2012. *The Souls of Black Folk.* New York: Signet.

Harper, Shaun. 2012. "Race without Racism: How Higher Education Researchers Minimize Racist Institutional Norms." *Review of Higher Education* 36 (1): 9–29.

Heifetz, Ron A., and Martin Linsky. 2002. *Leadership on the Line: Staying Alive through the Dangers of Leading.* Boston: Harvard Business Review Press.

Komives, Susan R., and Wendy Wagner and associates. 2009. *Leadership for a Better World: Understanding the Social Change Model of Leadership Development.* San Francisco: Jossey-Bass.

Lensmire, Timothy J., Shannon K. McManimon, Jessica Dockter Tierney, Mary E. Lee-Nichols, Zachary A. Casey, Audrey Lensmire, and Bryan M. Davis. 2013. "McIntosh as Synecdoche: How Teacher Education's Focus on White Privilege Undermines Antiracism." *Harvard Educational Review* 83 (3): 410–431.

Leonardo, Zeus. 2013. *Race Frameworks: A Multidimensional Theory of Racism and Education.* New York: Teacher's College Press.

May, Vivian M. 2015. *Pursuing Intersectionality, Unsettling Dominant Imaginaries.* New York: Routledge.

Mills, Charles W. 1997. *The Racial Contract.* Ithaca, NY: Cornell University Press.

Montoya, Margaret E. 1994. "Mascaras, Trenzas, y Greñas: Un/masking the Self While Un/braiding Latina Stories and Legal Discourse." *Chicano-Latino Law Review* 15 (1): 1–37.

———. 2000. "Silence and Silencing: Their Centripetal and Centrifugal Forces in Legal Communication, Pedagogy and Discourse." *Michigan Journal of Race & Law* 5: 847–911.

Said, Edward W. 1978. *Orientalism.* New York: Vintage Books, Random House.

Salvatore, Jessica, and J. Nicole Shelton. 2007. "Cognitive Costs of Exposure to Racial Prejudice." *Psychological Science* 18 (9): 810–815.

Solórzano, Daniel, Miguel Ceja, and Tara Yosso. 2000. "Critical Race Theory, Racial Microaggressions, and Campus Racial Climate: The Experiences of African American College Students." *Journal of Negro Education* 69 (1/2): 60–73.

Sue, Derald Wing. 2010. *Microaggressions in Everyday Life: Race, Gender, and Sexual Orientation.* Hoboken, NJ: John Wiley & Sons.

Utsey, Shawn O., and Joseph G. Ponterotto. 1996. "Development and Validation of the Index of Race-Related Stress (IRRS)." *Journal of Counseling Psychology* 43 (4): 490–501.

PART IV LIFE AMONG PAPERWORK AND BUREAUCRACY

Staff Identities and Experiences

12 · INTERSECTING IDENTITIES AND STUDENT AFFAIRS PROFESSIONALS

OPHELIE ROWE-ALLEN AND MEREDITH SMITH

Institutions of higher education are being challenged to enter into a phase of transformational change partly due to demands and expectations from students, faculty, and governmental agencies (Keeling 2004). The demands and expectations are inextricably connected to one another. Institutions are examining their historical structures, designed for a different demographic than who they are currently serving; a key example is Ivy League and Jesuit institutions, which were founded by men for men. Today, colleges and universities serve more women than men; yet tenured faculty and senior leadership do not reflect this demographic. Women held only 30 percent of college and university presidencies in 2016 (Johnson 2016). Women hold fewer tenured faculty positions than their male counterparts at every type of higher education institution (Johnson 2016). Despite these challenges, organizations such as the American Council on Education are promoting programs to address disparities between men and women in higher education.

Moreover, there are other demographic disparities; in particular, the campus climate continues to be a challenge for faculty and staff of color, especially at predominantly white institutions (PWIs). Faculty and staff of color have a higher likelihood of experiencing isolation, marginalization, tokenization, and alienation within campus communities. A study by Turner, Gonzalez, and Wood (2008) showed that faculty of color made up only 17 percent of all full-time faculty in 2005. Among full professors, the proportion fell to 12 percent. Finally, female professors of color represented less than 3 percent of faculty who held the rank of full professor (Turner, González, and Wood 2008).

However, there is a lack of research on staff experiences and advancement related to campus climate. One study focusing on African American student affairs administrators identified barriers for recruitment and retention of qualified staff (Jackson and Flowers 2003). For staff of color, these barriers include lack of mentorship, working conditions, compensation, and lack of professional identity (Jackson and Flowers 2003). The lack of professional identity stems from the constant attention given to staff of color related to their ethnic/cultural/racial backgrounds and the expectation to manage any situations related to diversity, such as student activism, and incidents of bias involving students of color. This disproportionate reliance on staff of color to attend to diversity-related crises increases the salience of their *racial* identity in the workplace but decreases the salience of their *professional* identity.

The identities—in particular, race, ethnicity, and gender—of student affairs professionals are sometimes tied to how they exercise their professional responsibilities. While these identities provide opportunities for student affairs professionals to be innovative and transformational, they are not without systemic limitations and pitfalls. These limitations unearth a lack of power and agency, which affects how student affairs professionals think and practice within the structure of academia (Chavez 2009). Thus, Harper (2008) encourages student affairs professionals to utilize research and theory to understand the complexities of the intersectionality of their identities and what they encounter in their role.

Student affairs professionals understand that their identities are expressed in the way they lead, supervise, make decisions, and form relationships. Their identities also manifest in their negotiation skills in addition to the myriad responsibilities they are accountable for in their different roles. Therefore, the essential question to explore is, How do student affairs professionals reconcile navigating their own identities with competing priorities such as student needs while working within historically white and male-dominated institutions? This question will serve as a guiding framework to identify how the work of student affairs professionals intersects with their *ways of being* and *ways of doing*.

Despite the lack of research on student affairs professionals and their experiences, the authors believe there is a similar lack of diversity and advancement for student affairs practitioners. The face of this profession is not changing to reflect the demographics in higher education. According to Sagana and Johnsrud (1991), "By increasing the minority presence in student affairs, student services divisions can cultivate a more racially and culturally diverse campus environment, which can in turn enhance the achievement of minority students" (105). Chávez and Sanlo (2013, 9) state that "identity influences experiences and perceptions of power or lack thereof and affects how we think about and practice within the power structures of colleges and universities.". Thus, institutional structures can contribute to or inhibit diversity and inclusion and one's sense of belonging within an organization.

The decision-making process for entering the field of student affairs is not well understood. There are no undergraduate majors directly linked to graduate study in student affairs. The profession is not well known to undergraduates as a career possibility unless students are involved in the student life (resident assistants, orientation leaders, student activities, etc.). According to Brown (1987), individuals' interests in student affairs careers come by way of chance, not by design. Additionally, Evans (1983) speculates that students pursuing a degree in student personnel can sometimes have an unrealistic image of the profession and vague understanding for pursuing this degree. Anecdotally, for many of us, our lived experiences, critical incidents, convergence of our identities, shared values, and influence from those in the field have drawn us to this profession.

The following narratives are from two student affairs professionals who have different experiences related to the intersection of their identities and their roles within a Catholic PWI of higher education. Their stories give a personal account of the influence of gender in relation to race, religion, privilege, oppression, and the working environment. Also, these narratives examine how their gender was perceived in various sociocultural contexts. The first narrative is from a woman of color who was the first black female to work in the Residence Life department at her institution and some of the challenges she faced in this leadership role. This narrative explores how her salient identities shaped her experiences over the years. The second narrative is from a woman who identifies as white and Catholic, working in the Office of Residence Life for over seven years. Her story demonstrates how lack of awareness of identity and perception can be its own obstacle to advancement and effectiveness when working with others.

LEADING AND SERVING WITH MY BLACKNESS

This narrative gives an insight of my life and multiple identities as I have navigated the field of higher education over the past ten years. I am currently working in Student Affairs at a private, religious PWI. Beyond conveying my personal and professional experiences, this narrative describes the approaches and practices I have cultivated over the years to achieve the positive outcomes of who I am. I highlight how I embrace my fluid identities of being a woman, black, and an immigrant. My story contributes to the many stories documenting the journey of working on predominantly white campuses. It is also an acknowledgment that we need to continue to advocate for and research the lived experiences of people of color working in the field of higher education, in particular on predominantly white campuses.

My most salient identities, my racial/ethnic background and gender, as a professional in the field of student affairs have shaped my professional life along with the many different experiences that affected my perceptions and convictions to continue in higher education. Within higher education there are only a few women of color at the highest levels of leadership. More women, including persons of color, are in midlevel student affairs positions; however, only a few are in dean, vice president, provost, or president positions (Chávez 2009). I have recently noticed that some student affairs professional organizations highlight when people of color advance to any of these positions, given their rarity. As a woman of color in an associate dean's position, I was blessed to land some unexpected and professionally rewarding opportunities that afforded me the chance to develop who I am and how I am called to be.

My story begins in my first year as a residential life area coordinator, the same year the university incorporated an overarching goal of diversity into its strategic plan. The strategy was to increase the number of students, staff, and faculty of color. However, owing to the overuse of the term "diversity," coupled with the negative interactions from both students of color and white students, the question of sense of belonging was on my mind each day when I stepped into my office. At one point, someone approached me in the lobby to let me know that I was the first person of color to work in my department. I did not know how to react to this comment as I was already questioning my intentions and where I belong at this university.

The university where I work affirms the development of a greater sense of community, shared common goals, a commitment to the core values that will guide and drive individuals in leadership to act, and education of the whole person. Thus, I incorporate these values into the work I do and encourage others to use them as well. These values have broadened my understanding of cultural and global differences and increased my civic engagement. Although it is through these values that I continue to find assurance that I belong, there are still personal challenges that I face each day as a woman who identifies as black.

According to Lloyd-Jones (2009), education and hard work are an inseparable pair that will lead to a life of social equity and greater career opportunities even for marginalized groups. Even so, I cannot forget the message that is widely shared by students of color and the few staff of color I have met. This "old" message is that people of color feel they must work twice as hard for recognition compared with those of the dominant race. For people of color, the intersection of race and social class remains a strong barrier to the achievement of social equity for career advancement. One quickly learns that there are informal guidelines for climbing up the ladder not by advanced degrees but rather by a willingness to "play the game" sometimes. Rather than be recognized by skill acquisition, student affairs professionals are identified or acknowledged by the networks they belong to, or their ability to ingratiate themselves with higher-ups.

On many occasions I have seen evidence of the intersection of race and gender in my capacity at the institution. I took on the responsibility of going above and beyond in whatever I do—I never say no to a task. I imposed this performance pressure on myself because of the "old" rule—the ideology that hard work will

overcome lack of racial and gender privilege. This ideology was taught and reinforced by family members, mentors, and colleagues. For me, it was necessary to
gain respect and credibility with students, colleagues, and supervisors so that my
race/ethnicity and gender would not undermine my efforts.

Research has shown that black women's qualifications are held to a higher
standard than those of any other group (Biernat and Kobrynowicz 1997). Black
women have to be better qualified and more articulate, yet have fewer opportunities than men to ascend the ladder of success. Intersecting identities (race, gender, and ethnicity) have consequences, creating tensions between educational
success and experiences of social inequity. These racial and gender identity constructs additionally highlight the complexities of my status as an administrator.

Within my first few years on the job, I experienced racism, sexism, isolation,
loneliness, and lack of trust. These barriers created insecurities around my racial
and gender identities when engaging with administrators who were different from
me. I have seen that black men's experiences within a PWI were more satisfying
than those of women of color. I have seen others exhibit more positive treatment
toward men of color than women of color. With the limited research available,
scholars contend that much is focused on black men and not on the scholarship
or intellectual ability of black women (Turner 2002). Thus, the intersection of race
and gender places me in a unique situation and has positioned me to experience
what it means to be black and a woman at the same time.

These two simultaneous identities intersected with other dilemmas experienced in my work with students and staff. I was very aware of the demographics
of my working environment, but I was not prepared for the negative attention
attributed to my identities. At times I did not feel that I could make decisions in
my capacity although I had demonstrated notable competence as an effective
leader. My decisions were constantly criticized by white male counterparts, which
led to skepticism of who I am as a leader and my ability to manage a department
as a woman of color. I compare my abilities with those of others around me and
think that others may be more intelligent than I am. For me, this is a sign of the
imposter syndrome, in which I begin to evaluate myself and compare my abilities with those of my male colleagues. The imposter syndrome allows women to
feel they will be found out or exposed as unworthy of the success they have attained
or the positions they have won (Vinnicombe and Singh 2002).

Furthermore, I felt disempowered within a system that questioned my abilities
and challenged my identities. These challenges came in the form of microaggressions from colleagues, parents, and students. According to Harwood et al. (2012),
the "subtle and often unconscious nature of racial microaggressions makes it hard
for people of color to decide whether they are being 'too sensitive' or are indeed
facing a new form of racism" (162). These microaggressions, which encourage
silence and become a burdensome cycle, are common among black women in
leadership positions (Stanley 2006). The microaggressions I experienced relate to

racial and gender discrimination and manifest in subtle ways. For example, my leadership position was questioned when others saw my male white colleague, whom I supervise, as more competent. I was also criticized for attending a protest held by students of color, although my white colleagues were present at that same protest.

Despite a plethora of research on faculty of color and their experiences, little research exists on staff members' lived experiences at PWIs. Stanley (2006) concluded that faculty of color are not able to candidly express their experiences, which impacts their feelings of acceptance. Similarly in my experience, staff members of color are not able to express themselves because a great deal of our time is spent on "invisible labor," particularly mentoring underrepresented students. We engage in organic mentoring relationships to provide support for students of color and be a positive change in their lives. These mentoring relationships and close connections with students place student affairs professionals of color in a position to be seen as experts on matters of diversity by members of their campus communities. This sentiment was echoed throughout my time attending the National Conference on Race and Ethnicity (NCORE). This conference provides safe and brave spaces for many to tell their stories relating to racial and gender identities and their experiences at different institutions. The stories of workplace bias, sense of belonging, and recognition resonated with me.

Many of the NCORE conversations focus on the attempts made to garner support to highlight issues around diversity on college campuses; however, many are saddened by a lack of interest and the need for change among members of their communities. Additionally, many participants voiced their concerns about the demand placed on them to do diversity work without the title or compensation. As I reflected on what I heard at the conference, I remembered times when racial incidents impacted my campus and I was called on to manage situations primarily because of my racial identity. Participating in these events can be challenging due to the additional burdens for staff of color to lead difficult conversations and advise students who may feel unsafe during these incidents.

Once, a senior administrator was asked who was doing the diversity work on campus and it was quickly mentioned that it was me and another female of color in the division. However, this was not part of our job descriptions at that time. This situation highlights how gender and racial bias can be subtle in the workplace even with the best intentions. We are being recognized mostly because of our skin color, not our talents, which creates a lesser sense of inclusion and belonging. Nonetheless, I was always ready to participate because I was secure with my *blackness* and because I knew I could be a voice for the students and staff who remained silent.

James (2002) argues that the cultural paradigm that permeates the American higher education system is white and noncommunal, and it is the expectation that all employees and students should succeed under this model. This is due to the difference in power, privilege, and positionality that is attributed to the voices and preferences of the dominant group. During protests, for example, I have seen that when the dominant group (whites) speaks there is a tremendous impact. Likewise, the dominant group influences policies and decision-making processes pertaining to social justice and diversity. There are numerous reasons why people of color have not attained equity at PWIs. Chief among them, however, is the lack of a critical mass of faculty, staff, and students of color, which reduces their ability to effectively advocate for change.

As the director of residence life and student diversity and multicultural affairs, I developed effective strategies on how to navigate a predominantly white campus. I learned many things during my ten years of leadership while embracing my racial and gender identities. In the conclusion, I share what I have learned, in the hopes that others will use these insights as tools for maintaining their value and integrity while navigating campus identities on the margins.

BREAKING DOWN MY PRIDE AND PRIVILEGE

When I first began my work in student affairs, I had a high opinion of myself and my ability to serve as a positive change agent. I believed in my own resilience as a professional, and that no matter what candidate pool I would be in, I would emerge as one of the strongest candidates because of my educational background, which included college and graduate degrees from highly prestigious institutions. As a white woman, I recognized the value in my undergraduate and graduate experiences because they exposed me to students and colleagues with identities very different from my own. In these settings, I prided myself on being not only the most studious but also the least confrontational. I had the privilege of using all of my experiences to learn and add to my knowledge of student affairs practice.

These qualities as a professional helped me to work at institutions that were not considered a PWI. I worked closely with mostly women colleagues with identities different from my own. From an intellectual standpoint, I enjoyed my experience in these environments, but in terms of emotions, I became weary because I felt my values and beliefs were consistently challenged. I can identify these feelings now, as being defensive about various aspects of my identity, especially my Catholic/Christian faith tradition and my whiteness. In those moments of challenge I would verbalize how I was different from my white peers by saying things like, "I'm part Middle Eastern" and "my family fled oppression and genocide in the early 1900s" when they immigrated to the United States.

I also found myself reflecting on the positive aspects of my Anglo-American ancestors, including stories of family members who fought in the American Revolution and later on fought to end segregation in a 1950s southern town. All these facts about my identities were true, but in the instances I brought them up they showcased a lack of awareness on my part to the experiences of others, including colleagues and students of color. I was trying to sympathize rather than empathize with my colleagues. In some circumstances I may have even subconsciously tried to one-up the experiences of others to justify my worldview instead of taking the time to listen to what others were saying. My weariness with being challenged and my defensiveness related to my identities exemplify an early stage of my own racial identity development. My actions at that time can now be identified as the reintegration stage of Helms's (1995) white identity model, where I idealized my socioracial group while being dismissive of the experiences of others.

When I changed settings from non-PWIs to a Catholic PWI, my experiences shifted a great deal. For the first time I felt that I could breathe easy and be myself without fear that my identities or opinions might challenge others or even inadvertently hurt another. At first, it was easy for me to fit in with my colleagues and with the tradition of my institution, because in many ways we shared a common set of values and beliefs. I was unaware, however, that my ability to fit in was also related to my belonging to the dominant race of both colleagues and students. Despite my previous experiences and education related to different identities, I was yet to critically examine my own identities because in many ways I lacked a reason or need to do so. It was not until I was faced with an overwhelming internal dissonance related to my gender and my institution's hidden structures that I understood the disconnect between my identities and my actions in wanting to be a better student affairs professional.

In my specific student affairs capacity in residence life, I encounter students in my office setting, and in my home, which consists of an apartment in an undergraduate residential building. A residence life professional's proximity to students makes it easy and effective for us to hold students accountable for unhealthy behaviors and to respond in emergency situations. In one of my encounters living in the residence hall as a professional, I recall sitting in my living room, reading a book, when I heard the sound of ripping paper outside my apartment. I opened my door to find a student ripping down the bulletin board. I glared at him and he in turn yelled a derogatory expletive related to my gender and ran through the exit door laughing. I was shocked and confused. In that moment, I questioned how someone could behave that way, especially at a Catholic institution. In my righteous innocence and feeling wounded as a female staff member, I confided what had happened to a male colleague the following day. My colleague was a bit surprised by how upset I was and brushed off my feelings, telling me that "these things happen in college," which essentially implied to me to "get over it." I remember looking at him, even more hurt because he failed to empathize with my experience. I reminded myself that colleagues at my alma mater would have handled this situation much differently and would have immediately expressed their concern because terms like the one used toward me were unacceptable at all times. When I was an undergraduate, similar incidents had resulted in student activism and discussion at the highest levels of administration.

Now, however, for the first time in my career, I became keenly aware of my own identity as a woman because of how easily my male colleague had minimized my feelings and experience. I became even more aware as a female when my male colleagues consistently provided feedback that my "emotions" were getting in the way of my "effectiveness" and how I was viewed in the workplace. In my mind, these were stereotypically female traits that were not spoken about in my previous work experiences. I began to construct a narrative in my head that this institution was not built for me or for women in general based on my experiences. My narrative was confirmed when male colleagues were promoted more readily than female colleagues. Sandberg (2013) pointed out that men are typically hired or promoted for their potential, whereas women are hired or promoted based on experience alone. Because of the lack of gender diversity within senior-level positions, these prevalent practices often go unnoticed. For example, at one point I was told that my experience did not yet warrant a promotion; meanwhile, a male colleague who had less experience received a promotion.

In conversations with female colleagues at other institutions, I realized that these patterns are not uncommon to higher education. Despite working long hours and working harder than my male colleagues, I felt stuck in place and that my work ethic and energy were taken for granted, especially by male colleagues. I also did not recognize how I was contributing to this unhealthy pattern of overwork. When asked about a project that I spearheaded, I never took recognition, whereas my male colleagues would brag about the very same project. I became a caricature of the modest, humble, and nurturing female colleague. Flynn, Heath, and Holt (2011) state that "it's no surprise we are willing to share the credit and play down our own accomplishments. . . . We feel inclined to discount our accomplishments" (59). I now realize that I was playing into the traditional gendered expectations previously described (Flynn, Heath, and Holt 2011).

However, through reflection and critical examination of my own identities (Catholic, white, female), I was able to understand how to navigate these patterns more effectively and to challenge some of the obstacles that provide me privilege over others. This process began with understanding that my identities were a key factor in developing my perspectives on seeing and working with others. As a woman of faith, I was raised to be compassionate, to seek justice, and to be a light for others. The desire to seek justice creates dissonance with my privileges based on my whiteness. In initial interactions with new students, parents, or colleagues, it is often assumed that I am the more senior ranking individual when compared with my colleagues of color who have the same or higher title or position. As a white woman, I needed to prove my experience through my actions and know when to speak up against gendered oppression and when to step back against undue racial privilege.

It is now many years from when I started in my role, and I am successfully climbing the ladder in my professional development. I am grateful for the willingness of others to engage with me on this journey and to challenge me through this process. One key factor in my own growth was a willingness to engage with the messier aspects of my identities and to continually challenge my words and actions. For me, this translated into creating a support system that includes both mentors and colleagues whom I trust to be honest with me and provide formative feedback rather than validation. To find these mentors, I had to build relationships outside of my comfort zone with both men and women, and take ownership of my own professional experience. A mentoring relationship requires a place where both individuals can be authentic. This type of relationship continues to be a brave space where I can explore questions about my identities, perspectives, and actions. Furthermore, by being mentored, I am able to also serve as a mentor for others finding themselves similarly stuck.

CONCLUSION AND PROMISING PRACTICES

This chapter draws on two student affairs professionals' lived experiences, their identities as a black woman and a white Catholic woman, and their commitment to identifying how various forms of identities intertwine with their work. Personal identity development and self-awareness remain necessary for student affairs personnel in their work with students. However, little research is available on student affairs professionals' own lived experiences, especially at PWIs. Research on these experiences can help us understand the intersectionality, tensions, and silence that often occur on campus with staff members with different identities.

Although many in the workplace take a dispassionate approach to issues of diversity and inclusion, students and faculty often have a choice in accepting or challenging their institutional cultures because they are governed by the principles of academic freedom. Yet, it must be noted that student affairs professionals, by the nature of our work as at will employees, do not have this liberty. Student affairs professionals must walk a fine line between institutional loyalty and navigating their own identities. Moreover, the behaviors associated with their institutional campus climate play a critical role in their experiences. Sometimes the story of the institution does not reflect "one size fits all."

To help student affairs professionals navigate college campuses, we have identified a few strategies that could be applicable to personal and professional development. First, create key principles of your personal vision so that your behavior is a product of your own conscious choices and values, rather than a product of conditions and feelings. As women, we often go into a "fix, repair, and assist" mode, which can feed gendered stereotypes. We may work twice as hard, stay at work late, or arrive early, trying to be all things to all people. Subconsciously, we internalize this operation to prove ourselves, especially for student affairs professionals of color. The challenge is for you to reincorporate yourself, become proactive, and make conscious choices to how you respond to your environment. According to

Covey (2013), "Proactive people can carry their own weather with them. Whether it rains or shines makes no difference to them. They are value driven and if their value is to produce good quality work it isn't a function of whether the weather is conducive to it or not" (79). The actions you take should not depend solely on your personal identities but reflect the values you hold and how those values show up in the work you do.

Second, to remain value-driven, student affairs professionals should seek out mentors and build networks to navigate the expected and the unexpected. Student affairs professionals who are in leadership roles should be mentors to young professionals and should also have mentors themselves. We do formally and informally mentor students; however, we may not recognize the mentoring opportunities from professionals to professionals. Mentoring relationships can be highly structured, formally planned by your department to meet organizational objectives, or they can be done informally, from one-off meetings to discuss problems, to listen to one another, or to share special knowledge based on lived experiences. These kinds of relationships remain an invaluable resource and can help traverse how you view yourself, your position, and your career trajectory. Moreover, mentors are fundamental to retention and promotion, especially for people of color in student affairs who are at institutions with limited support or resources.

Earlier in the chapter we indicated the systemic structures that made it difficult for us to navigate our institutions. Surviving in such systems involves using a delicate blend of knowing the ins and outs of your institution and maneuvering within these structures. Particularly for the underrepresented staff members, there may be feelings of isolation—as if they are the "only one." This could mean you are the only woman, the only person of color, the only nonreligious person, the only one speaking out, and so on. In addition to finding mentors, it may be helpful to network and professionally socialize for the purpose of meeting others to exchange ideas. These vital tools may not only manage your sanity but remind you that you are not alone. Use these tools as shock absorbers and support systems to help you grow professionally and handle situations that you think happen only to you.

Third, we recommend creating brave and safe spaces for staff members. Each professional should build a personal practice of reflection for self-awareness to help identify how their identities impact them as professionals within an organization. However, not many spaces are provided for staff members from different backgrounds to openly express themselves and discuss issues impacting their identities. One suggestion for student affairs professionals who are white is to engage in practices of examining their privilege. Most times, white staff members tend to remove themselves from racial incidents and leave staff of color to handle these situations. Sue and Constantine (2007) examined racial privilege among white people and identified fears including appearing racist, confronting their own white privilege, and taking responsibility for change. In spite of all this, it is critical that we, as professionals, become multiculturally competent individuals. Most of student affairs work is central to student development, and so it is imperative that we engage in difficult dialogue, however uncomfortable. Experiencing these moments is part of the process of identifying and unlearning certain practices of privilege and understanding how identity shapes responses to others who are different. To do this, when you seek out professional development, do not shy away from opportunities that challenge your personal identity. If you have internal professional development in your department, suggest topics that will engage everyone in a discussion on racial and identity development. Theoretical models that examine racial identity development, such as Helms's (1995) Racial Identity Model and Harro's (2008) Cycle of Socialization, can help bridge the gap from theory to practice.

In conclusion, student affairs professionals must have knowledge of different worldviews and a systemic understanding of how their environment operates. These worldviews and systems have the potential to influence the identities and experiences of others. These systems include the institutional policies, practices, and facilities that represent the needs of everyone in the college arena. Therefore, the strategies listed above are for student affairs professionals to take personal responsibility and not to wait for institutional change to make a difference for themselves and others. There are many other strategies that allow us to draw on a wide array of perspectives as we examine our identities and emotional intelligence to respond to the complex issues within the changing landscape of higher education.

REFERENCES

Biernat, Monica, and Diane Kobrynowicz. 1997. "Gender- and Race-Based Standards of Competence: Lower Minimum Standards but Higher Ability Standards for Devalued Groups." *Journal of Personality and Social Psychology* 72 (3): 544–557.

Brown, Robert D. 1987. "Professional Pathways and Professional Education." *New Directions in Student Services* 37: 5–18.

Chávez, Alicia F. 2009. "Leading in the Borderlands: Negotiating Ethnic Patriarchy for the Benefit of Students." *NASPA Journal about Women in Higher Education* 2 (1): 41–67.

Chávez, Alicia F., and Ronni Sanlo. 2013. *Identity and Leadership: Informing Our Lives, Informing Our Practice.* Washington, DC: NASPA.

Covey, Stephen R. 2013. *The 7 Habits of Highly Effective People: Powerful Lessons in Personal Change.* New York: Free Press.

Evans, Nancy J. 1983. "Environmental Assessment: Current Practices and Future Directions." *Journal of College Student Personnel* 24 (4): 293–299.

Flynn, Jill, Kathryn Heath, and Mary Davis Holt. 2011. *Break Your Own Rules: How to Change the Patterns of Thinking That Block Women's Paths to Power.* San Francisco: John Wiley & Sons.

Harper, Shaun R. 2008. *Creating Inclusive Campus Environments: For Cross-Cultural Learning and Student Engagement.* Washington, DC: NASPA.

Harro, Bobbie. 2008. "Updated Version of the Cycle of Socialization (2000)." In *Readings for Diversity and Social Justice*, 2nd ed., edited by Maurianne Adams, Warren J. Blummfeld, Heather W. Hackman, Madeline L. Peters, and Ximena Zuniga, 45–52. New York: Routledge.

Harwood, Stacy A., Margaret Browne Huntt, Ruby Mendenhall, and Jioni A. Lewis. 2012. "Racial Microaggressions in the Residence Halls: Experiences of Students of Color at a Predominantly White University." *Journal of Diversity in Higher Education* 5 (3): 159–173.

Helms, Janet E. 1995. "An Update of Helm's White and People of Color Racial Identity Models." In *Handbook of Multicultural Counseling*, edited by J. G. Ponterotto, J. M. Casas, L. A. Suzuki, and C. M. Alexander, 181–198. Thousand Oaks, CA: Sage.

Jackson, Jerlando F., and Lamont A. Flowers. 2003. "Retaining African American Student Affairs Administrators: Voices from the Field." *College Student Affairs Journal* 22 (2): 125–136.

James, P. 2002. "When Intellectual World's Collide." In *Our Stories: The Experiences of Black Professionals on Predominantly White Campuses*, edited by Mordean Taylor-Archer and Sherwood Smith, 99–102. Cincinnati, OH: John D. O'Bryant National Think Tank for Black Professionals in Higher Education on Predominately White Campuses (JDOTT).

Johnson, Heather L. 2016. *Pipelines, Pathways, and Institutional Leadership: An Update on the Status of Women in Higher Education*. Washington, DC: American Council on Education.

Keeling, Richard P. (Ed.). 2004. *Learning Reconsidered: A Campus-Wide Focus on the Student Experience*. Washington, DC: National Association of Student Administrators & American College Personnel Association.

Lloyd-Jones, Brenda. 2009. "Implications of Race and Gender in Higher Education Administration: An African American Woman's Perspective." *Advances in Developing Human Resources* 11 (5): 606–618.

Sagana, Mary Ann, and Linda K. Johnsrud. 1991. "Recruiting, Advancing, and Retaining Minorities in Student Affairs: Moving from Rhetoric to Results." *NASPA Journal* 28 (2): 105–120.

Sandberg, Sheryl. 2013. *Lean In: Women, Work, and the Will to Lead*. New York: Random House.

Stanley, Christine A. 2006. "Coloring the Academic Landscape: Faculty of Color Breaking the Silence in Predominantly White Colleges and Universities." *American Educational Research Journal* 43 (4): 701–736.

Sue, Derald Wing, and Madonna G. Constantine. 2007. "Racial Microaggressions as Instigators of Difficult Dialogues on Race: Implications for Student Affairs Educators and Students." *College Student Affairs Journal* 26 (2): 136–143.

Turner, Caroline S. V. 2002. "Women of Color in Academe: Living with Multiple Marginality." *Journal of Higher Education* 73 (1): 74–93.

Turner, Caroline S. V., Juan Carlos González, and J. Luke Wood. 2008. "Faculty of Color in Academe: What 20 Years of Literature Tells Us." *Journal of Diversity in Higher Education* 1 (3): 139–168.

Vinnicombe, Susan, and Val Singh. 2002. "Women-Only Management Training: An Essential Part of Women's Leadership Development." *Journal of Change Management* 3 (4): 294–306.

13 · STUDYING STEM WHILE BLACK

How Institutional Agents Prepare
Black Students for the Racial Realities
of STEM Environments

TONISHA B. LANE

Increasing attention has focused on the persistence, retention, and success of underrepresented groups in the science, technology, engineering, and mathematics (STEM) fields (Museus et al. 2011). Recent statistics indicate that communities of color make up a small fraction of the baccalaureate holders in STEM (National Science Foundation [NSF] 2017). As a group, their degree attainment constitutes only 20 percent of degree recipients. Within the past twenty years, blacks increased their degree attainment in the biological sciences, but there were significant declines in other areas, specifically mathematics and statistics. In 2014, black individuals with STEM degrees earned these degrees in the following areas: slightly under 10 percent in computer sciences, 6 percent in biological sciences, 5 percent in physics, slightly over 4 percent in mathematics, and just under 4 percent in engineering (NSF 2017). Recent research elucidates factors contributing to the underrepresentation of racial and ethnic minorities in STEM (Ong et al. 2011; Museus et al. 2011). These studies suggest that because of their minoritized status, students of color experience unique challenges within STEM disciplines (Ong et al. 2011; Museus et al. 2011).

In STEM contexts, negative perceptions about black students are used as tools to perpetuate discrimination and inequities (Fries-Britt, Johnson, and Burt 2013). Educators and administrators point to inadequate K–12 education, low math and science scores on standardized tests, and a lack of exposure to STEM role models and mentors as rationales for black students' underachievement (Moore,

Madison-Colmore, and Smith 2003). Because of this tendency to emphasize individual attributes over systemic inequalities, policies and practices designed to broaden participation in STEM often fall short of addressing anti-black sentiments and other forms of oppression experienced by black students (Seymour and Hewitt 1997). Given these issues, black students need strategies and support for navigating such hostile and unwelcoming climates.

Evidence indicates that racial-ethnic socialization (RES) can aid students in understanding and negotiating racialized contexts. Informants of RES typically are parents (Hughes et al. 2006). However, as students matriculate into new educational settings, institutional agents may be better equipped to render context-specific advice and resources (Museus and Neville 2012). Thus, the purpose of this study is to investigate how institutional agents help black students understand and navigate the racial realities of the STEM disciplines. Institutional agents are "high-status, non-kin, agents who occupy relatively high positions in the multiple dimensional stratification system, and who are well positioned to provide key forms of social and institutional support" (Stanton-Salazar 2011, 1067). While a number of studies show black students enacting their own agency to persist in STEM amid poor race relations, we know little about the role institutional agents play in helping students make sense of these environments. To this end, two research questions guide this study: (1) How do institutional agents inform black students about the racial realities of the STEM context at a large, public, predominantly white research university? (2) What messages do institutional agents directly or indirectly convey to students about their racialized identities in these environments? Further, this study is situated within postsecondary STEM educational research and race-centered frameworks to illuminate how institutional agents disrupt systems of oppression that undermine the college-going experiences of black STEM students.

LITERATURE REVIEW

Racialized Experiences in STEM

The competitive nature of the STEM disciplines juxtaposed with the lack of critical mass of students of color contributes to the often-reported alienation and isolation that students of color encounter in these fields (Fries-Britt et al. 2013; Ong et al. 2011). Previous research indicates that the STEM culture imposes a number of academic and heuristic demands (Carlone and Johnson 2007; Seymour and Hewitt 1997). The curriculum is highly theoretical and uniquely challenging (Seymour and Hewitt 1997). Students are expected to be able to communicate and demonstrate STEM knowledge and competencies (e.g., an ability to explain and use scientific tools and materials). Recognition by faculty and peers for such abilities is often touted as an indicator of success as well (Carlone and Johnson 2007).

While these characteristics of the STEM culture may not be exclusive to these disciplines, this notion of STEM culture is regularly cited in the literature as a barrier to the success for marginalized groups in STEM (Fries-Britt et al. 2013).

Poor racial climate also has an impact on the academic and social adjustment of black STEM students (McGee and Martin 2011; Moore et al. 2003). STEM students who perceive institutional contexts as hostile may experience negative effects in regard to a sense of belonging and academic outcomes (Ong et al. 2011). In a landmark study, Seymour and Hewitt (1997) found that students of color underperform owing to factors related to the campus climate. The "chilly climate" metaphor has also been used to describe the psychological aspects of STEM environments (Fries-Britt et al. 2013; Ong et al. 2011). Within these environments, black students report feeling like outsiders, not being appropriately credited for their contributions to group projects, and being exposed to explicit forms of racism and sexism (Fries-Britt et al. 2013; Ong et al. 2011).

Intersectionality and STEM

Intersectionality illuminates how the convergence of one's multiple identities is complicated by structures of privilege and subordination (Crenshaw 1991). To this end, intersectionality can be used as an analytical tool to unearth and critique dominant structures that reinforce bias and discrimination in educational contexts (Dill and Zambrana 2009). For instance, Ong and colleagues (2011) point out that women of color confront an uncomfortable existence with their "double-bind" status as they assert themselves in STEM fields. The double-bind construct emphasizes the experience of a doubly oppressive state for being a woman and a person of color in white, male-dominated fields. In a study investigating sense of belonging in STEM living learning communities, Johnson (2012) uncovered that women of color find it difficult to develop relationships with faculty and peers. She also found that black women experience challenges establishing study groups when other women of color are not involved (Johnson 2012). Some black women also report an inability to be their "whole" selves in STEM environments (Ong et al. 2011). They feel compelled to change their appearance, attire, or mannerisms to fit in. This fragmentation behavior poses unique challenges for black women and their struggle to thrive in STEM settings (Fries-Britt et al. 2013).

Lane and colleagues (forthcoming) found that applying intersectionality as a lens in STEM educational research has become increasingly prominent. Relative to the current study, Fries-Britt and colleagues' (2013) qualitative study investigated the experiences of black students at the intersections of race, gender, class, and academic abilities. In the study, the students pointed out that in predominantly white institutions they questioned their cognitive capabilities because they were members of a minoritized racial group. They also encountered unwelcoming experiences in the classroom environment and laboratory settings. Common among female participants were difficulties with faculty and peers, identifying partners for class assignments, and being assigned administrative instead of technical tasks in group projects.

In a more recent article, Ireland and colleagues (2018) synthesized literature on black women and girls in STEM. They noted "the rhetorical focus on 'women and minorities' in STEM risks treating these two groups as mutually exclusive and obscuring the particular experiences of individuals who exist as members of both groups" (227). Thus, the authors integrate intersectional and psychological dimensions to illuminate the experiences of black women and girls in STEM. Through their analysis, they show how elements such as confidence, ability perceptions, and achievement are influenced by the co-construction of one's identities. Stated another way, if students have a poor self-concept concerning their academic abilities because of their race, gender, and/or other marginalized identities, they may be less likely to succeed and persist (Sedlacek 2017). The current chapter contributes to these previous findings by showing how black students experience STEM contexts, and the role institutional agents may play in helping students persevere despite difficult racial climates.

Dealing with Bias in STEM

To mitigate bias, some black students engage in behaviors that include finding ways to outperform their white peers or actively resist stereotypes about their academic abilities (Moore et al. 2003). More recently, McGee and Martin (2011) advanced the concept of stereotype management to articulate the connection between high achievement and resilience among blacks in STEM. They defined this concept as the "tactical responses to ubiquitous forms of racism and racialized experiences" across academic and nonacademic contexts (McGee and Martin 2011, 1349) and noted how students deal with racism intermingled with their racial, gender, and mathematics identity development. In this study, students evolved from being concerned with "proving stereotypes wrong" about their intellectual capabilities to identifying "self-defined reasons to achieve" (McGee and Martin 2011, 1347). While these studies demonstrate how students enact agency to negotiate the racial realities of STEM, little is known about how institutional agents help students navigate these environments. Museus and Nelville (2012) contended that institutional agents play a critical role in helping students of color navigate higher education. Additionally, when institutional agents share the same racial-ethnic backgrounds as students, they are more likely to build rapport and be perceived as reliable sources of information (Museus and Nelville 2012). To this end, a closer examination of bias in STEM and how institutional agents aid students in navigating such environments is warranted.

Theoretical Framework

The current study uses RES theory as a theoretical framework to understand how institutional agents transmit messages about the racial climate in STEM environments to black students. The RES framework comprises four dimensions: cultural socialization, preparation for bias, promotion of mistrust, and egalitarianism (Hughes et al. 2006). Cultural socialization corresponds to the strategies and practices informants (e.g., parents, peers, other adults) indirectly or directly engage in to promote racial or ethnic pride, share heritage and history, and pass on customs and traditions. Preparation for bias is how informants teach individuals about racism, discrimination, and prejudice endured by people of color. The research also denotes this dimension as racism awareness training (Stevenson 1994) and cautious/defensive socialization (Hughes et al. 2006). Not only are individuals made aware of biased circumstances and contexts, but they may also be instructed on how to cope with and/or actively resist racism. Egalitarianism is the promotion of individual abilities and attributes over racial and ethnic group membership (Hughes et al. 2006). As such, informants might explicitly encourage the individual to focus on acquiring skills and dispositions that perceivably contribute to value and status within the dominant culture rather than aligning one's self with their native or minority culture (Hughes et al. 2006). Moreover, the current study examined how and what information gets transmitted from institutional agents to black collegians given their identities and positions in STEM.

METHODS

Study Design

The current study is part of a larger study that investigated how a STEM enrichment program contributed to the successful outcomes of underrepresented groups within these disciplines at a large, predominantly white, public research university. I employed a case study methodological approach for the following reasons: (1) an emphasis on in-depth analysis, (2) context as central to the phenomenon being studied, and (3) usage of multiple sources of data (Yin 2013). Data collection took place over an eleven-month period. Data generated from interviews of institutional agents and students and participant observations of program-related meetings and activities informed the current study.

Institutional and Program Context

Jefferson State University (JSU, pseudonym) is located in a rural area of a Midwestern state. The institution has more than 40,000 students, representing a diverse economic, racial and ethnic, and international population. The racial-ethnic makeup of the institution is 8 percent black, 4 percent Latinx, 5 percent Asian, and 67 percent white.

The Comprehensive STEM Program (CSP) at JSU began in 2007 to acclimate first-year students to the academic, psychosocial, and environmental aspects of postsecondary education. The program was designed to ensure the success of students pursuing a rigorous STEM-focused curriculum. Specifically, the program sought to support students until they were admissible into their given college. With the exception of one of the university's STEM colleges, there is a dual admission process such that students are first admitted to JSU, and by junior status they must meet specific criteria to be admissible to their particular college.

CSP contains eight components: summer bridge program, residential housing, clustered courses, weekly recitation sessions, peer mentoring, academic advising, freshman seminar, and an undergraduate research experience. I selected CSP because of the successful outcomes of its participants. The program boasted a 95 percent first to second year retention rate, the average grade point average (GPA) of its participants was 3.0, and math placement scores increased after participation in its summer bridge programs. CSP is housed within a multicultural engineering program (MEP). The MEP office was established in the 1960s to meet the needs of an increasingly diverse student population. The office provides a number of programs to facilitate academic, professional, and personal development of pre-college, undergraduate, and graduate students studying engineering.

Interviews

Semi-structured, audio-recorded interviews served as the primary data source for this study. I conducted twenty-four interviews total—three with black, male institutional agents (two administrators and one instructor within the program) and twenty-one with black students. Students included four first-years, three sophomores, three juniors, and eleven seniors. Only first-year students are considered current participants. Other class levels are program alumni; however, many of them maintain contact with the program through serving as mentors, and a significant portion of them receive services from the MEP. Thirteen students were men and eight were women. Interview questions covered students' experiences with racial discrimination and prejudice in STEM contexts and how institutional agents discussed such matters with students within the program. Each interview lasted between forty-five and sixty minutes. Given the purpose of this study, I center the perspectives of the three institutional agents: Phil, Collin, and Mr. Drew (all names are pseudonyms). However, I use the other eighteen interviews to elucidate the experiences black students reported in the STEM disciplines, their recollections of how institutional agents prepared them for such environments, and why institutional agents felt such instruction was necessary.

Data Analysis

All interviews were transcribed verbatim. I noted all instances of discussion of race, racism, prejudice, and discrimination to organize the data and generate categories. I engaged in thematic analysis, making note of recurring themes about the students' racial realities in STEM and how the institutional agents prepared students to navigate these environments. I read and re-read the transcripts to understand the essence of the participants' statements. My data analysis included two cycles of coding (Saldaña 2015). I began with coding transcripts line by line, jotting down notes in the margins. These notes entailed identifying recurring terms that emerged from the interviews, key concepts from the literature, and tenets within the theoretical framework. The second cycle of coding entailed organizing these codes within broader themes (Saldaña 2015). I focused on the institutional agents' responses and reactions to the racial climate in STEM environments and ways they helped students make meaning of, navigate, and negotiate such environments. Similarly, I compared and contrasted their responses to the existing literature and RES theory.

I used peer debriefing to ensure that my codes and themes are what they should be (Miles, Huberman, and Saldaña 2014). Findings were shared with three researchers to discern that the findings are consistent with the data collected. These individuals also challenged me to consider alternative ways of examining the data.

Institutional Agents

At the time of data collection, the institutional agents Phil and Collin were in their late thirties and Mr. Drew was in his late twenties. Phil was in his eighth year of a continuing appointment as director of the MEP. His bachelor's degree was in advertising, and his master's degree was in student affairs administration. Before working at JSU, he worked in a number of for-profit and nonprofit organizations. He integrated his business acumen into his work with the MEP. For example, he helped students with budgeting and finance. He once stated that the students were both JSU's product and service. Collin, the assistant director of MEP, had completed his sixth year in that role. He had a professional background in engineering. Both his bachelor's and master's degrees were in mechanical engineering. Before working at JSU, he worked in the automotive industry.

Through the interviews, I learned that their undergraduate experiences, in addition to present-day realities as professionals within the university, influenced their thinking and actions regarding how they socialized students in the program. Both Collin and Phil faced their own encounters with structural racism and bias. On one occasion, I overheard them discussing how the college of engineering and computer science decided not to invest in their MEP space and instead created a new student study space down the hall from their location. Many of the white students tended to occupy this space while the students of color studied in the MEP. The MEP contained dated furniture and carpet and relatively older computers than the other location. Unlike the other location, the MEP did not have cable television. Despite these stark differences, students of color called the MEP their "academic home."

Mr. Drew was a high school science teacher and an instructor in CSP. He had a bachelor's degree in chemistry and was working on a master's degree in science education. At the time of data collection, Mr. Drew was undergoing his second experience with the summer bridge program. He saw his work as integral to shaping future scientists and engineers. As part of his pedagogy, he provided his version of the "hidden curriculum" for excelling in college-level chemistry.

FINDINGS

Three themes emerged from the practices of institutional agents to support black students' RES in STEM: (1) having difficult conversations, (2) focusing on performance and building competencies, (3) reinforcing students' belongingness and capacity to contribute to STEM disciplines. These findings illuminate how institutional agents influence the RES process of black students within STEM environments.

Have Difficult Conversations

Institutional agents prepared students for the STEM environment at JSU through having difficult conversations about being a student of color and handling bias. These conversations often took place during residential floor meetings during the summer bridge program. Collin explained how program staff transmitted this information: "The support network is a really big thing for the program so we try to set up a support network so that students can come to staff members and older students that have already gone through the program and talk to them about some of the challenges that they are facing when they walk into these situations where they may be a minority from an ethnicity standpoint or from a gender standpoint."

Institutional agents in CSP created a network of students, staff, and instructors to support students' academic and psychosocial adjustment. Collin indicated in the previous quote that institutional agents leveraged this network to inform students about what they may encounter in these academic environments and how to manage their minoritized identity. Collin mentions both race and gender, noting that either identity or the convergence of these identities could make the academic environment feel alienating or isolating. While institutional agents prepared students for the racial realities of the STEM disciplines, no mention of gender or the intersection of racial and gender oppression was discussed except for Collin's brief comment.

Several students recalled engaging in these difficult conversations with the program's institutional agents. Vanessa, a senior in applied engineering sciences, shared what she remembered about these conversations: "Phil talked about [it] a lot, how you will be many of the few black engineers and it will be kinda tough to get used to but to not make it an obstacle . . . but use it as motivation to prove yourself and things like that. We had a lot of talks, especially in some of the courses that we took in CSP, they would always tell us, you gotta work a little bit harder than everyone else. So, we were prepared a lot. It wasn't something that I didn't expect."

According to Vanessa, Phil informed the CSP participants about the potential racial realities within the STEM disciplines. Phil's actions aligned with RES's preparation for bias tenet wherein he underscored the hypervisibility of minoritized students in STEM classroom settings. While many participants disclosed feeling prepared for what they might encounter in the classroom environment, Phil's advice for dealing with bias still seemed to follow an egalitarianism point of view emphasizing hard work and determination.

Focus on Performance and Building Competencies

CSP facilitates opportunities for students to enrich their math and science knowledge, skills, and abilities. These opportunities include a summer bridge program, special recitation sessions, academic advising, and access to free tutoring. Consequently, institutional agents encouraged students to use their academic performance and competencies to navigate chilly racial classroom settings. Phil explained:

> The way to eliminate [prejudice beliefs] is [through] performance. My experience has been once faculty, staff and other students see you perform those other things don't happen . . . for the most part. Yes, they still do happen but those people aren't gonna change their minds, [or] their opinion of . . . others anyway. . . . But . . . as a student's reputation grows and they are known for performance, then you don't have that issue. We have the biggest impact [in] how we . . . show students how to become [successful] in our programs and how we help them in those areas where they need help. . . . So those are the areas . . . we can help the student overcome those things.

According to Phil, the most effective way to combat bias and discrimination is to focus on building competencies and performing in the classroom environment. While Phil acknowledged there still may be instances in which students face discrimination because of their race, regardless of their academic prowess, he displayed egalitarianism when he surmised it was more important for students to focus less on those circumstances and more on intellectual development. He also noted that CSP was better equipped to help students build their individual attributes through providing academic services and advising than to dismantle the racist structure that persisted in the STEM environment.

Although some student participants shared similar sentiments as Phil for negotiating their racialized identities, focusing on academic performance and competencies did not necessarily warrant acceptance into the dominant culture. Students had to work harder for recognition, or white students had to perceive there were no other options before they were willing to interact with black students. Participants reported that white students assumed they knew less about the content areas because of their black identity. For example, when I inquired about William's experiences as a black person in STEM at JSU, he indicated:

> [White] students might be a bit resistant at first because they feel you may not know as much as them or you don't deserve to be there. I don't really let that deter me [because] I know I'm here for one thing. But my experience as a black male in [STEM]. It's been like the resistance from the students . . . trying to get help from them to understand something. Take group assignments [for example], they may not feel like you're capable of some task when actually you may know more than them. [They] try to avoid you. You ask them a question [and] they blow you off. They think you don't know things and, in a group, and they give you the non-technical task like organizing things.

William's perceptions and experiences illustrate how black students have to combat negative stereotypes even when they have the intellectual capacity to contribute to an assignment. As Phil previously mentioned, these white students may be ignorant and not worth proving one's cognitive prowess. However, many students in the study experienced frustrations with such racial realities and contemplated leaving JSU.

Reinforce Students' Belongingness and Contribution to STEM

Institutional agents regularly discussed the uniqueness of the students' backgrounds and diverse experiences as critical for advancing scientific research and discovery. Given the racialized identities of the students, the institutional agents wanted to ensure that black students had a positive academic self-concept, especially when interacting with peers who were less open to diversity. Collin elaborated on this practice: "Yeah, in the program, we talk a lot about you know, especially in engineering and science, many times you're going to be working in groups. And a lot of times, we try to get them to embrace the diversity that they bring to the table. We talk a lot about how your [viewpoints] may be different from the [viewpoints of your group members] but that diversity is valuable to the generation of good ideas in a group setting. And so, the support is critical there but we do really emphasize to them that, yeah, you are different, but your difference is an asset in the situation that you're in as opposed to a liability."

Collin's quote illustrated some of the ways institutional agents were instrumental in promoting racial pride among the students. Some students mentioned how these messages helped them circumvent racial tension in group settings. Other students reported knowing their self-worth and ability to address STEM-related problems whether in the classroom, the workplace, or society was important and would be eventually rewarded. For example, junior and senior students who had completed internships pointed out that colleagues in the workplace were more concerned with who was able to solve the problem than beliefs about racialized ineptness. Kari, a senior in chemical engineering, discussed this difference in his interview: "I don't know but that's something you encounter in school but in the work environment, like things were different. People were more open to like ideas from everybody. I think they had passed that. They were reaching out to everybody. If they needed a solution, they'd use all their resources and not just concentrate on one particular group. I think everybody realized at the end of the day, you gotta come up with a solution because that's . . . your purpose of being there. So, no matter who comes up with it or how they come up with it, they know, that's their job and it's expected of them to accomplish that."

Kari's experiences illustrated what Mr. Drew hoped to convey to students when he worked as an instructor in the summer program. He desired to reassure students that they belonged in the STEM disciplines and that their achievement in these areas would position them to make a lasting impact within this field. For example, Mr. Drew explained: "One of my biggest motivations for teaching the chemistry class was to encourage the students to understand that even though they may be in the minority, by population, in the chemistry class or engineering classes, that their skills, their talents, and what they're getting now in the program is preparing them to be a member of that classroom or a member of the science society . . . and play their role by being in that class and prove it to themselves, not to anyone else, that they belong in engineering." Mr. Drew indicated a strong interest in affirming students in their intellectual abilities and supporting them through his work in the summer program. As discussed in his interview, having been a student of color in the STEM disciplines at JSU, he had an understanding of what the students might face. He believed his role was to prepare them to be a "member" of the classroom environment and society at large, because they had something to offer (i.e., skills and talents). Finally, Mr. Drew insisted that students "prove to themselves and not to anyone else" that they belonged in the STEM disciplines. While some participants expressed feeling empowered to prove people wrong about their cognitive abilities, other students reported feeling overwhelmed by this positioning. Hence, Collin communicated how the program staff reinforced students' assets and what they brought to the classroom environment.

DISCUSSION

My study illuminates how institutional agents supported black students with understanding the racial realities of the STEM disciplines and negotiating their racialized identities within these contexts. To this end, RES was a helpful framework for examining the practices and implicit and explicit ways that institutional agents informed students about the racialized STEM environment and how to navigate such spaces. Engaging CSP participants in difficult conversations about racial realities provided opportunities for institutional agents to prepare students for the bias they may encounter in these contexts and help them identify strategies to deal with these circumstances. For example, Collin mentioned using the network of students, staff, and instructors within CSP to share information and strategies for managing the racial climate. Though valuable, agents' focus on racialized identities still failed to fully engage the complexities of racism and how such acts can cause psychological distress in college, barriers to advancement in the STEM fields, and diminished opportunities for black individuals to use their intellects to address societal problems with STEM knowledge.

I also found that institutional agents suggested students focus on their competencies and performance to circumvent a negative racial climate. Such responses, however, could have an unexpected negative effect. Coping mechanisms that focus on performance alone without helping students understand and navigate a poor racial climate may result in attrition (Seymour and Hewitt 1997). While some students find "proving others wrong" about their intellectual capabilities to be an effective strategy for managing bias (Moore et al. 2003), other students may find this strategy adds stress to their academic careers (Johnson et al. 2014). This finding also corresponds to behaviors associated with the egalitarianism dimension of RES. In order to assimilate within (and be accepted by) mainstream culture, individuals are taught to focus on personal attributes rather than calling out racialized inequities (Hughes et al. 2006). In the current study, Phil recognized that some institutional stakeholders (e.g., faculty, students) would maintain stereotypical beliefs about black students regardless of their achievements; however, others would change their views once black students demonstrated their intelligence. Yet, at the time of the study, students were still combating these negative stereotypes even though many of them maintained GPAs above 3.0. This demonstrates that high scholastic achievement was not enough to dismantle prejudicial beliefs about black students. In fact, previous research shows high-achieving students may be most vulnerable to stereotype threat (Steele 1997).

The third finding of this study revealed that institutional agents engaged in cultural socialization whereby informants directly or indirectly promote racial pride. In the context of STEM, these CSP agents showed students how their intellectual abilities were assets rather than deficits in the STEM community. They had the capacity to not only contribute to teams and group projects in curricular settings but could also have an impact in scientific research and discovery. While it seemed that students were not being valued much for their intellectual abilities at JSU, students such as Kari learned in his internship that race was not as significant of an issue in industry as it was in the college context. This distinction may be due to the types of students who attend JSU. Being a land-grant institution, it attracts many of its students from within the state. In contrast, a STEM-based company may draw its professionals from a variety of places in the United States and broader global community.

Finally, little attention was given to the intersectional marginalization black women and black men encounter. In fact, gender was brought up only once by an institutional agent. One student also indicated his gender when responding to questions about his black identity in STEM contexts. The lack of attention to this matter raises concerns given the increased attention to black men in higher education (Moore et al. 2003) and women of color in STEM (Ong et al. 2011). Collin suggested that program staff desire to create a welcoming environment for CSP students to share information and receive tailored support; however, black women may not feel comfortable with seeking assistance when combating gendered racism if institutional agents are not including any discussion of gender or intersectional bias as they socialize students within these contexts.

IMPLICATIONS

The findings indicate that educational leaders should consider instituting mandatory implicit bias training or diversity courses for all postsecondary education students. Black students in this study shared how they struggled with relevancy and inclusion in STEM contexts mostly because of white peers who did not believe they had the requisite intellectual ability. Institutional agents countered these perceptions by reminding students of their assets and how their backgrounds and identities were critical to the classroom environment. While these efforts are commendable, institutional leaders need to take greater responsibility for minimizing marginalization if the United States is to increase the number of individuals who earn STEM degrees, especially among underrepresented groups (McGee and Martin 2011). This study also shows how the lack of an intersectional lens falls short in disrupting exclusive STEM environments. Over thirty scholarly articles show that women of color encounter a double-bind that affects their pathways in STEM (Ong et al. 2011). Future studies should examine how institutional agents can help marginalized students whose identities vary along intersectional categories of difference navigate STEM climates that remain biased, and identify mechanisms for supporting them. Like Fries-Britt and colleagues (2013), researchers should also investigate how family income and class may disadvantage or advantage marginalized groups in STEM. For example, Fries-Britt found that black second-generation students had experiences similar to those of their white middle-class peers in terms of educational attainment and familial and social capital. However, for many students of color, this is not the case. Policies such as differential tuition as one matriculates to upper-division courses in engineering have been shown to disadvantage students at the intersections of race and class (George-Jackson, Rincón, and Martinez 2012).

CONCLUSION

This qualitative case study illuminated how institutional agents help black students understand and negotiate their racialized identities in the STEM disciplines at a large, public, predominantly white research university in the Midwest. Using RES as an analytic lens, findings revealed that institutional agents engaged in three practices: (1) have difficult conversations, (2) focus on performance and building competencies, and (3) reinforce students' belongingness and capacity to contribute to the STEM disciplines. While the institutional agents provided some useful strategies for navigating racial climate, additional efforts should be geared toward unpacking institutional and systemic racism, sexism, and the intersectionality of racial and gender bias (Ong et al. 2011). Given students' experiences with racial microaggressions in these disciplines, I also recommend that implicit bias training or diversity courses be required for all postsecondary education students. Both institutional agents and students discussed the chilly climate for marginalized populations and experiences of being alienated in the classroom environment. Similar to the institutional agents in this study, educators should also identify ways to promote racial pride among black students in STEM.

REFERENCES

Carlone, Heidi B., and Angela Johnson. 2007. "Understanding the Science Experiences of Successful Women of Color: Science Identity as an Analytic Lens." *Journal of Research in Science Teaching* 44 (8): 1187–1218.

Crenshaw, Kimberle. 1991. "Mapping the Margins: Intersectionality, Identity Politics, and Violence against Women of Color." *Stanford Law Review* 43 (6): 1241–1299.

Dill, Bonnie T., and Ruth E. Zambrana. 2009. "Critical Thinking about Inequality: An Emerging Lens." In *Emerging Intersections: Race, Class, Gender in Theory, Policy, and Practice*, edited by B. T. Dill and R. E. Zambrana, 1–21. New Brunswick, NJ: Rutgers University Press.

Fries-Britt, Sharon, Jennifer Johnson, and Brian Burt. 2013. "Students in Physics: The Intersection of Academic Ability, Race, Gender, and Class." In *Living at the Intersections: Social Identities and Black Collegians*, edited by T. Strayhorn, 21–39. Charlotte, NC: Information Age Press.

George-Jackson, Casey E., Blanca Rincón, Mariana G. Martinez. 2012. "Low-Income Engineering Students: Considering Financial Aid and Differential Tuition." *Journal of Student Financial Aid* 42 (2): 4–24.

Hughes, Diane, James Rodriguez, Emilie P. Smith, Deborah J. Johnson, Howard C. Stevenson, and Paul Spicer. 2006. "Parents' Ethnic-Racial Socialization Practices: A Review of Research and Directions for Future Study." *Developmental Psychology* 42 (5): 747–770.

Ireland, Danyelle T., Kimberly E. Freeman, Cynthia E. Winston-Proctor, Kendra D. DeLaine, and Stacey M. Lowe. 2018. "(Un)hidden Figures: A Synthesis of Research Examining the Intersectional Experiences of Black Women and Girls in STEM Education." *Review of Research in Education* 42 (1): 226–254.

Johnson, Dawn R. 2012. "Campus Racial Climate Perceptions and Overall Sense of Belonging among Racially Diverse Women in STEM Majors." *Journal of College Student Development* 53 (2): 336–346.

Johnson, Dawn R., Timothy H. Wasserman, Nilay Yildirim, and Barbara A. Yonai. 2014. "Examining the Effects of Stress and Campus Climate on the Persistence of Students of Color and White Students: An Application of Bean and Eaton's Psychological Model of Retention." *Research in Higher Education* 55 (1): 75–100.

Lane, Tonisha B., Blanca Rincón, Renata A. Revelo, and Kali Morgan. Forthcoming. "Addressing Multiculturalism in STEM: An Analysis of Theories That Inform our Research." In *Multicultural Education in the 21st Century: Innovative Research and Practice*, edited by Christopher B. Newman, Adriel A. Hilton, Brandi Hinnant-Crawford, and C. Spencer Platt. Charlotte, NC: Information Age Publishing.

McGee, Ebony O., and Danny B. Martin. 2011. "'You Would Not Believe What I Have to Go through to Prove My Intellectual Value!' Stereotype Management among Academically Successful Black Mathematics and Engineering Students." *American Educational Research Journal* 48 (6): 1347–1389.

Miles, M. B., A. Michael Huberman, and Johnny Saldaña. 2014. *Qualitative Data Analysis: A Methods Sourcebook*. Thousand Oaks, CA: Sage.

Moore, James L., III, Octavia Madison-Colmore, and Dionne M. Smith. 2003. "The Prove-Them-Wrong Syndrome: Voices from Unheard African-American Males in Engineering Disciplines." *Journal of Men's Studies* 12 (1): 61–73.

Museus, Samuel D., and Kathleen M. Neville. 2012. "Delineating the Ways That Key Institutional Agents Provide Racial Minority Students with Access to Social Capital in College." *Journal of College Student Development* 53 (3): 436–452.

Museus, Samuel D., Robert T. Palmer, Ryan J. Davis, and Dina Maramba, 2011. *Racial and Ethnic Minority Student Success in STEM Education: ASHE Higher Education Report* 36 (6). San Francisco: John Wiley and Sons.

National Science Foundation, National Center for Science and Engineering Statistics. 2017. *Women, Minorities, and Persons with Disabilities in Science and Engineering: 2017*. Special Report NSF 17-310. Arlington, VA. Accessed August 18, 2017. www.nsf.gov/statistics /wmpd/.

Ong, Maria, Carol Wright, Lorelle Espinosa, and Gary Orfield. 2011. "Inside the Double Bind: A Synthesis of Empirical Research on Undergraduate and Graduate Women of Color in Science, Technology, Engineering, and Mathematics." *Harvard Educational Review* 81 (2): 172–209.

Saldaña, J. 2015. *The Coding Manual for Qualitative Researchers*. Thousand Oaks, CA: Sage.

Sedlacek, William. 2017. *Measuring Noncognitive Variables: Improving Admissions, Success and Retention for Underrepresented Students*. Sterling, VA: Stylus Publishing.

Seymour, Elaine, and Nancy M. Hewitt. 1997. *Talking about Leaving: Why Undergraduates Leave the Sciences*. Boulder, CO: Westview Press.

Stanton-Salazar, Ricardo D. 2011. "A Social Capital Framework for the Study of Institutional Agents and Their Role in the Empowerment of Low-Status Students and Youth." *Youth and Society* 43 (3): 1066–1109.

Steele, Claude M. 1997. "A Threat in the Air: How Stereotypes Shape Intellectual Identity and Performance." *American Psychologist* 52: 613–629.

Stevenson, Howard C., Jr. 1994. "Validation of the Scale of Racial Socialization for African American Adolescents: Steps Toward Multidimensionality." *Journal of Black Psychology* 20 (4): 445–468.

Yin, Robert K. 2009. *Case Study Research: Design and Methods*. Thousand Oaks, CA: Sage.

14 · EXCLUSION, PERSPECTIVE TAKING, AND THE LIMINAL ROLE OF HIGHER EDUCATION STAFF IN SUPPORTING STUDENTS WITH DISABILITIES

ANNEMARIE VACCARO AND
EZEKIEL KIMBALL

The percentage of students with disabilities pursuing a postsecondary degree has grown rapidly, but degree attainment rates for students with disabilities still lag behind peers without disabilities (NCES 2016). Students with disabilities often face a chilly campus climate while contending with prevailing societal disability stigmas (Baker, Boland, and Nowik 2012; Trammell 2009). Higher education staff are expected to actively promote inclusion on campus (ACPA/NASPA 2015). Yet, little research documents how student affairs practitioners work to effectively support students with disabilities (Kimball, Vaccaro, and Vargas 2016; Vaccaro et al. 2015). This chapter helps rectify this problem by sharing the findings from a study anchored in a constructivist grounded theory approach of the ways postsecondary staff members from twenty-one institutions in the northeastern United States conceptualized and responded to disability on campus. During focus groups, professionals described a range of observed behaviors directed toward students with disabilities by campus peers without disabilities. To combat uncivil and exclusionary peer behavior, staff members navigated their liminal role to foster inclusion by teaching, modeling, and creating conditions for civil behavior and perspective taking. This chapter offers insight into the intersected nature of campus inclusion and exclusion through the lens of both social identity and institutional positionality.

LITERATURE REVIEW

The Americans with Disabilities Act (ADA) of 1990 defines disability as a physical or mental impairment that substantially limits a major life activity such as "communicating and working as well as caring for oneself, performing manual tasks, seeing, hearing, eating, walking, standing, lifting, bending, speaking, and breathing" (1990, Chapter 126, Sec. 12102). Eighteen years after passing, the ADA was amended to include cognitive activities such as learning disabilities and mental health disorders when they impair the life activities listed above (ADAA 2008).

Throughout the U.S. educational pipeline, students with disabilities are legally afforded different types of access and support. For instance, the Individuals with Disabilities Education Act (IDEA) requires students with disabilities be afforded a Free and Appropriate Public Education (FAPE) through high school graduation or age twenty-one. Students are not guaranteed a FAPE after high school graduation or after age twenty-one. However, a 2004 amendment to the IDEA specifies that higher education institutions should provide accommodations for students with disabilities and be accessible to all. Meanwhile, the ADAA (2008) specifies that students with disabilities have a legal right to access higher education institutions and to receive any necessary and reasonable accommodations necessary to do so. The intent of this legal framework is to create parity with peers without disabilities in terms of the accessibility of spaces, programs, and events. While there are a variety of accommodation guidelines for higher education institutions (Bryan and Myers 2006; Burke, Friedl, and Rigler 2010), many colleges and universities are not fully prepared to support the accommodation needs of students with disabilities (Belch and Marshak 2006; Kimball, Vaccaro, and Vargas 2016). The end result is a complex, often vexing support environment for students with disabilities, their peers, their instructors, and student affairs staff given the multitude of ways students with the same diagnoses and documentation might require support (Lee 2014; White and Vo 2006).

For peers, instructors, and even disability services staff members, the complex nature of disability itself may make understanding the need and creating an inclusive campus community more difficult: disability is simultaneously a social construction, medical diagnosis, legal status, and a part of a person's sense of self (Friedensen and Kimball 2017). Many people can hide their disabilities— either deliberately or inadvertently—from the view of others (Riddell and Weedon 2014; Tinklin, Riddell, and Wilson 2004). Further, statutory regulations require that records related to accommodations remain confidential, which means most staff, faculty, and peers have no right to know the disability status of a university student. Consequently, members of a campus community may not know when a disability is shaping their interactions with a student. This lack of knowledge may be especially problematic for higher education staff members who consider identity development as they create programs, services, and environmental conditions for individual and community development.

One of the reasons why students may not disclose a disability is because they perceive the campus climate to be unsupportive of students with disabilities based on a lifetime of navigating societal disability stigmas (Baker, Boland, and Nowik 2012; Trammell 2009). Students with disabilities face a prevailing social stigma that holds that they are less capable than their peers (Markoulakis and Kirsh 2013; May and Stone 2010). Perceived acceptance by and support from peers and faculty play an important role in students' sense of belonging and perceptions of campus climate (Daly-Cano, Vaccaro, and Newman 2015). Some studies show students with disabilities have difficulty developing positive relationships with, or receiving support from, faculty (Barnard-Brak, Lechtenberger, and Lan 2010; Olney and Brockelman 2003) and peers (Adams and Proctor 2010; Megivern, Pellerito, and Mowbray 2003).

Equally troubling, we know almost nothing about the perceptions and experiences of higher education staff who, by the nature of their work, are called on to intervene when interactions between students with and without disabilities go wrong because of underlying stigmas, stereotypes, and misinformation. Only one recent study examined the interconnected campus experiences of staff members and students with disabilities—with student affairs professionals reporting a lack of preparedness to support this population of students (Kimball, Vaccaro, and Vargas 2016). The dearth of empirical research is especially troubling since higher education professionals are expected to have the awareness, knowledge, skills, and dispositions to facilitate the holistic development of *all* college students—including students with disabilities.

The literature reviewed above makes the case that students with disabilities are actively minoritized and marginalized on college campuses from multiple groups, not just peers. As a result, both individual students and institutional climates benefit when students, staff, and faculty participate in stigma reduction interventions (Junco and Salter 2004; Milligan 2010). These efforts are part of a broader institutional imperative to foster perspective taking among campus community members "to create more welcoming, and ultimately, transformative environments where meaningful interactions, policies, and practices can prevail" (Ortiz and Patton 2012, 24–25). Most of this work has focused on formal interventions for faculty members. Thus, more work is needed on the intersected experiences of students (both with and without disabilities) and the staff members who work with them (again, both with and without disabilities). This chapter begins to fill that gap.

METHODS

We used focus group methods to generate data for a constructivist grounded theory study (Charmaz 2006; Morgan 1997). Six of seven focus groups took place at
a regional conference for higher education and student affairs professionals. The
seventh focus group and one peer debriefing session were conducted at a small,
private liberal arts college and a medium-sized public research university after the
conference. All focus groups utilized a loosely structured protocol that included
the following questions: (1) How do you define disability? (2) What role does
thinking about people with disabilities play in your work as a higher education
professional? (3) Tell us about your experiences with disability or with people
with disabilities on campus. (4) What people and offices provide support for students with disabilities or leadership on disability-related issues? (5) What obstacles exist on your campus in working with students with disabilities? More detailed
data collection practices for this study can be found elsewhere (Kimball, Vaccaro,
and Vargas 2016).

Sample

Participants were recruited using both purposive (the conference gave us access
to higher education staff from an array of functional areas and institutional types)
and convenience strategies (anyone who volunteered could participate). Focus
groups varied in size from two to nine participants. Our sample included thirty-
one participants from twenty-one higher education institutions across New
England. Roughly a third of the participants worked at four public institutions,
while the majority came from seventeen private postsecondary schools. There was
considerable heterogeneity in the higher education role, level of education, and
experience levels of participants. The focus groups were attended by fourteen
senior-level, five midlevel, eight entry-level, and four graduate-level professionals. Four participants had bachelor degrees, twenty had master degrees, and seven
had doctoral degrees. Participants represented departments including Residential Life $(n=14)$, Student Activities/Leadership $(n=6)$, Disability Services
$(n=2)$, Health Services $(n=1)$, and Student Affairs/Dean's Offices $(n=8)$. A total
of nineteen women and twelve men self-identified as white $(n=26)$, black $(n=3)$,
and Latino $(n=1)$. One participant did not specify their race and/or ethnicity.
Eight staff participants reported having a disability. To protect participants, we
use pseudonyms and remove identifying information throughout.

Data Analysis and Trustworthiness

We used a grid analysis framework immediately after each focus group to examine variations in perspective within each focus group, across focus groups, within
each question, and across questions (Morgan 1997). Subsequently, we used constant comparative analysis to systematically explore data from all seven focus

group transcripts (Charmaz 2006). During the analytic process, we revisited preliminary themes from our grid analysis and compared them with grounded, open codes that emerged from transcript analysis. Next, we generated axial codes by combining similar open codes. Those focused codes were then synthesized into themes. Throughout this process we used member checking, peer reviews, negative case analysis, and triangulation to enhance the trustworthiness of our analysis (Jones, Torres, and Arminio 2014). Our grounded theory model highlighting core themes is presented elsewhere (Kimball, Vaccaro, and Vargas 2016). In this chapter, we draw on axial codes not addressed in our prior work to explain staff observations of student (in)civility toward students with disabilities and practitioners' efforts to foster inclusion by teaching civility and perspective taking.

Limitations

Our study has several limitations. First, with any focus group that moves quickly toward consensus (as ours did), there is a possibility that divergent opinions held by participants were not shared. Second, our participants were mostly white, had traditional student affairs work experience, and came from private institutions in a relatively narrow geographic region. These limitations make transferability to other professional populations and campuses potentially problematic. Another limitation is that data were collected solely from staff members. Since assessing, and responding to, student behaviors through the lens of law, policy, and theory is a hallmark of many staff positions in higher education, we argue that our data—based on practitioner observations and interactions with students—are a valuable point of entry to campus climate for students with disabilities, civility, and campus inclusion. Future research, however, should collect paired data directly from students and staff to examine these topics further.

FINDINGS

A prominent theme from the focus groups concerned the perceptions of communities of students without disabilities who acted in mostly exclusionary ways toward peers with disabilities as well as the reactions of students with disabilities to this behavior. Higher education staff members either directly observed or had reported to them by students with disabilities these student behavior incidents. The findings—separated into two sections—highlight the experiences of students with disabilities and their peers without disabilities, as well as the experiences of staff members who attempted to create inclusive campus environments.

The interconnected experiences between students with disabilities and those without disabilities compose our first finding. Professionals in our study perceived a range of attitudes and behaviors toward students with disabilities, including (1) acceptance, (2) unawareness, frustration, and questioning the legitimacy of accommodations, and (3) outright bullying. Since little literature documents the ways students with disabilities are treated by peers, we felt it was important to highlight the range of behaviors, noting the predominantly uncivil ones that warranted staff members' interventions. In the second section, we share findings exemplifying the various ways higher education staff responded to incivility toward students with disabilities. Through individual interactions, role modeling, and programming, postsecondary staff members taught civility and perspective taking in order to create inclusive campus communities.

(Un)Civil Communities for Students with Disabilities

In this section, we highlight the intersected campus experiences of students with and without disabilities as observed by higher education staff. It is possible that staff members were more prone to relate negative cases and utilized the focus group as a form of collective problem solving. However, it is still striking that across seven focus groups *only one* narrative emerged wherein practitioners reported students without disabilities collectively behaved in an inclusive and compassionate manner toward students with disabilities. One staff member explained how an entire community stepped up to support a peer with a disability without prompting: "We had two residents, quadriplegic residents who moved into one of our residence halls. . . . And one of our students lost their personal care attendant. So, she started advertising for a fellow resident to become that personal care attendant. What was fascinating to me with that situation was how engrossed the whole community became with that process and cared for that one student." While heartening, this case also reveals one of the paradoxical elements of many forms of disability: they are often hidden from the view of peers. In this case, the students in question had a very visible form of disability and actively requested support from the community via their attempt to hire a personal care attendant.

Despite this positive example, most stories reflected a lack of awareness and knowledge about students with nonapparent disabilities by peers without disabilities. Two examples highlight how students without disabilities did not understand why particular students needed accommodations. In the first case, a personal assistant for a student with a disability was given a room key, which made the roommates uncomfortable. Karma explained: "We would have personal aids coming in. . . . They would have keys to the room. . . . What happens when [the roommates are] like, 'No way do I want some random woman having a key to our room coming in all hours of the day and night.'" This situation posed a potential conflict between students with disabilities and those without disabilities and the staff members who worked with them. Legally, practitioners cannot disclose any information about a student's disability, and in practice, students assume that they have a right to privacy in their own residence hall rooms. While ethically and legally the needs of the student with the disability should be met, that standard of privacy was questioned by community members whose lives were impacted by an accommodation.

In another incident, students complained about a service animal and demanded a reason why someone could have a dog but they could not. The fact that the student with an invisible disability was not a model community member complicated the situation further. Fabio explained: "Part of the problem with the service animal is the student was not washing the dog. It was smelling and it was causing allergies for somebody else in the room and that presented more of a [challenge. Students wondered] 'Why does this person have the animal or have the dog?' We had to have a discussion about [how] . . . everybody functions in a different way. We could not disclose her disability. [. . .] In a way [my role] was being a mediator . . . to help build . . . a respectful community." While it is unreasonable and unfair to expect that students with disabilities will behave perfectly in order to avoid these complex situations, higher education staff, like Fabio, are asked to mediate between two unenviable positions when they do not. In both of these instances, it was clear that community members were not aware of the issues faced by, or the legal rights of, students with disabilities. Moreover, they showed little capacity or willingness to engage in basic levels of perspective taking. As Fabio explained, he tried to get the complainants to understand that "everybody functions in a different way." Unfortunately, these students seemed to focus only on their own needs and concerns and did not engage in perspective taking.

Responding to unaware students who lacked perspective-taking skills was a challenge, but it was even more difficult for staff to manage incivility and outright discrimination when they emerged. A number of disturbing stories highlighted uncivil behaviors perpetrated against students with disabilities. One professional shared the following example of an entire community engaging in harmful behavior against a former friend: "I actually had a student come to me very concerned. She has a severe allergy to nuts. . . . When she came to me and she was distraught . . . She disclosed [her allergy] to some friends on the floor. Things had gone wrong [and they were no longer friends], and so they thought it would be funny . . . putting peanut butter or peanut butter oil on their hands. It was public bathrooms so they would touch different things all over the place. . . . She told me that she had been to the health center on campus or to the ER three times already within the start of the semester." The person sharing this example further revealed that they thought that the students who perpetrated the bullying likely did not realize the seriousness of their actions and were not seeing the interaction from the standpoint of the student with a peanut allergy.

In another example, Dalyn explained how community members "picked on" a student by using his disability against him. She was disappointed in the behavior and deeply empathetic toward a student with a disability who had to endure bullying from peers. "There was a situation earlier this year that was particularly heartbreaking. There was a student who identified to a [staff member] that he had

Asperger's. The people on his floor . . . noticed he was exhibiting some socially inappropriate behaviors, perhaps he was standing at people's doorway maybe longer than what the other students would have preferred. . . . The students had started picking on him a little bit. There were some rude notes on his door." Since this student did not want to disclose his disability to anyone but residence life staff, Dalyn struggled with the right response. On the one hand, as a student affairs staff member she had an obligation to educate those involved in discriminatory behavior, but doing so was difficult without revealing confidential information. On the other hand, Dalyn might be able to have a conversation with the student about the social norms of the residence hall, but doing so would raise issues about the potential to blame the victim. Another participant, Emma, nicely summarized this dilemma for higher education staff members: "It's never okay to pick on anybody, but how do you educate [other students] about appropriate behavior and how do you get resources to the student [with the disability?] . . . How do you get help for a student who doesn't want to be identified?" For Emma and many other participants, the imperfect answer came down to teaching all students about civility and perspective taking.

Working toward Inclusion by Teaching Civility and Perspective Taking

For our participants, the professional and ethical responsibility to educate students about perspective taking, respect, and civility led to many different ways of doing social justice work on campus—not merely through formal means such as classrooms and educational programs. Practitioners used individual conversations and role modeling inclusive behavior. They also worked to create empowering environments where students with disabilities could succeed and debunk stereotypes. For example, many staff members educated students about civility and perspective taking through individual conversations. Palmer focuses on respect, empathy, perspective taking, and setting behavioral expectations when using individual conversations as a means of civility education. He said, "Usually I have to call the students in to talk to them about their behavior. I think that our students have the ability to be empathetic, but they don't know when to do it. They need some ground rules, some understanding to understand why the person or individual is behaving that way." In addition to one-to-one interventions, participants talked about educating students about perspective taking through programmatic interventions. Abby's office was planning a campaign to educate the general population about disabilities and to also inspire potential activism among the general student population.

Another way practitioners educated students about civility and attempted to foster inclusion was by serving as a role model for inclusion. Staff members felt obligated to walk the talk and show the campus community what it meant to understand the needs of others and stand up for their rights—even when it was unpopular. Morris explained how he canceled a student retreat when a student who used a wheelchair could not access the bus: "This bus company . . . did not bring the bus that had the lift on it (even though one was requested). Their drivers and their owner said, 'That's all right, we'll just lift her on.' I said, 'Oh no you won't.' It became quite an altercation with the company. . . . Initially [my institution was] not pleased with my response. Of course [the student with a disability] somehow found out about it later and was very appreciative but very humble. But, this was not about her. This was about the bus company and about all of our students having a fair, enjoyable and safe time." Morris role modeled inclusion not merely to show support for an individual student but also to educate *all* students (and his colleagues) about the importance of perspective taking.

As part of their strategy for fostering inclusion by teaching perspective taking and civility, some staff members intentionally sought to debunk stereotypes and reduce the stigma of disability. Genuine perspective taking can happen only when students see their peers through authentic versus stereotypical and stigmatized lenses. In many cases, offices or departments engaged in educational programming (as described by Abby earlier) to accomplish this goal. Others intentionally crafted environments where students with disabilities were empowered to shine and debunk stereotypes through everyday, self-directed behaviors. The art faculty member in the following example created a space for a student with a disability to shine (and thus debunk stereotypes) by highlighting a student's artistic masterpiece during a regularly scheduled weekly critique. Mia, a staff member who worked with the student regularly, recounted the story: "The student is diagnosed with Cerebral Palsy (CP) and is nonverbal and has limited mobility in his hands. . . . And I think that people saw him and had very little ability to interact with him initially and had, as a result, very low expectations. And, in the first round of assignments and critiques a faculty member posted one of the pieces of work. Students were just amazed and wondering who had done it. And when they said it was this student with CP, I think it was a major shift for a lot of students around challenging expectations of what they had assumed he would be capable of doing and producing." We are not advocating the responsibility for challenging stereotypes and stigma should belong to students with disabilities. That burden is given all too often to members of marginalized communities. We do, however, want to note the importance of encouraging self-determination and self-advocacy for all students, including students with disabilities. When higher education staff members create environments where students with disabilities can self-advocate and succeed, stereotypes and stigma can be exposed and debunked more easily. Another participant conveyed the delicate balance of providing necessary accommodations, ensuring safety, engaging community support, and self-advocacy. Tabitha shared, "It's empowering to students [with disabilities when] they share their own information to advocate for themselves, but you don't want to put them in a complicated position. I think it's things like trying to make sure you're prepared and can serve them without crossing any boundaries or putting a student in an uncomfortable position and have to do that for themselves." In sum, higher education staff members engaged in a variety of tactics to teach students about perspective taking and civility to create inclusive campus communities for students with disabilities who were excluded and stigmatized.

DISCUSSION AND IMPLICATIONS

Higher education staff members in our study revealed important new insight concerning the role of disability in the creation of inclusive communities on college campuses. Interconnections between students with disabilities and those without disabilities varied, but often included uncivil and bullying behaviors. Our findings highlight the extent to which the position of higher education staff members in these interactions is a liminal one. During interactions between students with disabilities and their peers without disabilities, there is often information asymmetry wherein each party is largely unaware of the thinking, motivation, and intent of the other. In many cases, students were ignorant of the fact that a peer had a disability and right to a particular accommodation. Of course, part of the ignorance stems from the right to privacy and confidentiality of medical records. Students with disabilities seldom knew how disgruntled their peers were until an issue resulted in uncivil behavior. As a consequence of this lack of information, students may be fundamentally unable to engage in the sort of perspective taking that would lead to inclusive campus communities (Ortiz and Patton 2012). In many cases, higher education staff members have more complete information than students and can play a mediating role in the creation of an inclusive campus community. However, managing this liminal role is rarely straightforward. Even when educators and staff themselves know a student has a disability, privacy and confidentiality regulations mean they cannot divulge this information to other students or professional colleagues who have no legitimate educational reason to know (ADA 1990; ADAA 2008). Instead, they must draw on the more general practices that support the creation of an inclusive campus community while also being attentive to the more specific needs of students with disabilities (ACPA/NASPA 2015; Kimball, Vaccaro, and Vargas 2016).

Navigating these competing pressures would be made easier by a more complete understanding of the way in which disability intersects with the perspective-taking capacity of college students. Our findings offer preliminary insight that suggests the interface might be quite problematic. Students without disabilities struggled to comprehend the prospect that a "hidden" aspect of a peer's personhood might result in differential treatment while also being equitable (Riddell and Weedon 2014; Tinklin, Riddell, and Wilson 2004). Educators have an ethical responsibility to create environments wherein students with disabilities can engage in self-advocacy, debunk stereotypes, and in turn reduce stigma (Adams and Proctor 2010; Test et al. 2005). The staff members in our study recognized the intersected nature of campus identities (i.e., disability), experiences, and positions (staff, students) and were thus sensitive to the complex nature of this type of inclusion work.

Despite their liminal role, staff members utilized a variety of interventions intended to create inclusive environments for all students, but especially the historically minoritized population of students with disabilities. Those strategies included educating community members about perspective taking and civility and role modeling inclusion. Consistent with literature on student affairs practice, the venues for these strategies included one-on-one conversations, formal educational programs, and alterations to existing policies and practices (Kimball, Vaccaro, and Vargas 2016). These interventions allowed staff members to alter student behaviors and educate entire communities without breaching the anonymity to which students with disabilities are entitled. Given the limited scholarship available to support these interventions, higher education staff could benefit from the use of structured thinking about the intention, design, and impact of programs as a way of mitigating potentially deleterious implicit theories based on stigma, stereotype, or misinformation (Reason and Kimball 2012).

Higher education literature suggests that professional staff members have a responsibility to foster inclusion on campus (ACPA/NASPA 2015; Ortiz and Patton 2012). Our findings demonstrate the dire need for campuses to engage in proactive efforts to increase civility and improve the climate for students with disabilities. Staff members can lead these efforts, but the realities of the intersected nature of college campuses suggest that they cannot achieve inclusion by working alone. Staff members must partner with faculty and students to mitigate their complicity in perpetuating the marginalization of students with disabilities.

Campuses can begin the work of fostering inclusion by assessing the climate for people with disabilities (see Stodden, Brown, and Roberts 2011) and conceptualizing disability as a key component of institutional diversity (Vaccaro and Kimball 2016). While a great deal of attention has been paid to other social identities as they relate to institutional diversity, less attention has focused on students with disabilities, which can intersect with other identities to compound students' experience of marginalization on college campuses. We contend that disability should be included as a key element in campus conversations about diversity. These discussions should focus on disability as a marginalized identity and as an identity that intersects with race, gender, class, sexuality, and religion to shape the life experiences of students in unique ways.

Drawing on research showing formal programs may provide a catalyst for stigma reduction (Junco and Salter 2004; Milligan 2010), campuses must regularly provide disability awareness workshops (for students, staff, and faculty) with information about hidden and visible disabilities, rights/accommodations, and stigma. The uncivil and exclusionary behaviors described here also suggest disability awareness must be combined with perspective taking and civility education.

Graduate programs in higher education and student affairs play an important role in preparing novice professionals to navigate the legal, behavioral, and moral complexities related to the topics covered in this chapter. As scholars have noted, higher education staff report feeling underprepared to support college students with disabilities, typically because their graduate programs included little information about disability (Kimball, Vaccaro, and Vargas 2016). Yet, the most recent professional competencies for student affairs professionals suggest practitioners need to have the awareness, knowledge, skills, and dispositions to support students with all abilities and backgrounds (ACPA/NASPA 2015). Therefore, graduate programs must infuse disability topics throughout the curriculum so that emerging higher education practitioners have a foundation of law, theory, and best practices to draw on when they are faced with the liminal role of supporting students with disabilities, combating disability incivility, and teaching perspective taking to all students. Students in graduate preparation programs must know how to answer questions related to law, theory, and practice. At a minimum, students must have a strong understanding of the complex legal and ethical considerations related to disability support in the postsecondary learning environment. Typically, that understanding entails knowledge of both federal legislation (e.g., ADA, ADAA, IDEA) and relevant case law. Students should also be taught the various theoretical paradigms related to disability and be able to describe how different theoretical lenses (e.g., critical disability versus medical model) would lead to very different strategies for student affairs practice.

However, knowing the programs, services, and accommodations to which students are legally entitled is not enough: graduate students should also learn how to foster inclusion beyond what is legally required. One way to do this is to teach graduate students universal design principles (Burgstahler and Cory 2008) and require students to infuse the principles into assignments and practice. Another strategy is to encourage students to learn about promising practices from literature (Vance, Lipsitz, and Parks 2014) and develop new ones based on their core understandings of good student affairs practice (Kimball, Vaccaro, and Vargas 2016).

CONCLUSION

Our study offers preliminary insight into disability, perspective taking, and civility within campus communities. Our data suggest a wide range of uncivil and exclusionary behaviors are directed at students with disabilities by their peers. These findings may stem from an inability of students without disabilities to engage in perspective taking. By examining the intersected nature of disability identity, we exposed persistently exclusionary student-to-student behaviors. The simultaneous focus on the intersected nature of institutional positionality additionally afforded us the opportunity to document the liminal role of higher education staff members as they attempted to foster inclusive campus communities by role modeling inclusion and educating students about civility and perspective taking. Future research should continue to focus on better understanding the thoughts and behaviors of those members of the campus community (e.g., peers, student affairs practitioners, faculty members) whose actions profoundly shape learning environments for students with disabilities as well as how educators can support students with disabilities as they react to unwelcoming learning environments.

REFERENCES

ACPA/NASPA. 2015. *ACPA/NASPA Professional Competency Areas for Student Affairs Educators.* Washington, DC: ACPA/NASPA.

Adams, Katharine S., and Briley F. Proctor. 2010. "Adaptation to College for Students with and without Disabilities: Group Differences and Predictors." *Journal of Postsecondary Education and Disability* 22 (3): 166–183. https://www.ahead.org/publications/jped.

Americans with Disabilities Act of 1990. 42 U.S.C.A. § 12101 et seq.

Americans with Disabilities Amendments Act of 2008, Pub.L. No. 110-325, 29 U.S.C.S. § 705.

Baker, Kerrie Q., Kathleen Boland, and Christine M. Nowik. 2012. "A Campus Survey of Faculty and Student Perceptions of Persons with Disabilities." *Journal of Postsecondary Education and Disability* 25 (4): 309–329. http://www.ahead.org/publications/jped.

Barnard-Brak, Lucy, DeAnn Lechtenberger, and William Y. Lan. 2010. "Accommodation Strategies of College Students with Disabilities." *Qualitative Report* 15 (2): 411–429. http://nsuworks.nova.edu/tqr/vol15/iss2/10.

Belch, Holley A., and Laura E. Marshak. 2006. "Critical Incidents Involving Students with Psychiatric Disabilities: The Gap between State of the Art and Campus Practice." *NASPA Journal* 43 (3): 464–483.

Bryan, Anne, and Karen A. Myers. 2006. "Students with Disabilities: Doing What's Right." *About Campus* 11 (4): 18–22.

Burgstahler, Sheryl E., and Rebecca C. Cory. 2008. *Universal Design in Higher Education: From Principles to Practice.* Cambridge, MA: Harvard Education Press.

Burke, Lisa A., John Friedl, and Michelle Rigler. 2010. "The 2008 Amendments to the Americans with Disabilities Act: Implications for Student Affairs Practitioners." *Journal of Student Affairs Research and Practice* 47 (1): 63–77.

Charmaz, Kathy. 2006. *Constructing Grounded Theory: A Practical Guide through Qualitative Analysis.* Thousand Oaks, CA: SAGE.

Daly-Cano, Meada, Annemarie Vaccaro, and Barbara Newman. 2015. "College Student Narratives about Learning and Using Self-Advocacy Skills." *Journal of Postsecondary Education and Disability* 28 (2): 209–223. http://www.ahead.org/publications/jped.

Friedensen, Rachel, and Ezekiel Kimball. 2017. "Disability as Identity: A Critical Examination of a Multivalent Construct." In *Theory and Method in Higher Education Research*, edited by Jeroen Huisman and Malcolm Tight, 229–247. Somerville, MA: Emerald Publishing.

Jones, S. R., Vasti Torres, and Jan Arminio. 2014. *Negotiating the Complexities of Qualitative Research in Higher Education: Fundamental Elements and Issues.* 2nd ed. New York: Routledge.

Junco, Reynol, and Daniel W. Salter. 2004. "Improving the Campus Climate for Students with Disabilities through the Use of Online Training." *Journal of Student Affairs Research and Practice* 41 (2): 263–276.

Kimball, Ezekiel W., Annemarie Vaccaro, and Nadia Vargas. 2016. "Student Affairs Professionals Supporting Students with Disabilities: A Grounded Theory Model." *Journal of Student Affairs Research & Practice* 53 (2): 175–189.

Lee, Barbara A. 2014. "Students with Disabilities: Opportunities and Challenges for Colleges and Universities." *Change: The Magazine of Higher Learning* 61 (1): 40–45.

Markoulakis, Roula, and Bonnie Kirsh. 2013. "Difficulties for University Students with Mental Health Problems: A Critical Interpretive Synthesis." *Review of Higher Education* 37 (1): 77–100.

May, Alison L., and C. Addison Stone. 2010. "Stereotypes of Individuals with Learning Disabilities: Views of College Students with and without Disabilities." *Journal of Learning Disabilities* 43 (6): 483–499.

Megivern, Deborah, Sue Pellerito, and Carol Mowbray. 2003. "Barriers to Higher Education for Individuals with Psychiatric Disabilities." *Psychiatric Rehabilitation Journal* 23 (3): 217–231.

Milligan, Nancy V. 2010. "Effects of Training about Academic Accommodations on Perceptions and Intentions of Health Science Faculty." *Journal of Allied Health* 39 (1): 54–62.

Morgan, David L. 1997. *Focus Groups as Qualitative Research*. 2nd ed. Thousand Oaks, CA: Sage.

NCES (National Center for Education Statistics). 2016. *Digest of Education Statistics, 2014*. Washington, DC: NCES.

Olney, Marjorie F., and Karin F. Brockelman. 2003. "Out of the Disability Closet: Strategic Use of Perception Management by Select University Students with Disabilities." *Disability & Society* 18 (1): 35–50.

Ortiz, Anna M., and Lori D. Patton. 2012. "Awareness of Self." In *Why Aren't We There Yet? Taking Personal Responsibility for Creating an Inclusive Campus*, edited by Jan Arminio, Vasti Torres, and Raechele L. Pope, 9–31. Sterling, VA: Stylus.

Reason, Robert, and Ezekiel W. Kimball. 2012. "A New Theory-to-Practice Model for Student Affairs: Integrating Scholarship, Context, and Reflection." *Journal of Student Affairs Research & Practice* 49 (4): 359–376.

Riddell, Sheila, and Elisabet Weedon. 2014. "Disabled Students in Higher Education: Discourses of Disability and the Negotiation of Identity." *International Journal of Educational Research* 63: 38–46.

Stodden, Robert A., Steven E. Brown, and Kelly Roberts. 2011. "Disability-Friendly University Environments: Conducting a Climate Assessment." *New Directions for Higher Education* 154: 83–92. https://doi.org/10.1002/he.437.

Test, David W., Catherine H. Fowler, Wendy M. Wood, Denise M. Brewer, and Steven Eddy. 2005. "A Conceptual Framework of Self-Advocacy for Students with Disabilities." *Remedial and Special Education* 26 (1): 43–54.

Tinklin, Teresa, Sheila Riddell, and Alastair Wilson. 2004. *Disabled Students in Higher Education: A Center for Higher Educational Sociology (CES) Briefing*. Centre for Educational Sociology. http://www.ces.ed.ac.uk/PDF%20Files/Brief032.pdf.

Trammell, Jack. 2009. "Postsecondary Students and Disability Stigma: Development of the Postsecondary Student Survey of Disability-Related Stigma (PSSDS)." *Journal of Postsecondary Education and Disability* 22 (2): 106–116. https://www.ahead.org/publications/jped.

Vaccaro, Annemarie, Meada Daly-Cano, and Barbara Newman. 2015. "A Sense of Belonging among College Students with Disabilities: An Emergent Theoretical Model." *Journal of College Student Development* 56 (7): 670–686. http://dx.doi.org/10.1353/csd.2015.0072.

Vaccaro, Annemarie, and Ezekiel Kimball. 2016. "'It's a Very Deep, Layered Topic': Student Affairs Professionals on the Marginality and Intersectionality of Disability." In *Disability as Diversity in Higher Education: Policies and Practices to Enhance Student Success*, edited by Eunyoung Kim and Katherine C. Aquino, 138–152. New York: Routledge.

Vaccaro, Annemarie, Ezekiel W. Kimball, Ryan S. Wells, and Benjamin J. Ostiguy. 2015. "Researching Students with Disabilities: The Importance of Critical Perspectives." *New Directions for Institutional Research* 2014 (163): 25–41. doi:10.1002/ir.20084

Vance, Mary Lee, Neal E. Lipsitz, and Kaela Parks, eds. 2014. *Beyond the Americans with Disabilities Act: Inclusive Policy and Practice for Higher Education*. Washington, DC: National Association of Student Personnel Administrators.

White, Glen W., and Yen T. H. Vo. 2006. "Requesting Accommodations to Increase Full Participation in Higher Education: An Analysis of Self-Advocacy Training for Postsecondary Students with Learning and Other Disabilities." *Learning Disabilities: A Multidisciplinary Journal* 14 (1): 41–56. http://www.ldaamerica.org.

PART V INTERSECTIONALITY AND EQUITY EFFORTS AMONG CAMPUS COMMUNITIES

15 · MAKING ROOM FOR GENDERED POSSIBILITIES

Using Intersectionality to Discover Transnormative Inequalities in the Women's College Admissions Process

MEGAN NANNEY

National attention turned to Smith College, an elite women's college in Massachusetts, as it denied admission to Calliope Wong, an Asian American trans*[1] woman, in the spring of 2013. At the time of Wong's college search, Smith lacked a clear admissions policy for trans* applicants, a situation Wong (2012b) calls "problematic *un*policies." Smith stated that the institution would consider trans* students on a case-by-case basis. Wong was advised that Smith would consider her as long as her application materials reflected her *gender* identity as a woman, which could be accomplished by one of three methods: (1) submitting all application materials as female, (2) submitting online applications as male and submitting a paper application to Smith as female, or (3) submitting online application materials to coeducational institutions as male and, with the Common Application's help, change gender markers for online application materials sent to women's colleges (Wong 2012a). Upon following this advice, however, Smith rejected Wong's application because her optional Free Application for Federal Student Aid (FAFSA) form indicated her *sex* as male. As Wong's (2013) rejection letter read, "Thank you again for your interest in Smith College. . . . As you may remember from our previous correspondence, Smith is a women's college, which means that undergraduate applicants to Smith must be female at the time of admission. Our expectation is that it is consistently reflected throughout the application that the student is a woman. Upon reviewing your file, this is not the case. Your FAFSA indicates your gender as male. Therefore, Smith cannot process your application." Since then, nineteen women's colleges[2] in the United States have adopted transgender inclusive admissions policies (hereafter: trans* admissions policies) that codify up to fourteen different combinations of sex, gender, and legal criteria that define who is included and excluded from the category of "woman" and therefore who may and may not apply to their institutions (Nanney and Brunsma 2017).

Though many have celebrated what appears to be trans* inclusion within these gendered spaces (Marine 2009; Nanney 2017; Weber 2016), others note the limited reach such policies have for the day-to-day realities of trans* students (Fogg Davis 2017; Nanney and Brunsma 2017; Wong 2015). The introduction of transition-related requirements in these admissions policies raises the question of how these policies can simultaneously exclude and further marginalize trans* people based on precisely the same criteria. In other words, how does expanding admissions to *some* trans* people—albeit differently across institutions—limit the mission of trans* inclusion to only those most privileged trans* students who can access such transition-related criteria of womanhood? These seemingly neutral administrative criteria do not merely sort and manage pre-existing identities; rather, they produce the very categories that they seek to accommodate. Consequently, they reproduce inequality by focusing on transness as a singular and all-encompassing identity experience—as if trans* people experience *only* gender. What is missing are simultaneous analyses of race, class, and their relationships to binaries such as sex/gender and trans*/cis. Understanding trans* admissions policies, therefore, requires examining the interrelated influences of class and race on the lived experiences of trans* students in relation to legal documentation, medical services, and safety, among other experiences.

Drawing on an intersectional, critical trans* framework, I contend that sex and gender are not the sole institutional barriers for trans* college students. Instead, multiple intersecting barriers are codified within the language and implementation of these policies that result in seemingly inclusive policies reproducing inequitable outcomes. Through an inductive analysis grounded in the policy text and application materials at nineteen women's colleges, I call for higher education practitioners and policy makers to rethink adding trans* identities to pre-existing nondiscrimination policies that invite students into broken systems. I advocate for trickle-up justice and policy building (Dockendorff, Nanney, and Nicolazzo, forthcoming; Nicolazzo 2017; Spade 2015), led by students, to address the multiple, interlocking systems of inequalities preventing full inclusion in postsecondary systems of education for trans* students.

HISTORIES OF EXCLUSION

Institutions of higher education—regardless of their demographic composition—are "inequality regimes": the "interrelated practices, processes, actions and meanings that result in and maintain [intersecting] class, gender and race inequalities within particular organizations" (Acker 2006, 443). On the one hand, theorizing postsecondary institutions in terms of these regimes suggests that the institution comprises formal, rational policies and practices—called the ostensive routine. On the other hand, how the organization actually functions—called the performative routine—may diverge from the expressed values of the organization. Thus, even well-intentioned policies may result in unequal outcomes (Ahmed 2012; Lewis and Diamond 2015). These can be both achievement-based outcomes—including enrollment, test scores, and graduation rates—and qualitative inequities such as accessing certain resources on campus (Bilodeau 2007; Nanney and Brunsma 2017; Nicolazzo 2017). For example, it is well documented that while women enroll, test, and graduate at higher rates than men (DiPrete and Buchman 2013), women—especially women of color—also experience significant qualitative inequities including which fields they major in, quality of classroom and instructor interaction, and persistence within career pipelines (Carbonaro, Ellison, and Covay 2011; Mickelson 1989; Morris and Perry 2017). While significant strides have been made to level the playing field, an *equality* regime can operate as an *inequality* regime given new form, maintaining and reproducing the inequalities that are ostensibly being remedied (Acker 2006; Ahmed 2012). As a result, as organizations change over time, even the best-intentioned inclusive practices may perpetuate inequality regimes or create new ones.

Over their 250-year history, women's colleges in the United States have creatively adapted to the changing needs, norms, and requirements of women's education (Harwarth, Maline, and DeBra 1997; Marine 2009; Tidball et al. 1999; Wolf-Wendel 2002). Before the late eighteenth century, educational institutions excluded women because they were considered to be "intellectually inferior—incapable, merely by reason of being a woman, of great thoughts" (Tidball et al. 1999, 4–5). Early women's education activists founded the first girls' schools and women's colleges to challenge ideas about inherent, biological differences by providing women *the same* academic resources as men (Marine 2009; Tidball et al. 1999; Wolf-Wendel 2002). However, it would be misleading to suggest women's colleges have always been open to all women. Race, class, religion, and sexuality were (and still are) organizing features of elite women's colleges. Throughout their histories, both the explicit policies and the informal practices of women's colleges have constructed an environment of "properly educable womanhood" as defined by exclusion (Harwarth, Maline, and DeBra 1997; Horowitz 1984; Marine 2009; Perkins 1998).

For example, Perkins (1998) documents how black women were "strongly advised not to apply" to the Seven Sisters[3] between the 1880s and the 1960s. These institutions admitted black women in token numbers—often only one or two per class year—though Perkins suggests that many more were admitted unknowingly. If the applicant was light-skinned, was upper-class, and came from a highly educated family, they often passed as white on campus. For example, Anita

Hemmings graduated from Vassar while passing as white. However, upon learn-ing that she identified as black, administrators threatened to rescind her diploma (Marine 2009).

Similar patterns of exclusion still occur on women's college campuses today. Though women's colleges have adopted ostensive values of inclusivity and diver-sity, marginalized students' daily lives are full of performative incidents producing a pervasive feeling of not embodying the *ideal* womanhood that the school embraces (Ahmed 2012; Davis 2017). For instance, Vaccaro (2017) juxtaposes dominant, yet unquestioned, ideologies that position women's colleges as warm, welcoming, and empowering spaces with women of color's counternarratives of isolation and exclusion on campus. One respondent detailed how, when she reported incidents of racism, administrators dismissed her as taking everything too personally: "When I took it to the staff, it was really downplayed to the point where I had to say, 'No! You're going to deal with this. I'm not going to let it go. I'd much rather resolve it here, but . . . I can call an attorney.' [The administrators argued] 'Oh, she didn't mean it. She didn't mean it, so it's okay.' And I'm like, 'I don't care what she meant. You need to recognize the fact that that's offensive to me'" (Vac-caro 2017, 273–274). The administrative response in this case upheld the white woman's actions as acceptable while diminishing the respondent's exclusion and marginalization on campus, in effect silencing her protest. As a result, while women's colleges today may formally have the goal of educating diverse groups of women, their policies and practices clearly demarcate their *ideal* student. Thus, not *all* women are included within the women's college narrative (see Nanney 2017).

As trans* students become more visible on campus, women's colleges face a new iteration of the "woman question": *who is a woman in a women's college,* and *how do we determine that our students are women?* Though conversations regarding trans* students at women's colleges have occurred for over a decade (see, for exam-ple, Davis 2017; Marine 2009), Calliope Wong's publicized rejection from Smith served as a catalyst by which these institutions began to formally address these questions en masse. While the answer to the woman question, at first glance, seems simple—a woman is not a man—it is also necessary that these colleges define who the ideal woman *is* in order to include them while excluding others. This is particu-larly complicated when considering the nuanced and varied embodiments, lived experiences, and identities that could potentially constitute womanhood. Is a woman a woman because of her biology? Identity? Legal or social recognition? Par-ticular life experiences? To answer the woman question, then, is to define the gen-dered possibilities of who is and who is not properly educable at women's colleges.

METHODS

To examine how these seemingly inclusive policies reproduce intersectional bar-riers to admissions, I draw on an inductive analysis grounded in the administrative scripts appearing in trans* admissions policies and materials across nineteen women's colleges. Drawing from the database of current women's colleges and trans* policies by Nanney and Brunsma (2017), I obtained the policies using a search with the terms "transgender admissions policy," "transgender policy," "single-sex admissions," and "admissions policy" on each institution's website and included preamble text explaining the policy-development process, the mission of the institution, the policy itself, and any FAQ sections about admissions. Based on the text of the policy, I then gathered the required application materials for applicants, including application questions and financial aid applications. Table 15.1 describes each school included in the sample. Primed with coding cues from Nicolazzo (2017), Fogg Davis (2017), and Spade (2015), I reviewed these policies and materials in chronological order of adoption, including the rationale behind the policy change, the meaning of womanhood and the tradition of the college's mission, and the specific sets of criteria (such as biological markers, legal status, or identity) that determine sex/gender and, thus, potential admittance. Using intersectionality as an analytical strategy (Dill and Zambrana 2009), I interrogated how these policies function through maintaining, replicating, or changing practices that determine admissibility while addressing interconnected systems of access and power. Rather than simply locating individuals within a matrix of domination and privilege, this chapter engages with intersectionality as a method to analyze how privilege, marginalization, and inequality are embedded and (re)produced by institutions, "even in movements designed to further social justice and institutional change" (Acker 2006; Wijeyesinghe and Jones 2014, 10).

SEEMINGLY INCLUSIVE TRANS* POLICY

The purpose of admissions policies is to outline the institutional criteria by which applicants will be judged and, thus, potentially accepted to attend. Therefore, trans* applicants simply want to know, Can I apply to [insert name] women's college? Looking across the nineteen policies, each follows a similar structure and pattern including an overview of who may apply, a brief history and mission of the college evoking values of feminist tradition and inclusion, and detailed information regarding the status of the college, defined application criteria, and application processes. Considered the gold standard of admissions policies among trans* advocates and activists (Diamond, Erlick, and Wong 2015; Nanney and Brunsma 2017; Weber 2016), Mount Holyoke's admissions policy reads:

> Mount Holyoke College welcomes applications for our undergraduate program from any qualified student who is female or identifies as a woman. . . .
>   Mount Holyoke remains committed to its historic mission as a women's college. Yet, we recognize that what it means to be a woman is not static. Traditional binaries around who counts as a man or woman are being challenged by those

TABLE 15.1   Trans* Admissions Policies at U.S. Women's Colleges

Institution	State	Founded	Policy adopted	Enrollment	% White	% Financial aid
Agnes Scott	GA	1889	unknown	905	35	97
Barnard	NY	1889	2015	2,520	52	46
Bennett	NC	1873	2017	424	0	86
Bryn Mawr	PA	1885	2015	1,474	42	71
Cedar Crest	PA	1867	2017	1,303	58	73
College of Saint Benedict	MN	1913	2016	2,127	78	100
Converse	SC	1889	2017	905	56	84
Cottey	MO	1884	n/a	285	64	99
Hollins	VA	1842	2007	723	66	98
Mills	CA	1852	2014	843	44	95
Moore College of Art & Design	PA	1848	unknown	362	57	100
Mount Holyoke	MA	1837	2014	2,238	47	79
Russell Sage	NY	1916	2017	1,033	64	89
Salem College	NC	1772	2017	943	56	88
Scripps	CA	1926	2014	1,029	52	60
Simmons	MA	1899	2014	1,834	65	94
Spelman	GA	1881	2017	2,196	0	62
Smith	MA	1875	2015	2,536	47	67
Wellesley	MA	1870	2015	2,580	36	58
Wesleyan	GA	1836	2016	601	41	74

SOURCES: Integrated Postsecondary Education Data System (IPEDS); Nanney and Brunsma (2017).

NOTE: Total full-time undergraduate enrollment in 2016–2017 reported; percentage of students enrolled by race/ethnicity in the fall of 2016 included in undergraduate enrollment; percentage of students receiving financial aid includes all undergraduate students receiving any grant or institutional financial aid in 2015–2016.

whose gender identity does not conform to their biology. . . . Just as early feminists argued that the reduction of women to their biological functions was a foundation for women's oppression, we must acknowledge that gender identity is not reducible to the body. Instead, we must look at identity in terms of the external context in which the individual is situated. It is this positionality that biological and trans-women share, and it is this positionality that is relevant when women's colleges open their gates for those aspiring to live, learn, and thrive within a community of women. (Mount Holyoke College 2018)

The policy then outlines exactly who is allowed to attend the institution, with the sole exclusion being "biologically born male[s], identifies as man." Meanwhile, six bio-legal-socio identity combinations that were previously considered inadmissible, such as "biologically born female; identifies as a man," "biologically born male; identifies as a woman," and "biologically born female; does not identify as either woman or man," are included within the organizational logic of womanhood.

Such policies, at first glance, gesture toward trans* inclusion and equality. The intersectional legal theorist Kimberlé Crenshaw (1991) suggests, however, that policies focusing on a singular axis of identity disadvantage those who experience oppression from multiple interconnected systems of inequality. Trans* admissions policies focus on expanding admissions only on the basis of sex and gender. Without acknowledging the intersecting barriers of class and race, this leads to unintended barriers for trans* populations while simultaneously reproducing an understanding of trans* experiences that upholds white cis womanhood as the norm (Johnson 2016; Spade 2015). For instance, while Mount Holyoke's policy expands the criteria for womanhood, numerous other combinations are not included. The policy includes both intersex and nonbinary individuals, but it does not list the possibility of an applicant with intersex anatomy who *also* identifies as nonbinary. Turning to other colleges' policies, these criteria become more restrictive: both Smith and Barnard specify eight different identity combinations that are excluded from attending, while Converse, Salem, and Hollins note that any student who transitions away from an identity as a woman during matriculation is asked to leave the university.[4]

Further, many of the policies distinguish between self-identification (such as Mount Holyoke) and legal documentation or medical recognition (such as Scripps) to determine eligibility, wherein students must be able to *prove* that they are (1) really trans, and (2) really a woman (see Nanney and Brunsma 2017; Westbrook and Schilt 2014). For instance, Bryn Mawr's (2018) policy states that "individuals assigned female at birth who have . . . taken medical or legal steps to identify as male" are ineligible for admission, while Scripps determines eligibility through the applicant's sex marked on the Common Application. Yet, scholars critique the use of such legal or medical criteria for admissions as it limits the possibility of who can be considered a woman to only those who are most economically advantaged (Davis 2017; Spade 2015).

Take the Common Application, for example. Annually, over 750 colleges accept 4 million applications from 1 million students by means of the Common Application (2018) because of its relative simplicity. Applicants may complete one application (with the exception of a few supplemental questions) and submit it to multiple schools, making the consideration process fairly equal across institutions. While the purpose of using such an application is rational in many ways, the problem lies with women's colleges using the application to exclude potential applicants on the basis of sex/gender. After the applicant creates an account on the website and provides one's name, the first required question is one's sex, with only two options: male or female. An optional box provided below the question reads, "If you would like the opportunity, we invite you to share more about your gender identity below." As Fogg Davis (2017, 104) writes: "When an application form prompts a prospective student to check a male or female box, what definition of sex identity is the person being asked to disclose? Is it a first-person self-understanding of being a male or being a female? Or is it a third-person perception of how others may perceive the person in relation to the social and legal scheme of binary sex? What should an applicant do when these two conceptions diverge? What about the person who wants to check both male and female boxes, or neither?" Previous iterations of the Common Application site included icons providing more information regarding the question, but these were removed in 2016 (Fogg Davis 2017). Thus, applicants must decide for themselves what definition of sex the application requires, and how they fit within that definition.

Assuming, as suggested by the Scripps policy, that the question is implying the "legal sex" of applicants as listed on one's birth certificate, this creates almost insurmountable barriers for many trans* students. To change one's gender marker on legal documents is not a simple task but rather a maze of bureaucratic red tape that requires a precise order of operations. In most states, the majority of ID-issuing agencies require proof of having undergone some form of gender-confirming health care in order to obtain updated documents such as driver's licenses, passports, or birth certificates—and a change on one document may be required before another document can be obtained. This may include undergoing a particular surgery (such as a hysterectomy, bilateral mastectomy, implants, genital reconstruction, electrolysis), hormone use, or a doctor's letter(s) affirming a diagnosis of gender dysphoria and attesting to the permanence of one's gender identity. Yet, through an intersectional lens, this medical requirement to prove one's "transness" is accessible only to economically privileged people. The majority of private health insurance and state Medicaid programs consider such gender-affirming health care as "elective," which means it is often paid out-of-pocket by the patient (Spade 2015). As a result of the wide range of policies and practices for such changes across states, a person born and living in Arizona might have a birth certificate and passport she cannot change from "M" to "F" because she has not undergone gender reassignment surgery, while her driver's license correctly reflects her gender because of a doctor's note. Another person with the same medical evidence might have a completely different set of documents because they were born in Nevada but live in Connecticut (National Center for Transgender Equality 2018; Spade 2015). Obtaining such documents for trans* college applicants is particularly difficult, as most are under the legal age of eighteen, thus requiring an adult family member to co-sign and pay for such changes. Grant et al. (2011) report, however, that nearly 40 percent of trans* individuals are rejected by their family members when they come out, placing them at higher risk for high school dropout, homelessness, and incarceration. Family rejection occurred at an even higher rate for trans* people of color (ranging between 41 percent and 49 percent for Asians, Latinx, American Indian, and multiracial groups) and those earning $20,000 or less annually (48 percent). Thus, the "legal sex" requirement places a significant barrier to prospective trans* students being included within the organizational logic of womanhood. Moreover, this barrier varies intersectionally by race/ethnicity and income.

Calliope Wong faced these predicaments when she applied to Smith, leading to her ultimate rejection. Smith provided three ways to navigate *around*, rather than address, the barriers that the Common Application provides for trans* students regarding the sex/gender question. After addressing that first barrier, however, Calliope's application was still rejected because her sex marker on her FAFSA, a technically optional financial aid form,[5] indicated her sex as male. A closer look at the FAFSA (see Figure 2) reveals that sex information is collected not for *financial* purposes but for the purpose of ensuring males comply with mandatory military draft registration. As a result, while Calliope's application was formally denied due to her *sex/gender*, because the school used her financial status form to screen her identity, Calliope was rejected because of how her trans* identity is shaped (and outed) by her class status. If Calliope did not need financial aid, if she wanted (and been able to access) legal or medical transition, and/or if Smith did not use a nonacademic source as a determining factor of Calliope's identity, then it is possible that her application would have been considered. Instead, the institutional practices of requiring sex information outed her as trans, which then barred her from accessing both the institution and institutionally sanctioned womanhood.

While Smith has since rescinded its policy of using financial aid forms as a source of admissions exclusion criteria (Fogg Davis 2017), the damage has already been done. By codifying transition-related requirements into policy, a new womanhood is produced: one in which some trans* people may be recognized as women, but which reduces that identity to a normative alignment of embodiment, experience, and legality (Johnson 2016; Spade 2015). As in the case of Calliope, and especially low-income, nonbinary, and people of color, however, many trans* applicants may not "read" as women within the logic of the women's college owing to financial, emotional, or other social constraints. In other words, these seemingly inclusive policies fall short due to their performative actions that reproduce inequality.

INTERSECTIONAL POLICY

After the rapid adoption of trans* policies at women's colleges during the 2014–2015 academic year, there was a distinct pause in policy adoptions. By that point,

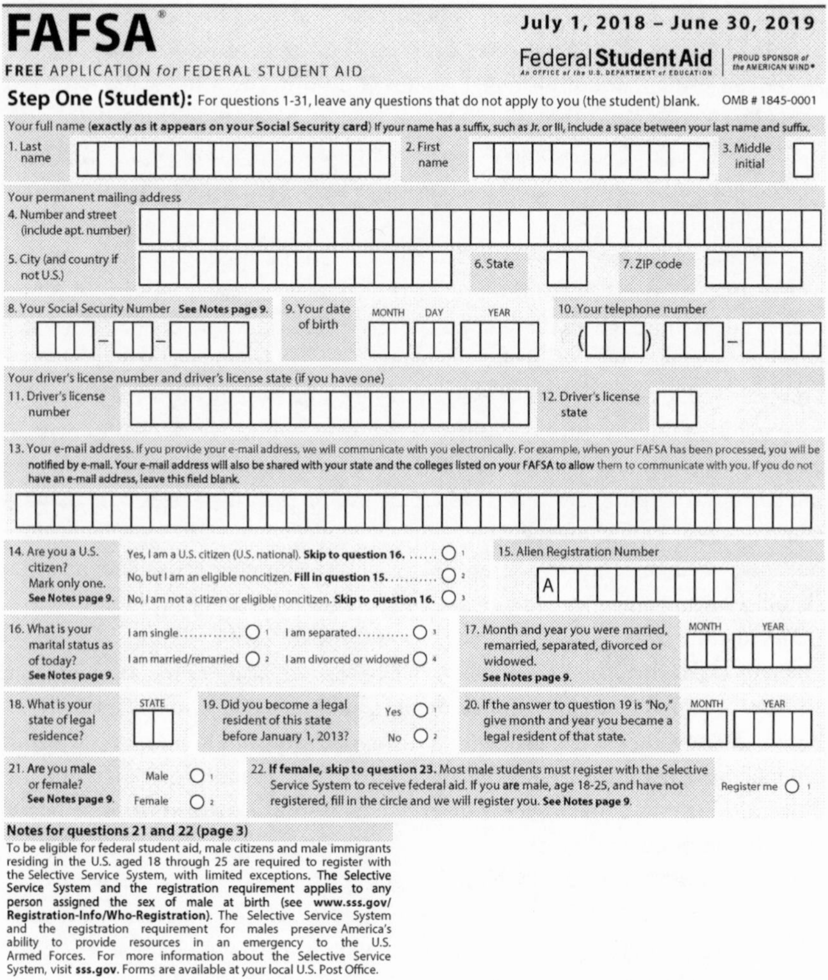

FAFSA®
FREE APPLICATION *for* FEDERAL STUDENT AID

July 1, 2018 – June 30, 2019

Federal Student Aid | PROUD SPONSOR *of* the AMERICAN MIND®
An OFFICE of the U.S. DEPARTMENT of EDUCATION

Step One (Student): For questions 1-31, leave any questions that do not apply to you (the student) blank.   OMB # 1845-0001

Your full name (**exactly as it appears on your Social Security card**) If your name has a suffix, such as Jr. or III, include a space between your last name and suffix.

1. Last name   2. First name   3. Middle initial

Your permanent mailing address
4. Number and street (include apt. number)

5. City (and country if not U.S.)   6. State   7. ZIP code

8. Your Social Security Number See Notes page 9.   9. Your date of birth MONTH DAY YEAR   10. Your telephone number

Your driver's license number and driver's license state (if you have one)
11. Driver's license number   12. Driver's license state

13. Your e-mail address. If you provide your e-mail address, we will communicate with you electronically. For example, when your FAFSA has been processed, you will be notified by e-mail. Your e-mail address will also be shared with your state and the colleges listed on your FAFSA to allow them to communicate with you. If you do not have an e-mail address, leave this field blank.

14. Are you a U.S. citizen? Mark only one. See Notes page 9.
Yes, I am a U.S. citizen (U.S. national). **Skip to question 16.** ○ 1
No, but I am an eligible noncitizen. **Fill in question 15.** ○ 2
No, I am not a citizen or eligible noncitizen. **Skip to question 16.** ○ 3

15. Alien Registration Number
A

16. What is your marital status as of today? See Notes page 9.
I am single ○ 1   I am separated ○ 3
I am married/remarried ○ 2   I am divorced or widowed ○ 4

17. Month and year you were married, remarried, separated, divorced or widowed. See Notes page 9. MONTH YEAR

18. What is your state of legal residence? STATE

19. Did you become a legal resident of this state before January 1, 2013? Yes ○ 1 No ○ 2

20. If the answer to question 19 is "No," give month and year you became a legal resident of that state. MONTH YEAR

21. Are you male or female? See Notes page 9. Male ○ 1 Female ○ 2

22. **If female, skip to question 23.** Most male students must register with the Selective Service System to receive federal aid. If you are male, age 18-25, and have not registered, fill in the circle and we will register you. See Notes page 9. Register me ○ 1

Notes for questions 21 and 22 (page 3)
To be eligible for federal student aid, male citizens and male immigrants residing in the U.S. aged 18 through 25 are required to register with the Selective Service System, with limited exceptions. **The Selective Service System and the registration requirement applies to any person assigned the sex of male at birth** (see www.sss.gov/ Registration-Info/Who-Registration). The Selective Service System and the registration requirement for males preserve America's ability to provide resources in an emergency to the U.S. Armed Forces. For more information about the Selective Service System, visit **sss.gov.** Forms are available at your local U.S. Post Office.

FIGURE 15.1. Screenshot of the FAFSA form

only large, historically recognized women's colleges, all of which were predominantly white and wealthy, had adopted these policies, while smaller women's colleges did not seem to be entertaining such ideas (Nanney and Brunsma 2017). After a two-year hiatus, the two remaining historically black women's colleges, Bennett and Spelman, adopted trans* admissions policies in 2017. Like their sister schools, both colleges framed their decision to adopt a policy as a "contemporary" move recognizing that womanhood is not limited to cisgender identity (Heilman 2017). Unlike other women's colleges that were lauded for their policies, both schools experienced backlash from trans* students of color, critiquing the move as "hasty" and devoid of true dedication to trans* inclusion. As one student stated on Twitter:

Spelman College is NOT ready to admit [trans] students. Regardless of what "studies" have been done, Spelman is not safe for queer folx/ Let alone black trans women. Spelman has no idea what to do with situations, there are not mental health profs knowledgeable on- / -trans health. There are no physicians knowledgeable on trans health. Teachers/faculty/staff have OPTIONAL LGBTQIA+ training/ As well as public safety. Can we think about what being stopped by public safety is going to do to trans women? . . . Other women's* institutions have been admitting trans/ Gender queer folx for years & now Spelman feels the pressure and has made a hasty decision without first making sure that campus is ready. . . . So Spelman can now claim progression & inclusion, so they can have their name associated with rainbows.[6]

As this student argues, Spelman does not have an adequate infrastructure to support trans* students, including health care resources, faculty and staff training, and public safety, especially noting the heightened risk of police violence that trans* women of color are subject to (see Ritchie 2017). While Spelman may have had the right *intention* with its policy, treating the admissions process as the sole barrier trans* students face—without addressing the intersectional identities that simultaneously shape trans* experiences—puts trans* students at risk.

I conclude with this example of historically black women's colleges and universities because it represents a prime example of the possible consequences when trans* inclusive policies focus only on transness as a singular and all-encompassing identity experience. Historically black colleges and universities serve as an important space for inclusion of marginalized students, but intersectionally, inclusion on the basis of race does not necessarily transcend to full inclusion and remove marginality across identities. Though revising admissions policies appears to be a step toward inclusion for trans* students, too often these become Band-Aid fixes that *accommodate* students instead of addressing the underlying organizational structures that hold trans* students back (Nicolazzo 2017; Spade 2015). Best practices such as transforming one restroom per building, adding gender expression and identity to nondiscrimination policies, allowing trans* students to have single dorm rooms on a case-by-case basis, and having trans* admissions policies end up *differentiating* and *tokenizing* trans* students from the majority student population and thus treat them as problems that need fixing. This is not to argue that changes to physical spaces and practices are not necessary. Rather, I argue that aligning institutional status with historically white women's colleges with trans* policies and surface-level changes (being "associated with rainbows") are not enough to address the intersecting inequalities that trans* students face.

While there is not one clear-cut solution to the problems embedded within these policies, I point to Nicolazzo's (2017) application of Spade's (2015) *trickle up activism* within postsecondary institutions as an insightful strategic intervention for intersectional trans* justice. Spade (2015) re-orients epistemological practices of activism by calling for a re-centering of those who are most vulnerable and marginalized in order to advance gender justice. This is done through addressing four interlocking pillars of social justice: *intersectional* policy development, *rethinking* power, *consistently and actively participating* in consciousness raising, and engaging service *with* trans* communities. Nicolazzo (2017) applies this concept to hir concept of *trickle up education,* whereby trans* students are at the center of their liberation—including being involved in the policy creation and implementation process (see also Dockendorff, Nanney, and Nicolazzo, forthcoming). After all, if these policies are meant to *help* trans* students, it follows that students themselves deserve a say in what those policies look like.

As postsecondary institutions of all types increasingly implement changes to address trans* students' needs, such as housing, restroom, name change, and nondiscrimination policies, researchers and higher education practitioners must continually return to the question of where transgender students "belong" in the university (Nicolazzo 2017). The college years are associated with independence and the ability to come into one's own through holistic development (Nicolazzo 2017; Rodgers 1990). They can also be anxiety-provoking for transgender students who are forced to navigate policies and practices that, while well intentioned, may perpetuate inequalities (Marine 2009; Nicolazzo 2017). While the overall population at women's colleges is small (1%–3% of college enrollment) (Wolf-Wendel 2002), and the number of trans* students within this is even smaller, examining how these policies affect students' lives is important if we are to create safe and inclusive college environments, especially for, by, and with trans* students. What is needed, consequently, is not more policies but *better* policies, as well as an awareness of how inclusivity and inequality are not mutually exclusive. Perhaps the better question to ask is not *who is an educable woman,* but *how can our policies make room for a multitude of gendered possibilities?*

NOTES

1. As argued throughout this chapter, the boundaries of what trans* means shift in relation to intersecting categories (Valentine 2007). I use the asterisk to demarcate the multiple lived possibilities that encompass trans* embodiment, identity, and experiences.
2. I use Marine's (2009) definition of policy—a formalized, public, and codified official stance toward an issue or population.
3. The Seven Sisters, a consortium of elite, private women's colleges founded in the 1800s, comprises Barnard, Bryn Mawr, Mount Holyoke, Smith, Radcliffe, Vassar, and Wellesley.
4. Should cis women, however, have a mastectomy, hysterectomy, and/or used hormonal therapy, they would not be asked to leave the university. As a result, while all bodies are subject to codified standards of womanhood, trans* bodies in particular are held to more stringent gender-conforming norms in order to be "trans* enough" as well as "woman enough."
5. I refer to the FAFSA as technically "optional" because, though not required, the form is not really optional for those who cannot otherwise afford college. Colleges' treatment of the FASFA as optional thus suggests that low-income trans* students who cannot afford to "opt out" of

financial aid are to blame for incorrect sex/gender assignments, rather than universities' own policies.

6. Tweets from Bello Bioni (@Keo_Gogh) on September 5, 2017. This Twitter account has since been deactivated.

REFERENCES

Acker, Joan. 2006. "Inequality Regimes: Gender, Class and Race in Organizations." *Gender & Society* 20 (4): 441–464.

Ahmed, Sara. 2012. *On Being Included: Racism and Diversity in Institutional Life.* Durham, NC: Duke University Press.

Bilodeau, Brent Laurence. 2007. "Genderism: Transgender Students, Binary Systems and Higher Education." PhD diss., Department of Educational Administration, Michigan State University, 3264140.

Bryn Mawr College. 2018. "Transgender Applicants." https://www.brynmawr.edu/admissions /transgender-applicants.

Carbonaro, William, Brandy J. Ellison, and Elizabeth Covay. 2011. "Gender Inequalities in the College Pipeline." *Social Science Research* 40 (1): 120–35.

Common Application. 2018. https://www.commonapp.org/.

Crenshaw, Kimberlé. 1991. "Mapping the Margins: Intersectionality, Identity Politics, and Violence against Women of Color." *Stanford Law Review* 43: 1241–1299.

Davis, Sam [Director]. 2017. *In Our Own Words: Being Trans at Smith.* Northampton, MA.

Diamond, Danie, Eli Erlick, and Calliope Wong. 2015. "Model Policy on Transgender Students at Women's Colleges." Trans Student Educational Resources. Accessed December 2, 2017. www.transstudent.org/womenscolleges.

Dill, Bonnie Thornton, and Ruth Enid Zambrana. 2009. *Emerging Intersections: Race, Class, and Gender in Theory, Policy and Practice.* New Brunswick, NJ: Rutgers University Press.

DiPrete, Thomas A., and Claudia Buchman. 2013. *The Rise of Women: The Growing Gender Gap in Education and What It Means for American Schools.* New York: Russell Sage Foundation.

Dockendorff, Kari J., Megan Nanney, and Z. Nicolazzo. Forthcoming. "Trickle up Policy-Building: Envisioning Possibilities for Trans*Formative Change in Postsecondary Education." In *Rethinking Lgbtqia Students and Collegiate Contexts: Identity, Policies, and Campus Climate*, edited by E. M. Zamani-Gallaher, D. D. Chouduri, and J. L. Taylor. New York: Routledge.

Fogg Davis, Heath. 2017. *Beyond Trans: Does Gender Matter?* New York: New York University Press.

Grant, Jaime M., Lisa A. Mottet, Justin Tanis, Jack Harrison, Jody L. Herman, and Mara Keisling. 2011. *Injustice at Every Turn: A Report of the National Transgender Discrimination Survey.* Washington, DC: National Center for Transgender Equality and National Gay and Lesbian Task Force.

Harwarth, Irene, Mindi Maline, and Elizabeth DeBra. 1997. *Women's College in the United States: History, Issues and Challenges.* Washington, DC: US Department of Education.

Heilman, Becca. 2017. "'A Space That's Safer': Transgender and Nonbinary Enrollment at Women-Only Colleges in North Carolina." *Daily Tar Heel*, November 5. http://www .dailytarheel.com/article/2017/11/a-space-thats-safer-transgender-and-non-binary-enrollment -at-women-only-colleges-in-north-carolina.

Horowitz, Helen Lefkowitz. 1984. *Alma Mater: Design and Experience in the Women's Colleges from Their Nineteenth-Century Beginnings to the 1930s.* New York: Alfred A. Knopf.

Johnson, Austin H. 2016. "Transnormativity: A New Concept and Its Validation through Documentary Film about Transgender Men." *Sociological Inquiry* 86 (4): 465–491.

Lewis, Amanda, and John B. Diamond. 2015. *Despite the Best Intentions: How Racial Inequality Thrives in Good Schools.* New York: Oxford University Press.

Marine, Susan B. 2009. "Navigating Discourses of Discomfort: Women's College Student Affairs Administrators and Transgender Students." PhD diss., Boston College.

Mickelson, Roslyn Arlin. 1989. "Why Does Jane Read and Write So Well? The Anomaly of Women's Achievement." *Sociology of Education* 62 (1): 47–63.

Morris, Edward W., and Brea L. Perry. 2017. "Girls Behaving Badly? Race, Gender, and Subjective Evaluation in the Discipline of African American Girls." *Sociology of Education* 90 (2): 127–148.

Mount Holyoke College. 2018. "Admission of Transgender Students." https://www.mtholyoke .edu/policies/admission-transgender-students.

Nanney, Megan. 2017. "'I'm Part of the Community, Too': Women's College Alumnae Responses to Transgender Admittance Policies." In *Gender Panic, Gender Policy*, edited by V. Demos and M. T. Segal, 133–154. Bingley, UK: Emerald Publishing.

Nanney, Megan, and David L. Brunsma. 2017. "Moving beyond Cis-Terhood: Determining Gender through Transgender Admittance Policies at U.S. Women's Colleges." *Gender & Society* 31 (2): xx.

National Center for Transgender Equality. 2018. "Id Documents Center." https://transequality .org/documents.

Nicolazzo, Z. 2017. *Trans* in College: Transgender Students' Strategies for Navigating Campus Life and the Institutional Politics of Inclusion.* Sterling, VA: Stylus.

Perkins, Linda M. 1998. "The African American Female Elite: The Early History of African American Women in the Seven Sister Colleges, 1880–1960." *Harvard Educational Review* 67 (4): 718–756.

Ritchie, Andrea J. 2017. *Invisible No More: Police Violence against Black Women and Women of Color.* Boston: Beacon Press.

Rodgers, Robert. 1990. "Recent Theories and Research Underlying Student Development." In *College Student Development: Theory and Practice for the 1990s*, edited by D. G. Creamer, 27–79. Alexandria, VA: American College Personnel Association.

Spade, Dean. 2015. *Normal Life: Administrative Violence, Critical Trans Politics, & the Limits of Law.* Durham, NC: Duke University Press.

Tidball, M. Elizabeth, Daryl G. Smith, Charles S. Tidball, and Lisa E. Wolf-Wendel. 1999. *Taking Women Seriously: Lessons and Legacies for Educating the Majority.* Phoenix, AZ: Oryx Press.

Vaccaro, Annemarie. 2017. "'Trying to Act Like Racism Is Not There': Women of Color at a Predominantly White Women's College Challenging Dominant Ideologies by Exposing Racial Microaggressions." *NASPA Journal about Women in Higher Education* 10 (3): 262–280.

Valentine, David. 2007. *Imagining Transgender: An Ethnography of a Category.* Durham, NC: Duke University Press.

Weber, Shannon. 2016. "'Womanhood Does Not Reside in Documentation': Queer and Feminist Student Activism for Transgender Women's Inclusion at Women's Colleges." *Journal of Lesbian Studies* 20 (1): 29–45.

Westbrook, Laurel, and Kristen Schilt. 2014. "Doing Gender, Determining Gender: Transgender People, Gender Panics, and the Maintenance of the Sex/Gender/Sexuality System." *Gender & Society* 28 (1): 32–57.

Wijeyesinghe, Charmaine L., and Susan R. Jones. 2014. "Intersectionality, Identity, and Systems of Power and Inequality." In *Intersectionality and Higher Education: Theory, Research and Praxis*, edited by J. Donald Mitchell, 9–19. New York: Peter Lang.

Wolf-Wendel, Lisa E. 2002. "Women's Colleges." In *Women in Higher Education*, edited by A. M. M. Aleman and K. A. Renn. Santa Barbara, CA: ABC-CLIO.

Wong, Calliope. 2012a. "Please read, share, and discuss." Trans Women @ Smith. Accessed May 1, 2017. http://calliowong.tumblr.com/post/34132356393/please-read-share-and-discuss.

———. 2012b. "Make Smith possible for trans women." Trans Women @ Smith. Accessed May 1, 2017. http://calliowong.tumblr.com/post/29467307825/make-smith-possible-for-trans-women.

———. 2013. "Thank you." Transwomen @ Smith. Accessed May 1, 2017. http://calliowong.tumblr.com/post/45074030481/thank-you.

———. 2015. "Good game." Trans Women @ Smith. Accessed May 1, 2017. http://calliowong.tumblr.com/post/118031024736/good-game.

16 · TROUBLING DIVERSITY

An Intersectional Analysis of Diversity Action
Plans at U.S. Flagship Universities

SUSAN V. IVERSON

More than a decade ago, Gerald and Haycock (2006) published
Engines of Inequality, a troubling assessment of college access at U.S. public flagship universities. In their view, these universities, "charged with special responsibilities for producing the future political, business and civic leaders of their
respective states," were "turning away" (3) from racial minorities and low-income
students, instead of investing financial resources in the "more affluent and less
racially and ethnically diverse" (5). A decade later, scholars are reporting similar
disturbing findings: public research universities continue to fall short in enrolling a critical mass of low-income and underrepresented racial minorities (Jaquette,
Curs, and Posselt 2016). Growth in the proportion of nonresident students is
associated with a decline in the proportion of low-income students and underrepresented racial minorities (Jaquette, Curs, and Posselt 2016).

Public universities were founded on the premise that U.S. higher education
should be more accessible, and these institutions sought to educate the masses
to ensure the strength and competitiveness of America's human capital (Campbell 1995; Johnson 1999). Further, flagship universities hold status in the higher
education community as their classification as research or doctoral institutions
meets "the prestige standard by which most colleges judge their progress" and
positions them—symbolically and in actuality—as a benchmark for other institutions, on local, regional, and national levels (Fairweather and Beach 2002, 99).
This standing holds the potential for the flagships to emerge as a social force in
higher education's response to the public concern of diversity. Yet, this alarming
assessment of college access suggests that flagship universities have abandoned
their "proud tradition serving as an engine of social mobility" (Gerald and Haycock 2006, 3). Jaquette et al. (2016) conclude that public research universities may

have shifted their organizational values "away from the public good emphasis on access and toward the self-interested emphases of academic profile and revenue generation" (33).

For decades, a principal mechanism for illustrating an institution-wide commitment to open access to the dream and the reality of this public good was through the codification of a commitment to diversity. Some scholars criticize this strategy, suggesting little to no relationship between planning and performance (Rudd et al. 2008); yet, policy making continues to be deployed as a strategy to codify solutions to problems. Diversity policy making holds significant appeal and perceived efficacy for institutions of higher education (Chang 2005). A search of nearly any college or university website reveals efforts related to diversity, equity, and inclusion, often codified in an action plan. These action plans, which I collectively refer to as "diversity action plans," serve as a primary means for universities to profess their commitment to a (more) inclusive and equitable climate for *all* members of the campus community (Iverson 2012).

More than a decade ago, I analyzed diversity action plans at public universities to enhance our collective understanding of these diversity policy documents, how they contribute to producing a particular cultural reality, and how they may (unwittingly) compromise the achievement of their own goals (Iverson 2007, 2008, 2012). Now, ten years later, with new data collected for a ten-year follow-up study, I offer an Intersectionality-Based Policy Analysis (IBPA) of diversity action plans at U.S. public flagship universities. This analytic lens (Hankivsky 2012) is guided by an *intersectionality* perspective that human lives cannot be reduced to singular and distinct categories (Crenshaw 1991; Purdie-Vaughns and Eibach 2008). Yet, the moniker of "diversity" risks serving as a singular placeholder for multiple identity statuses. IBPA also gives explicit attention to *power* in policy and the ways in which power "operates at discursive and structural levels to exclude particular knowledges and experiences" (Hankivsky et al. 2012b, 35).

This investigation reveals that despite progress made to date, there is still much work to be done to better understand policy effects, and who is benefiting and who remains marginalized by the policy priorities. As Waldegrave (2009) attests, "We need to deconstruct . . . policy making from the perspectives of culture, gender, and socioeconomic status and enquire as to the reasons for their hegemony and practice. Are they achieving equity?" (97). I argue that by adopting an intersectional approach, a case can be made for intersectionality in policy analysis, and potentially a paradigm shift could be facilitated to address root causes of sociopolitical problems.

POLICY ANALYSIS

Policy analysis is dominated by a conventional—sometimes called "rational"—approach that views policy making principally as a process of problem solving.

With this approach, policy makers employ formulaic steps in policy making—meaning the problem that the policy seeks to resolve is accepted as an unquestioned, objective fact, and attention is instead focused on identifying solutions to the (taken-for-granted) problem (Bacchi and Goodwin 2016). Policy authors, then, are managing rather than problematizing the "deep-seated assumptions and presuppositions" within policies (38). This is what Foucault (1994) refers to as the "unexamined ways of thinking" that give rise to "accepted practices" (456).

Alternative approaches to policy analysis exist. In contrast to treating policy and the problems it seeks to address as a given, Shore and Wright (2011) argue for policy analysis that views the policy itself as "a curious and problematic social and cultural construct that needs to be unpacked and contextualized" (90). I align with these alternative approaches, rooted in critical and poststructural perspectives that have influenced scholars to interrogate the taken-for-granted notions of policy (Allan, Iverson, and Ropers-Huilman 2010; Bacchi and Goodwin 2016). It is what the educational sociologist Ball (1993) refers to as "the way in which policy ensembles, or collections of related policies, exercise power through a *production* of 'truth' and 'knowledge'" (14, italics in original). Policy, then, is not neutral, objective, or rational, but it is an "expression of knowledge as power" (John 1998, 165). Policy constructs and constitutes the problems it seeks to redress. The IBPA framework encourages those examining policy discussions from an intersectionality perspective to pay attention to the framing of policy problems by asking: What is the policy "problem" under consideration? What assumptions (e.g., beliefs about what causes the problem and which populations are most affected) underlie this representation of the "problem"?

Policy, a form of institutional knowledge and site of power relations, has the power to define what is normal. With diversity action plans, this power derives from its location at the top of the institutional hierarchy—that is, from senior administration who legitimize policy with their official status. Institutions act, through policy, with the authority to classify, objectify, and normalize persons, discursively constituting "subjects." As Bacchi and Eveline (2010) put it, "Policies do not simply 'impact' on people; they 'create' people" (52), including their social locations, and access to power and resources.

THEORY OF INTERSECTIONALITY

This chapter draws on the theory of intersectionality to critically interrogate diversity as framed in diversity action plans and to illuminate how dimensions of identity (i.e., race, gender, sexuality) are socially constructed and constituted in policy. Black feminist thought introduced the concept of intersectionality as a lens to see "distinctive systems of oppression as being part of one overarching structure of domination" (Collins 1990, 122). Crenshaw (1991) offered the theoretical concept for researchers to account for multiple categories of identity. Yet, this concept is far more than just an accounting of differences regarding race, class, and sexuality, among other identity dimensions. The theory of intersectionality destabilizes identity categories (Jennrich and Kowalski-Braun 2014) and emphasizes "the process by which social structures and power relations are written into identities and bodily repertoires and thus *shape* experience" (Phipps 2010, 360, italics in original).

While scholars have variously defined and deployed intersectionality (see Andersen and Collins 2004; BacaZinn, Hondagneu-Sotolo, and Messner 2000; Ken 2008), this theory has several shared tenets:

Identity is multidimensional, not monolithic.

Social categories, such as race, gender, sexuality, and ability, are socially constructed, fluid, and flexible.

"Social locations are inseparable and shaped by interacting and mutually constituting social processes and structures, which, in turn, are shaped by power and influenced by both time and place" (Hankivsky et al. 2012a, 17).

Attention to "how power and power relations are maintained and reproduced" is paramount (Hankivsky et al. 2010, 3).

Some critique the limited tools for applying intersectionality theory to policy (Hankivsky and Cormier 2011); yet, Manuel (2006) asserts that it is "incredibly useful" as an analytic lens for policy scholars "who wish to strengthen the explanatory power of policy models that evaluate policy impacts and outcomes" (175). For instance, Iverson (2017) draws on intersectionality theory to uncover embedded assumptions and predominant meanings constructed through sexual assault policies. Employing an intersectional analysis, Iverson reveals how an over-reliance on one-dimensional analyses (meaning assumptions that all women experience sexual violence the same as white, cisgender, economically privileged women) contributes to misunderstandings of sexual violence. In another example, Rudrum (2012) conducted an intersectional critical discourse analysis of maternity care policy in British Columbia, to focus on gendered and racialized hierarchies, differences, and inequities among women. Through an intersectional lens, Rudrum revealed the ways in which systems of domination shape access to care and how advocacy for choice and autonomy in maternity care is undermined by the interlocking systems of privilege and oppression.

The current study utilized an intersectional lens, and specifically the method of IBPA, to investigate university diversity policies to understand how these documents frame diversity and what reality is produced by diversity action plans. An intersectional approach invites and responds to questions such as, What has produced this problem, what has given rise to this issue and leads us to view it in this way, and what contributes to the maintenance of this problem and may (unintentionally) undermine efforts to solve the problem (e.g., chilly climate for LGBT [lesbian, gay, bisexual, transgender, queer] students, attrition of underrepresented minorities, and slow-to-no advancement of women, among other concerns)?

METHODS

Sample and Data Collection

The data for this intersectional analysis consist of twenty-one diversity action plans issued at U.S. flagship universities and published between 2006 and 2016 (see appendix). These policies were collected from a search of the university websites for the identified "flagship" institution in each of the fifty states using the search function and keywords "diversity" and "diversity plan." All fifty universities possessed diversity-related content (e.g., multicultural student affairs, faculty committee on diversity in the curriculum, diversity workshops). Most of the universities had at least one diversity-related group (e.g., President's Council on Disabilities, President's Commission on Women, President's Commission on the Status of GLBT Issues, and Provost's Committee on the Status of People of Color) committed to one or more of the following concerns: the recruitment and retention of underrepresented populations, curriculum change, and campus climate. While diversity councils and documents have various titles, I was seeking policies that addressed diversity in the broadest sense. This parameter excluded status reports or plans generated by other committees charged by senior administrators with a narrower focus (e.g., commissions on women or disabilities). In the end, I collected twenty-one university-wide diversity policies that were generated by a diversity council charged by a senior administrator (president, chancellor, provost) and published within the last decade (2006–2016).

Analytic Process

The IBPA framework, developed by Hankivsky and colleagues (2012a), is a strategy for examining processes shaping power differentiation within and among populations, and the ways in which they come together to make particular perspectives more prominent than others. IBPA centers eight guiding principles in the analysis and poses two categories of questions: descriptive and transformative (explicated in Hankivsky et al. 2012b). The first set of questions, *descriptive*, attends "to the processes and mechanisms by which policy problems are identified, constructed and addressed . . . and what inequities and privileges are created by current policy responses" (Hankivsky et al. 2012b, 34). The second set of questions, *transformative*, identifies "alternative policy responses and solutions specifically aimed at social and structural change that reduce inequities and promote social justice" (34). While a total of twelve questions are available, analysts may focus on certain questions. Hankivsky et al. (2012b) note that it is "unnecessary to work through all of the IBPA questions in any policy analysis" (34).

For this analysis, a series of descriptive and transformative questions (adapted from Hankivsky et al. 2012b) were asked of the data in an effort to understand the policy "problems" and how they have come to be represented as they are, and to describe policy responses ("solutions") to the "problem" and in what ways these proposed policy responses reduce, or sustain, inequities. More specifically, the following questions guided this inquiry:

What is the policy "problem" under consideration?

How have representations of the "problem" come about? Or put another way, what (discursively) has given rise to this issue and framed it in this way?

What are the current policy responses, or solutions, to the "problem"?

How are groups affected by the problem representation? What realities do these policy problems, solutions, and representations construct?

DIVERSITY PROBLEMS AND SOLUTIONS

In this section, I describe and discuss the "problem" of access, the "solution" of inclusion, and in what ways diversity action plans challenge inequities at their source and demand "the interrogation of complex social and power relations" (Hankivsky et al. 2012b, 38). First, however, I explain how policies (fail to) define diversity and their consequential use of the placeholder of "diversity" as a single referent for multiple identity groups. Consistent with Thomas's (2017) critique, diversity served as both a "catch-all" for all possible differences, from race to geography, and from gender to talent (7), and a placeholder for particular demographics (e.g., "ethnic diversity in the student body and faculty"; see University of Alabama 2008, 2). The following excerpt is emblematic of the "ubiquitous emptiness" (Thomas 2017, 8) of diversity definitions in diversity action plans:

> *Broad* diversity encompasses all aspects of individuals that contribute to a robust academic, research, and campus environment including experience, perspectives, disciplines, geographic background, talent, socio-economic background, disability, ethnicity, race, gender, and other characteristics. Where "diversity" is used in this Action Plan, it implies *the broadest definition* of diversity. Some aspects of *broad diversity* have been achieved, while others have not and remain a significant focus. The components in this Action Plan are aimed at increasing *the missing aspects of broad diversity* that may change over time. (University of Florida 2011, 1, italics added)

This "broad" definition (seen throughout the policies) seems purposefully vague, leaves the reader unclear about the focus and/or what is "missing," and erases the importance of attention to inequalities. "Diversity work" (Ahmed 2012), then, is left open for interpretation. It both affirms inclusiveness and is a reputational symbol of excellence for an institution; yet, this work also resists change in the practices and organizational cultures that re/produce social inequality (Berrey 2015; Iverson 2007, 2008, 2012).

Problem: Access or Exclusion?

A persistent problem articulated in the diversity action plans is access—or rather lack of access. This problem, made visible through a discourse of *access*, is carried by two strands: entrée and representation. The challenge of entrée is in recruiting, retaining, and advancing members of diverse groups (whether students, faculty, or staff). Thus, institutions must identify and open points of entry, permitting diverse groups to participate in the institution. An intersectional analysis illuminates that, more precisely, the problem is difficulty recruiting *certain* members of diverse groups[1]—high ability, high performing, and high achieving, those with little or lesser risk who will enable the institution to sustain its exemplary status, its "excellence." The policies suggest there are very few "right" diverse individuals (the pools from which to recruit are considered shallow), and the competition for "them" is fierce. To determine who is "right," they (e.g., members of "historically underrepresented and underserved groups, first generation, low-income, and other diverse groups," according to the University of Delaware's policy) must be compared with and measured against a standard, "us," that is implicitly defined as the norm. This "normalizing judgment" that "hierarchizes qualities, skills and aptitudes" (Foucault [1977] 1995, 181) produces the at-risk outsider, enables comparisons to be made between "us" and "them," and ensures conformity to a standard "that is at once a field of comparison, a space of differentiation and the principle of a rule to be followed" (182). For instance, the diversity action plan at the University of Maryland (2010) asserts: "If students feel marginalized because they are *different from those in the mainstream*, if faculty or staff members feel that their contributions are not valued, or if any individual feels isolated and excluded by a climate that is unfriendly or uninterested, the university community is diminished. A welcoming, supportive climate is essential (16, italics added)." Yet, the policies are absent any interrogation of "those in the mainstream" and how they have been identified as the standard against which "others" are measured.

The second strand—representation—is evident in calls for increased visibility of diversity throughout the campus, in the student body, in the workforce, in leadership positions, on committees, and in curriculum. These data excerpts are illustrative of the representation strand:

> Strengthen current programs and design and implement new programs to support the progress of all junior faculty toward tenure, inclusive of mentoring, peer evaluations, research support, and opportunities for professional

development on and off-campus; ensure broad dissemination of the availability of such programs, especially for women, people of color, and members of other under-represented groups. (University of New Hampshire 2012, 15)

Establish a subcommittee of the campus master planning committee charged with making UM grounds/buildings more welcoming by highlighting diversity in the constructed environment and public art. (University of Montana 2009, 3)

Develop a leadership program for mid-career women and faculty from historically underrepresented and underserved groups who may be interested in pursuing chair and other administrative positions. (University of Delaware 2016, 12)

Analysis also revealed that most policies articulate concerns about the absence of diversity content in curricular offerings and delineate strategies to "infuse" or "integrate" diversity into the curriculum and "transform and diversify the curriculum." These data excerpts are illustrative:

Because the world is made up of diverse peoples, the University academic curricula must ensure that all students study diversity. The University intends to strengthen academic preparation of all students by infusing curricula with reputable scholarship and critical thinking skills regarding diversity. (University of Tennessee 2006, 6–7)

Promote the adoption of a diversity requirement or diversity attribute for all undergraduate students . . . [and] identify and promote existing diversity related interdisciplinary curriculum and research. (University of New Hampshire 2012, 13)

Provide opportunities for faculty to participate in course development workshops that focus on integrating diversity into the curriculum. (University of Montana 2009, 7)

Evaluate undergraduate curriculum and encourage departments and programs to consider the histories, cultures, and experiences of historically underserved, underrepresented, and international groups. (University of Delaware 2016, 15)

Ensuring the access of "others" situates the institution as accessible, and any failure to access must be located *within* the diverse individual, constituted as an *at-risk outsider*. Universities are committed to access, ready to be tolerant, and prepared to provide a positive experience. Diversity, then, as Mohanty (2003) explains, is a discourse of "benign variation," which "bypasses power as well as history to suggest a harmonious empty pluralism" (193). Diversity policies have "an ideological function in the 'manufacture of cohesion' and create the impression of 'more diversity'" (Ahmed 2012, 14). Representing the problem of (in)access in this way conceals any possibility that the institution is inaccessible or exclusionary. Policies fail to identify privileging conditions and practices that advantage some (namely white males) and marginalize others; they fail to question what produces a *risky* institution for some more than others.

Solution: Inclusive Excellence

The problem representation of some (diverse) groups not being able to have access constructs an "us-them" binary. The response (or solution) to this problem is two-fold: the institution must profess its commitment to and valuing of diversity, and assert that it is, and will continue to be, a welcoming, inclusive campus. In short, the solution to an outsider's inability to access the institution, and the "us-them" divide, is to remain committed to inclusion while also valuing, affirming, and celebrating difference.

Diversity action plans place great emphasis on inclusion—seemingly a panacea for so many problems articulated in the policies. The diversity action plans emphasize "common ground," "shared values," "integration," and "inclusion." A commitment to "a diverse, inclusive, and respectful campus community" (University of Alabama 2008, 6) that "promotes tolerance and values diversity" (14) pervades the policies. Diversity action plans proclaim to do better including (adding) others to the existing (or dominant) cultural project (Tierney 1992).

The diverse individual, then, must shed "otherness" in order to conform to the norm, "so that they might all be like one another" (Foucault [1977] 1995, 182). However, a seemingly paradoxical conclusion is that while diverse "others" must be the same as the majority, in order to be included and achieve insider status, they must also sustain their difference, an exotic otherness that enables the institution to benefit from their presence. As Ahmed (2012) notes, "To be included can thus be a way of sustaining and reproducing a politics of exclusion" (163). This illustrates the tension that exists between expectations to acculturate the outsider to an insider status (emphasizing sameness) and commodifying the (ornamental) value of diversity (emphasizing difference). As the policy of the University of Florida (2011) attests, in its goal to be "the model of inclusive excellence" (6), the solution is "to engage in interracial and intercultural peer-to-peer conversations that promote *common ground* values of respect and civility, justice and equity, and the cultural and social *understanding of human difference*" (16, my emphasis).

An intersectional analysis calls us to "trouble" what is, or is not, embedded within the notion of inclusion. One diversity policy asserts the need "to create a more inclusive community," noting that "many groups still encounter barriers to the promise and achievement of equality, justice, and the unprejudiced quest for knowledge" and that the university is "still too often perceived as ineffectively serving a society that is daily growing more diverse" (University of Tennessee 2006, 5). Yet, simply professing the need to be "more inclusive" will not itself "erase barriers" or "foster retention" (6). Diversity, as Ahmed (2012) argues, "is exercised as a repair narrative," and to "show our gratitude," she adds, "we must put racism behind us" (168).

Such statements, however, of "steadfast commitment to diversity, equity, and inclusion" (University of Delaware 2016, 6) may serve as a sleight of hand. These statements of commitment declare pride in what the institution values, and become "a form of compliance" (Ahmed 2012, 102)—offices and individuals are put in place "for coordinating the efforts, measuring and reporting institutional progress" to "transform [the University] into a more equitable and inclusive institution" (University of Delaware 2016, 18). Statements of commitment are also a form of "concealment"—a way of presenting the university as being good at doing diversity, while inequalities persist (Ahmed 2012; Berrey 2015). Doing diversity then becomes "a form of image management" (Ahmed 2012, 102). "Progress," as asserted in one policy, is ensured through "mechanisms of accountability" that "incentivize achievements" and identify "inclusiveness" as a core competency (University of California, Berkeley, 2009, 21).

Valuing diversity and being inclusive conceal from sight what the institution is (or is not) doing; they serve as public relations for elevating institutional reputation (Ahmed 2012; Berrey 2015). Herein also lies the benefit of coupling a commitment to inclusion with an emphasis on excellence: inclusive excellence. To attract and retain *excellent* "diverse students," is to make a strategic commitment to "continue progress in achieving diversity among faculty, staff, students, and administration" (University of Alabama 2008, 4). The institution can utilize diversity to its advantage (e.g., to advance the university's reputation). One policy states, "the University highly values diversity and believes it is essential for excellence" (University of Iowa 2006, 18). Diversity, then, is a commodity for achieving the goal of elevated institutional standing within the marketplace.

Challenging or Maintaining Inequities

In the decade since my previous analysis of diversity action plans (Iverson 2007), universities have adopted a commitment to equity. In some cases this is little more than the addition of the word "equity" to the title of an office or position. In other cases, policies assert strategic priorities to achieve equity in representation, hiring, and salaries. A focus on equity holds potential to shift attention to institutional practices and the production of unequal educational outcomes (Bensimon 2005). However, it is not evident how (if) a discursive shift to equity (can disrupt) disrupts the problem of exclusion (inaccessible and risky institutions) and the solution of inclusion. For instance, one university asserts that its "commitment to inclusive excellence" will foster "greater diversity, equity, inclusion and accountability" (University of New Hampshire 2010, 3). Yet, the "solution" of "being inclusive" seems to offer little explanation of how "under-represented groups and those who experience systemic inequity will have equal opportunities and feel welcome on our campus" (8). Caring about and being committed to diversity and inclusion will do little to confront and combat racism, sexism, homophobia, and other forms of oppression, discrimination, and marginalization that systemically produce inequities.

One move toward equity would be to include (beyond tokenism) those who are typically marginalized in the policy process. Diversity action plans are authored by institutional agents, faculty, administrators, and experts (at times guided by contracted consultants), and consequently these documents tell only one (part of the) story. IBPA is concerned about *diverse knowledges,* and additional sources of knowledge must be identified. Diversity action plans must purposefully include perspectives and worldviews of people who are typically marginalized or excluded (including those who are positionally marginalized, e.g., staff members), and give attention to the ways in which diverse knowledges can serve as a disrupting force of power. A cacophony of stories holds the potential to disrupt (erase) the organizational hierarchy (and valuing of "expert" knowledge) that may constrain systemic change-making possibilities.

An intersectional analysis reveals as problematic the additive (Andersen 2005; Bowleg 2008) or multiplicative (Hancock 2007) responses to the "problem" of diversity access, and how campuses are constituted as spaces into which outsiders are added or included (Ahmed 2012). The conceptualization of diversity as *inclusion* resonates with "that old adage that we must learn to live together" (Rutherford 1990, 26)—what Rodney King pleaded for in his question, Why can't we just all get along (in Johnson 2006)—that can (unwittingly) reinforce practices that support exclusion and inequity. The challenge is to move beyond the hope and promise of inclusion—or "happiness" as Ahmed (2012, 165) refers to it—to destabilize how structures privilege some and systematically disadvantage others. Policy authors, like policy analysts, must interrogate structural oppression to reveal how privilege and advantage operate systemically.

CONCLUSIONS

The findings of this study point to the need to resist and contest dominant conceptions of communities as inclusive, welcoming, and friendly environments, even as they situate some as outsiders to those communities; to interrogate and disrupt the problem of access—or how institutions are inaccessible to some while remaining (unquestionably) accessible to (privileged) others; and to illuminate how "problems" are positioned within and remain the burden of the at-risk outsiders, and that to achieve equity, policies must instead point to how problems of exclusion are an institutional, not individual, problem, and that inaccessible institutional spaces are shaped by some (privileged) bodies and not others (Ahmed 2012; Berrey 2015).

Policy is a place where the construction of identity and difference is produced and where agendas can be furthered. I conclude that rather than abandon the "tool" of policy, policy authors and analysts must consider the power

APPENDIX: Diversity Action Plans at Flagship Universities

State	Institution	Diversity Action Plan
Alabama	University of Alabama	Strategic Diversity Plan, 2008 (58 pp.)
California	University of California, Berkeley	Strategic Plan for Equity, Inclusion, & Diversity: Pathway to Excellence, 2009 (42 pp.)
Delaware	University of Delaware	Inclusive Excellence: An Action Plan for Diversity at UD, 2016–2021 (32 pp.)
Florida	University of Florida	Diversity Action Plan, 2011 (5 pp.)
Georgia	University of Georgia	Embracing Diversity and Inclusion at UGA: The University of Georgia Diversity Plan, 2011–2016 (13 pp.)
Illinois	University of Illinois at Urbana-Champaign	"Pursuing Diversity Excellence: A Plan to Transform the Campus for the Class of 2030," Chancellor's Committee on Race and Ethnicity, 2013 (22 pp.)
Iowa	University of Iowa	Diversity Action Committee Report & Recommendations, 2006 (36 pp.)
Kentucky	University of Kentucky	Diversity Plan, 2010; revised 2014 (5 pp.)
Maryland	University of Maryland, College Park	Transforming Maryland: Expectations for Excellence in Diversity and Inclusion, 2010 (32 pp.)
Massachusetts	UMass, Amherst	Diversity Plan, 2011 (35 pp.)
Michigan	University of Michigan	Many Voices, Our Michigan: Diversity, Equity & Inclusion Strategic Plan, 2016 (42 pp.)
Minnesota	University of Minnesota, Twin Cities	Reimagining Equity and Diversity: A Framework for Transforming the University of Minnesota, 2008 (20 pp.)
Mississippi	University of Mississippi	Diversity Matters: University of Mississippi Diversity Plan, 2016 (96 pp.)
Montana	University of Montana	Diversity Plan, 2009 (8 pp.)
New Hampshire	University of New Hampshire	2010–2020 Inclusive Excellence Strategic Plan, 2012 (24 pp.)
North Carolina	University of North Carolina at Chapel Hill	University of Carolina's Diversity Plan, 2006 (7 pp.)
Ohio	Ohio State University	Renewing the Covenant: Diversity Objectives and Strategies for 2007 to 2012, 2008 (24 pp.)

(cont.)

APPENDIX: Diversity Action Plans at Flagship Universities (*continued*)

State	Institution	Diversity Action Plan
Oregon	University of Oregon	Diversity Action Plan, 2007 (27 pp.)
Pennsylvania	Pennsylvania State University	A Framework to Foster Diversity at Penn State, 2010–2015 (44 pp.)
Tennessee	University of Tennessee	Diversity and the University of Tennessee: A Framework for Action, 2005–2010 (13 pp.)
Vermont	University of Vermont	Inclusive Excellence at the University of Vermont: A Framework for Building a More Diverse, Inclusive, and Multiculturally Competent Campus, 2016–2021 (12 pp.)

of language carried in these policy documents and endeavor to rewrite them. Through an intersectional analysis, we might advance institutional policy changes that will enable flagship universities to cease operating as engines of social inequality.

NOTE

1. I adopt a moniker used in the policies—referring to affected populations in ambiguous terms, for example, "diverse group populations," "diverse faculty," "diverse students," "diverse constituencies on campus."

REFERENCES

Ahmed, S. 2012. *On Being Included: Racism and Diversity in Institutional Life*. Durham, NC: Duke University Press.

Allan, E. J., S. V. Iverson, and R. Ropers-Huilman, eds. 2010. *Reconstructing Policy in Higher Education: Feminist Poststructural Perspectives*. New York: Routledge.

Andersen, M. L. 2005. "Thinking about Women: A Quarter Century's View." *Gender & Society* 19 (4): 437–455.

Andersen, M. L., and P. H. Collins, eds. 2004. *Race, Class, and Gender: An Anthology*. 5th ed. Belmont, CA: Wadsworth.

BacaZinn, M., P. Hondagneu-Sotolo, and M. Messner, eds. 2000. *Gender through the Prism of Difference*. 2nd ed. Boston: Allyn & Bacon.

Bacchi, C. L., and J. Eveline, eds. 2010. "Mainstreaming and Neoliberalism: A Contest Relationship." In *Mainstreaming Politics: Gendering Practices and Feminist Theory*, 39–60. Adelaide, Australia: University of Adelaide Press.

Bacchi, C. L., and S. Goodwin. 2016. *Poststructural Policy Analysis: A Guide to Practice*. New York: Palgrave.

Ball, S. J. 1993. "What Is Policy? Texts, Trajectories, and Toolboxes." *Discourse: Studies in the Cultural Politics of Education* 13 (2): 10–17.

Bensimon, E. M. 2005. "Closing the Achievement Gap in Higher Education: An Organizational Learning Perspective." *New Directions for Higher Education* (131): 99–111.

Berrey, E. 2015. *The Enigma of Diversity: The Language of Race and the Limits of Racial Justice.* Chicago: University of Chicago Press.

Bowleg, Lisa. 2008. "When Black + Lesbian + Woman ≠ Black Lesbian Woman: The Methodological Challenges of Qualitative and Quantitative Intersectionality Research." *Sex Roles* 59 (5–6): 312–325.

Campbell, J. R. 1995. *Reclaiming a Lost Heritage: Land-Grant and Other Higher Education Initiatives for the Twenty-First Century.* Ames: Iowa State University Press.

Chang, M. J. 2005. "Reconsidering the Diversity Rationale." *Liberal Education* 91 (1): 6–13.

Collins, P. H. 1990. *Black Feminist Thought: Knowledge, Consciousness and the Politics of Empowerment.* Boston: Unwin Hyman.

Crenshaw, K. 1991. "Mapping the Margins: Intersectionality, Identity Politics, and Violence against Women of Color." *Stanford Law Review* 43 (6): 1241–1299.

Fairweather, J. S., and A. L. Beach. 2002. "Variations in Faculty Work at Research Universities: Implications for State and Institutional Policy." *Review of Higher Education* 26 (1): 97–115.

Foucault, M. 1994. "So Is It Important to Think?" In *Power: Essential Works of Foucault 1954–1984,* vol. 3, edited by J. D. Faubion, translated by R. Hurley and others, 454–458. London: Penguin.

———. (1977) 1995. *Discipline and Punish: The Birth of the Prison.* 2nd ed. Translated by Alan Sheridan. New York: Vintage Books.

Gerald, D., and K. Haycock. 2006. *Engines of Inequality: Diminishing Equity in the Nation's Premier Public Universities.* Washington, DC: Education Trust.

Hancock, A. 2007. "When Multiplication Doesn't Equal Quick Addition: Examining Intersectionality as a Research Paradigm." *Perspectives on Politics* 5 (1): 63–79.

Hankivsky, O., ed. 2012. *An Intersectionality-Based Policy Analysis Framework.* Vancouver, BC: Institute for Intersectionality Research and Policy, Simon Fraser University.

Hankivsky, O., and R. Cormier. 2011. "Intersectionality and Public Policy: Some Lessons from Existing Models." *Political Research Quarterly* 64 (1): 217–229.

Hankivsky, O., D. Grace, G. Hunting, and O. Ferlatte. 2012a. "Introduction: Why Intersectionality Matters for Health Equity and Policy Analysis." In *An Intersectionality-Based Policy Analysis Framework,* edited by O. Hankivsky, 7–30. Vancouver, BC: Institute for Intersectionality Research and Policy, Simon Fraser University.

Hankivsky, O., D. Grace, G. Hunting, O. Ferlatte, N. Clark, A. Fridkin, M. Giesbrecht, S. Rudrum, and T. Laviolette. 2012b. "Intersectionality-Based Policy Analysis." In *An Intersectionality-Based Policy Analysis Framework,* edited by O. Hankivsky, 33–45. Vancouver, BC: Institute for Intersectionality Research and Policy, Simon Fraser University.

Hankivsky, O., C. Reid, R. Cormier, C. Varcoe, N. Clark, C. Benoit, and S. Brotman. 2010. "Exploring the Promises of Intersectionality for Advancing Women's Health Research." *International Journal for Equity in Health* 9 (5): 1–15.

Iverson, S. V. 2007. "Camouflaging Power and Privilege: A Critical Race Analysis of University Diversity Policies." *Educational Administration Quarterly* 43 (5): 586–611.

———. 2008. "Capitalizing on Change: The Discursive Framing of Diversity in U.S. Land-Grant Universities." *Equity and Excellence in Education* 41 (2): 1–18.

———. 2012. "Constructing Outsiders: The Discursive Framing of Access in University Diversity Policies." *Review of Higher Education* 35 (2): 149–177.

———. 2017. "Mapping Identities: An Intersectional Analysis of Sexual Violence Policies." In *Intersections of Identity and Sexual Violence on Campus: Centering Minoritized Students' Experiences,* edited by J. Harris and C. Linder, 214–232. Sterling, VA: Stylus.

Jaquette, O., B. R. Curs, and J. R. Posselt. 2016. "Tuition Rich, Mission Poor: Nonresident Enrollment Growth and the Socioeconomic and Racial Composition of Public Research Universities." *Journal of Higher Education* 87 (5): 635–673.

Jennrich, J., and M. Kowalski-Braun. 2014. "My Head Is Spinning": Doing Authentic Intersectional Work in Identity Centers." *Journal of Progressive Policy & Practice* 2: 199–211.

John, P. 1998. *Analyzing Public Policy.* New York: Routledge.

Johnson, A. G. 2006. *Privilege, Power, and Difference.* 2nd ed. Boston: McGraw Hill.

Johnson, E. L. 1999. "Misconceptions of Early Land-Grant Colleges." In *The History of Higher Education,* 2nd ed., edited by L. F. Goodchild and H. S. Wechsler, 222–233. ASHE Reader Series. New York: Simon & Schuster Custom Publishing.

Ken, I. 2008. "Beyond the Intersection: A New Culinary Metaphor for Race-Class-Gender Studies." *Sociological Theory* 26 (2): 152–172.

Manuel, T. 2006. "Envisioning the Possibilities for a Good Life: Exploring the Public Policy Implications of Intersectionality Theory." *Journal of Women, Politics and Policy* 28 (3–4): 173–203.

Mohanty, C. T. 2003. *Feminism without Borders: Decolonizing Theory, Practicing Solidarity.* Durham, NC: Duke University Press.

Phipps, A. 2010. "Violent and Victimized Bodies: Sexual Violence Policy in England and Wales." *Critical Social Policy* 30: 359–383.

Purdie-Vaughns, V., and R. P. Eibach. 2008. "Intersectional Invisibility: The Distinctive Advantages and Disadvantages of Multiple Subordinate-Group Identities." *Sex Roles* 59(5–6): 377–391.

Rudd, J. M., G. E. Greenley, A. T. Beatson, and I. N. Lings. 2008. "Strategic Planning and Performance: Extending the Debate." *Journal of Business Research* 61 (2): 99–108.

Rudrum, S. 2012. "An Intersectional Critical Discourse Analysis of Maternity Care Policy Recommendations in British Columbia." In *An Intersectionality-Based Policy Analysis Framework,* edited by O. Hankivsky, 47–66. Vancouver, BC: Institute for Intersectionality Research and Policy, Simon Fraser University.

Rutherford, J., ed. 1990. *Identity: Community, Culture, Difference.* London: Lawrence & Wishart.

Shore, C., and S. Wright. 2011. "Conceptualising Policy: Technologies of Governance and the Politics of Visibility." In *Policy Worlds: Anthropology and the Analysis of Contemporary Power,* edited by C. Shore, S. Wright, and D. Pero, 1–26. New York: Berghahn Books.

Thomas, J. M. 2017. "Diversity Regimes and Racial Inequality: A Case Study of Diversity University." *Social Currents,* 1–17. doi:10.1177/2329496517725335.

Tierney, W. G. 1992. *Official Encouragement, Institutional Discouragement: Minorities in Academe—the Native American Experience.* Norwood, NJ: Ablex Publishing.

Waldegrave, C. 2009. "Cultural, Gender, and Socioeconomic Contexts in Therapeutic and Social Policy Work." *Family Process* 48 (1): 85–101.

17 · TIPS OF ICEBERGS IN THE OCEAN

Reflections on Future Research for Embracing Intersectionality in Higher Education

W. CARSON BYRD, SARAH M. OVINK, AND RACHELLE J. BRUNN-BEVEL

Throughout this volume our contributors detail how marginalization and inequality operate within higher education in relation to privilege and mobility. As a key component of intersectionality (Collins 2000), none of the chapters levies calls that any one specific form of marginalization is privy to the title of "most oppressed" compared with the others. These examinations of students, faculty, and staff identify how the interpersonal, disciplinary, cultural, and structural domains of power (Collins and Bilge 2016) vary, yet are still interconnected. The authors show how marginalization is differentially shaped among groups on college campuses, including for white members of the campus community, who are often assumed to hold the most privileged positions. An important goal of this volume relates to the perspective shared by Cho, Crenshaw, and McCall (2013)— that scholars must not simply aim to cite particular sources or use terminology such as "diversity," "inclusive," "multiplicative," or "intersectionality" to make intersectional analyses; rather, through these analyses, scholars must "[emphasize] what intersectionality *does* rather than what intersectionality *is*" (795). Using a variety of positions and methods, our contributors carefully examine how members of our campus communities are not equitably treated. Identity and inequality organize each other in the power-laden university environment. Thus, intersectional analyses represent an integral feature of critical research on education and educational spaces. These contributions provide insights into how marginalization manifests in higher education, as well as how to work through efforts to correct the inequalities our institutions produce and reproduce.

As the chapter title suggests, we must recognize how different forms of marginalization on college campuses connect to broader cultural and structural inequality. Therefore, although each form of marginalization (icebergs) may seem disconnected, they relate to one another and important aspects of our campuses (ocean). We must engage in direct social action to simultaneously produce equitable foundations, support systems, and inclusive experiences. In doing so, we utilize intersectionality as a theoretical framework and methodological guide. We must examine our campuses both broadly and deeply to uncover how inequality and marginalization manifest visibly through policies and practices as well as how they are invisible through these same aspects of our institutions. In this chapter, we elaborate on how the findings contributed throughout this volume connect, in order to suggest practical approaches for lasting change. Utilizing an intersectional lens, we advocate for a radical transformation in higher education institutions—from "engines of inequality" to engines of equity and social justice.

APPROACHES TO INSTITUTIONAL CHANGE

Our volume offers important policy implications based on research findings that focus on the intersectional experiences of students, faculty, and staff at a variety of higher education institutions. At the heart of these implications are suggestions for institutional change that reflect Pettigrew and Martin's (1987) important call for simultaneous cultural and structural shifts within organizations. Without strong commitments for institutional change on multiple fronts, colleges and universities risk a repeated cycle of incomplete transformation and recurring inequalities.

One broad-based approach for institutional change is for scholars to utilize innovative research methodologies that capitalize on intersectional framing. As this volume establishes at the outset, discussions of intersectionality cannot be restricted to individual experiences using an additive approach to identity. To situate how individual experiences relate to an intersectional identity, the positioning of the individual in relation to other campus community members must be taken into account. Furthermore, relying on a single methodology can limit our understanding of the full picture of the college environment for marginalized groups. As Cuellar and Johnson-Ahorlu note (chapter 2), mixed-methods approaches can "get behind the numbers" to identify why students may rate their college's commitment to diversity as moderately strong while at the same time detailing experiences of discrimination they face on campus. Additionally, examining climate surveys to identify which marginalized groups are not included (e.g., students with disabilities) in these assessment programs could better inform policy decisions. Nanney (chapter 15) uses inductive textual analysis to demonstrate how women's colleges that seem to have trans* inclusive admissions policies in practice ignore or even exacerbate inequality by race and class. Nanney underscores that postsecondary institutions, despite espousing inclusive ideology via policy changes, often lack the necessary infrastructure to support trans* students. Scholars can use these innovative methodological approaches to not only amplify the voices of marginalized groups on campus but also strengthen policies and their implementation. Such efforts put pressure on institutions to move beyond the lip-service rhetoric of diversity and inclusion, as Iverson (chapter 16) poignantly notes, in order to cultivate broad-reaching efforts to support all students, faculty, and staff on campus.

As Iverson suggests, to assist administrators and their constituents in evaluating the changes needed on campus, a discursive shift to equity centers attempts to make the institution accessible and inclusive. If equity is the goal, then privilege and systemic disadvantage are its enemy. However, decisions about the benchmarks for equitable outcomes must not lie only with those who already hold positions of power; often, those who stand to be most negatively impacted by educational policy decisions are not included in such discussions at all. As Nanney's discussion of "trickle-up activism" notes, marginalized students who stand to be most affected by higher education policy changes deserve to have a hand in their creation. Additionally, these discussions must move from focusing on equity on campus to a more holistic consideration of how the institution influences equity in the surrounding community. Institutions cannot detach themselves from the communities they are embedded in, nor can they ignore how the marginalization of segments of their students impacts them after they leave campus, as graduates or not. For example, as institutions are further pressured to exhibit specific job-related outcomes for their graduates, institutions cannot assume they are adequately preparing all of their students for a competitive labor market when students are laying demands on their desk to eliminate the discrimination and unsupportive environment they must live and study in. This raises the question, What specific changes should institutions make to increase equity on campus?

Our authors offer many programmatic changes that can assist institutions to both reorient their efforts toward equity and boost academic excellence. Building on Warnock's suggestion (chapter 4), institutions should re-evaluate their orientation programs to make sure they do not make unwarranted assumptions about students' knowledge and resources. Orientation programs often rely on parents being present for certain tasks, but what if a student must come on their own because their parents are unable to take time away from work? Do our orientation programs provide the needed support for low-socioeconomic students and their families to make a successful transition to college? To facilitate dismantling structures of privilege and systemic inequalities, orientation programs should incorporate discussions of institutional history and equity so that students may begin to engage with these efforts from the very beginning of their college career. Often, a racial discrimination incident catches students off guard because of the presumption that educational systems have moved "beyond" the overtly racist practices of the past. Initiating these conversations during orientation can signal to students that the institution is a welcoming space and desires all campus community members to engage in equitable practices. College orientations could also include the initiation of intergroup dialogues so that students can grapple with how marginalization and oppression manifest in a variety of ways. Such dialogues, while difficult and sometimes uncomfortable, can push students' critical thinking skills and understanding of the importance of equity in society (Ford 2012; Ford and Mulaney 2012; Schoem and Hurtado 2001; Warikoo 2016; Zuniga et al. 2007).

Our authors detail how faculty can serve as anchors for intersectional conversations across fields of study. Moreover, administrators can sustain faculty work in this area by supporting curricular development. For faculty themselves, Cuellar and Johnson-Ahorlu (chapter 2), Gast, Matthews, and Brooms (chapter 10), and Lee and Maynard (chapter 7) argue for increasing faculty members' knowledge and use of inclusive pedagogies through workshops and faculty development initiatives. Through techniques such as critical race pedagogy, classrooms can incorporate conversations about power, diversity, and inequality, linking historical events to current realities in their fields of study. This work should not fall solely on the shoulders of the humanities and social sciences; these conversations also directly relate to research and practice in science, technology, engineering, and mathematics (STEM) fields. Further, these authors suggest faculty should encourage an open dialogue about their positioning, if possible, around issues of power and inequality. Although not without risks, these openings for personal dialogue can assist marginalized students with feeling less alone and perhaps finding a resource to expand conversations about their experiences. However, the power to adapt conversations and course content in relation to the responsibilities of instructors in the classroom can vary by the instructors' own intersecting identities and institutional context. Mohajeri, Rodriguez, and schneider (chapter 11) suggest incorporating a collaborative co-teaching practice to better inform how faculty from marginalized identities utilize silencing and naming of power dynamics. Such practices, they argue, necessitate ongoing discussion with one another to cultivate an intersectional pedagogical approach.

Faculty cannot improve campus dialogue and transform the curriculum alone. In support of faculty efforts, our authors suggest approaches for administrative units as well. One approach is to ensure that meaningful conversations are held in "diversity" classes by limiting class sizes. Burdening a faculty member with 140 students for an important course at the heart of an institution's diversity efforts sends the opposite signal of support; it signals that students must cram together once to take the course, then move on. Administrative support would reduce the class sizes, not the number of classes themselves, to have these important conversations. As Gast, Matthews, and Brooms note, to reduce class sizes, faculty diversity initiatives must increase the number of faculty who are equipped to lead these courses and buoy institutional efforts to become a leader in equity, inclusion, and academic excellence. As Richards (chapter 9) notes, these efforts could couple with changes to how faculty are assessed when they take on core diversity courses, because courses that incorporate contentious issues often result in polarizing student evaluations.

A related discussion by Goerisch (chapter 8) includes the need to increase conversations among faculty about the importance of care work, such as taking on mentorship roles. These conversations should directly confront the reality that faculty of color, especially women, are more likely to handle the care work for students of color. More equitably distributing care work responsibilities, particularly among white (male) faculty who are less likely to work with students of color, can assist with increasing student success among marginalized students. We must stop telling faculty of color and women of all races and ethnicities to simply "say no" to service work, and begin holding (white) men accountable for supporting students and the broader departmental community. Further, we must systematically situate faculty care work as valued and rewarded within academia. Faculty and administrative committees at different institutional levels could also explore how performance evaluations—including tenure and promotion metrics—could better recognize and reward care work undertaken by faculty.

Turning to programmatic changes to increase equity and inclusion on college campuses, our authors' research suggests a need for clear guidelines and communication around financial aid policies. As both Jones (chapter 3) and Warnock (chapter 4) highlight, for low-income, first-generation, undocumented, and other marginalized students, gaining an understanding of the full financial picture of college attendance can be difficult. Nanney illustrates how sex/gender questions on the Common Application and FAFSA (Free Application for Federal Student Aid) can actually prevent trans* students from being admitted to women's colleges. Consequently, the most economically vulnerable trans* students are those most negatively affected. Improving financial aid staff members' awareness of students who face financial precarity would help dismantle dangerous assumptions about the profile of the "typical" college student. Clearly communicated financial aid policies would further help staff better assist students in need. Similar discussions could also be held with staff members supervising internship and study abroad programs to help them understand why marginalized students might not take advantage of their programming. Such shifts in dialogue could provide staff members with opportunities to identify ways to increase the participation of historically marginalized groups in financial aid streams and important extended learning opportunities.

Additional dialogue may also facilitate needed changes to policies for student affairs practitioners and other institutional agents to more effectively support the needs of students from marginalized groups. Vaccaro and Kimball (chapter 14) emphasize the nearly complete stalemate many student affairs practitioners meet with when assisting students with disabilities. The necessity of maintaining confidentiality, particularly for students with disabilities that are "invisible," makes successfully advocating for students a complex issue. Developing workshops for campus community members to gain awareness of the variety of disability statuses that can exist on campus could foster important cultural shifts, ultimately easing the burden on student affairs practitioners to build bridges between faculty and students needing institutional accommodations. Lane's research (chapter 13) details how conversations in STEM support services rarely include broader conversations about how these programs marginalize students and faculty from different groups, particularly black women students. These programmatic and support recommendations directly connect to the need for more campus community members to gain important knowledge, pedagogical techniques, and training to enhance their professional development in the areas of diversity, equity, and inclusion.

Amending universities' physical social environments must also command our attention. Echoing a demand by student protests around the nation (Chessman and Wayt 2016), Cuellar and Johnson-Ahorlu suggest institutions seriously consider campus architecture and building names. At some institutions, a history of exclusion is literally encased in stone around campus, representing a powerful indicator to marginalized groups of whose lives are valued on campus. Clayton (chapter 5) taps a growing national discussion about whether colleges and universities ought to dismantle Greek life on campuses, given these organizations' support for racial, gender, and class hierarchies that promote life-threatening behaviors. Although wholesale removal may not gain universal support—we note that some Greek organizations were created with the goal of affirmatively supporting equity and pro-social values—we must ask ourselves why educational institutions should continue to support those Greek chapters repeatedly found in violation of campus rules, whose practices actively hinder efforts toward equity. Finally, though changes to the physical environment such as all-gender bathrooms may help some trans* students navigate higher education institutions, Nanney reminds us that Band-Aid solutions cannot replace the hard work of transforming underlying organizational structures that continue to marginalize trans* members of the university community.

As we have detailed throughout this section, our authors have utilized an intersectional lens to identify many areas of campus life that are ripe for reform efforts to increase equitable outcomes. Taken together, our volume offers a variety of avenues for staff, faculty, and students to pursue the ongoing project of ensuring equity in college experiences and outcomes. However, we would be remiss if we did not call attention to areas of intersectional research that are not represented here, to which scholars must next turn their attention. In the section that follows, we highlight recent data on representation among nonadministrative staff on college campuses and offer suggestions for bringing their largely invisible labor into the light. We close with suggestions for future directions in research examining intersectionality in higher education, including our call for a re-examination of what it means to be a "marginalized" or "traditional" campus community member in an economically precarious college-for-all context.

INVISIBLE LABOR AND INEQUALITY ON CAMPUS

One morning several years ago, the first author was walking into the office on a snow-covered campus with few people in sight. It was nearing 7:30 A.M. Though the campus slowly awakens at this time each day, that particular day was slightly different as a result of a sudden burst of snow. The snowfall barely tipped into the "several inches" category, but the timing led administrators to delay opening the campus to clear parking lots, roads, and sidewalks. As the author approached the door of their building, two housekeeping staff members were busily sweeping the area of the last remnants of snow. Bundled in jackets, scarves, and gloves, they quickly cleared one of four major entry points to the building. I waved good morning and said "thank you" for clearing the entry area, and made my way into the building.

Later, in a hallway of the building, I met one of the staff members who had been clearing the sidewalks. Our meeting was not an infrequent occurrence as we had often exchanged small talk in the halls over the years. Appearing somewhat exasperated, the staff member eventually mentioned what was bothering them. Many of the housekeeping, physical plant, and office staff cannot afford to live in the college town, and live as far away as a town that is fully two hours' distance, over mountain roads, from the university. Often arriving before 5:00 A.M., the staff were particularly troubled this morning as they had to traverse snow- and ice-covered roads before many of the snow plows had cleared the areas near their homes, in order to arrive at the university to clear the campus for faculty, upper-division staff, and students. The staff member noted that many people could not make it to campus on time because of the weather, and some feared that they would no longer have a job under a new restructuring of housekeeping staff under a private company contracted by the university. Wages for staff were higher compared with similar jobs in the region, but still only high enough to barely stay ahead of the bills. The new management seemed to push housekeeping staff to do more for less, and promised the university efficient results. If someone was not meeting the supposed benchmarks set by the company, their position may be terminated. On this snowy morning, the staff member worried that traveling on treacherous roads was not enough to protect a job their family counted on.

The staff members who braved the winter weather to open the campus are members of groups often recognized as marginalized on campus: racial and ethnic minorities, women, low-income, and employees with some forms of disability, among others. The struggle for visibility and respect happens across higher education institutions, from public regional colleges to elite private research universities (see Green 2016), and institutions in between. Yet, their experiences, which directly affect how faculty and students navigate the college environment, are frequently missing from narratives of how identity and inequality intertwine in higher education. An area vitally important to expanding conversations about intersectionality and higher education relates to staff members on college campuses. Often invisible in many ways, staff members occupy differing positions and vary in how they experience inequalities and marginalization on campus. Chapters 12 through 14 elaborate on a small segment of college staff member experiences, many of who serve in student or academic affairs positions, supporting students. When we began sifting through the many submissions for this volume, what became painfully obvious was how seldom scholars focus on how colleges and universities marginalize the staff members who literally make their institutions run each day. The housekeeping, dining hall, physical plant, administrative support and transportation staff, and many other staff members remain invisible in conversations about intersectionality and higher education. These members of campus communities are paid less, offered fewer (if any) benefits such as health insurance and retirement funds, and are more susceptible to institutional restructuring such as being placed under private-public partnerships for management purposes.

In the fall of 2013, nearly 3.9 million people were employed by colleges and universities across the United States (Snyder, de Brey, and Dillow 2016). Nearly 822,000 employees are present on our campuses working as office staff, in service and sales occupations, construction and maintenance, and production and transportation services, which represent 21.1 percent of all higher education employees. Of these staff members, 62.3 percent are white, 17.3 percent are black, 11.2 percent are Latina/o, 3.6 percent are Asian or Pacific Islander, and 0.7 percent are Native American employees. When we dissect these data further, we find disparities by race and gender for who is employed in different positions on campus.

Table 17.1 provides a snapshot of this race-gender breakdown of who is represented as faculty, staff, or administrators on college campuses. The percentages for nonadministrative staff members, management administrators, student affairs practitioners, and instructional and research faculty provide the occupational groupings for this discussion. The table presents the percentages of men and women in varying racial and ethnic groups by occupational categories. The first column displays the percentage of a particular race-gender group composing an occupational category. The second column displays the percentage of a particular race-gender group in an occupational category among all higher education employees of that race-gender group. The third column presents the percentage of a particular race-gender group in an occupational category among all higher education employees.

An examination of race-gender disparities by occupational categories provides a glimpse at the inequality on college campuses regarding who occupies certain positions that hold different resources and opportunities. Among nonadministrative staff members, a majority of staff members are white regardless of gender,

TABLE 17.1   Percentages of Employees in Each Occupational, Race-Gender, and Total Grouping at Postsecondary Institutions, Fall 2013

	Men			Women		
Racial/ethnic group	Occupational category	Race-gender group	Total in higher ed.	Occupational category	Race-gender group	Total in higher ed.
Nonadministrative staff	17.5	—	8.0	24.1	—	13.1
White	62.0	15.9	7.3	63.1	22.4	12.2
Black	17.1	37.9	14.1	17.5	37.7	23.7
Latina/o	11.6	33.9	14.4	10.9	38.6	22.3
Asian and Pacific Islander	3.6	9.8	4.7	3.6	15.0	7.8
Native American	0.8	27.9	12.0	0.7	29.9	17.1
Administration	6.4	—	2.9	6.5	—	3.6
White	79.7	7.5	3.4	75.9	7.3	4.0
Black	8.0	6.5	2.4	11.2	6.6	4.1
Latina/o	4.8	5.1	2.2	5.5	5.3	3.0
Asian and Pacific Islander	3.6	3.6	1.7	3.7	4.2	2.2
Native American	0.5	6.2	2.7	0.5	6.2	3.5
Student affairs	2.9	—	1.3	5.1	—	2.7
White	68.2	2.9	1.3	68.5	5.1	2.7
Black	11.4	4.2	1.6	13.2	5.9	3.7
Latina/o	7.8	3.8	1.6	7.7	5.7	3.3
Asian and Pacific Islander	4.3	2.0	0.9	3.8	3.4	1.7
Native American	0.9	4.9	2.1	0.8	7.3	4.1
Faculty	44.0	—	20.0	34.9	—	19.0
White	73.3	47.2	21.6	72.3	37.2	20.2
Black	5.3	29.3	10.9	8.4	26.1	16.4
Latina/o	4.3	31.3	13.2	4.5	22.9	13.2
Asian and Pacific Islander	7.5	51.6	24.9	6.1	37.3	19.4
Native American	0.4	38.3	16.4	0.5	31.9	18.2

SOURCE: Data from Snyder, de Brey, and Dillow (2016) used for calculations.

NOTE: Faculty includes only instructional and research faculty members regardless of work status (full/part); administration includes only management positions.

and comparable percentages of each racial and ethnic group exist across genders as well. However, when we examine the percentages of members in this occupational category as a total percentage of higher education employees from that particular group, a starkly different story emerges from the data. Nearly 40 percent of all black men employed in higher education work as nonadministrative staff members. Similarly, one-third of all Latino men and nearly one-third of all Native American men employed by universities work in nonadministrative staff positions. These percentages drastically overshadow the small percentages of all Asian and Pacific Islander men and white men employed in similar positions on college campuses. A related trend is found among women in these positions as well, with nearly 40 percent of all black and Latina women and nearly one-third of all Native American women employed in higher education working in nonadministrative staff positions. Women in these positions represented much smaller percentages of all Asian and Pacific Islander women and white women employed on college campuses. Overall, the percentage of women in nonadministrative staff positions was higher compared with men in all racial and ethnic groupings.

Turning to people employed in campus management positions, white men and women hold the largest number of these positions, with most racial and ethnic groups representing less than 10 percent each of such administrative groups. With the exception of whites and Native Americans, women in the remaining racial and ethnic categories were slightly more represented than men in these positions, which contrasts with other occupations on campus. Although white men and women in these administrative positions have the highest representation within their respected racial-gender groupings compared with other racial-gender groups, their percentages are only slightly higher overall. An important point about these data is the positions aggregated under the administrative category are not restricted to the highest and most visible senior-level administrators, such as presidents, vice presidents, provosts, and deans. Thus, it may seem surprising that women occupy higher percentages in these positions than men for some groups; however, these data do not indicate who is often in charge of these units compared with who is represented among the staff in a provost's office, for example.

As found among the previous occupational categories, white men and women compose the majority of men and women working in student affairs positions. Women have higher representation in these positions than men. Interestingly, Native American men and women have the highest race-gender representation compared with all other groups. That is, 7.3 percent of all Native American women and 4.9 percent of all Native American men working in colleges and universities are employed as student affairs practitioners. Black and Latino/a men and women had the next highest representation of all members of those groups working in student affairs, while white and Asian and Pacific Islander men and women had the lowest representation in this higher education occupation.

Instructional and research faculty members present similar composition as the aforementioned occupational categories, but illustrate the often discussed narrative of underrepresentation concerning scholars of color. Men hold a larger percentage of faculty positions compared with women across race and ethnicity, though some groups have more comparable percentages in the faculty ranks. Asian and Pacific Islander men and women are the most represented among faculty members in higher education with slightly more than half of all Asian and Pacific Islander men and nearly 40 percent of all Asian and Pacific Islander women located in faculty positions. Quite similar to Asian and Pacific Islander employees in higher education, white men and women are the second most represented among faculty as almost half of all white men in higher education are faculty members and nearly 40 percent of white women are also faculty members. Native American men and women were slightly more represented in faculty ranks among their specific race-gender groupings compared with black and Latino men and women, though these groups hovered between a quarter and one-third representations of their particular race-gender groups.

The aggregated data described above provide an overview of the (under)representation of men and women in different positions on college campuses by race and ethnicity. As noted with regard to the administrative calculations, these data fall short of providing a full picture of who holds power and privilege on college campuses within these occupational categories. Although the National Center for Education Statistics (NCES) provides data for the racial, ethnic, and gender breakdown of management positions, these positions are not restricted to only the most visible senior-level administrators. Additionally, these calculations are not broken down by work status (i.e., full time or part time), which would indicate how groups are over- or underrepresented in particular positions further as previous research notes the prevalence of racial and ethnic minority employees, particularly women, being overrepresented in part-time positions including faculty positions. Taken together, more research on how nonadministrative and non–student affairs staff members are incorporated into our discussions about marginalization and inequality on college campuses would provide a more holistic account of what obstacles still exist for the staff who ensure that our campuses open on time and run effectively and efficiently. If their experiences are not represented in our conversations about intersectionality in higher education, then we are not fully considering higher education intersectionally and our policies and practices will continue to fall short.

FUTURE DIRECTIONS FOR COLLEGE CAMPUSES

Our conversation about intersectionality and higher education is broad-reaching, with important insights focusing on faculty, staff, students, and campus communities. Our contributors provide an extensive overview of how inequality and marginality manifest on our campuses, and provide key perspectives on how to begin redressing such issues and experiences. However, it would be disingenuous to fail to acknowledge areas of research not fully incorporated into our volume. Ongoing discussions will continue to elaborate on aspects of identities intertwined with inequalities on college campuses.

There is a dearth of research addressing the unique experiences and needs of veterans attending and working in postsecondary institutions. Iverson (2014) uses her intersectional analysis of interviews with female student veterans to advance a "constellations of identity" metaphor. In this model, the "apparent magnitude" of interviewees' salient identities (race, class, having a disability, being a veteran, having children, etc.) varies across time and place (Iverson 2014). In short, the "traditional college student"—eighteen- to twenty-two-year-old first-time freshmen who enroll full time in colleges and universities immediately after high school graduation—is a diminishing share of the undergraduate population at most postsecondary institutions in the United States. Despite the rapidly changing demographic profile of the "typical" college student, tertiary education—and especially four-year residential colleges and universities—continues to cater to this idealized "traditional" student (Hamilton and Armstrong 2012).

Though discussions of gender and sexualities are included in some chapters (most notably in Nanney, chapter 15), our volume does not fully elaborate on how aspects of sexual identity affect student, faculty, and staff experiences on college campuses. We direct the interested reader toward the many extant explorations of how a person's sexuality and positioning within different institutional contexts can inform their experiences of privilege and marginalization (Narui 2014; Strayhorn and Tillman-Kelly 2013; Tillapaugh 2015). Olive (2015) and Thomas-Card and Ropers-Huilman (2014) call for combining queer theory and intersectionality to help better understand the experiences of LGBTQ (lesbian, gay, bisexual, transgender, queer) students. The current volume's contributors elaborate on whether, and when, these aspects of interlocking power dynamics come through in their analyses, but it should not be forgotten that this dimension of identity is an integral part of intersectional conversations about higher education.

As Victor Ray's contribution (chapter 6) points out, the experiences of underrepresented graduate students are too often "still furious." Research on graduate students that builds on this critical intersectional work, amid today's academic uncertainties—including the erosion of tenure-line positions as a proportion of all university instructors—should continue to uncover avenues for increasing inclusion in graduate education. Maintaining a reflexive perspective about our own work is an integral part of intersectionality as praxis (Collins and Bilge 2016). Similarly, and as noted above, institutions that wish to critically examine their practices must avoid too narrowly framing aspects of marginalization and inequality on campus. With this volume, we hope to participate in and help direct this ongoing conversation. In this way, we hope to show how intersectional analyses may serve to enhance emancipatory efforts toward equity and social justice on our college campuses and by our institutions.

REFERENCES

Chessman, Holly, and Lindsay Wayt. 2016. "What Are Students Demanding?" *Higher Education Today: A Blog by ACE.* http://higheredtoday.org/2016/01/13/what-are-students-demanding/.

Cho, Sumi, Kimberlé Crenshaw, and Leslie McCall. 2013. "Toward a Field of Intersectionality Studies: Theory, Applications, and Praxis." *Signs* 38 (4): 785–810.

Collins, Patricia Hill. 2000. *Black Feminist Thought: Knowledge, Consciousness, and the Politics of Empowerment*. 2nd ed. New York: Routledge.

Collins, Patricia Hill, and Sirma Bilge. 2016. *Intersectionality*. Malden, MA: Polity Press.

Ford, Kristie A. 2012. "Shifting White Ideological Scripts: The Educational Benefits of Inter- and Intraracial Curricular Dialogues on the Experiences of White College Students." *Journal of Diversity in Higher Education* 5 (3): 138–158.

Ford, Kristie A., and Victoria A. Mulaney. 2012. "'I Now Harbor More Pride in My Race': The Educational Benefits of Inter- and Intraracial Dialogues on the Experiences of Students of Color and Multiracial Students." *Equity & Excellence in Education* 45 (1): 14–35.

Green, Adrienne. 2016. "Cleaning After Hours." *The Atlantic*, September 6. http://www .theatlantic.com/business/archive/2016/09/janitor/498776.

Hamilton, Laura, and Elizabeth A. Armstrong. 2012. "The (Mis)Education of Monica and Karen." *Contexts* 11 (4): 22–27.

Iverson, Susan. 2014. "Identity Constellations: An Intersectional Analysis of Female Student Veterans." In *Intersectionality & Higher Education: Theory, Research, & Praxis*, edited by D. Mitchell Jr. with C. Y. Simmons and L. A. Greyerbiehl, 135–145. New York: Peter Lang.

Narui, Mitsu. 2014. "Hidden Populations and Intersectionality: When Race and Sexual Orientation Collide." In *Intersectionality & Higher Education: Theory, Research, & Praxis*, edited by D. Mitchell Jr. with C. Y. Simmons and L. A. Greyerbiehl, 185–200. New York: Peter Lang.

Olive, James L. 2015. "Queering the Intersectional Lens: A Conceptual Model for the Use of Queer Theory in Intersectional Research." In *Intersectionality in Educational Research*, edited by D. J. Davis, R. J. Brunn-Bevel, and J. L. Olive, 19–30. Sterling, VA: Stylus.

Pettigrew, Thomas F., and Joanne Martin. 1987. "Shaping the Organizational Context for Black American Inclusion." *Journal of Social Issues* 43 (1): 41–78.

Schoem, David, and Sylvia Hurtado, eds. 2001. *Intergroup Dialogue: Deliberative Democracy in School, College, Community, and Workplace*. Ann Arbor: University of Michigan Press.

Snyder, Thomas D., Cristobal de Brey, and Sally A. Dillow. 2016. *Digest of Education Statistics 2015* (NCES 2016-014). Washington, DC: National Center for Education Statistics, Institute of Education Sciences, U.S. Department of Education.

Strayhorn, Terrell L., and Derrick L. Tillman-Kelly. 2013. "When and Where Race and Sexuality Collide with Other Social Locations: Studying the Intersectional Lives of Gay Men in College." In *Living at the Intersections: Social Identities and Black Collegians*, edited by T. Strayhorn, 237–257. Charlotte, NC: Information Age Publishing.

Thomas-Card, Traci, and Rebecca Ropers-Huilman. 2014. "Heteronormativity Fractured and Fused: Exploring the College Experiences of Multiple Marginalized LGBT Students." In *Intersectionality & Higher Education: Theory, Research, & Praxis*, edited by D. Mitchell Jr. with C. Y. Simmons and L. A. Greyerbiehl, 78–87. New York: Peter Lang.

Tillapaugh, Daniel. 2015. "'Writing Our Own Rule Book': Exploring the Intersectionality of Gay College Men." In *Intersectionality in Educational Research*, edited by D. J. Davis, R. J. Brunn-Bevel, and J. L. Olive, 172–188. Sterling, VA: Stylus.

Warikoo, Natasha. 2016. *The Diversity Bargain: And Other Dilemmas of Race, Admissions, and Meritocracy at Elite Universities*. Chicago: University of Chicago Press.

Zuniga, Ximena, Biren A. Nagada, Mark Chessler, and Adena Cytron Walker. 2007. *Intergroup Dialogue in Higher Education: Meaningful Learning about Social Justice*. ASHE Higher Education Report, 32 (4). San Francisco: Jossey-Bass.

NOTES ON CONTRIBUTORS

EDITORS

W. CARSON BYRD is associate professor of sociology at the University of Louisville. His research examines race and educational inequality, inter- and intra-racial interactions and their influence on identities and ideologies, and the connections among race, science, and knowledge production. These three areas intertwine under a broader research umbrella examining how educational institutions, particularly colleges and universities, can simultaneously operate as centers for social mobility and engines of inequality. His scholarship has appeared in numerous academic journals, including the *Annals of the American Academy of Political and Social Science, Du Bois Review, Equity, Excellence & Education*, and *Ethnic and Racial Studies*, among other journals. He is also the author of *Poison in the Ivy: Race Relations and the Reproduction of Inequality on Elite College Campuses* (Rutgers University Press, 2017). Byrd received his bachelor's degree in sociology from Mars Hill College, and his master's degree and doctorate in sociology from Virginia Tech. He would like to acknowledge the generous financial support for this volume from the Commonwealth Center for the Humanities and Society at the University of Louisville.

RACHELLE J. BRUNN-BEVEL is associate professor of sociology and anthropology at Fairfield University. Her research examines how students' race, ethnicity, class, gender, and immigrant status intersect to influence their educational experiences and outcomes. She has published her scholarship in several academic journals, including the *Du Bois Review: Social Science Research on Race, Humanity & Society* and *Race and Social Problems*. She is the co-editor (with Dannielle Joy Davis and James L. Olive) of *Intersectionality in Educational Research* (Stylus, 2015). She is the co-author (with Kristin Richardson) of *"Let's Move!* with Michelle Obama" featured in *Michelle Obama's Impact on African American Women and Girls*, edited by Michelle Duster, Paula Marie Seniors, and Rose Thevenin (Palgrave MacMillan, 2018). Brunn-Bevel received a bachelor of arts, with distinction, in sociology and political science at the University of Delaware and a master of arts and PhD in sociology with a graduate certificate in urban studies from the University of Pennsylvania. She would like to acknowledge her appreciation for the financial support from the College of Arts & Sciences Publication Fund at Fairfield University for this publication.

SARAH M. OVINK is associate professor of sociology at Virginia Tech. Her research focuses primarily on inequalities in students' higher education pathways by race/ethnicity, gender, and income, using mixed methods of inquiry. Her publications have appeared in a variety of journals, including *Gender & Society*, *Social Currents, Research in Higher Education*, and *Socius*. She is the author of *Race, Class and Choice in Latino/a Higher Education: Pathways in the College-for-All Era* (Palgrave Macmillan, 2017). Ovink received her bachelor of arts in sociology at Kalamazoo College, and her master of arts and PhD in sociology at the University of California, Davis.

CONTRIBUTORS

DERRICK R. BROOMS is faculty in sociology and Africana studies at the University of Cincinnati and serves as a youth worker as well. His research and activism focus on educational equity, race and racism, diversity and inequality, and identity. His education research primarily centers on black male schooling experiences in both secondary and postsecondary institutions, with particular focus on school culture, engagement, resilience, identity, and sense of self. He is the author of *Being Black, Being Male on Campus: Understanding and Confronting Black Male Collegiate Experiences*.

KRISTEN A. CLAYTON is assistant professor of sociology at Oglethorpe College. Clayton's research lies at the intersections of sociology of race and ethnicity, sociology of gender, sociology of higher education, and social psychology. Much of Clayton's current research compares black-white biracial students' experiences within historically white and historically black colleges and universities. Her work has been published in *Law & Social Inquiry* and is forthcoming in *Sociology of Race and Ethnicity*.

MARCELA G. CUELLAR is assistant professor in the School of Education at the University of California, Davis. Her research focuses on access and equity in higher education, Latina/o college student success, and Hispanic-Serving Institutions (HSIs). More specifically, her research explores Latina/o students' experiences and outcomes at HSIs and emerging HSIs. She has published in the *Review of Higher Education, Teachers College Record*, and *Community College Review*.

MELANIE JONES GAST is assistant professor of sociology at the University of Louisville. Gast's research focuses on mechanisms of inclusion/exclusion and the structuring of support in schools and community programs serving racial and ethnic minority youth and families. She has other work examining information and resource gaps and the transition to college. She has published in journals such as the *Du Bois Review, Journal of Adolescent Research, Journal of Ethnic and Migration Studies, Social Science Research, Sociological Perspectives, Teachers College Record, Journal of Higher Education*, and *Urban Education*.

DENISE GOERISCH is assistant professor of liberal studies at Grand Valley State University. Her research focuses on the socioeconomic lives of children and young people. She is currently researching college students' engagement with the costs of pursuing higher education in the United States, not just the financial costs but also the sociocultural and emotional costs of attending college. She has published on topics related to emotional labor and girlhood, children's work and play, and leadership in informal educational spaces.

SUSAN V. IVERSON is professor and coordinator of higher education leadership at Manhattanville College. Iverson's research interests include equity and diversity, status of women in higher education, feminist pedagogy, and the role of policy (e.g., sexual violence) in shaping problem representation. In addition to articles and chapters, she has two co-edited volumes: *Feminist Community Engagement: Achieving Praxis* and *Reconstructing Policy Analysis in Higher Education: Feminist Poststructural Perspectives*. Before becoming faculty, Iverson worked as a student affairs administrator for more than ten years.

R. NICOLE JOHNSON-AHORLU is director of juvenile justice and education at the Center for Policing Equity. In this capacity, she supports education and law enforcement partners in addressing the "school-to-prison pipeline" in their jurisdictions. This includes designing empirical studies to inform solutions regarding racially disparate outcomes for youth in education and the justice system. She has an MA in African studies and a PhD in education, both from UCLA.

TERRY-ANN JONES is associate professor of sociology and anthropology at Fairfield University. She studies international and domestic migration, particularly between and within Latin America, the Caribbean, and North America. Her comparative study of the racial and ethnic settings and labor markets of Miami and Toronto, *Jamaican Immigrants in the United States and Canada: Race, Transnationalism, and Social Capital*, was published in 2008. Her other current projects include research on undocumented students' access to tertiary education. She is co-editor of *Undocumented and in College: Students and Institutions in a Climate of National Hostility*.

EZEKIEL KIMBALL is assistant professor of higher education and the associate director of the Center for Student Success Research at the University of Massachusetts Amherst. His recent research has examined the way that student affairs professionals use scholarly knowledge in practice and the way that disability status shapes student success in higher education. His publications on the experiences of students with disabilities appear in the *Journal of Diversity in Higher Education, Higher Education: Handbook of Theory and Research, the Journal of Student Affairs Research and Practice*, and *New Directions in Institutional Research*.

TONISHA B. LANE is assistant professor of higher education and student affairs at the University of South Florida. Lane's research agenda broadly examines diversity, equity, and inclusion in postsecondary education. Her primary research strand investigates the experiences and outcomes of underrepresented groups in science, technology, engineering, and mathematics (STEM). Using qualitative methodologies, she has explored access and success for underserved students of color in STEM and STEM intervention programs. Her secondary research strand focuses on blacks in higher education. Most recently, Lane served as a principal investigator on the national Black Doctoral Women Study.

ELIZABETH M. LEE is assistant professor of sociology at Ohio University. Her work on education and inequality has been published in *Sociology of Education, Sociology Compass,* and *Poetics,* as well as in her book *Class and Campus Life: Managing and Experiencing Inequality at an Elite College.* She is also the co-editor of a volume of collected works entitled *College Students' Experiences of Power and Marginality: Sharing Spaces and Negotiating Differences.*

ANTRON D. MAHONEY is a doctoral candidate in the Department of Pan-African Studies and the Graduate Certificate Program in Women's and Gender Studies at the University of Louisville. His research and scholarship interests include critical explorations of race, gender, and sexuality. In this context, he explores race/gender/sexuality theories and politics as well as leadership and social justice education—specifically examining experiences and performances (inter)relating to African American/African diaspora, black masculine/male identities, black feminist/queer organizing, mass media, and U.S. higher education. His work has been published in *New Directions in Student Leadership, Journal of Leadership Studies,* and forthcoming in *Maryland Law Journal for Race, Religion, Gender and Class.*

ERVIN (MALIQ) MATTHEW is assistant professor of sociology at the University of Cincinnati. His work examines racial gaps in academic and occupational outcomes, as well as broader theoretical questions about how social stratification processes operate in society.

TONYA MAYNARD is a doctoral student in the Department of Sociology at the University of Oklahoma. Her research interests include deviant subcultures, gender, sexualities, and religion.

ORKIDEH MOHAJERI is assistant professor of higher education policy and student affairs in the Department of Educational Foundations and Policy Studies at West Chester University. Her current work focuses on individuals and groups who are ambiguously located along contemporary schema of racial difference and seeks to problematize how discourses act on bodies, and how bodies act on discourses, to produce material effects.

MEGAN NANNEY is a doctoral candidate in the Department of Sociology with a concentration in women's and gender studies at Virginia Tech. Megan's research focuses on seemingly gender-inclusive social movements, communities, social panics, and policies. Their current projects examine gender nonconformity and transgender admissions policies at women's colleges, trans-exclusionary radical feminism and gender critical perspectives, and women's experiences within craft beer culture.

VICTOR E. RAY is assistant professor of sociology at the University of Tennessee. His academic work examines race and gender discrimination in organizations and has been published in the *Sociology of Race and Ethnicity, Ethnic and Racial Studies, Annals of the American Academy of Political and Social Science, Journal of Marriage and Family, Sociological Theory,* and *Contexts.* His commentary has appeared in *Newsweek, Boston Review, Gawker,* and *Inside Higher Ed.*

BEDELIA N. RICHARDS is associate professor of sociology at the University of Richmond. Her research interrogates the role of educational institutions in reproducing racialized identities and outcomes. Her work has appeared in the *Sociology of Race and Ethnicity, Ethnic and Racial Studies, International Journal of Teaching and Learning in Higher Education, Black Women, Gender and Families,* and as chapters in edited volumes. She is co-editor of a forthcoming book, *Clearing the Path for First Generation College Students: Intersectional Examinations on Educational Mobility.* Richards's new research agenda focuses on how to create a racially inclusive environment on college campuses. She is available to conduct workshops on this and other related issues.

FERNANDO RODRIGUEZ currently serves as assistant director for social justice and inclusion in housing at residential life at the University of Minnesota. He hails from the border city of El Paso, Texas, and has either worked alongside, and learned with, diverse student populations attending a broad range of institutions as a result of his educational and career endeavors. His research centers on examining how Mexican American gay men who were born along the U.S.-Mexico border construct masculinity, and how these constructs impact their college experience.

OPHELIE ROWE-ALLEN is associate dean / director of residence life & student diversity and multicultural affairs at Fairfield University. Her background is in counselor education and supervision. Some of her administrative responsibilities include serving on the Diversity and Mission Leadership Councils, chairing the Bias Response Team, and leading Living and Learning initiatives at Fairfield University. She is also Fairfield University's institutional representative for the ACE Women's Network and a facilitator for the Ignatian Colleagues Program.

FINN SCHNEIDER is a doctoral student in the Department of Organizational Leadership, Policy & Development at the University of Minnesota.

MEREDITH SMITH is associate director for living & learning and leadership development in the Office of Residence Life at Fairfield University. She co-authored "Mentors and College Student Leadership Outcomes," published in the *Review of Higher Education,* and was a member of the Multi-Institutional Student of Leadership research team from 2007 to 2010.

ANNEMARIE VACCARO is associate professor of human development and director of the College Student Personnel Graduate Program at the University of Rhode Island. Vaccaro's research interests focus on the intersections between college student development and gender, race, class, ability, and sexual orientation. Her scholarship is inspired by critical and feminist perspectives that call attention to underlying inequalities embedded in society and social structures such as higher education. She uses qualitative methods to examine the rich and complicated higher education experiences of diverse students, faculty, and staff.

DEBORAH M. WARNOCK is sociology faculty at Bennington College. Her research focuses on transitions to and from, as well as experiences of, higher education for underrepresented students, with a focus on low-income and first-generation students. Her work has appeared in the *Journal of Diversity in Higher Education, Journal of College Student Development,* and *Innovative Higher Education.* Together with other faculty, staff, and students, she founded FLOW, a support network for first-generation, low-income, and/or working-class students at Bennington.

INDEX

Note: page numbers followed by *f* and *t* refer to figures and tables, respectively.

insufficient, 28, 160; importance of including undocumented persons in commitment to, 56; increase in, 27; as term collapsing multiple identity statuses, 243, 247; as term obscuring factors producing social inequality, 6

diversity, universities' rhetoric on: as hindrance to real action, 152, 153, 154; as moral credentialing, 98; premise of racial equality underlying, 152, 153–154; vs. reality of color-blind racism, 141–142, 143; students' exposure to, 153–154; ubiquity of, 152–153; watering-down of racial component of, 153–154

diversity action plans at flagship universities, 253t–54t; as common strategy for declaring commitment to diversity, 243; and diversity as public relations commodity, 251; effects of, as under-studied, 243; emptiness of definitions of diversity in, 247–248; failure to consider underlying power relations in, 248–249; focus on "inclusion" in, as call for diverse individual to shed otherness, 250; focus on visible commitment to diversity rather than actual change, 248–249, 250; and framing of issue as individuals' failure to access welcoming environment, 249, 250; lack of concrete action in, 251–252; and limiting of access to high-achieving individuals similar to "us," 248; and need for destruction of existing power structure rather than "inclusion" within it, 252; need for inclusion of diverse knowledges of marginalized in, 252; policy changes in, as often cosmetic, 251

diversity action plans at flagship universities, IBPA analysis of, 243, 245–246; descriptive and transformative types of questions in, 246–247; methods in, 246–247. See also Intersectionality-Based Policy Analysis (IBPA)

DLE. See Diverse Learning Environments (DLE) study

Dodson, Leigh, 126

domains of power, in matrix of domination, 6–7

dominant ideology in higher education: changes over twentieth century, 12–13; history of racism in, 9–12; marginalized

subjects' challenges to, 9; radical changes in, after 1960s, 13–14

DREAM Act. See Development, Relief, and Education for Alien Minors (DREAM) Act

Du Bois, W.E.B.: and black education, 11, 12; sociologists' neglect of, 98

education, as "great equalizer," 93

egalitarianism: and Comprehensive STEM Program at Jefferson State University, 201, 202–203, 205; in RES framework, 198

elite white institutions: assumed low-income background of students of color at, 58, 59; assumed wealth of white students at, 58, 59; marginalization of students of color at, 58; predominance of wealthy students at, 59

elite white institutions, LIFGWC students at: and cleft *habitus*, 59, 70; experience of unmet needs in, 58; increased salience of class for, 59; and invisibility of class, 59; lack of place within diversity narrative, 59; out-of-place feeling of, 59; seeking out of similar peers, 59; and working-class values of, vs. values of elites, 59. See also Primrose College, LIFGWC students at

Ellison, John, 4

Embrick, David, 99

emotional labor: devaluing of, 126; as gendered, 123, 125–126; increasing susceptibility to exploitation, 126; intersectionality in, as under-theorized, 125; jobs requiring, as typically underpaid, 126

emotional labor in academia: effect of precarity on, 123–124, 129, 132; faculty care work as, 123, 125; by male faculty, 130–131. See also faculty care work

Engines of Inequality (Gerald and Haycock), 242

enslaved Africans, pursuit of education by, 10, 12

equity, discursive shift to, and pressure of institutions to change, 259

ethnic studies programs: as contested, 158; as cosmetic change, 89; value of, 158

eugenics movement, 12

Evaline, J., 244

Evans, Nancy J., 183